Psychoanalysis and Woman

Psychoanalysis and Woman

A Reader

Edited by Shelley Saguaro

NEW YORK UNIVERSITY PRESS
Washington Square, New York

First published in the U.S.A. in 2000 by
NEW YORK UNIVERSITY PRESS
Washington Square
New York, NY 10003

Library of Congress Cataloging-in-Publication Data
Psychoanalysis and woman: a reader/edited by Shelley Saguaro.
p. cm.
Includes bibliographical references and index.
ISBN 0–8147–9770–9 (alk. paper) – ISBN 0–8147–9771–7 (pbk.: alk. paper)
1. Sex (Psychology). 2. Psychoanalysis. 3. Women and psychoanalysis.
4. Psychoanalysis and feminism. 1. Saguaro, Shelley.
BF175.5.S48 P795 2000
155.3'33—dc21   99–056793

This book is printed on paper suitable for recycling and
made from fully managed and sustained forest sources.

10	9	8	7	6	5	4	3	2	1
09	08	07	06	05	04	03	02	01	00

Printed in Hong Kong

TO JENNY

Contents

Preface

It was while teaching a second-year undergraduate course entitled 'Psychoanalysis, Feminism, Writing' that I realized how difficult it was to find, and make available for study, accessible and/or collated primary material. The course was designed to present a selection of texts, written by women, which engaged with psychoanalysis from its inception to the present. It aimed to interrogate the ways in which these women found psychoanalysis to be plausible and defensible – or not. Freud's own work was readily available, but that of such contemporaries of his as Ruth Mack Brunswick or Helene Deutsch was not. Moreover, it would have been most useful, I believed, to read these women theorists *alongside* Freud, a strategy which was less easy to implement than it was with Jacques Lacan and the work of several 'new French feminists'. Many of the students, hailing from the disciplines of Women's Studies and English, were familiar (and largely happy) with the work of, say, Hélène Cixous or Luce Irigaray, but had, at the same time, very superficial (and prejudiced) notions about Freud's premises. While these very premises were undoubtedly being challenged by Cixous and Irigaray, it was also the case that these theorists were dependent upon and continuing to engage with those Freudian paradigms which my students avowedly rejected, but without being unable to recognize them.

The prejudicial bracketing-off of Freud, and the misrecognition of much Freudian thought, has simultaneously belied the status and complexity of earlier theorists and denied the extent of the relation of contemporary theorists to those prior psychoanalytic positions. Thus, Lacan's more acceptable (though less accessible) work could be referred to 'parrot-fashion' as a 'return to Freud' by students who had themselves never been there. Equally, the work of Jung, and particularly other Jungians, is exceptional in that it is quite comprehensively excluded from academic consideration, and yet such work is increasingly popular and in demand for the contribution it makes to those offspring of psychoanalysis: psychotherapy and counselling. Contemporary theorists were thus also skewed, and appeared falsely original, by the lack of context with earlier theorists, and indeed, with the more occluded earlier *women* theorists. However, to include on a course the range of material that was needed, and in concise form, was a financial and practical impossibility at that time.

The present *Reader* represents an attempt to rectify this situation. When the proposal for such a source-book was accepted, therefore, it gave me the opportunity to include a section on Jung and the Jungians. The rationale for this particular inclusion was not dissimilar to that which pertained to Freud: the juxtaposition of theorists was contextually imperative and sometimes gave rise to startling insights, while its inclusion at once showed up unexpected correlatives, as well as being illustrative of the better-known dissension between Freud and Jung. It is the overall aim of this collection, then, to make available materials which have often been lost sight of, and in a form which will, I believe, give rise to new discussions and discernments in the field of women and psychoanalysis.

Acknowledgements

The editor and publishers wish to thank the following for permission to use copyright material:

Judith Butler, for material from *Gender Trouble: Feminism and the Subversion of Identity* (1990), pp. 1–13, 28–33, by permission of Routledge, Inc; Nancy Chodorow, for material from *The Reproduction of Mothering: Psychoanalysis and the Sociology of Gender* (1978), pp. 191–205. Copyright © The Regents of the University of California, by permission of University of California Press; Hélène Cixous, for 'Castration or Decapitation?', *Signs*, Autumn (1981), pp. 41–55, translated by Annette Kuhn, by permission of The University of Chicago Press; Helene Deutsch, for 'The Significance of Masochism in the Mental Life of Women', *International Journal of Psycho-Analysis*, XI (1930), p. 48 ff., by permission of *The International Journal of Psycho-Analysis*; Jane Flax, for material from *Disputed Subjects: Essays on Psychoanalysis, Politics and Philosophy* (1993), pp. 47–58, by permission of Routledge; Marie-Louise von Franz, for Lecture 1 'The Feminine in Fairy Tales' from *Problems of the Feminine in Fairytales* (1972/1993), pp. 1–20, by permission of Shambhala Publications, Inc; Sigmund Freud, for material from *On Sexuality* (1931), PFL Vol. 7, (ed.) Angela Richards (1977), pp. 371–88, by permission of Sigmund Freud Copyrights; Karen Horney, for 'The Flight from Womanhood', *International Journal of Psycho-Analysis*, VII (1926), pp. 324–39, by permission of *The International Journal of Psycho-Analysis*; Luce Irigaray, for 'Ce sexe qui n'en n'est pas un' in *Ce sexe qui n'en est pas un*. Copyright © 1977 by Editions de Minuit. English translation from *New French Feminisms*, (eds) Elaine Marks and Isabelle de Courtivron. Copyright © 1980 by The University of Massachusetts Press, by permission of Editions de Minuit for original text and The University of Massachusetts Press for English translation; Carl G. Jung, for material from *Aspects of the Feminine* (1982), pp. 77–100. Copyright 1982 by Princeton University Press, by permission of Princeton University Press and Routledge; Melanie Klein, for 'Early Stages of the Oedipus Complex', *International Journal of Psycho-Analysis*, IX (1928), by permission of *The International Journal of Psycho-Analysis*; Julia Kristeva, for 'About Chinese Women' in *The Kristeva Reader*, Blackwell Publishers (1974), pp. 139–58, extracts from *Folle vérité*, collective work directed by Julia Kristeva. Copyright © Editions du Seuil, 1979, by permission of Editions du Seuil; Jeanne Lampl de Groot, for 'The Evolution of the Oedipus Complex in Women', *International Journal of Psycho-Analysis*, IX (1928), p. 332, by permission of *The International Journal of Psycho-Analysis*; Jacques Lacan, for 'The Meaning of the Phallus'

(1958) in *Feminine Sexuality*, (ed.) Juliet Mitchell and Jacqueline Rose, trs. Jacqueline Rose (1982), pp. 75–85. Translation copyright © 1982 by Jacqueline Rose. Copyright © 1966, 1968, 1975 by Editions du Seuil. Copyright © 1975 by Le Graphe, by permission of Macmillan Ltd and W. W. Norton & Company, Inc; Juliet Mitchell, for material from *Women: The Longest Revolution*, Virago (1984), pp. 296–313. Copyright © Juliet Mitchell, 1984, by permission of Rogers, Coleridge & White Ltd on behalf of the author; Noreen O'Connor and Joanna Ryan, for material from *Wild Desires and Mistaken Identities: Lesbianism and Psychoanalysis* (1993), pp. 73–83. Copyright © 1993 Columbia University Press, by permission of Virago Press and Columbia University Press; Camille Paglia, for material from *Sexual Personae: Art and Decadence from Nefertiti to Emily Dickinson* (1990), pp. 1–5, 8–14, 16–20, by permission of Yale University Press; Joan Riviere, for 'Womanliness as a Masquerade', *International Journal of Psycho-Analysis*, X (1929), by permission of *The International Journal of Psycho-Analysis*; Jacqueline Rose, for material from *Sexuality in the Field of Vision* (1986), pp. 224–33, by permission of Verso; Maria Torok, for 'The Meaning of "Penis Envy" in Women' (1963), *differences: A Journal of Feminist Cultural Studies*, 4:1 (1992), pp. 3–15, by permission of Indiana University Press; Marion Woodman, for material from *The Pregnant Virgin: A Process of Psychological Transformation* (1985), pp. 32–42, by permission of Inner City Books.

Every effort has been made to trace the copyright holders but if any have been inadvertently overlooked the publishers will be pleased to make the necessary arrangement at the first opportunity.

Introduction: Psychoanalysis and Woman

. . . feminist suspicion watches over any man's attempt to help define the uniqueness of womanhood, as though by uniqueness he could be expected to mean inborn inequality. Yet it still seems to be amazingly hard for many women to say clearly what they feel most deeply, and to find the right words for what to them is most acute and actual, without saying too much or too little and without saying it with defiance or apology.[1]

> A woman like that is not a woman, quite.
> I have been her kind.[2]

The present *Reader* is a collection of essays on psychoanalysis, 'woman' and female sexuality (in psychoanalytic terms). More specifically, these are essays predominantly written *by* women. As a selection, this *Reader* has a history and a rationale as outlined in the Preface, but overall it takes no one particular line and, in its format of an edited volume, it offers no conclusions. Neither does it constitute a specific defence of psychoanalysis, and yet it is a collection which aims to show the persistent viability of psychoanalytic tenets and the range of debate these continue to engender. It shows that, while psychoanalysis undoubtedly has been biased and male-dominated, it has nevertheless, and since its inception, engaged women theorists who have been keen to challenge and to revise variously and partially (in both senses of the word). What is evident, particularly in the work which is contemporaneous with that of Freud and Jung, is an allegiance to and gratitude for the liberating aspects of psychoanalysis. Despite the fact that female sexuality is seen by Freud as a foreign and obscure 'dark continent', it was at least – and at last – seen to be acknowledged. Women theorists' responses to the claims of psychoanalysis, therefore, are largely an attempt, not to refute but to reply to, and thus modify; to establish 'a woman's point of view'; and to counteract the predominance of the male. Nevertheless, the point of view of women on the subject of 'woman', it seems, has never been as consensual as the point of view of men on that same subject, and this is confirmed by the inconclusiveness that the present collection reveals.

The definitions and dicta first outlined by Freud (and always under revision by

Freud himself) are broadly reflective of the prevailing views of 'patriarchy' – in which, of course, women participate or are complicit, and are not merely alien and subjected. But when a 'woman's perspective' is brought to bear on such dicta, what ultimately emerges is the arbitrariness and indefinability of the very term and concept 'woman'. For instance, the category is also intersected by other specificities such as race, class, caste, ethnicity, and so forth. As a consequence, there has been a black backlash against some of the presuppositions of the predominantly white, middle-class, 'second-wave' feminism of the 1960s and 1970s, which tended to assume that 'woman', in all cultures and communities, was subject to oppression from men, and thus that certain universal claims could be made about female experience. Black feminists responded by pointing out that white feminism could not begin to presume to speak for all women, and that to do so was merely another act of colonization. They pointed out the complexity of their own allegiances: for example, to black men of their own culture and community – despite oppressions – over white women. Indeed, both psychoanalysis and feminism have been indicted for their tendency to universalize while using white, bourgeois paradigms.

What, then, may be the truth (without problematizing the very notion of 'truth' for the moment) about 'woman': how can we identify, if at all, genuine womanliness and essential femaleness? Is it possible to define 'woman', after all this patriarchal time, without perpetual reference to 'man'? Is what we tend readily to identify as a woman born – or made? How far are biological and anatomical differences constituent of psychical ones – or is it the social and cultural reception of a creature sexed as female that inscribes 'woman' in terms both of sex (biology) and gender (culture)? What is there about womanhood that is essential, inherent or 'natural', and what is nurtured, culturally specific or constructed? How can a woman claim equality with men when she also needs to overcome, not just relative physical smallness, say, or muscular weakness, but also the periodic inconvenience and psychical impact of menstruation, pregnancy, childbirth, lactation, menopause (although not every woman 'suffers' all, or necessarily any, of these)? Does a woman really suffer 'penis envy', as Freud and his followers outline it, or does she rather envy it merely as the arbitrary token to which cultural power and prestige automatically accrue? To what extent do men envy or fear women's reproductive power, the primacy of mothers, the hiddenness and plurality of female sexual organs? To what extent are women the fetishized objects which must work to appease men's castration anxiety? Is *everything* a woman should be merely a strategic and compensatory fantasy for both sexes?

Throughout this *Reader*, questions such as these abound, as does contestation, overlap and proliferation, since the questions raised seem only to generate yet more uncertainties. At times, indeed, there appears a profound scepticism on 'subjects' which have hitherto seemed to us *given*, most obvious, most natural. For instance, when it comes to sexed bodies, can we believe our eyes, or have our very 'eyes' been regulated to see what we expect to believe in particular arbitrary but normative ways? Judith Butler puts it more eloquently:

> The concept of 'sex' is itself troubled terrain, formed through a series of contestations over what ought to be decisive criterion [sic] for distinguishing between the two sexes; the concept of sex has a history . . . Through what regulatory norms is sex itself materialized? And how is it that treating the materiality of sex as a given presupposes and consolidates the normative conditions of its own emergence?[3]

Just when we thought that anatomical sexual difference and the materiality of bodies was an indisputable given, we are challenged with the notion that sex, sexuality and the discourses pertaining to sexual acts have a history of interpretation and regulation. To try to step outside such 'performative'[4] and normative postulates of any culture is exceedingly difficult, even perhaps impossible as a specific and targeted endeavour. However, to begin to do so would be radically to rethink the sexual 'activity', say, of the male body and the passivity of the receptive, conceptive role of the female. The personification of sexual organs has been so pervasive that to begin to characterize them otherwise is a great challenge. In a very crude way, one could suggest that the presumed activity, drive and dominance of the male is, instead, indicative of alienation, frenzied seeking and insecurity. Again, one could suggest that woman's 'inner space' – bearing in mind Erik Erikson's question: 'how does the identity formation of women differ by dint of the fact that their somatic design harbors an "inner space" destined to bear the offspring of chosen men . . .?'[5] – needs to be re-materialized (in Foucauldian terms: '[re]invested with power'[6]), so that this 'space' is not cited as the marker of lack, or of an emptiness waiting to be filled – and thus *ful*filled. Similarly, one might aim to subvert the convention which posits female penetrability (and fragility) as opposed to male impenetrability (and power). Judith Butler, for example, offers a complex discussion on the presumed stability of difference propounded by this western metaphysical, heterosexual matrix of penetrator and penetrated (which male homosexuality most obviously threatens), and speculates on disruptions to this – including 'a full-scale confusion over what qualifies as "penetration" anyway'.[7]

Having arrived at this profoundly sceptical pass, seeking a woman's 'point-of-view' or perspective is severely problematized. But the fact remains that from the time anatomical difference is assigned, the inscription of sexual identity begins; as Francette Pacteau puts it:

> From the instant my biological sex is determined, my identity is defined in difference – I am either a boy or a girl. I shall consequently take up my position in society on one side of the sexual divide, behave according to the genderized codes, reaffirm the difference.[8]

The major 'difference' to be reaffirmed is that 'man' will desire 'woman'; woman will desire to bear his children; and the incest taboo will regulate this heterosexual desire.[9] Anything that falls outside this paradigm is considered deviant, perverse and, within psychoanalysis, as indicative of failure in the resolution of Oedipal complexities. In an influential essay of 1980, 'Compulsory Heterosexuality and Lesbian Existence', Adrienne Rich registered her dismay at the number of feminists whose work continued to be unquestioning about the 'assumption that "most women are innately heterosexual" ',[10] hence ignoring 'the extent and elaboration of measures designed to keep women within a male sexual purlieu'.[11] To some extent anticipating a theorist such as Judith Butler, Rich called for a thorough-going investigation of the institutionalization of 'compulsory heterosexuality' (in the perpetuation of which, psychoanalysis has played a large part):

> The assumption that 'most women are innately heterosexual' stands as a theoretical and political stumbling block for feminism. It remains a tenable assumption partly because lesbian existence has been written out of history or catalogued under disease, partly because it has been treated as exceptional rather than intrinsic, partly because to acknowledge that for women heterosexuality may not be a 'preference' at all but something that has had to be imposed, managed, organized, propagandized, and maintained by force is an immense step to take if you consider yourself freely and 'innately' heterosexual. Yet the failure to examine heterosexuality as an institution is like failing to admit that the economic system called capitalism or the caste system of racism is maintained by a variety of forces, including both physical violence and false consciousness. To take the step of questioning heterosexuality as a 'preference' or 'choice' for women – and to do the intellectual and emotional work that follows – will call for a special quality of courage in heterosexually identified feminists . . .[12]

It is to the relations between 'feminism' and psychoanalysis that I now turn.

Feminism – which aims to articulate the arbitrariness of the inequity identified by Rich above, to vindicate woman's rights and abilities, and to lobby for change – pre-dates psychoanalysis. Mary Wollstonecraft's rhetorical question of 1792, posited more than a century before Freud coined the term 'psychoanalysis' in 1896 (the word 'feminism' was itself first coined in France by Charles Fourier in 1837), remained just as apposite by the time Freud was developing his own universalizing judgements:

> Who made man the exclusive judge, if woman partake with him of the gift of reason? In this style argue tyrants of every denomination, from the weak king to the weak father of a family; they are all eager to crush reason, yet always

assert that they usurp its throne only to be useful. Do you not act a similar part when you *force* all women, by denying them civil and political rights, to remain immured in their families groping in the dark?[13]

In outlining the exigencies of the Oedipus complex, and the effects of 'castration' for the boy and girl, Freud specifically confronts 'the feminists' and their project. With a 'scientific' rationale and an apparently universal sexology to elaborate, he proffers a consequential view of woman which readily provokes a further challenge along the lines of Wollstonecraft's prior one:

> In girls the motive for the demolition of the Oedipus complex is lacking. Castration has already had its effect [she is always and already castrated while the boy will continue to dread the possibility, which the girl's castration demonstrates as able to be accomplished] . . . I cannot evade the notion (though I hesitate to give it expression) that for women the level of what is ethically normal is different from what it is in men. Their super-ego is never so inexorable, so impersonal, so independent of its emotional origins as we require it to be in men. Character-traits which critics of every epoch have brought up against women – that they show less sense of justice than men, that they are less ready to submit to the great exigencies of life, that they are more often influenced in their judgements by feelings of affection or hostility – all these would be amply accounted for by the modification in the formation of their super-ego . . . We must not allow ourselves to be deflected from such conclusions by the denials of the feminists, who are anxious to force us to regard the two sexes as completely equal in position and worth . . . .[14]

In classical psychoanalysis, as will become apparent from essays included in this book, the development of the female to the point where, realizing her castration, 'the girl has turned into a little woman',[15] seems to be entirely negative in comparison to the development of the male. He has the penis, which she will envy; her clitoris, the analogous organ, on the other hand, is decidedly inferior, and this apprehension will inflict a permanent 'wound to her narcissism'. Moreover, she must renounce her initial clitoral activity and take up instead the passivity attendant on the vagina, which is now, Freud claims, her prime (and feminine) sexual organ. Thus, with disavowal, disappointment, repression and anger (at her mother for not *having* the penis, and for not *bequeathing* her daughter one), she must turn from the mother who was her first love object, but who is now perceived as 'castrated', to her father (who has/is everything to be desired), and then to a male father-surrogate. This will constitute the course of her 'normal' – that is, heterosexual – female development. The boy, of course, must repress everything that is 'feminine' in order to evade the dreaded condition of castration, and to establish an incontrovertible difference from both his castrated mother and all women. The wounded girl will now seek, in psychical and symbolic terms, to bear her father a gift: that is, a child. Repudiating this incestuous desire, she then turns to her father-surrogate partner and begins her child-bearing career. For her, according to Freud, this child will represent a compensatory substitute-penis – which is all that she can achieve under the circumstances of her anatomical destiny.

Of course, women readers and analysts reacted indignantly to this devaluation and sought to provide a different emphasis. In this search, the general debasement of women was countered most often by a valorization of motherhood. (This in itself has left something of a negative legacy, since not all women will be, or want to be, mothers. According to the maternalist imperative, however, such women will be 'doubly' failed: failed by virtue of their very being – as 'woman' – and then failed by virtue of not being 'woman enough'.) Several female theorists, who otherwise operated within conventional psychoanalytic terms of reference, sought to recuperate a much more positive assessment of motherhood than Freud seemed to offer. They asked: is this all one can say about motherhood and its crucial importance in the very perpetuation of human life? Since Freud had acknowledged what later theorists tended to underline (that 'in both cases the mother is the original object')[16] they asked: what about the significance of the mother as the prime carer and first love-object for all offspring, male and female? The earliest and symbiotic relation of child to mother is followed by separation and 'object relations',[17] with the subsequent perception (however distorted)[18] of 'self' and of 'other'. In this way, the mother is both the first 'self' (symbiotically) and the first 'other' (by virtue of separation and loss). As the separation proceeds, the power and plenitude of the mother, and thus the child's dependency and need, engender envy and fear in the child. Thus, the first and fundamental envy, for boys and for girls, is envy of the mother: mother-envy therefore pre-dates (and pre-figures) penis-envy. Juliet Mitchell usefully highlights a distinction between the approaches of Freud and his female contemporary, Melanie Klein, in this regard:

> Psychically the mother in Freud's scheme is important when she goes away . . . the penis when it is not there (penis-envy). Klein's concept of envy (interestingly enough also the bedrock of her theory and therapy) is for a mother who has everything . . . This mother who has everything is not 'feminine'; she is complete.[19]

One might want to go on to suggest here that being as replete and complete as she is – at least until the vicissitudes of the castration complex – she *is* 'the phallus'. It is not that she *has* the penis, but rather that she *is* phallic: originary, upright, potent, entire.

To introduce the concept of 'the phallus', which is not the same as (having) the frail, corporeal penis, is to introduce a key concept of Lacanian theory. Lacan returns to Freud, bringing with him the insights afforded by modern linguistic analysis. Lacan's interest in the relation of the linguistic signifier to the signified involves a post-structuralist modification of Saussurean notions of the, albeit arbitrary, inseparability of these two components of the linguistic sign. Instead, Lacan indicates the gap between signifier and signified, and the signifier's dislocation as it occludes the signified and circulates without stable signification. What he certainly refutes is the notion of the speaker's autonomy, intention and control: rather, language drives – indeed determines – the subject who speaks. Freud, of course, had been extremely attentive to language, to all those slips and displacements, denials, repetitions and silences which liberated a repressed tale, and a tale of repression, without the conscious effort or effective control of the speaker. Lacan, 'following' Freud, incorporates his 'modern linguistic analysis', so that the emphasis on 'penis-envy' shifts to the signification of the phallus. As Lacan explains in 'The Meaning of the Phallus' (see pp. 222–30 here):

> . . . the signifier then becomes a new dimension of the human condition, in that it is not only man who speaks, but in man and through man that it speaks, that his nature is woven by effects in which we can find the structure of language, whose material he becomes, and that consequently there resounds in him, beyond anything ever conceived of by the psychology of ideas, the relation of speech.

According to this model, the gendered pronouns notwithstanding, all human subjects, male and female, are 'spoken' by language. Lacan refers to this 'structure of language' as the 'Symbolic Order', into which human subjects are inserted rather as if they were themselves signs in a linguistic system. Such a system of differences (without positive terms)[20] needs its organizing principles (as do human subjects), and for Lacan, anatomical difference aligns them in relation to the *linguistic* transcendental signifier – the phallus.

A large amount of work has been done by Lacan and others in elaboration of this premise (an indicative list is included at the end of Chapter 4). What is most important to note here is Lacan's reiteration that the phallus is *not* the penis; indeed, the phallus reveals male subjects as lacking, too, for nothing they possess can stand up to the sustained turgidity of the phallus. Of course, by this, female subjects are lacking in this lack. The penis, which lacks in relation to the phallus (the penis, which the phallus is *not),* is missing and has never been there (enough) to be under any threat.

All human subjects, in order to avoid psychosis or death, in order to move out of a pre-Oedipal 'puddle', must align themselves with the phallus and enter the Symbolic Order of paternal legitimation, or the Law of the Father (at least, this is the *myth* we all live with and re-enact). However, even if the phallus is *not* the penis it is nevertheless metonymically related to it; and while the phallus does not *signify* the penis, having a penis nonetheless signifies a privileged relation to the phallus. The transcendent phallus thus becomes a signified – each and every bearer of the penis signifies the phallus by bearing its metonymic attribute – while those without a penis cannot signify or be signified, and thus remain 'outside'. Judith Butler discusses Luce Irigaray's notion that:

> . . . women constitute a paradox, if not a contradiction, within the discourse of identity itself. Women are the 'sex' which is not 'one'. Within a language pervasively masculinist, a phallogocentric language, women constitute the *unrepresentable*. In other words, women represent the sex that cannot be thought, a linguistic absence [as the penis is absent] and opacity. Within a language that rests on univocal signification, the female sex constitutes the unconstrainable and undesignatable. In this sense, women are the sex which is not 'one', but multiple.[21]

'Order', 'Law', 'Father', 'Phallus', 'One': there is no denying that Lacanian revisionism has done little if anything to shift patriarchy's privileged terms.

Most of the essays collected here, with their differing theoretical affiliations, are engaged in a consideration of the intransigence of these terms. Is the primacy of the phallus inevitable? Why is the father's penis an uncontested token of power and prestige? How does one explain the persistence of castration anxiety and penis-envy as the apparent driving forces of human subjectivity and cultural organization? Lacan suggests that :

> The phallus is the privileged signifier of that mark where the share of the logos is wedded to the advent of desire. One might say that this signifier is chosen as what stands out as most easily seized upon in the real of sexual copulation, and also as the most symbolic in the literal (typographical) sense of the term, since it is equivalent in that relation of the (logical) copula. One might also say that by virtue of its turgidity, it is the image of the vital flow as it is transmitted in generation.[22]

Elizabeth Grosz summarizes the features of the phallus – which is presumed to be so different from the penis – and is led to conclude that: 'It is thus simultaneously and indissolubly the mark of sexual difference (and identity), the signifier of the speaking position in language, and the order governing exchange relations.'[23] Prior to this order was the realm of undifferentiation, of pulsional drives and echolalia. Lacan's term for this un-order is 'the Imaginary', while Kristeva and others discuss it as the 'semiotic' or 'semiotic chora'.[24] In classical psychoanalysis, it is the perceived intervention of the father, the apprehension of the mother's castration, and the consequent need to develop language and 'identity' attendant on the mother's loss (castration and separation), which instigate the transition. The identification of the phallus (and penis) is seen to be crucial to this development: 'by means of the phallus, the subject comes to occupy the position of "I" in discourse'.[25] If the phallus is the means by which subjects occupy the position of 'I' in discourse, it is also easy to see the phallus emblematized *by* this

'I'. Monumental, monolithic, upright, a phallic 'I': the phallus = 'I'. (One is reminded of Maxine Hong Kingston's view, as an Asian American, of the Western monumental 'I' which is 'so straight')[26] Hence, only male subjects who bear the penis can aspire to take up the subject position that approximates to 'I', which renders women as 'O': 'O' for Other, 'O' for 'Object'; 'O' denoting the hole where the 'I' should be: 'O' the sign of a cipher (although it could just as easily denote the plenitude of a *full* circle).

The variety of material presented in this *Reader*, however, argues against the *inevitability* of the perception and institutionalization of women's lack. There are theories which proclaim the primacy of the female – Jean Strouse, for example, claiming that:

> Although genetic sex is determined at fertilization, the influence of the sex genes does not begin until some weeks after conception has occurred. During these first weeks the foetus is morphologically female. Enough androgen at the appropriate time will produce in both sexes a normal penis. The absence of androgen at this time will produce in both sexes a normal clitoris. In other words, only the male embryo has to go through a differentiation process in genital development, when the hormone androgen masculinizes the genital tract. Female development proceeds normally by itself. Contrary, therefore, to Freud's assumption, the clitoris is not a smaller, undeveloped penis; instead, it is ontogenetically correct to say that the penis is an androgenized clitoris.[27]

Others discuss the overriding role of the Mother as the first carer, as the primary law-giver, and as the initial instructor in language. Her predominant presence and her power – to prohibit, to withhold, to withdraw, to fulfil – is enormous. The far-reaching effects of this are the bedrock of psychoanalysis: how often is a complex or crisis traced back to Mother, to a case of 'the mother's fault', or, more inevitably, to a long lineage of mothers' faults? Melanie Klein, as has already been noted, was certainly one to underline the power of the mother, and it led her to elaborate the subsequent strength of infantile feelings of rage, envy and aggression.

There is a metonymic aspect to consider here, too. The breast becomes a part-object standing in for the mother, symbolizing the mother's power to fulfil and her power to deny: the good breast and the bad breast. (This is discussed further in Part 2 of this book: 'Klein and Object Relations'.) Klein's work on the breast is interestingly extended in the work of Wilfred Bion. He suggests the importance in symbolization and speech-formation, not of the penis first and foremost, but of the nipple. Julia Segal summarizes:

> Wilfred Bion maintained that phantasies deriving from the nipple were used not only to understand penises and ultimately men but also to give meaning

and 'body' to words and speech. These, like the nipple, are experienced as the link between mother and child; between a source of goodness, the breast, and the child who needs it. Words both bring mother and child together and also illustrate the separation and difference between them. The fact of needing to speak implies that mother and baby are not one, indivisible, inside each other and knowing each other's mind.[28]

According to this, the mother's body presents the first '(logical) copula' – 'by virtue of its turgidity' and 'vital flow' (see Lacan's explanation for the inevitability of the phallus, above) – not the penis. Might this view not modify the primacy of the phallus? Why not, then, the 'transcendental nipple'?

Other theorists again elaborate on the ways in which the female body generally has too much rather than too little. In a western culture obsessed with straightforward binary oppositions and equivalencies, the female body exceeds neat correlatives. A list of sexual attributes, constructed in oppositional columns, demonstrates this:

penis –   clitoris (the penile failure *or* the originary organ)
testicles –   ovaries
                vagina
                womb
                breasts

Moreover, a woman's genitalia are hidden from view, and what is hidden and secret may generate fantasy and fear. Her 'difference' makes her an object of desire, but of a desire that is constituted as 'epistemophilia' and 'scopophilia' – the compulsion to know and the compulsion to look – manifest in extreme form in pornography. Such a compulsive curiosity might itself be construed as envy. Many, variously, have suggested that the aggrandizement of the phallus is indeed an indication of a male insecurity complex. Male power is always belated in relation to the maternal body. *Mutual* envy, Bruno Bettelheim, amongst others, has attested, may, of course, be the case, but this acknowledgement of reciprocity does little to change the prevailing imbalance in societal and familial power-structures. [29]

In the era dominated by women's liberation, equal rights and the 'sexual revolution' – in particular the 1960s and 1970s – further data was gathered to prove the equivalence of the sexes and, on occasion, the stupendous superiority of the female 'equipment'. Hence we have Mary Jane Sherfey, in the essay collected here, proclaiming the innate 'hypersexual drive' of the female: 'theoretically, a woman could go on having orgasms indefinitely if physical exhaustion did not intervene'. Stephen Heath, in *The Sexual Fix*, discusses our late twentieth-century fixation with orgasmic facility, where the woman excels, but the markers are resiliently 'masculine':

Equality of the orgasm, of course. The friends of the naked ape have assured us that among all the primates only the human female experiences orgasm . . . Moreover, the woman corresponds to the man, is every bit his equal; . . . 'the female way of getting pleasure . . . corresponds to the muscular dance of male ejaculation'. Indeed, she ejaculates just the same as he does; according to *Playboy* in 1980, Dr John Perry, a Vermont psychologist, has identified 'a urethral discharge during sex' by women which is an 'ejaculation-like emission'.[30]

Luce Irigaray, while less empirical, would argue that woman's orgasmic pleasure, her *jouissance* (a term which resists strict definition, but is used to denote an orgasmic pleasure which incorporates the pulsional forces of the pre-Oedipal 'semiotic'), is entirely her own kind; and continuing in the combative and competitive vein, that it far exceeds that of man's: for 'woman has sex organs more or less everywhere'. Different from, as good as, the same as, more or less than: the arguments and demonstrations continue – and continue to be fixed by those very oppositional paradigms which situated women negatively, since this works merely as inversion, rather than subversion or conversion. Meanwhile, the bodies being measured are metamorphosing.

The sexed human body, which has been considered the most 'natural' of phenomena, aligned with the given and intrinsic features of the animal kingdom, is increasingly artificial. Reproductive technologies and other advancements in medical science have intervened for some time. From dental work to pacemakers, from medical prostheses to cosmetic surgery and silicone implants, the 'natural' body is re-created variously and for different reasons. At a time when epidemics such as cancer and Aids cause terror over the medical interventions and bodily mutations that may ensue, more and more women in particular are seeking surgery and other medical regimens in order to remake themselves. The persistently youthful, death-defying images often chosen are not very various and suggest cloning and stereotype (again) more than individual preference. Such women choose to be made 'woman', picked and mixed, as it is culturally prescribed. Thus, a 1994 newspaper article presents one 'Orlan':

> For the past three years, this 46-year-old French performance artist has undergone seven major cosmetic surgery operations in an attempt to fit her face to a digital image culled from the mythic icons of feminine beauty.[31]

Orlan's work may be ironic and parodic (as well as painful), but her body-pastiche parodies an increasingly common phenomenon. Orlan is 'fortunate', however, in having a feminist surgeon: 'Prior to that', the article explains, '. . . the cosmetic surgeons she worked with had always refused to countenance her wilder designs. "I think it was because they were always men. They wanted to keep me cute," ' she states. Instead, Orlan goes for a composite image made up from those of famous – yes, male – artists: Mona Lisa's forehead; Botticelli's Venus for the chin. There are other females, however, who choose surgery, not to make them stereotypically 'woman', but precisely to remove those features which most readily impose gender. Double mastectomies and hysterectomies, but without phalloplasty, are most common for 'transgenderists' whose aim is not to become the 'opposite sex' but neuter[32] – literally, a sex which is *not* one.

At what point does a 'cyborg' – ' a hybrid of machine and organism, a creature of social reality as well as a creature of fiction'[33] – become one, eclipsing or transmuting the prior 'natural' creature? (We might further ask, by this definition, if a woman hasn't always been one?) Where does natural end and artificial begin? With clothes? cosmetics? surgery, hormones and prostheses? The boundary between the natural and artificial, which has been complicated enough in terms of gender, is now becoming just as complex in terms of human bodies and agency. Transsexualism, transgenderism and hermaphroditism have been well-documented in medical and popular media; and there is a pervasive knowledge of, if not acceptance that, our most 'natural' fact – that is, sex – is not necessarily for keeps and may be engineered according to our (not necessarily individual) fantasies, fancies and deepest beliefs about what we should have been had we been consulted or would like to be at any particular moment. In 1994, another article, in the *Independent on Sunday*, announced the creation of 'The Third Sex' with the following caption: 'Tessa Souter meets the women taking the male hormone testosterone, not to become men, but in an attempt to create an entirely new gender'. The article explains:

> . . . Stafford and Jordy are not ordinary women. In fact, they may no longer be completely women at all . . . They are among a growing number of predominantly lesbian and bisexual women in America who are taking testosterone with no intention of turning themselves into men . . . the goal is androgyny, and the result, some claim, is the creation of an entirely new sex.
>
> 'I never felt like a girl. Now I don't feel like a man. I just feel like me. I feel the balance is finally there,' says Stafford . . . Her flatmate Jordy . . . says that in an ideal world she would like to be a 'fully functioning hermaphrodite'.
>
> . . . Stafford also finds that she now prefers 'super-feminine' women.[34]

The article doesn't conjecture whether the 'super-feminine women' to whom she is attracted were born that way – or were made. Possibly, as in Neil Jordan's film, *The Crying Game*, the 'super-feminine' woman has a penis inside her frilly knickers. There are those who contend that a concept of androgyny – even of a 'third sex' – is still too conscious of 'two', arguing instead for a 'transgender' continuum where a gendered subject is always in process: negotiated and re-negotiated, acting and acted upon, in multiple ways. Thus there may be as many sexes as subjects – and one need not be the same sex or subject twice or for long.

Sex has been 'queered'; the binary oppositionalism demanded of 'compulsory heterosexuality' is being subverted continually, and yet the prior terms are difficult to dislodge. Judith Butler, in the last chapter of *Bodies that Matter*, entitled 'Critically Queer', cautions:

> The risk of offering a final chapter on 'queer' is that the term will be taken as the summary moment, but I want to make a case that it is perhaps only the most recent. In fact, the temporality of the term is precisely what concerns me here: how is it that a term that signaled degradation has been turned – 'refunctioned' in the Brechtian sense – to signify a new and affirmative set of meanings? . . . Is this a reversal that retains and reiterates the abjected history of the term? . . . Much of the straight world has always needed the queers it has sought to repudiate . . . . If the term is now subject to a reappropriation, what are the conditions and limit of that significant reversal? Does the reversal reiterate the logic of repudiation by which it was spawned? Can the term overcome its constitutive history of injury?[35]

Although the issues are not identical, one could substitute the word 'woman' for 'queer' in the extract above to good effect in the line of enquiry posited by the present *Reader*. 'Woman' has always been 'queer' in relation to the male paradigms but if she was not 'womanly', as outlined by this prevailing view, she was queerer still. No one should underestimate the pain and injury attendant on abjection. The notion of therapy and 'cure' posited by psychoanalysis is thus a complicated – and political – matter. The notion of 'cure' has very specific and normative criteria: what then – what *now* – would constitute a 'cure', and is it necessarily the abjected subject who is in need of it?

The valorization of 'woman', like the attempts to valorize 'queer', soon becomes enmeshed in a 'history of injury' and a 'logic of repudiation'. Grappling with these issues, however, merely uncovers – ironically, in terms of psychoanalysis – something that is not there. Joan Riviere's own response, in 1929, to an anticipated question, reverberates in this regard:

> The reader may now ask how I define womanliness or where I draw the line between genuine womanliness and the 'masquerade'. My suggestion is not, however, that there is any such difference; whether radical or superficial, they are the same thing.[36]

The discussions presented in the following sections try to ascertain, variously, whether there is or can be a 'natural' female sexuality, a 'genuine' womanliness, an 'authentic' perspective by and for women. The overwhelming answer may be: 'there is no such thing' – or, as Jacques Lacan puts it: '*The* woman can only be written with ~~The~~ crossed through. There is no such thing as *The* woman, where the definite article stands for the universal.'[37] There have been plenty of people telling her who she is – and what she cannot be – and why. Psychoanalysis has read and re-read the scripts and continues to consider the problem of casting a role for a creature that simply may not *be*: the ~~Woman~~.

NOTES

1. Erik H. Erikson, 'Womanhood and Inner Space' (1968), in Jean Strouse (ed.), *Women and Analysis* (New York: Grossman, 1974), p. 293.
2. Anne Sexton, 'Her Kind', *The Complete Poems* (Boston: Houghton Mifflin, 1982), p. 15.
3. Judith Butler, *Bodies that Matter: On the Discursive Limits of 'Sex'* (New York and London: Routledge, 1993), pp. 5 and 10.
4. Judith Butler has extended her discussion and analysis of 'performativity' in *Gender Trouble: Feminism and the Subversion of Identity* (London and New York: Routledge, 1990) and *Bodies that Matter* (1993). See also an interview in October 1993, where she summarizes her use of 'performativity': 'Gender as Performance: An Interview with Judith Butler', by Peter Osborne and Lynne Segal, *Radical Philosophy*, 67, Summer, 1994, p. 33.
5. Erik H. Erikson, 'Womanhood and Inner Space' (1968) collected with Erikson's response 'Once More the Inner Space: Letter to a Former Student' (1974), in J. Strouse, op. cit., p. 295.
6. See Judith Butler (1993), pp. 22 and 34.
7. Ibid., p. 51.
8. Francette Pacteau, 'The Impossible Referent: representations of the androgyne', *Formations of Fantasy*, Victor Burgin, James Donald and Cora Kaplan (eds), (London and New York: Methuen, 1994), p. 63.
9. Freud discusses the 'barrier against incest' at some length in 'Three Essays on the Theory of Sexuality' (1905). See bibliography for full reference and editions of Freud's work.
10. Adrienne Rich, 'Compulsory Heterosexuality and Lesbian Existence', *Blood, Bread and Poetry* (London: Virago, 1987), p. 50.
11. Ibid., p. 49.
12. Ibid., pp. 50–1.
13. Mary Wollstonecraft, *Vindication of the Rights of Woman* (1792), M. B. Kramnick (ed.), (Harmondsworth: Penguin, 1983), p. 87.
14. Sigmund Freud, 'Some Psychical Consequences of the Anatomical Distinction Between the Sexes' (1927), PFL 7, p. 342. In Freud's tripartite psychical structure of id, ego and super-ego, the super-ego performs a parental or policing function.
15. Ibid., p. 340.
16. Ibid., p. 334.
17. The term is also used more specifically to describe a school of thought developed, in particular, by Melanie Klein. See this *Reader*, pp. 93ff.
18. See, for instance, Jacques Lacan's 'The Mirror Stage' in *Écrits: A Selection* (London: Tavistock, 1974), p. 4.
19. Juliet Mitchell, 'The Question of Femininity and the Theory of Psychoanalysis', *Women: The Longest Revolution* (London: Virago, 1984), pp. 310 and 312.
20. See Ferdinand de Saussure, *Course in General Linguistics* (Glasgow: Fontana/ Collins, 1974 [1915]).
21. Judith Butler (1990) op. cit., p. 9.

22. See 'The Meaning of the Phallus' at pp. 222-30 in this *Reader*.

23. Elizabeth Grosz, *Jacques Lacan: A Feminist Introduction* (London and New York: Routledge, 1990), p. 126. Also in E. Grosz, 'The Penis and the Phallus' in Sue Vice (ed.), *Psychoanalytic Criticism: a Reader* (Cambridge: Polity, 1996), p. 145.

24. See in particular 'Section 2: The Semiotic <u>Chora</u> Ordering the Drives', 'Revolution in Poetic Language' in *The Kristeva Reader,* Toril Moi (ed.), (Oxford: Blackwell, 1986), p.93ff.

25. Elizabeth Grosz (1990), op. cit., p. 125 and in Sue Vice (1996), op. cit., p. 145.

26. Maxine Hong Kingston, *The Woman Warrior: Memoirs of a Girlhood Among Ghosts* (London: Picador, 1977), p. 150.

27. Jean Strouse, 'Introduction', *Women and Analysis* (New York: Grossman, 1974), p. 7.

28. Julia Segal, *Melanie Klein* (London: Sage, 1992), p. 119.

29. Bruno Bettelheim, *Symbolic Wounds: Puberty Rites and the Envious Male* (London: Thames and Hudson, 1955). See also, for example, Erik H. Erikson, 'Once More the Inner Space: Letter to a Former Student', in Jean Strouse (ed.) (1974).

30. Stephen Heath, *The Sexual Fix* (London: Macmillan, 1986 [1982]), p. 148.

31. Jim McClellan, 'The extensions of woman' 'Life', *Observer,* 17 April 1994, p. 38.

32. See Julie Wheelright, 'I'm just a sweet transgenderist', *Independent*, 27 March 1995 and 'Sex Acts', BBC 1, *QED,* broadcast, 28 March 1995.

33. Donna Haraway, 'A Manifesto for Cyborgs: Science, Technology, and Socialist Feminism in the 1980s', *Feminism/Postmodernism*, Linda J. Nicholson (ed.), (New York and London: Routledge, 1990), p. 191.

34. Tessa Souter, *Independent on Sunday*, 9 October 1994, p. 23

35. Judith Butler (1993) op. cit., p. 223.

36. Joan Riviere, 'Womanliness as a Masquerade' collected here, p. 70–8.

37. Jacques Lacan 'God and the <u>Jouissance</u> of ~~The~~ Woman. A Love Letter' in *Feminine Sexuality*, J. Mitchell and J. Rose (eds), (London: Macmillan, 1985), p. 144.

Editor's Note

The notes and references that follow each of the essays collected here are the author's original notes. Any additional information or explanation has been provided in square brackets by the editor of this volume. Occasionally, notes have been provided by another editor or a translator; these also appear in square brackets.

PART I: FREUD

This section begins with Freud's 1931 essay, 'Female Sexuality', which explores the differences and correlations in the development of adult sexuality, or of what Freud calls, with reference to women, 'the final normal female attitude'. The 'Editor's Note'[1] explains that the 1931 piece is 'in essence a restatement' of those findings first outlined in Freud's 1925 paper, 'Some Psychical Consequences of the Anatomical Distinction between the Sexes'. Although he acknowledges, in the essay of 1931, the impossibility of finding the girl's and the boy's progression as analogous and parallel, this does little to change the prevailing view that a boy's development is paradigmatic and the female's a puzzle. As he wrote famously (and notoriously): 'the sexual life of adult women is a '"dark continent" for psychology'.[2] Freud frequently (and disarmingly) acknowledges his own limitations in unravelling the mystery of such a complex, disappointed creature as a woman: prone to hysteria, to disavowal and to a 'masculinity complex' in her own attempts to come to terms with her psycho-sexual peculiarities. Of particular interest here is the consideration of the extent of a girl's unwilling renunciation, not just of her 'phallic activity', but of her mother as her primary love-object.

The essays included in this section, ranging in date from 1926 to 1965, have one aspect in common: they all acknowledge and work with Freud's fundamental concepts of the Oedipal scenario: the ensuing castration complex, and, for women, penis-envy. This is not to say, however, that the essays agree with Freud in every regard, or indeed with each other. They do, though, show common attention to the complexities of a women's psycho-sexual development and thus to the complex strategies which a woman must adopt to negotiate her way towards what may, outwardly at least, be perceived as the accomplishment of 'the final normal female attitude'.

Each of the 'responses' collected here has a particular and unique contribution to make. Karen Horney, for instance, places a much greater stress on the social and cultural reasons why women envy 'the penis'; for her, it is not the corporeal penis that they envy, but rather all the privileges and freedom that bearing the penis affords: 'Our whole civilization is a masculine civilization'. There are other advantages in having a penis too, which, while of anatomical origin, are bound up in gendering prohibitions. The little girl is forbidden to touch her genitalia, but every time the boy urinates he must touch his. The boy's genitalia are visible and 'up front'; as well as being in view of others, the penis is also able to be seen by the bearer. The little girl's genitalia are not so, but are enfolded and hidden, so that, even to herself, she is an object of curiosity. In a later section of the *Reader* (see pp. 99ff.), Melanie Klein discusses the developing child's 'early feeling of *not knowing*' and the frustration and fear it can engender. For the female child, this impulse to know and explore what is so difficult to apprehend (her sex) combines with the stronger prohibitions against her developing sexuality and the explorations of touching and looking. In Freud's terms, she also experiences the crucial recognition that she does not have what she should have: she stands as a cautionary tale, inevitably abject, and an emblem of what it means to have been found guilty and punished – with castration. According to Freud, she will renounce the clitoris, the failed phallus, and move to the passivity and interiority of the vagina (although the notion of the 'passive vagina' is challenged here by Helene Deutsch). Thus female masturbation and the complexity of this taboo (external prohibition and/or narcissistic renunciation) figure, and are variously interpreted, in the essays collected here.

Each of the pieces, Freud's included, stresses the importance of the mother as the first love-object for both boys and girls. But it is the girl, through disillusionment (the mother is not *the* phallus; she has not got the phallus; she has not given the phallus) and resentment (the mother has not given her the penis, but neither will the mother give her the father), who marks her adult heterosexuality by turning from a same-sex object choice to the 'other' as love-object. The complexities of the girl's relation to the mother – to her primal plenitude, then perceived lack, and the girl's desire for/envy of the penis – is addressed by each of the contributors. Female homosexuality, the continuation of same-sex object choice, which for Freud is a failure of the teleological endeavour to arrive at the 'normal adult female attitude', is seen to be fundamental and persistent. (Essays in other sections will also address this.) The mother as prior love-object has particular impact upon the evolution of the Oedipus complex for women; the importance of women analysts for women, as a mother-surrogate in analytical transference, for instance, is found to be integral to the particularity of the female complex. As Jeanne Lampl de Groot suggested, and as Freud later acknowledged, in terms of transference,[3] it is a mother-figure and not a father-figure which often needs recuperation in the clinical situation. The implications for female homosexuality of the double renunciation of her own sex (her sex is not adequate, therefore she must renounce the clitoris; her sex is her mother's and must therefore be renounced as her love-object choice) are also addressed here and extended in later sections.

The papers by Helene Deutsch and Jeanne Lampl de Groot pre-date Freud's 1931 'Female Sexuality' essay, but are a response to his fundamental 1925 essay on anatomical distinction. Both aim to revise Freud's theorizing of female sexuality by making a contribution from *women* analysts who, by virtue of gendered transference, can introduce fuller details of daughter/mother relations. Deutsch and Lampl de Groot also discuss the still difficult issues of female masochism, rape-fantasies, frigidity and over-compensation. We have Lampl de Groot's claim that 'she is constantly subjecting herself to castration', and Deutsch's view that the girl moves seamlessly from the rebellious denial – 'I won't be castrated' – to the masochistically punitive: 'I want to be castrated'. These papers must be set in the context of Freud's retraction of his first views on childhood sexual abuse (see note no. 3 to 'Female Sexuality', p. 34 in this *Reader*), since their authors are working with the view that such (common) allegations are most often wishful and strategic fantasies arising from the castration complex.[4]

Both Joan Riviere, a contemporary of Deutsch and Lampl de Groot, and more recently, Maria Torok, are attentive to the strategies and 'subterfuges' adopted by women. As Riviere's client revealed, an ardent femininity is 'assumed and worn as a mask both to hide the possession of masculinity and to avert the reprisals expected if she was found to possess it'. 'Masculinity', of course, pertains to intellectual activity, public address, sexual virility. The 'double-act' of competence and deprecation dramatizes the hysteric's 'simultaneous acceptance and refusal of the organization of sexuality under patriarchal capitalism'.[5] Of his own hysterics, Freud noted that they were almost always women remarkable for their intellectual capacity and artistic ability; it is also worth remembering that many of his female colleagues were first his hysterical clients.

We see in the essays by Riviere and Torok an attention to the complex negotiations of envy, frustration and guilt but there is also an interrogation of the emphatic male *projection* of envy and lack upon the woman. Maria Torok's essay questions the adequacy of theories of biological inferiority and anatomical lack in explaining the 'radical depreciation' of the female sex. Akin to Riviere's 'masquerade' is her notion of penis-envy as a 'subterfuge' where 'nothing matters less than the penis itself'. Rather, this 'partial object' is 'a stopgap invented to camouflage a desire', a desire which has been misconstrued yet has been impossible to explain aright.

Thus, these women psychoanalysts psychoanalyse not just their female patients, but also male psychoanalytic discourse for its own symptomatic strategies. To varying degrees, they take Freud's theoretical models and use them to explore contradictions, illogicality, bias, disavowal and displacement, rather than seeing them as incontrovertibly true (albeit culturally and psycho-sexually enacted and manifest). The dramas Freud discussed were indeed recognized and resonant; but the motive forces behind them demanded more thorough investigation.

NOTES

1. Angela Richards (ed.), PFL 7, pp. 369–70.
2. S. Freud, 'The Question of Lay Analysis' (1926), PFL 15, p. 313.
3. In analysis 'transferences' take place as the analysand substitutes the analyst for figures

from past, repressed relations and situations which are worked through. Freud outlined the term in the case history of 'Dora'; see PFL 8, pp. 157–8.

4. Jeffrey M. Masson's *The Assault on Truth: Freud's Suppression of the Seduction Theory* (Harmondsworth: Penguin, 1985) provides a further explanation of Freud's change of opinion.

5. This is Juliet Mitchell's description of hysteria – and of the woman writer who is, she argues, necessarily hysteric. See 'Femininity, Narrative and Psychoanalysis', *Women: The Longest Revolution* (London: Virago, 1984), pp. 289–90.

1

Female Sexuality

Sigmund Freud

1

During the phase of the normal Oedipus complex we find the child tenderly attached to the parent of the opposite sex, while its relation to the parent of its own sex is predominantly hostile. In the case of a boy there is no difficulty in explaining this. His first love-object was his mother. She remains so; and, with the strengthening of his erotic desires and his deeper insight into the relations between his father and mother, the former is bound to become his rival. With the small girl it is different. Her first object, too, was her mother. How does she find her way to her father? How, when and why does she detach herself from her mother? We have long understood that the development of female sexuality is complicated by the fact that the girl has the task of giving up what was originally her leading genital zone – the clitoris – in favour of a new zone – the vagina. But it now seems to us that there is a second change of the same sort which is no less characteristic and important for the development of the female: the exchange of her original object – her mother – for her father. The way in which the two tasks are connected with each other is not yet clear to us.

It is well known that there are many women who have a strong attachment to their father; nor need they be in any way neurotic. It is upon such women that I have made the observations which I propose to report here and which have led me to adopt a particular view of female sexuality. I was struck, above all, by two facts. The first was that where the women's attachment to her father was particularly intense, analysis showed that it had been preceded by a phase of exclusive attachment to her mother which had been equally intense and passionate. Except for the change of her love-object, the second phase had scarcely added any new feature to her erotic life. Her primary relation to her mother had been built up in a very rich and many-sided manner. The second fact taught me that the *duration* of this attachment had also been greatly underestimated. In several cases it lasted until well into the fourth year – in one case into the fifth year – so that it covered by far the longer part of the period of early sexual efflorescence. Indeed, we had to reckon with the possibility that a number of women remain arrested in their original attachment to their mother and never achieve a true change-over towards men. This being so, the pre-Oedipus phase in women gains an importance which we have not attributed to it hitherto.

Since this phase allows room for all the fixations and repressions from which we trace the origin of the neuroses, it would seem as though we must retract the universality of the thesis that the Oedipus complex is the nucleus of the neuroses. But if anyone feels reluctant about making this correction, there is no need for him to do so. On the one hand, we can extend the content of the Oedipus complex to include all the child's relations to both parents; or, on the other, we can take due account of our new findings by saying that the female only reaches the normal positive Oedipus situation after she has surmounted a period before it that is governed by the negative complex. And indeed during that phase a little girl's father is not much else for her than a troublesome rival, although her hostility towards him never reaches the pitch which is characteristic of boys. We have, after all, long given up any expectation of a neat parallelism between male and female sexual development.

Our insight into this early, pre-Oedipus, phase in girls comes to us as a surprise, like the discovery, in another field, of the Minoan-Mycenaean civilization behind the civilization of Greece.

Everything in the sphere of this first attachment to the mother seemed to me so difficult to grasp in analysis – so grey with age and shadowy and almost impossible to revivify – that it was as if it had succumbed to an especially inexorable repression. But perhaps I gained this impression because the women who were in analysis with me were able to cling to the very attachment to the father in which they had taken refuge from the early phase that was in question. It does indeed appear that women analysts – as, for instance, Jeanne Lampl de Groot and Helene Deutsch – have been able to perceive these facts more easily and clearly because they were helped in dealing with those under their treatment by the transference to a suitable mother-substitute. Nor have I succeeded in seeing my way through any case completely, and I shall therefore confine myself to reporting the most general findings and shall give only a few examples of the new ideas which I have arrived at. Among these is a suspicion that this phase of attachment to the mother is especially intimately related to the aetiology of hysteria, which is not surprising when we reflect that both the phase and the neurosis are characteristically feminine, and further, that in this dependence on the mother we have the germ of later paranoia in women.[1] For this germ appears to be the surprising, yet regular, fear of being killed (? devoured) by the mother. It is plausible to assume that this fear corresponds to a hostility which develops in the child towards her mother in consequence of the manifold restrictions imposed by the latter in the course of training and bodily care and that the mechanism of projection is favoured by the early age of the child's psychical organization.

2

I began by stating the two facts which have struck me as new: that a woman's strong dependence on her father merely takes over the heritage of an equally strong attachment to her mother, and that this earlier phrase has lasted for an unexpectedly long period of time. I shall now go back a little in order to insert these new findings into the picture of female sexual development with which we are familiar. In doing this, a certain amount of repetition will be inevitable. It will help our exposition if, as we go along, we compare the state of things in women with that in men.

First of all, there can be no doubt that the bisexuality, which is present, as we believe, in the innate disposition of human beings, comes to the fore much more clearly in women than in men. A man, after all, has only one leading sexual zone, one sexual organ, whereas a woman has two: the vagina – the female organ proper – and the clitoris, which is analogous to the male organ. We believe we are justified in assuming that for many years the vagina is virtually non-existent and possibly does not produce sensations until puberty. It is true that recently an increasing number of observers report that vaginal impulses are present even in these early years. In women, therefore, the main genital occurrences of childhood must take place in relation to the clitoris. Their sexual life is regularly divided into two phases, of which the first has a masculine character, while only the second is specifically feminine. Thus in female development there is a process of transition from the one phase to the other, to which there is nothing analogous in the male. A further complication arises from the fact that the clitoris, with its virile character, continues to function in later female sexual life in a manner which is very variable and which is certainly not yet satisfactorily understood. We do not, of course, know the biological basis of these peculiarities in women; and still less are we able to assign them any teleological purpose.

Parallel with this first great difference there is the other, concerned with the finding of the object. In the case of a male, his mother becomes his first love-object as a result of her feeding him and looking after him, and she remains so until she is replaced by someone who resembles her or is derived from her. A female's first object, too, must be her mother: the primary conditions for a choice of object are, of course, the same for all children. But at the end of her development, her father – a man – should have become her new love-object. In other words, to the change in her own sex there must correspond a change in the sex of her object. The new problems that now require investigating are in what way this change takes place, how radically or how incompletely it is carried out, and what the different possibilities are which present themselves in the course of this development.

We have already learned, too, that there is yet another difference between the sexes, which relates to the Oedipus complex. We have an impression here that what we have said about the Oedipus complex applies with complete strictness to the male child only and that we are right in rejecting the term 'Electra complex' which seeks to emphasize the analogy between the attitude of the two sexes. It is only in the male child that we find the fateful combination of love for the one parent and simultaneous hatred for the other as a rival. In his case it is the discovery of the possibility of castration, as proved by the sight of the female genitals, which forces on him the transformation of his Oedipus complex, and which leads to the creation of his super-ego and thus initiates all the processes that are designed to make the individual find a place in the cultural community. After the paternal agency has been internalized and become a super-ego, the next task is to detach the latter from the figures of whom it was originally the psychical representative. In this remarkable course of development it is precisely the boy's narcissistic interest in his genitals – his interest in preserving his penis – which is turned round into a curtailing of his infantile sexuality.

One thing that is left over in men from the influence of the Oedipus complex is a certain amount of disparagement in their attitude towards women, whom they regard as being castrated. In extreme cases this gives rise to an inhibition in their choice of object, and, if it is supported by organic factors, to exclusive homosexuality.

Quite different are the effects of the castration complex in the female. She acknowledges the face of her castration, and with it, too, the superiority of the male and her own inferiority; but she rebels against this unwelcome state of affairs. From this divided attitude three lines of development open up. The first leads to a general revulsion from sexuality. The little girl, frightened by the comparison with boys, grows dissatisfied with her clitoris, and gives up her phallic activity and with it her sexuality in general as well as a good part of her masculinity in other fields. The second line leads her to cling with defiant self-assertiveness to her threatened masculinity. To an incredibly late age she clings to the hope of getting a penis some time. That hope becomes her life's aim; and the phantasy of being a man in spite of everything often persists as a formative factor over long periods. This 'masculinity complex' in women can also result in a manifest homosexual choice of object. Only if her development follows the third, very circuitous, path does she reach the final normal female attitude, in which she takes her father as her object and so finds her way to the feminine form of the Oedipus complex. Thus in women the Oedipus complex is the end-result of a fairly lengthy development. It is not destroyed, but created, by the influence of castration; it escapes the strongly hostile influences which, in the male, have a destructive effect on it, and indeed it is all too often not surmounted by the female at all. For this reason, too, the cultural consequences of its break-up are smaller and of less importance in her. We should probably not be wrong in saying that it is this difference in the reciprocal relation between the Oedipus and the castration complex which gives its special stamp to the character of females as social beings.[2]

We see, then, that the phase of exclusive attachment to the mother, which may be called the *pre-Oedipus* phase, possesses a far greater importance in women than it can have in men. Many phenomena of female sexual life which were not properly understood before can be fully explained by reference to this phase. Long ago, for instance, we noticed that many women who have chosen their husband on the model of their father, or have put him in their father's place, nevertheless repeat towards him, in their married life, their bad relations with their mother. The husband of such a woman was meant to be the inheritor of her relation to her father, but in reality he became the inheritor of her relation to her mother. This is easily explained as an obvious case of regression. Her relation to her mother was the original one, and her attachment to her father was built up on it, and now, in marriage, the original relation emerges from repression. For the main content of her development to womanhood lay in the carrying over of her affective object attachments from her mother to her father.

With many women we have the impression that their years of maturity are occupied by a struggle with their husbands, just as their youth was spent in a struggle with their mother. In the light of the previous discussions we shall conclude that their hostile attitude to their mother is not a consequence of the rivalry implicit in the Oedipus complex, but originates from the preceding phase and has merely been reinforced and exploited in the Oedipus situation. And actual analytic examination confirms this view. Our interest must be directed to the mechanisms that are at work in her turning away from the mother who was an object so intensely and exclusively loved. We are prepared to find, not a single factor, but a whole number of them operating together towards the same end.

Among these factors are some which are determined by the circumstances of infantile sexuality in general, and so hold good equally for the erotic life of boys. First and foremost we may mention jealousy of other people – of brothers and sisters, rivals, among whom the father too has a place. Childhood love is boundless; it demands exclusive possession, it is not content with less than all. But it has a second characteristic: it has, in point of fact, no aim and is incapable of obtaining complete satisfaction; and principally for that reason it is doomed to end in disappointment and to give place to a hostile attitude. Later on in life the lack of an ultimate satisfaction may favour a different result. This very factor may ensure the uninterrupted continuance of the libidinal cathexis, as happens with love-relations that are inhibited in their aim. But in the stress of the process of development it regularly happens that the libido abandons its unsatisfying position in order to find a new one.

Another, much more specific motive for turning away from the mother arises from the effect of the castration complex on the creature who is without a penis. At some time or other the little girl makes the discovery of her organic inferiority – earlier and more easily, of course, if there are brothers or other boys about. We have already taken note of the three paths which diverge from this point: (*a*) the one which leads to a cessation of her whole sexual life, (*b*) the one which leads to a defiant over-emphasis of her masculinity, and (*c*) the first step towards definitive femininity. It is not easy to determine the exact timing here or the typical course of events. Even the point of time when the discovery of castration is made varies, and a number of other factors seem to be inconstant and to depend on chance. The state of the girl's own phallic activity plays a part; and so too does the question whether this activity was found out or not, and how much interference with it she experienced afterwards.

Little girls usually discover for themselves their characteristic phallic activity – masturbation of the clitoris; and to begin with this is no doubt unaccompanied by phantasy. The part played in starting it by nursery hygiene is reflected in the very common phantasy which makes the mother or nurse into a seducer. Whether little girls masturbate less frequently and from the first less energetically than little boys is not certain; quite possibly it is so. Actual seduction, too, is common enough; it is initiated either by other children or by someone in charge of the child who wants to soothe it, or send it to sleep or make it dependent on them. Where seduction intervenes it invariably disturbs the natural course of the developmental processes, and it often leaves behind extensive and lasting consequences.

A prohibition of masturbation, as we have seen, becomes an incentive for giving it up; but it also becomes a motive for rebelling against the person who prohibits it – that is to say, the mother, or the mother-substitute who later regularly merges with her. A defiant persistence in masturbation appears to open the way to masculinity. Even where the girl has not succeeded in suppressing her masturbation, the effect of the apparently vain prohibition is seen in her later efforts to free herself at all costs from a satisfaction which has been spoilt for her. When she reaches maturity her object-choice may still be influenced by this persisting purpose. Her resentment at being prevented from free sexual activity plays a big part in her detachment from her mother. The same motive comes into operation again after puberty, when her mother takes up her duty of guarding her daughter's chastity. We shall, of course, not forget that the mother is similarly opposed to a boy's masturbating and thus provides him, too, with a strong motive for rebellion.

When the little girl discovers her own deficiency, from seeing a male genital, it is only with hesitation and reluctance that she accepts the unwelcome knowledge. As we have seen, she clings obstinately to the expectation of one day having a genital of the same kind too, and her wish for it survives long after her hope has expired. The child invariably regards castration in the first instance as a misfortune peculiar to herself; only later does she realize that it extends to certain other children and lastly to certain grown-ups. When she comes to understand the general nature of this characteristic, it follows that femaleness – and with it, of course, her mother – suffers a great depreciation in her eyes.

This account of how girls respond to the impression of castration and the prohibition against masturbation will very probably strike the reader as confused and contradictory. This is not entirely the author's fault. In truth, it is hardly possible to give a description which has general validity. We find the most different reactions in different individuals, and in the same individual the contrary attitudes exist side by side. With the first intervention of the prohibition, the conflict is there, and from now on it will accompany the development of the sexual function. Insight into what takes place is made particularly difficult by the fact of its being so hard to distinguish the mental processes of this first phase from later ones by which they are overlaid and are distorted in memory. Thus, for instance, a girl may later construe the fact of castration as a punishment for her masturbatory activity, and she will attribute the carrying out of this punishment to her father, but neither of these ideas can have been a primary one. Similarly, boys regularly fear castration from their father, although in their case, too, the threat most usually comes from their mother.

However this may be, at the end of this first phase of attachment to the mother, there emerges, as the girl's strongest motive for turning away from her, the reproach that her mother did not give her a proper penis – that is to say, brought her into the world as a female. A second reproach, which does not reach quite so far back, is rather a surprising one. It is that her mother did not give her enough milk, did not suckle her long enough. Under the conditions of modern civilization this may be true often enough, but certainly not so often as is asserted in analyses. It would seem rather that this accusation gives expression to the general dissatisfaction of children, who, in our monogamous civilization, are weaned from the breast after six or nine months, whereas the primitive mother devotes herself exclusively to her child for two or three years. It is as though our children had remained for ever unsated, as though they had never sucked long enough at their mother's breast. But I am not sure whether, if one analysed children who had been suckled as long as the children of primitive peoples, one would not come upon the same complaint. Such is the greed of a child's libido!

When we survey the whole range of motives for turning away from the mother which analysis brings to light – that she failed to provide the little girl with the only proper genital, that she did not feed her sufficiently, that she compelled her to share her mother's love with others, that she never fulfilled all the girl's expectations of love, and, finally, that she first aroused her sexual activity and then forbade it – all these motives seem nevertheless insufficient to justify the girl's final hostility. Some of them follow inevitably from the nature of infantile sexuality; others appear like rationalizations devised later to account for the uncomprehended change in feeling. Perhaps the real fact is that the attachment to the mother is bound to perish, precisely because it was the first and was so intense; just as one can often see happen in the first marriages of young women which they have entered into when they were most passionately in love. In both situations the attitude of love probably comes to grief from the disappointments that are unavoidable and from the accumulation of occasions for aggression. As a rule, second marriages turn out much better.

We cannot go so far as to assert that the ambivalence of emotional cathexes is a universally valid law, and that it is absolutely impossible to feel great love for a person without its being accompanied by a hatred that is perhaps equally great, or vice versa. Normal adults do undoubtedly succeed in separating those two attitudes from each other, and do not find themselves obliged to hate their love-objects and to love their enemy as well as hate him. But this seems to be the result of later developments. In the first phases of erotic life, ambivalence is evidently the rule. Many people retain this archaic trait all through their lives. It is characteristic of obsessional neurotics that in their object-relationships love and hate counterbalance each other. In primitive races, too, we may say that ambivalence predominates. We shall conclude, then, that the little girl's intense attachment to her mother is strongly ambivalent, and that it is in consequence precisely of this ambivalence that (with the assistance of the other factors we have adduced) her attachment is forced away from her mother – once again, that is to say, in consequence of a general characteristic of infantile sexuality.

The explanation I have attempted to give is at once met by a question: 'How is it, then, that boys are able to keep intact their attachment to their mother, which is certainly no less strong than that of girls?' The answer comes equally promptly: 'Because boys are able to deal with their ambivalent feelings towards their mother by directing all their hostility on to their father.' But, in the first place, we ought not to make this reply until we have made a close study of the pre-Oedipus phase in boys, and, in the second place, it is probably more prudent in general to admit that we have as yet no clear understanding of these processes, with which we have only just become acquainted.

3

A further question arises: 'What does the little girl require of her mother? What is the nature of her sexual aims during the time of exclusive attachment to her mother?' The answer we obtain from the analytic material is just what we should expect. The girl's sexual aims in regard to her mother are active as well as passive and are determined by the libidinal phases through which the child passes. Here the relation of activity to passivity is especially interesting. It can easily be observed that in every field of mental experience, not merely that of sexuality, when a child receives a passive impression it has a tendency to produce an active reaction. It tries to do itself what has just been done to it. This is part of the work imposed on it of mastering the external world and can even lead to its endeavouring to repeat an impression which it would have reason to avoid on account of its distressing content. Children's play, too, is made to serve this purpose of supplementing a passive experience with an active piece of behaviour and of thus, as it were, annulling it. When a doctor has opened a child's mouth, in spite of his resistance, to look down his throat, the same child, after the doctor has gone, will play at being the doctor himself, and will repeat the assault upon some small brother or sister who is as helpless in his hands as he was in the doctor's. Here we have an unmistakable revolt against passivity and a preference for the active role.

This swing-over from passivity to activity does not take place with the same regularity or vigour in all children; in some it may not occur at all. A child's behaviour in this respect may enable us to draw conclusions as to the relative strength of the masculinity and femininity that it will exhibit in its sexuality.

The first sexual and sexually coloured experiences which a child has in relation to its mother are naturally of a passive character. It is suckled, fed, cleaned, and dressed by her, and taught to perform all its functions. A part of its libido goes on clinging to those experiences and enjoys the satisfactions bound up with them; but another part strives to turn them into activity. In the first place, being suckled at the breast gives place to active sucking. As regards the other experiences the child contents itself either with becoming self-sufficient – that is, with itself successfully carrying out what had hitherto been done for it – or with repeating its passive experiences in an active form in play; or else it actually makes its mother into the object and behaves as the active subject towards her. For a long time I was unable to credit this last behaviour, which takes place in the field of real action, until my observations removed all doubts on the matter.

We seldom hear of a little girl's wanting to wash or dress her mother, or tell her to perform her excretory functions. Sometimes, it is true, she says: 'Now let's play that I'm the mother and you're the child'; but generally she fulfils these active wishes in an indirect way, in her play with her doll, in which she represents the mother and the doll the child. The fondness girls have for playing with dolls, in contrast to boys, is commonly regarded as a sign of early awakened femininity. Not unjustly so; but we must not overlook the fact that what finds expression here is the *active* side of femininity, and that the little girl's preference for dolls is probably evidence of the exclusiveness of her attachment to her mother, with complete neglect of her father-object.

The very surprising sexual activity of little girls in relation to their mother is manifested chronologically in oral, sadistic, and finally even in phallic trends directed towards her. It is difficult to give a detailed account of these because they are often obscure instinctual impulses which it was impossible for the child to grasp psychically at the time of their occurrence, which were therefore only interpreted by her later, and which then appear in the analysis in forms of expression that were certainly not the original ones. Sometimes we come across them as transferences on to the later, father-object, where they do not belong and where they seriously interfere with our understanding of the situation. We find the little girl's aggressive oral and sadistic wishes in a form forced on them by early repression, as a fear of being killed by her mother – a fear which, in turn, justifies her death-wish against her mother, if that becomes conscious. It is impossible to say how often this fear of the mother is supported by an unconscious hostility on the mother's part which is sensed by the girl. (Hitherto, it is only in men that I have found the fear of being eaten up. This fear is referred to the father, but it is probably the product of a transformation of oral aggressivity directed to the mother. The child wants to eat up its mother from whom it has had its nourishment; in the case of the father there is no such obvious determinant for the wish.)

The women patients showing a strong attachment to their mother in whom I have been able to study the pre-Oedipus phase have all told me that when their mother gave them enemas or rectal douches they used to offer the greatest resistance and react with fear and screams of rage. This behaviour may be very frequent or even the habitual thing in children. I only came to understand the reason for such a specially violent opposition from a remark made by Ruth Mack Brunswick, who was studying these problems at the same time as I was, to the effect that she was inclined to compare the outbreak of anger after an enema to the orgasm following genital excitation. The accompanying anxiety should, she thought, be construed as a transformation of the desire for aggression which had been stirred up. I believe that this is really so and that, at the sadistic-anal level, the intense passive stimulation of the intestinal zone is responded to by an outbreak of desire for aggression which is manifested either directly as rage, or, in consequence of its suppression, as anxiety. In later years this reaction seems to die away.

In regard to the passive impulses of the phallic phase, it is noteworthy that girls regularly accuse their mother of seducing them. This is because they necessarily received their first, or at any rate their strongest, genital sensations when they were being cleaned and having their toilet attended to by their mother (or by someone such as a nurse who took her place). Mothers have often told me, as a matter of observation, that their little daughters of two and three years old enjoy these sensations and try to get their mothers to make them more intense by repeated touching and rubbing. The fact that the mother thus unavoidably initiates the child into the phallic phase is, I think, the reason why, in phantasies of later years, the father so regularly appears as the sexual seducer. When the girl turns away from her mother, she also makes over to her father her introduction into sexual life.[3]

Lastly, intense *active* wishful impulses directed towards the mother also arise during the phallic phase. The sexual activity of this period culminates in clitoridal masturbation. This is probably accompanied by ideas of the mother, but whether the child attaches a sexual aim to the idea, and what that aim is, I have not been able to discover from my observations. It is only when all her interests have received a fresh impetus through the arrival of a baby brother or sister that we can clearly recognize such an aim. The little girl wants to believe that she has given her mother the new baby, just as the boy wants to; and her reaction to this event and her behaviour to the baby is exactly the same as his. No doubt this sounds quite absurd, but perhaps that is only because it sounds so unfamiliar.

The turning-away from her mother is an extremely important step in the course of a little girl's development. It is more than a mere change of object. We have already described what takes place in it and the many motives put forward for it; we may now add that hand in hand with it there is to be observed a marked lowering of the active sexual impulses and a rise of the passive ones. It is true that the active trends have been affected by frustration more strongly; they have proved totally unrealizable and are therefore abandoned by the libido more readily. But the passive trends have not escaped disappointment either. With the turning-away from the mother clitoridal masturbation frequently ceases as well; and often enough when the small girl represses her previous masculinity a considerable portion of her sexual trends in general is permanently injured too. The transition to the father-object is accomplished with the help of the passive trends in so far as they have escaped the catastrophe. The path to the development of femininity now lies open to the girl, to the extent to which it is not restricted by the remains of the pre-Oedipus attachment to her mother which she has surmounted.

If we now survey the stage of sexual development in the female which I have been describing, we cannot resist coming to a definite conclusion about female sexuality as a whole. We have found the same libidinal forces at work in it as in the male child and we have been able to convince ourselves that for a period of time these forces follow the same course and have the same outcome in each.

Biological factors subsequently deflect those libidinal forces (in the girl's case) from their original aims and conduct even active and in every sense masculine trends into feminine channels. Since we cannot dismiss the notion that sexual excitation is derived from the operation of certain chemical substances, it seems plausible at first to expect that biochemistry will one day disclose a substance to us whose presence produces a male sexual excitation and another substance which produces a female one. But this hope seems no less naïve than the other one – happily obsolete today – that it may be possible under the microscope to isolate the different exciting factors of hysteria, obsessional neurosis, melancholia, and so on.

Even in sexual chemistry things must be rather more complicated. For psychology, however, it is a matter of indifference whether there is a single sexually exciting substance in the body or two or countless numbers of them. Psychoanalysis teaches us to manage with a single libido, which, it is true, has both active and passive aims (that is, modes of satisfaction). This antithesis and, above all, the existence of libidinal trends with passive aims, contains within itself the remainder of our problem.

4

An examination of the analytic literature on the subject shows that everything that has been said by me here is already to be found in it. It would have been superfluous to publish this paper if it were not that in a field of research which is so difficult of access every account of first-hand experiences or personal views may be of value. Moreover, there are a number of points which I have defined more sharply and isolated more carefully. In some of the other papers on the subject the description is obscured because they deal at the same time with the problems of the super-ego and the sense of guilt. This I have avoided doing. Also, in describing the various outcomes of this phase of development, I have refrained from discussing the complications which arise when a child, as a result of disappointment from her father, returns to the attachment to her mother which she had abandoned, or when, in the course of her life, she repeatedly changes over from one position to the other. But precisely because my paper is only one contribution among others, I may be spared an exhaustive survey of the literature, and I can confine myself to bringing out the more important points on which I agree or disagree with these other writings.

Abraham's (1921) description of the manifestations of the castration complex in the female is still unsurpassed; but one would be glad if it had included the factor of the girl's original exclusive attachment to her mother. I am in agreement with the principal points in Jeanne Lampl de Groot's important paper (1927). In this the complete identity of the pre-Oedipus phase in boys and girls is recognized, and the girl's sexual (phallic) activity towards her mother is affirmed and substantiated by observations. The turning-away from the mother is traced to the influence of the girl's recognition of castration, which obliges her to give up her sexual object, and often masturbation along with it. The whole development is summed up in the formula that the girl goes through a phase of the 'negative' Oedipus complex before she can enter the positive one. A point on which I find the writer's account inadequate is that it represents the turning-away from the mother as being merely a change of object and does not discuss the fact that it is accompanied by the plainest manifestations of hostility. To this hostility full justice is done in Helene Deutsch's latest paper, on feminine masochism and its relation to frigidity (1930), in which she also recognizes the girl's phallic activity and the intensity of her attachment to her mother. Helene Deutsch states further that the girl's turning towards her father takes place *via* her passive trends (which have already been awakened in relation to her mother). In her earlier book (1925) the author had not yet set herself free from the endeavour to apply the Oedipus pattern to the pre-Oedipus phase, and she therefore interpreted the little girl's phallic activity as an identification with her father.

Fenichel (1930) rightly emphasizes the difficulty of recognizing in the material produced in analysis what parts of it represent the unchanged content of the pre-Oedipus phase and what parts have been distorted by regression (or in other ways). He does not accept Jeanne Lampl de Groot's assertion of the little girl's active attitude in the phallic phase. He also rejects the 'displacement backwards' of the Oedipus complex proposed by Melanie Klein (1928), who places its beginnings as early as the commencement of the second year of life. This dating of it, which would also necessarily imply a modification of our view of all the rest of the child's development, does not in fact correspond to what we learn from the analyses of adults, and it is especially incompatible with my findings as to the long duration of the girl's pre-Oedipus attachment to her mother. A means of soft-ening this contradiction is afforded by the reflection that we are not as yet able to distinguish in this field between what is rigidly fixed by biological laws and what is open to movement and change under the influence of accidental experience. The effect of seduction has long been familiar to us and in just the same way other factors – such as the date at which the child's brothers and sisters are born or the time when it discovers the difference between the sexes, or again its direct observations of sexual intercourse or its parents' behaviour in encouraging or repelling it – may hasten the child's sexual development and bring it to maturity.

Some writers are inclined to reduce the importance of the child's first and most original libidinal impulses in favour of later developmental processes, so that – to put this view in its most extreme form – the only role left to the former is merely to indicate certain paths, while the [psychical] intensities which flow along those paths are supplied by later regressions and reaction-formations. Thus, for instance, Karen Horney (1926) is of the opinion that we greatly overestimate the girl's primary penis-envy and that the strength of the masculine trend which she develops later is to be attributed to a *secondary* penis-envy which is used to fend off her feminine impulses and, in particular, her feminine attachment to her father. This does not tally with my impressions. Certain as is the occurrence of later reinforcements through regression and reaction-formation, and difficult as it is to estimate the relative strength of the confluent libidinal components, I nevertheless think that we should not overlook the fact that the first libidinal impulses have an intensity of their own which is superior to any that come later and which may indeed be termed incommensurable. It is undoubtedly true that there is an antithesis between the attachment to the father and the masculinity complex; it is the general antithesis that exists between activity and passivity, masculinity and femininity. But this gives us no right to assume that only one of them is primary and that the other owes its strength merely to the force of defence. And if the defence against femininity is so energetic, from what other source can it draw its strength than from the masculine trend which found its first expression in the child's penis-envy and therefore deserves to be named after it?

A similar objection applies to Ernest Jones's view (1927) that the phallic phase in girls is a secondary, protective reaction rather than a genuine developmental stage. This does not correspond either to the dynamic or the chronological position of things.

NOTES

[The notes have been renumbered for this volume.]
1. In the well-known case of delusional jealousy reported by Ruth Mack Brunswick (1928), the direct source of the disorder was the patient's pre-Oedipus fixation (to her sister).
2. It is to be anticipated that men analysts with feminist views, as well as our women analysts, will disagree with what I have said here. They will hardly fail to object that

such notions spring from the 'masculinity complex' of the male and are designed to justify on theoretical grounds his innate inclination to disparage and suppress women. But this sort of psychoanalytic argumentation reminds us here, as it so often does, of Dostoevsky's famous 'knife that cuts both ways'. The opponents of those who argue in this way will on their side think it quite natural that the female sex should refuse to accept a view which appears to contradict their eagerly coveted equality with men. The use of analysis as a weapon of controversy can clearly lead to no decision.

3. [Angela Richards, the editor of the Pelican Freud Library, volume 7, in which this essay is collected, notes: This is the last phase of a long story. When, in his early analyses, Freud's hysterical patients told him that they had been seduced by their father in child-hood, he accepted these tales as the truth and regarded the traumas as the cause of their illness. It was not long before he recognized his mistake, and grasped the important fact that these apparently false memories were wishful phantasies, which pointed the way to the existence of the Oedipus complex. It was only in the present passage, however, that Freud gave his full explanation of these ostensible memories. He discusses this whole episode at greater length in Lecture 33 of his *New Introductory Lectures* (1933a), *PFL*, 2, 154. and the reference pp. 386–7 n.]

2

The Flight from Womanhood: The Masculinity-Complex in Women, as Viewed by Men and by Women

Karen Horney

In some of his latest works Freud has drawn attention with increasing urgency to a certain one-sidedness in our analytical researches. I refer to the fact that till quite recently the mind of boys and men only was taken as the object of investigation.

The reason for this is obvious. Psycho-analysis is the creation of a male genius, and almost all those who have developed his ideas have been men. It is only right and reasonable that they should evolve more easily a masculine psychology and understand more of the development of men than of women.

A momentous step towards the understanding of the specifically feminine was made by Freud himself in discovering the existence of penis-envy, and soon after the work of van Ophuijsen and Abraham shewed how large a part this factor plays in the development of women and in the formation of their neuroses. The significance of penis-envy has been extended quite recently by the hypothesis of the 'phallic phase'. By this we mean that in the infantile genital organization in both sexes only one genital organ, namely the male, plays any part, and that it is just this which distinguishes the infantile organization from the final genital organization of the adult.[1] According to this theory, the clitoris is conceived of as a phallus, and we assume that little girls as well as boys attach to the clitoris in the first instance exactly the same value as to the penis.[2]

The effect of this phase is partly to inhibit and partly to promote the subsequent development. Helene Deutsch has demonstrated principally the inhibiting effects. She is of the opinion that, at the beginning of every new sexual function (e.g. at the beginning of puberty, of sexual intercourse, of pregnancy and childbirth), this phase is re-animated and has to be overcome every time before a feminine attitude can be attained. Freud has elaborated her exposition on the positive side, for he believes that it is only penis-envy and the overcoming of it which gives rise to the desire for a child and thus forms the love-bond to the father.[3]

The question now arises whether these hypotheses have helped to make our insight into feminine development (insight which Freud himself has stated to be unsatisfactory and incomplete) more satisfactory and clearer.

Science has often found it fruitful to look at long familiar facts from a fresh point of view. Otherwise there is a danger that we shall involuntarily continue to classify all new observations amongst the same clearly defined groups of ideas.

The new point of view of which I wish to speak came to me by way of philosophy, in some essays by Georg Simmel.[4] The point which Simmel makes there and which has been in many ways elaborated since, especially from the feminine side,[5] is this: Our whole civilization is a masculine civilization. The State, the laws, morality, religion and the sciences are the creation of men. Simmel by no means deduces from these facts, as is commonly done by other writers, an inferiority in women, but he first of all gives considerable breadth and depth to this conception of a masculine civilization: 'The requirements of art, patriotism, morality in general and social ideas in particular, correctness in practical judgement and objectivity in theoretical knowledge, the energy and the profundity of life – all these are categories which belong as it were in their form and their claims to humanity in general, but in their actual historical configuration they are masculine throughout. Supposing that we describe these things, viewed as absolute ideas, by the single word "objective", we then find that in the history of our race the equation objective = masculine is a valid one.'

Now Simmel thinks that the reason why it is so difficult to recognize these historical facts is that the very standards by which mankind has estimated the values of male and female nature are 'not neutral, arising out of the difference of the sexes, but in themselves essentially masculine'. 'We do not believe in a purely "human" civilization, into which the question of sex does not enter, for the very reason that prevents any such civilization from in fact existing, namely, the (so to speak) naïve identification of the concept "human being"[6] and the concept "man",[7] which in many languages even causes the same word to be used for the two concepts. For the moment I will leave it undetermined whether this masculine character of the fundamentals of our civilization has its origin in the essential nature of the sexes or only in a certain preponderance of force in men, which is not really bound up with the question of civilization. In any case this is the reason why in the most varying fields inadequate achievements are contemptuously called "feminine", while distinguished achievements on the part of women are called "masculine" as an expression of praise.'

Like all sciences and all valuations, the psychology of women has hitherto been considered only from the point of view of men. It is inevitable that the man's position of advantage should cause objective validity to be attributed to his subjective, affective relations to the woman, and according to Delius[8] the psychology of women hitherto does actually represent a deposit of the desires and disappointments of men.

An additional and very important factor in the situation is that women have adapted themselves to the wishes of men and felt as if their adaptation were their true nature. That is, they see or saw themselves in the way that their men's wishes demanded of them; unconsciously they yielded to the suggestion of masculine thought.

If we are clear about the extent to which all our being, thinking and doing conform to these masculine standards, we can see how difficult it is for the individual man and also for the individual woman really to shake off this mode of thought.

The question then is how far analytical psychology also, when its researches have women for their object, is under the spell of this way of thinking, in so far as it has not yet wholly left behind the stage in which frankly and as a matter of course masculine development only was considered. In other words, how far has the evolution of women, as depicted to us today by analysis, been measured by masculine standards and how far therefore does this picture fail to present quite accurately the real nature of women.

If we look at the matter from this point of view our first impression is a surprising one. The present analytical picture of feminine development (whether that picture be correct or not) differs in no case by a hair's breadth from the typical ideas which the boy has of the girl.

We are familiar with the ideas which the boy entertains. I will therefore only sketch them in a few succinct phrases, and for the sake of comparison will place in a parallel column our ideas of the development of women.

The Boy's Ideas:	*Our Ideas of Feminine Development:*
Naïve assumption that girls as well as boys possess a penis.	For both sexes it is only the male genital which plays any part.
Realization of the absence of the penis.	Sad discovery of the absence of the penis.
Idea that the girl is a castrated, mutilated boy.	Belief of the girl that she once possessed a penis and lost it by castration.
Belief that the girl has suffered punishment which also threatens him.	Castration is conceived of as the infliction of punishment.
The girl is regarded as inferior.	The girl regards herself as inferior. Penis-envy.
The boy is unable to imagine how the girl can ever get over this loss or envy.	The girl never gets over the sense of deficiency and inferiority and has constantly to master afresh her desire to be a man.
The boy dreads her envy.	The girl desires throughout life to avenge herself on the man for possessing something which she lacks.

The existence of this over-exact agreement is certainly no criterion of its objective correctness. It is quite possible that the infantile genital organization of the little girl might bear as striking a resemblance to that of the boy as has up till now been assumed.

But it is surely calculated to make us think and take other possibilities into consideration. For instance, we might follow Georg Simmel's train of thought and reflect whether it is likely that female adaptation to the male structure should take place at so early a period and in so high a degree that the specific nature of a little girl is overwhelmed by it. Later I will return for a moment to the point that it does actually seem to me probable that this infection with a masculine point of view occurs in childhood. But it does not seem to me clear off-hand how everything bestowed by nature could be thus absorbed into it and leave no trace. And so we must return to the question I have already raised: whether the remarkable parallelism which I have indicated may not perhaps be the expression of a onesidedness in our observations, due to their being made from the man's point of view.

Such a suggestion immediately encounters an inner protest, for we remind ourselves of the sure ground of experience upon which analytical research has always been founded. But at the same time our theoretical scientific knowledge tells us that this ground is not altogether trustworthy, but that all experience by its very nature contains a subjective factor. Thus, even our analytical experience is derived from direct observations, dreams and symptoms and from the interpretations which we make or the conclusions which we draw from this material. Therefore, even when the technique is correctly applied, there is in theory the possibility of variations in this experience.

Now, if we try to free our minds from this masculine mode of thought, nearly all the problems of feminine psychology take on a different appearance.

The first thing that strikes us is that it is always, or principally, the genital difference between the sexes which has been made the cardinal point in the analytical conception and that we have left out of consideration the other great biological difference, namely, the different parts played by men and by women in the function of reproduction.

The influence of the man's point of view in the conception of motherhood is most clearly revealed in Ferenczi's extremely brilliant genital theory.[9] His view is that the real incitement of coitus, its true, ultimate meaning for both sexes, is to be sought in the desire to return to the mother's womb. During a period of contest man acquired the privilege of really penetrating once more, by means of his genital organ, into a uterus. The woman, who was formerly in the subordinate position, was obliged to adapt her organization to this organic situation and was provided with certain compensations. She had to 'content herself' with substitutes of the nature of phantasy and above all with harbouring the child, whose bliss she shares. At the most, it is only in the act of birth that she perhaps has potentialities of pleasure which are denied to the man.[10]

According to this view the psychic situation of a woman would certainly not be a very pleasurable one. She lacks any real primal impulse to coitus, or at least she is debarred from all direct – even if only partial – fulfilment. If this is so, the impulse towards coitus and pleasure in it must undoubtedly be less for her than for the man. For it is only indirectly, by circuitous ways, that she attains to a certain fulfilment of the primal longing – i.e. partly by the roundabout way of masochistic conversion and partly by identification with the child which she may conceive. These, however, are merely 'compensatory devices'. The only thing in which she ultimately has the advantage over the man is the, surely very questionable, pleasure in the act of birth.

At this point I, as a woman, ask in amazement, and what about motherhood? And the blissful consciousness of bearing a new life within oneself? And the ineffable happiness of the increasing expectation of the appearance of this new being? And the joy when it finally makes its appearance and one holds it for the first time in one's arms? And the deep pleasurable feeling of satisfaction in suckling it and the happiness of the whole period when the infant needs her care?

Ferenczi has expressed the opinion in conversation that in that primal period of conflict which ended so grievously for the female, the male as victor imposed upon her the burden of motherhood and all that it involves.

Certainly, regarded from the standpoint of the social struggle, motherhood *may* be a handicap. It is certainly so at the present time, but it is much less certain that it was so in times when human beings were closer to nature.

Moreover, we explain penis-envy itself by its biological relations and not by social factors; on the contrary, we are accustomed without more ado to construe the woman's sense of being at a disadvantage socially as the rationalization of her penis-envy.

But from the biological point of view woman has in motherhood, or in the capacity for motherhood, a quite indisputable and by no means negligible physiological superiority. This is most clearly reflected in the unconscious of the male psyche in the boy's intense envy of motherhood. We are familiar with this envy as such, but it has hardly received due consideration as a dynamic factor. When one begins, as I did, to analyse men only after a fairly long experience of analysing women, one receives a most surprising impression of the intensity of this envy of pregnancy, childbirth and motherhood, as well as of the breasts and of the act of suckling.

In the light of this impression derived from analysis one must naturally enquire whether an unconscious masculine tendency to depreciation is not expressing itself intellectually in the above-mentioned view of motherhood? This depreciation would run as follows: In reality women do simply desire the penis; when all is said and done motherhood is only a burden which makes the struggle for existence harder, and men may be glad that they have not to bear it.

When Helene Deutsch writes that the masculinity-complex in women plays a much greater part than the femininity-complex in man, she would seem to overlook the fact that the masculine envy is clearly capable of more successful sublimation than the penis-envy of the girl, and that it certainly serves as one, if not as the essential, driving force in the setting-up of cultural values.

Language itself points to this origin of cultural productivity. In the historic times which are known to us this productivity has undoubtedly been incomparably greater in men than in women. Is not the tremendous strength in men of the impulse to creative work in every field precisely due to their feeling of playing a relatively small part in the creation of living beings, which constantly impels them to an over-compensation in achievement?

If we are right in making this connection we are confronted with the problem why no corresponding impulse to compensate herself for her penis-envy is found in women? There are two possibilities; either the envy of the woman is absolutely less than that of the man or it is less successfully worked off in some other way. We could bring forward facts in support of either supposition.

In favour of the greater intensity of the man's envy we might point out that an actual anatomical disadvantage on the side of the woman exists only from the point of view of the pregenital levels of organization.[11] From that of the genital organization of adult women there is no disadvantage, for obviously the capacity of women for coitus is not less but simply other than that of men. On the other hand, the part of the man in reproduction is ultimately less than that of the woman.

Further, we observe that men are evidently under a greater necessity to depreciate women than conversely. The realization that the dogma of the inferiority of women had its origin in an unconscious male tendency could only dawn upon us after a doubt had arisen whether in fact this view was justified in reality. But if there actually are in men tendencies to depreciate women behind this conviction of feminine inferiority, we must infer that this unconscious impulse to depreciation is a very powerful one.

Further, there is much to be said in favour of the view that women work off their penis-envy less successfully than men from a cultural point of view. We know that in the most favourable case this envy is transmuted into the desire for a husband and child, and probably by this very transmutation it forfeits the greater part of its power as an incentive to sublimation. In unfavourable cases, however, as I shall presently show in greater detail, it is burdened with a sense of guilt instead of being able to be employed fruitfully, whilst the man's incapacity for motherhood is probably felt simply as an inferiority and can develop its full driving power without inhibition.

In this discussion I have already touched on a problem which Freud has recently brought into the foreground of interest:[12] namely, the question of the origin and operation of the desire for a child. In the course of the last decade our attitude towards this problem has changed. I may therefore be permitted to describe briefly the beginning and the end of this historical evolution.

The original hypothesis[13] was that penis-envy gave a libidinal reinforcement both to the wish for a child and the wish for the man, but that the latter wish arose independently of the former. Subsequently the accent became more and more displaced on to the penis-envy, till in his most recent work on this problem Freud expressed the conjecture that the wish for the child arose only through penis-envy and the disappointment over the lack of the penis in general, and that the tender attachment to the father came into existence only by this circuitous route – by way of the desire for the penis and the desire for the child.

This latter hypothesis obviously originated in the need to explain psychologically the biological principle of heterosexual attraction. This corresponds to the problem formulated by Groddeck, who says that it is natural that the boy should retain the mother as a love-object, 'but how is it that the little girl becomes attached to the opposite sex?'[14]

In order to approach this problem we must first of all realize that our empirical material with regard to the masculinity-complex in women is derived from two sources of very different importance. The first is the direct observation of children, in which the subjective factor plays a relatively insignificant part. Every little girl who has not been intimidated displays penis-envy frankly and without embarrassment. We see that the presence of this envy is typical and understand quite well why this is so; we understand how the narcissistic mortification of possessing less than the boy is reinforced by a series of disadvantages arising out of the different pregenital cathexes: the manifest privileges of the boy in connection with urethral erotism, the scoptophilic instinct, and onanism.[15]

I should like to suggest that we should apply the term *primary* to the little girl's penis-envy which is obviously based simply on the anatomical difference.

The second source upon which our experience draws is to be found in the analytical material produced by adult women. Naturally it is more difficult to form a judgement on this, and there is therefore more scope for the subjective element. We see here in the first instance that penis-envy operates as a factor of enormous dynamic power. We see patients rejecting their female functions, their unconscious motive in so doing being the desire to be male. We meet with phantasies of which the content is: 'I once had a penis; I am a man who has been castrated and mutilated', from which proceed feelings of inferiority and which have for after-effect all manner of obstinate hypochondriacal ideas. We see a marked attitude of hostility towards men, sometimes taking the form of depreciation and sometimes of a desire to castrate or maim them, and we see how the whole destinies of certain women are determined by this factor.

It was natural to conclude – and especially natural because of the male orientation of our thinking – that we could link these impressions on to the primary penis-envy and to reason *a posteriori* that this envy must possess an enormous intensity, an enormous dynamic power, seeing that it evidently gave rise to such effects. Here we overlooked the fact, more in our general estimation of the situation than in details, that this desire to be a man, so familiar to us from the analyses of adult women, had only very little to do with that early, infantile, primary penis-envy, but that it is a secondary formation embodying all that has miscarried in the development towards womanhood.

From beginning to end my experience has proved to me with unchanging clearness that the Oedipus complex in women leads (not only in extreme cases where the subject has come to grief, but *regularly*) to a regression to penis-envy, naturally in every possible degree and shade. The difference between the outcome of the male and the female Oedipus complexes seems to me in average cases to be as follows. In boys the mother as a sexual object is renounced owing to the fear of castration, but the male role itself is not only affirmed in further development but is actually over-emphasized in the reaction to the fear of castration. We see this clearly in the latency and pre-pubertal period in boys and generally in later life as well. Girls, on the other hand, not only renounce the father as a sexual object but simultaneously recoil from the feminine role altogether.

In order to understand this flight from womanhood we must consider the facts relating to early infantile onanism, which is the physical expression of the excitations due to the Oedipus complex.

Here again the situation is much clearer in boys, or perhaps we simply know more about it. Are these facts so mysterious to us in girls only because we have always looked at them through the eyes of men? It seems rather like it when we do not even concede to little girls a specific form of onanism but without more ado describe their auto-erotic activities as male; and when we conceive of the difference, which surely must exist, as being that of a negative to a positive, i.e. in the case of anxiety about onanism, that the difference is that between a castration threatened and castration that has actually taken place! My analytical experience makes it most decidedly possible that little girls have a specific feminine form of onanism (which incidentally differs in technique from that of boys), even if we assume that the little girl practises exclusively clitoral masturbation, an assumption which seems to me by no means certain. And I do not see why, in spite of its past evolution, it should not be conceded that the clitoris legitimately belongs to and forms an integral part of the female genital apparatus.

Whether in the early phase of the girl's genital development she has organic vaginal sensations is a matter remarkably difficult to determine from the analytical material produced by adult women. In a whole series of cases I have been inclined to conclude that this is so and later I shall quote the material upon which I base this conclusion. That such sensations should occur seems to me theoretically very probable for the following reasons. Undoubtedly the familiar phantasies that an excessively large penis is effecting forcible penetration, producing pain and haemorrhage and threatening to destroy something, go to show that the little girl bases her Oedipus phantasies most realistically (in accordance with the plastic concrete thinking of childhood) on the disproportion in size between father and child. I think too that both the Oedipus phantasies and also the logically ensuring dread of an internal, i.e. vaginal injury, go to show that the vagina as well as the clitoris must be assumed to play a part in the early infantile genital organization of women.[16] One might even infer from the later phenomena of frigidity that the vaginal zone has actually a stronger cathexis (arising out of anxiety and attempts at defence) than the clitoris, and this because the incestuous wishes are referred to the vagina with the unerring accuracy of the unconscious. From this point of view frigidity must be regarded as an attempt to ward off the phantasies so full of danger to the ego. And this would also throw a new light on the unconscious pleasurable feelings which, as various authors have maintained, occur at parturition or, alternatively, on the dread of childbirth. For (just because of the disproportion between the vagina and the baby and because of the pain to which this gives rise) parturition would be calculated to a far greater extent than subsequent sexual intercourse to stand to the unconscious for a realization of those early incest-phantasies, a realization to which no guilt is attached. The female genital anxiety, like the castration-dread of boys, invariably bears the impress of feelings of guilt and it is to them that it owes its lasting influence.

A further factor in the situation, and one which works in the same direction, is a certain consequence of the anatomical difference between the sexes. I mean that the boy can inspect his genital to see whether the dreaded consequences of onanism are taking place; the girl, on the other hand, is literally in the dark on this point and remains in complete uncertainty. Naturally this possibility of a reality-test does not weigh with boys in cases where the castration-anxiety is acute, but in the slighter cases of fear, which are practically more important because they are more frequent, I think that this difference is very important. At any rate the analytical material which has come to light in women whom I have analysed has led me to conclude that this factor plays a considerable part in feminine mental life and that it contributes to the peculiar inner uncertainty so often met with in women.

Under the pressure of this anxiety the girl now takes refuge in a fictitious male role.

What is the economic gain of this flight? Here I would refer to an experience which probably all analysts have had: they find that the desire to be a man is generally admitted comparatively willingly and that, when once it is accepted, it is clung to tenaciously, the reason being the desire to avoid the realization of libidinal wishes and phantasies in connection with the father. Thus the wish to be a man subserves the repression of these feminine wishes or the resistance against their being brought to light. This constantly recurring, typical experience compels us, if we are true to analytical principles, to conclude that the phantasies of being a man were at an earlier period devised for the very purpose of securing the subject against libidinal wishes in connection with the father. The fiction of male-ness enabled the girl to escape from the female role now burdened with guilt and anxiety. It is true that this attempt to deviate from her own line to that of the male inevitably brings about a sense of inferiority, for the girl begins to measure herself by pretensions and values which are foreign to her specific biological nature and confronted with which she cannot but feel herself inadequate.

Although this sense of inferiority is very tormenting, analytical experience emphatically shows us that the ego can tolerate it more easily than the sense of guilt associated with the feminine attitude, and hence it is undoubtedly a gain for the ego when the girl flees from the Scylla of the sense of guilt to the Charybdis of the sense of inferiority.

For the sake of completeness I will add a reference to the other gain which, as we know, accrues to women from the process of identification with the father which takes place at the same time. I know of nothing with reference to the importance of this process itself to add to what I have already said in my earlier work.

We know that this very process of identification with the father is one answer to the question why the flight from feminine wishes in regard to the father always leads to the adoption of a masculine attitude. Some reflections connected with what has already been said reveal another point of view which throws some light on this question.

We know that, whenever the libido encounters a barrier in its development, an earlier phase of organization is regressively activated. Now, according to Freud's latest work, penis-envy forms the preliminary stage to the true object-love for the father. And so this train of thought suggested by Freud helps us to some comprehension of the inner necessity by which the libido flows back precisely to this preliminary stage whenever and in so far as it is driven back by the incest-barrier.

I agree in principle with Freud's notion that the girl develops towards object-love by way of penis-envy, but I think that the nature of this evolution might also be pictured differently.

For when we see how large a part of its strength accrues to primary penis-envy only by retrogression from the Oedipus complex, we must resist the temptation to interpret in the light of penis-envy the manifestations of so elementary a principle of nature as that of the mutual attraction of the sexes.

Whereupon, being confronted with the question how we should conceive psychologically of this primal, biological principle, we should again have to confess ignorance. Indeed, in this respect the conjecture forces itself more and more strongly upon me that perhaps the causal connection may be the exact converse and that it is just the attraction to the opposite sex, operating from a very early period, which draws the libidinal interest of the little girl to the penis. This interest, in accordance with the level of development reached, acts at first in an auto-erotic and narcissistic manner, as I have described before. If we view these relations thus, fresh problems would logically present themselves with regard to the origin of the male Oedipus complex, but I wish to postpone these for a later paper. But, if penis-envy were the first expression of that mysterious attraction of the sexes, there would be nothing to wonder at either when analysis discloses its existence in a yet deeper layer than that in which the desire for a child and the tender attachment to the father occur. The way to this tender attitude towards the father would be prepared not simply by disappointment in regard to the penis but in another way as well. We should then instead have to conceive of the libidinal interest in the penis as a kind of 'partial love', to use Abraham's term.[17] Such love, might explain the process too by an analogy from later life: I refer to the fact that admiring envy is specially calculated to lead to an attitude of love.

With regard to the extraordinary ease with which this regression takes place I must mention the analytical discovery[18] that in the associations of female patients the narcissistic desire to possess the penis and the object-libidinal longing for it are often so interwoven that one hesitates as to the sense in which the words 'desire for it'[19] are meant.

One word more about the castration-phantasies proper, which have given their name to the whole complex because they are the most striking part of it. According to my theory of feminine development I am obliged to regard these phantasies also as a secondary formation. I picture their origin as follows: when the woman takes refuge in the fictitious male role her feminine genital anxiety is to some extent translated into male terms – the fear of vaginal injury becomes a phantasy of castration. The girl gains by this conversion, for she exchanges the uncertainty of her expectation of punishment (an uncertainty conditioned by her anatomical formation) for a concrete idea. Moreover, the castration-phantasy too is under the shadow of the old sense of guilt – and the penis is desired as a proof of guiltlessness.

Now these typical motives for flight into the male role – motives whose origin is the Oedipus complex – are reinforced and supported by the actual disadvantage under which women labour in social life. Of course we must recognize that the desire to be a man, when it springs from this last source, is a peculiarly suitable form of rationalization of those unconscious motives. But we must not forget that this disadvantage is actually a piece of reality and that it is immensely greater than most women are aware of.

Georg Simmel says in this connection that 'the greater importance attaching to the male sociologically is probably due to his position of superior strength', and that historically the relation of the sexes may be crudely described as that of master and slave. Here, as always, it is 'one of the privileges of the master that he has not constantly to think that he is master, whilst the position of the slave is such that he can never forget it'.

Here we probably have the explanation also of the under-estimation of this factor in analytical literature. In actual fact a girl is exposed from birth onwards to the suggestion – inevitable, whether conveyed brutally or delicately – of her inferiority, an experience which must constantly stimulate her masculinity complex.

There is one further consideration. Owing to the hitherto purely masculine character of our civilization it has been much harder for women to achieve any sublimation which should really satisfy their nature, for all the ordinary professions have been filled by men. This again must have exercised an influence upon women's feelings of inferiority, for naturally they could not accomplish the same as men in these masculine professions and so it appeared that there was a basis in fact for their inferiority. It seems to me impossible to judge to how great a degree the unconscious motives for the flight from womanhood are reinforced by the actual social subordination of women. One might conceive of the connection as an interaction of psychic and social factors. But I can only indicate these problems here, for they are so grave and so important that they require a separate investigation.

The same factors must have quite a different effect on the man's development. On the one hand they lead to a much stronger repression of his feminine wishes, in that these bear the stigma of inferiority; on the other hand it is far easier for him successfully to sublimate them.

In the foregoing discussion I have put a construction upon certain problems of feminine psychology which in many points differs from the views hitherto current. It is possible and even probable that the picture I have drawn is one-sided from the opposite point of view. But my primary intention in this paper was to indicate a possible source of error arising out of the sex of the observer, and by so doing to make a step forward towards the goal which we are all striving to reach: to get beyond the subjectivity of the masculine or the feminine standpoint and to obtain a picture of the mental development of woman which shall be truer to the facts of her nature – with its specific qualities and its differences from that of man – than any we have hitherto achieved.

NOTES

1. Freud, 'The Infantile Genital Organization of the Libido', *Collected Papers*, Vol. II, No. XX.
2. H. Deutsch, *Psychoanalyse der weiblichen Sexualfunktionen*, 1925.
3. Freud, 'Einige psychische Folgen der anatomischen Geschlechtsunterschiede', *Internationale Zeitschrift für Psychoanaluse*, Bd. XI. 1925.
4. Georg Simmel, *Philosophische Kultur*.
5. Cf. in particular Vaerting, *Männliche Eigenart in Frauenstaat und Weibliche Eigenart im Männerstaat*.
6. German *Mensch*.
7. German *Mann*.
8. Delius, *Vom Erwachen der Frau*.
9. Ferenczi, *Versuch einer Genitaltheorie* (1924).
10. Cf. also Helene Deutsch, *Psychoanalyse der Weiblichen Sexualfunktionem*; and Groddeck, *Das Buch vom Es*.
11. [Karen] Horney, 'On the Genesis of the Castration-complex in Women', *International Journal of Psycho-Analysis*, Vol. V, 1924.
12. Freud, 'Über einige psychische Folgen der anatomischen Geschlechtsunterschiede'.
13. Freud, 'On the Transformation of Instincts with special reference to Anal Erotism', *Collected Papers*, Vol. II, No. XVI.
14. Groddeck, *Das Buch vom Es*.
15. I have dealt with this subject in detail in my paper 'On the Genesis of the Castration-complex in Women'.
16. Since the possibility of such a connection occurred to me I have learnt to construe in

this sense, i.e. as representing the dread of vaginal injury, many phenomena which I was previously content to interpret as castration-phantasies in the male sense.

17. Abraham, *Versuch einer Entwicklungsgeschichte der Libido*, 1924.
18. Freud referred to this in *The Taboo of Virginity*.
19. German: *Haben-Wollen.*

3

The Significance of Masochism in the Mental Life of Women

Helene Deutsch

'FEMININE' MASOCHISM AND ITS RELATION TO FRIGIDITY.[1]

In the analysis of women we became familiar with the masculinity-complex before we learnt much about the 'femininity' which emerges from the conflicts accompanying development. The reasons for this later recognition were various. First of all, analysis comes to know the human mind in its discords rather than in its harmonies, and, when we turn the microscope of observation upon the woman, we see with special distinctness that the main source of her conflicts is the masculinity which she is destined to subdue. It followed that we were able to recognize the 'masculine' element in women earlier and more clearly than what we may term the nucleus of their 'femininity'. Paradoxical as it may sound, we approached the feminine element with greater interest when it formed part of a pathological structure and, as a foreign body, attracted a closer attention. When we encountered in men that instinctual disposition which we designate feminine and passive-masochistic, we recognized its origin and the weighty consequences it entailed. In the case of women we discovered that, even in the most feminine manifestations of their life – menstruation, conception, pregnancy and parturition – they had a constant struggle with the never wholly effaced evidences of the bisexuality of their nature. Hence, in my earlier writings[2] I shewed with what elemental force the masculinity-complex flares up in the female reproductive functions, to be once more subdued.

My aim in this paper is different. I want to examine the genesis of 'femininity', by which I mean the feminine, passive-masochistic disposition in the mental life of women. In particular I shall try to elucidate the relation of the function of feminine instinct to the function of reproduction, in order that we may first of all clarify our ideas about sexual inhibition in women, that is to say, about frigidity. The discussion will concern itself with theoretical premises rather than with the clinical significance of frigidity.

But first let us return to the masculinity-complex.

No one who has experience of analysis can doubt that female children pass through a phase in their libidinal evolution, in which they, just like boys, having abandoned the passive oral and anal cathexes, develop an erotogenicity which is actively directed to the clitoris as in boys to the penis. The determining factor in the situation is that, in a certain phase, sensations in the organs, which impel the subject to masturbation, tend strongly towards the genital and effect cathexis of that zone which in both sexes we have called the 'phallic'.

Penis-envy would never acquire its great significance were it not that sensations in the organs, with all their elemental power, direct the child's interest to these regions of the body. It is this which first produces the narcissistic reactions of envy in little girls. It seems that they arrive only very gradually and slowly at the final conclusion of their investigations: the recognition of the anatomical difference between themselves and boys. So long as onanism affords female children an equivalent pleasure they deny that they lack the penis, or console themselves with hopes that in the future the deficiency will be made good. A little girl, whom I had the opportunity of observing, reacted to the exhibitionistic aggression of an elder brother with the obstinate and often repeated assertion: 'Susie *has* got one', pointing gaily to her clitoris and labia, at which she tugged with intense enjoyment. The gradual acceptance of the anatomical difference between the sexes is accompanied by conflicts waged round the constellation which we term penis-envy and masculinity-complex.

We know that, when the little girl ceases to deny her lack of the penis and abandons the hope of possessing one in the future, she employs a considerable amount of her mental energy in trying to account for the disadvantage under which she labours. We learn from our analyses what a large part the sense of guilt connected with masturbation commonly plays in these attempts at explanation. The origin of these feelings of guilt is not quite clear, for they already exist in the phase in which the Oedipus complex of the little girl does not seem as yet to have laid the burden of guilt upon her.[3]

Direct observation of children shows beyond question that these first onanistic activities are informed with impulses of a primary sadistic nature against the outside world.[4] Possibly a sense of guilt is associated with these obscure aggressive impulses. It is probable that the little girl's illusion that she once had a penis and has lost it is connected with these first, sadistic, active tendencies to clitoral masturbation. Owing to the memory-traces of this active function of the clitoris, it is subsequently deemed to have had in the past the actual value of an organ equivalent to the penis. The erroneous conclusion is then drawn: 'I once did possess a penis'.

Another way in which the girl regularly tries to account for the loss is by ascribing the blame for it to her mother. It is interesting to note that, when the father is blamed for the little girl's lack of a penis, castration by him has already acquired the libidinal significance attaching to this idea in the form of the rape-phantasy. Rejection of the wish that the father should have been the aggressor generally betokens, even at this early stage, that rejection of the infantile feminine attitude to which I shall recur.

In his paper 'Some Consequences of the Anatomical Difference between the Sexes', Freud sees in the turning of the little girl to her father as a sexual object a direct consequence of this anatomical difference. In Freud's view, development from the castration to the Oedipus complex consists in the passing from the narcissistic wound of organ-inferiority to the compensation offered: that is to say, there arises the desire for a child. This is the source of the Oedipus complex in girls.

In this paper I shall follow up the line of thought thus mapped out by Freud. After the phallic phase, where the boy renounces the Oedipus complex and phallic masturbation, there is intercalated in the girl's development a phase which we may call 'post-phallic'; in this the seal is set upon her destiny of womanhood. Vaginal cathexis, however, is as yet lacking.

In spite of my utmost endeavours, I am unable to confirm the communications that have been made with reference to vaginal pleasure-sensations in childhood. I do not doubt the accuracy of these observations, but isolated exceptions in this case prove little. In my own observations I have had striking evidence in two instances of the existence of vaginal excitations and vaginal masturbation before puberty. In both, seduction with defloration had occurred very early in life.[5] If there were in childhood a vaginal phase, with all its biological significance, it surely could not fail to appear as regularly in our analytical material as do all the other infantile phases of development. I think that the most difficult factor in the 'anatomical destiny' of the woman is the fact that at a time when the libido is still unstable, immature and incapable of sublimation, it seems condemned to abandon a pleasure-zone (the clitoris as a phallic organ) without discovering the possibility of a new cathexis. The narcissistic estimation of the non-existent organ passes smoothly (to use a phrase of Freud's) 'along the symbolic equation: penis – child, which is mapped out for it'. But what becomes of the dynamic energy of the libido which is directed towards the object and yearns for possibilities of gratification and for erotogenic cathexes?

We must also reflect that the wish-phantasy of receiving a child from the father – a phantasy of the greatest significance for the future of a woman – is, nevertheless, in comparison with the reality of the penis, for which it is supposed to be exchanged, a very unreal and uncertain substitute. I heard of the little daughter of an analyst mother who, at the time when she was experiencing penis-envy, was consoled with the prospect of having a child. Every morning she woke up to ask in a fury: 'Hasn't the child come *yet*?' and no more accepted the consolation of the future than we are consoled by the promise of Paradise.

What, then, does happen to the actively directed cathexis of the clitoris in the phase when that organ ceases to be valued as the penis? In order to answer this question we may fall back on a familiar and typical process. We already know that, when a given activity is denied by the outside world or inhibited from within, it regularly suffers a certain fate – it turns back or is deflected. This seems to be so in the instance before us: the hitherto active-sadistic libido attached to the clitoris rebounds from the barricade of the subject's inner recognition of her lack of the penis and, on the one hand, regressively cathects points in the pregenital development which it had already abandoned, while, on the other hand, and most frequently of all, it is deflected in a regressive direction towards masochism. In place of the active urge of the phallic tendencies, there arises the masochistic phantasy: 'I want to be castrated', and this forms the erotogenic masochistic basis of the feminine libido. Analytic experience leaves no room for doubt that the little girl's first libidinal relation to her father is masochistic, and the masochistic wish in its earliest distinctively feminine phase is: 'I want to be castrated by my *father*'.[6]

In my view this turning in the direction of masochism is part of the woman's 'anatomical destiny', marked out for her by biological and constitutional factors, and lays the first foundation of the ultimate development of femininity, independent as yet of masochistic reactions to the sense of guilt. The original significance of the clitoris as an organ of activity, the masculine-narcissistic protest: 'I won't be castrated' are converted into the desire: 'I want to be castrated'. This desire assumes the form of a libidinal, instinctual trend whose object is the father. The woman's whole passive-feminine disposition, the entire genital desire familiar to us as the rape-phantasy, is finally explained if we accept the proposition that it originates in the castration-complex. *My view is that the Oedipus complex in girls is inaugurated by the castration-complex.* The factor of pleasure resides in the idea of a sadistic assault by the love-object and the narcissistic loss is compensated by the desire for a child, which is to be fulfilled through this assault. When we designate this masochistic experience by the name of the wish for castration, we are not thinking merely of the biological meaning – the surrender of an organ of pleasure (the clitoris) – but we are also taking into account the fact that the whole of this deflection of the libido still centres on that organ. The onanism belonging to this phase and the masochistic phantasy of being castrated (raped) employ the same organ as the former active tendencies. The astonishing persistency of the feminine castration-complex (including all the organic vicissitudes with which is associated a flow of blood) as we encounter it in the analyses of our female patients is thus explained by the fact that this complex contains in itself not only the masculinity-complex, but also the whole infantile set towards femininity.

At that period there is a close connection between the masochistic phantasies and the wish for a child, so that the whole subsequent attitude of the woman towards her child (or towards the reproductive function) is permeated by pleasure-tendencies of a masochistic nature.

We have an illustration of this in the dream of a patient whose subsequent analysis unequivocally confirmed what had been hinted in the manifest content of her dream; this occurred in the first phase of her analysis before much insight had been gained.

'Professor X. and you (the analyst) were sitting together. I wanted him to notice me. He went past my chair and I looked up at him and he smiled at me. He began to ask me about my health, as a doctor asks his patient; I answered with reluctance. All of a sudden he had on a doctor's white coat and a pair of obstetrical forceps in his hand. He said to me: "Now we'll just have a look at the little angel". I clearly saw that they were obstetrical forceps, but I had the feeling that the instrument was to be used to force my legs apart and display the clitoris. I was very much frightened and struggled. A number of people, amongst them you and a trained nurse, were standing by and were indignant at my struggling. They thought that Professor X. had specially chosen me for a kind of experiment, and that I ought to submit to it. As everyone was against me, I cried out in impotent fury: "No, I will not be operated on, you shall not operate on me".'

Without examining the dream more closely here, we can see in its manifest content that castration is identified with rape and parturition, and the dream-wish which excites anxiety is as follows: 'I want to be castrated (raped) by my father and to have a child' – a three-fold wish of a plainly *masochistic character*.

The first, infantile identification with the mother is always, independently of the complicated processes and reactions belonging to the sense of guilt, *masochistic*, and all the active birth-phantasies, whose roots lie in this identification, are of a bloody, painful character, which they retain throughout the subject's life.[7]

In order to make my views on frigidity intelligible I had to preface them with these theoretical considerations.

I will now pass on to discuss those forms of frigidity which bear the stamp of the masculinity-complex or penis-envy. In these cases the woman persists in the original demand for possession of a penis and refuses to abandon the phallic organization. Conversion to the feminine-passive attitude, the necessary condition of vaginal sensation, does not take place.

Let me mention briefly the danger of the strong attachment of all sexual phantasies to clitoris-masturbation. I think I have made it clear that the clitoris has come to be the executive organ, not only of active but of passive masochistic phantasies. By virtue of its past phase of masculine activity, a kind of organ-memory constitutes it the great enemy of any transference of pleasure-excitation to the vagina. Moreover, the fact that the whole body receives an increased cathexis of libido (since it has failed to find its focus) brings it about that, in spite of an often very vehement manifestation of the sexual instinct, the libido never attains to its centralized form of gratification.

In far the largest number of cases, feminine sexual inhibition arises out of the vicissitudes of that infantile-masochistic libidinal development which I have postulated. These vicissitudes are manifold, and every form they assume may lead to frigidity. For instance, as a result of the repression of the masochistic tendencies a strong narcissistic cathexis of the feminine ego may be observed. The ego feels that it is threatened by these tendencies, and takes up a narcissistic position of defence. I believe that, together with penis-envy, this is an important source of so-called feminine narcissism.

Akin to this reaction of repression is another reaction-formation which Karen Horney calls 'the flight from femininity', and of which she has given a very illuminating description. This flight from the incest-wish is, in my view, a shunning not only of the incestuous object (Horney), but most of all of the masochistic dangers threatening the ego which are associated with the relation to this object. Escape into identification with the father is at the same time a flight from the masochistically determined identification with the mother. Thus there arises the masculinity-complex, which I think will be strong and disturbing in proportion as penis-envy has been intense and the primary phallic active tendencies vigorous.

Repression of the masochistic instinctual tendencies may have another result in determining a particular type of object-choice later in life. The object stands in antithesis to the masochistic instinctual demands and corresponds to the requirements of the ego. In accordance with these the woman chooses a partner whose social standing is high or whose intellectual gifts are above the average, often a man whose disposition is rather of an affectionate and passive type. The marriage then appears to be peaceful and happy, but the woman remains frigid, suffering from an unsatisfied longing – the type of the 'misunderstand wife'. Her sexual sensibility is bound up with conditions whose fulfilment is highly offensive to her ego. How often do such women become the wretched victims of a passion for men who ill-treat them, thus fulfilling the woman's unconscious desires for castration or rape.

I have also observed how frequently – indeed, almost invariably – women whose whole lives are modelled on the lines of masculine sublimation-tendencies are markedly masochistic in their sexual experiences. They belong to that reactive masculine type which yet has failed to repress its original masochistic instinctual attitude. My experience is that the prospect of cure in these cases of relative frigidity, in which sexual sensation depends on the fulfilment of masochistic conditions, is very uncertain. It is peculiarly difficult to detach these patients from the said conditions and, when analysis has given them the necessary insight, they have consciously to choose between finding bliss in suffering or peace in renunciation.

The analyst's most important task is, of course, the abolition of the sexual inhibition in his patients, and the attainment of instinctual gratification. But sometimes, when the patient's instincts are so unfortunately fixed and yet there are good capacities for sublimation, the analyst must have the courage to smooth the path in the so-called 'masculine' direction and thus make it easier for the patient to renounce sexual gratification.

There are women who have strong sexual inhibition and intense feelings of inferiority, the origin of which lies in penis-envy. In such cases it is evidently the task of analysis to free these patients from the difficulties of the masculinity-complex and to convert penis-envy into the desire for a child, i.e. to induce them

to adopt their feminine role. We can observe that during this process the 'masculine aims' become depreciated and are given up. Nevertheless we often find that,
if we can succeed in making it easier for such women to sublimate their instincts
in the direction of 'masculine tendencies' and so to counter the sense of inferiority, the capacity for feminine sexual sensibility develops automatically in a striking manner. The theoretical explanation of this empirically determined fact is
self-evident.

It is but rarely in analytic practice that we meet with such cases of conditioned
frigidity as I have described or indeed with any cases of frigidity unaccompanied
by pathological symptoms, i.e. of sexual inhibition without symptoms of suffering. When such a patient comes to us, it is generally at the desire of the husband,
whose narcissism is wounded, and who feels uncertain of his masculinity. The
woman, actuated by her masochistic tendencies, has renounced the experience of
gratification for herself, and, as a rule, her desire to be cured is so feeble that the
treatment is quite unsuccessful.

As we know, hysteria which expresses itself in symptom-formation is extraordinarily capricious and varied as regards the nature of the sexual inhibition
displayed. One type of hysterical patient is driven by an everlasting hunger for
love-objects, which she changes without inhibition: her erotic life appears free,
but she is incapable of genital gratification. Another type is monogamous and
remains tenderly attached to the love-object, but without sexual sensibility; she
exhibits other neurotic reactions which testify to her morbid state. Such women
often dissipate the sexual excitation in the fore-pleasure, either owing to the
strong original cathexis of the pregenital zones or because by a secondary and
regressive reaction they are endeavouring to withhold the libido from the genital
organ which prohibitions and their own anxiety have barricaded off. Here one
often receives the impression that all the sense-organs, and indeed the whole
female body, are more accessible to sexual excitation than is the vagina, the organ
apparently destined for it. But conversion-symptoms turn out to be the seat of
false sexual cathexes. Behind the hysterical, pleasure-inhibiting, genital anxiety
we discover the masochistic triad: castration, rape and parturition. The fixation of
these wish-phantasies to the infantile object here becomes, as we know, the
motive factor in the neuroses. If this attachment is revolved by analysis, sexual
sensibility as a rule develops.

In touching briefly on the question of frigidity accompanying phobias and
obsessions, mention must be made of the remarkable fact that in these cases the
sexual disturbance is emphatically not in direct ratio to the severity of the neurosis. There are patients who remain frigid long after they have overcome their anxiety, and even after they have got rid of the most severe obsessional symptoms, and
the converse is also true. The uncertainty of obsessional neurosis – in so far as the
genital capacity of female patients is concerned – is most plainly manifested in
certain cases (several of which have come under my observation) in which the
most violent orgasm may result from hostile masculine identifications. The

vagina behaves like an active organ, and the particularly brisk secretion is designed to imitate ejaculation.

At the beginning of this paper I endeavoured to show that the masochistic triad constantly encountered in the analyses of women corresponds to a definite phase of feminine libidinal development and represents, so to speak, the last act in the drama of the vicissitudes of the 'feminine castration-complex'. In neurotic diseases, however, we meet above all with the reactions of the sense of guilt, and hence we find this primary-libidinal feminine masochism already so closely inter-woven and interlocked with the moral masochism, originating under pressure of the sense of guilt, that we miss the significance of that which is in origin libidi-nal. Thus many obscure points in connection with the feminine castration-complex became clearer if we recognize that, behind the castration-anxiety, there is further the repressed masochistic wish characteristic of a definite infantile phase of development in the normal feminine libido.

The task of psycho-analysis is to resolve the conflicts of the individual exis-tence. The instinctual life of the individual, which is the object of analytical scrutiny, strives towards the ultimate goal, amidst conflicts and strange vicissi-tudes, of *attainment of pleasure*. The preservation of the race lies outside these aims, and, if there be a deeper significance in the fact that the same means are employed to achieve the racial aim as to subserve the pleasure-tendency of man's instincts, that significance is outside the scope of our individualistic task.

Here I think we have a fundamental and essential difference between 'femi-nine' and 'masculine'. In the woman's mental life there is *something* which has nothing at all to do with the mere fact of whether she has or has not actually given birth to a child. I refer to the psychic representatives of motherhood which are here long before the necessary physiological and anatomical conditions have developed in the girl. For the tendency of which I am speaking the attaining of the child is the main goal of existence, and in woman the exchange of the racial aim for the individual one of gratification may take place largely at the expense of the latter. No analytical observer can deny that in the relation of mother to child – begun in pregnancy and continued in parturition and lactation – libidinal forces come into play which are very closely allied to those in the relation between man and woman.

In the deepest experience of the relation of mother to child it is masochism in its strongest form which finds gratification in the bliss of motherhood.

Long before she is a mother, long after the possibility of becoming one has ended, the woman has ready within her the maternal principle, which bids her take to herself and guard the real child or some substitute for it.

In coitus and parturition the masochistic pleasure of the sexual instinct is very closely bound up with the mental experience of conception and giving birth; just so does the little girl see in the father, and the loving woman in her beloved – a child. For years I have traced out in analyses this most intimate blending of the sexual instinct with that of the reproductive function in women, and always the question has hovered before my mind: When does the female child begin to be a woman and when a mother? Analytic experience has yielded the answer: *simultaneously*, in that phase when she turns towards masochism, as I described at the beginning of this paper. Then, at the same time as she conceives the desire to be castrated and raped, she conceives also the phantasy of receiving a child from her father. From that time on, the phantasy of parturition becomes a member of the masochistic triad and the gulf between instinctual and the reproductive tendencies is bridged by masochism. The interruption of the little girl's infantile sexual development by the frustration of her desire for the child gives to the sublimation-tendencies of the woman a very definite stamp of masochistic maternity. If it is true that men derive the principal forces which make for sublimation from their sadistic tendencies, then it is equally true that women draw on the masochistic tendencies with their imprint of maternity. In spite of this symbiosis, the two opposite poles, the sexual instinct and the reproductive function, may enter into conflict with one another. When this occurs, the danger is the greater in proportion as the two groups of tendencies are in close proximity.

Thus, a woman may commandeer the whole of her masochistic instinctual energy for the purpose of direct gratification and abandon sublimation in the function of reproduction. In the relation of the prostitute to the *souteneur* we have such an unadulterated product of the feminine masochistic instinctual attitude.

At the opposite end of the pole, yet drawing upon the same source, we have the *mater dolorosa*, the whole of whose masochism has come to reside in the relation of mother to child.

From this point I return to my original theme. There is a group of women who constitute the main body figuring in the statistics which give the large percentage of frigidity. The women in question are psychically healthy, and their relation to the world and to their libidinal object is positive and friendly. If questioned about the nature of their experience in coitus, they give answers which show that the conception of orgasm as something to be experienced by themselves is really and truly foreign to them. During intercourse what they feel is a happy and tender sense that they are giving keen pleasure and, if they do not come of a social environment where they have acquired full sexual enlightenment, they are convinced that coitus as a sexual act is of importance only for the man. In it, as in other relations, the woman finds happiness in tender, maternal giving.

This type of woman is dying out and the modern woman seems to be neurotic if she is frigid. Her sublimations are further removed from instinct and therefore, while on the one hand they constitute a lesser menace to its direct aims, they are, on the other, less well adapted for the indirect gratification of its demands. I think that this psychological change is in accordance with social developments and that it is accompanied by an increasing tendency of women towards masculinity. Perhaps the women of the next generation will no longer submit to defloration in the normal way and will give birth to children only on condition of freedom from pain.

And then in after-generations they may resort to infibulation and to refinements in the way of pain – ceremonials in connection with parturition. It is this masochism – the most elementary force in feminine mental life – that I have been endeavouring to analyse.

Possibly I have succeeded in throwing light on its origin, and, above all, on its importance and its application in the function of reproduction. This employing of masochistic instinctual forces for the purpose of race-preservation I regard as representing in the mental economy an act of sublimation of the part of the woman. In certain circumstances it results in the withdrawal from the direct gratification of instinct of the energy involved and in the woman's sexual life becoming characterized by frigidity without entailing any such consequences as would upset her mental balance and give rise to neurosis.

Let me now at the close of my paper give its main purport: *Women would never have suffered themselves throughout the epochs of history to have been withheld by social ordinances on the one hand from possibilities of sublimation, and on the other from sexual gratifications, were it not that in the function of reproduction they have found magnificent satisfaction for both urges.*

NOTES

1. Read at the Eleventh International Psycho-Analytical Congress, Oxford, 27 July 1929.
2. Helene Deutsch, *Psychoanalyse der weiblichen Sexualfunktionen*, Neue Arbeiten zur ärztlichen Psychoanalyse, Nr. V.
3. Freud, 'Some Psychological Consequences of the Anatomical Difference between the Sexes' ([*International Journal of Psycho-Analysis*], Vol. VIII, 1927). The argument in this paper of Freud's is that the Oedipus complex does not develop in girls until after the phase of phallic onanism. Cf. also Deutsch, op. cit.
4. In his paper on 'The Economic Problem in Masochism' (*Collected Papers*, Vol. II), Freud points out that the important task of the libido is to conduct into the outside world the instinct of destruction primarily inherent in living beings, transforming it into the 'instinct of mastery'. This is effected by means of the organ of motility, the muscular system. It appears to me that part of these destructive tendencies remains attached to the subject's own person in the earliest form of masturbation, which has as yet no libidinal object, and that it is thus intercalated between organic pleasure and motor discharge into the outside world. At any rate I have been able, with some degree of certainty, to establish the fact that children who are specially aggressive and active have a particularly strong urge to masturbation. (I am speaking here of the earliest masturbation, which is as yet autoerotic.) We see too that in little children frustration may provoke an outburst of rage and at the same time attempts at masturbation.
5. Even if further observations should prove the occurrence of vaginal sensations in childhood, the subsequent cathexis of the vagina as a sex-organ would still seem to be scarcely affected by the question of whether it had transitorily been a zone of excitation, very soon repressed so as to leave scarcely a trace, or whether it were only in later years of development that it assumed for the first time the role of the genital apparatus. The same difficulties arise in either case.

6. That 'feminine' masochism has its origin in this regressive deflection of the libido is clear evidence of the identity of 'erotogenic' and 'feminine' masochism.

7. In the second section of this paper I will revert to the part that the sense of guilt plays in feminine masochistic phantasies. In the present argument I am indicating the purely libidinal origin of feminine masochism, as determined by the course of evolution.

4

The Evolution of the Oedipus Complex in Women

Jeanne Lampl de Groot

One of the earliest discoveries of psycho-analysis was the existence of the Oedipus complex. Freud found the libidinal relations to the parents to be the centre and the acme of the development of childish sexuality and soon recognized in them the nucleus of the neuroses. Many years of psycho-analytical work greatly enriched his knowledge of the developmental processes in this period of childhood; it gradually became clear to him that in both sexes there is both a positive and a negative Oedipus complex and that at this time the libido finds physical outlet in the practice of onanism. Hence the Oedipus complex makes its appearance only when the phallic phase of libido-development is reached and, when the tide of infantile sexuality recedes, that complex must pass in order to make way for the period of latency during which the instinctual tendencies are inhibited in their aim. Nevertheless, in spite of the many observations and studies by Freud and other authors, it has been remarkable how many obscure problems have remained for many years unsolved.[1]

It seemed that one very important factor was the connection between the Oedipus and the castration complexes, and there were many points about this which were obscure. Again, understanding of the processes in male children has been carried much further than with the analogous processes in females. Freud ascribed the difficulties in elucidating the early infantile love-relations to the difficulty of getting at the material relating to them: he thought that this was due to the profound repression to which these impulses are subjected. The greater difficulty of understanding these particular mental processes in little girls may arise on the one hand from the fact that they are in themselves more complicated than the analogous processes in boys and, on the other, from the greater intensity with which the libido is repressed in women. Horney thinks that another reason is that, so far, analytical observations have been made principally by men.

In 1924 and 1925 Freud published two works which threw much light on the origin of the Oedipus complex and its connection with the castration complex. The first of these: 'The Passing of the Oedipus Complex',[2] shows what happens to that complex in little boys. It is true that several years previously in the 'History of an Infantile Neurosis'[2] and again, in 1923, in the paper entitled 'A Neurosis of Demoniacal Possession in the Seventeenth Century',[2] its fate in certain individual cases had been described. But in 'The Passing of the Oedipus Complex' we have the general application and the theoretical appreciation of this discovery and also the further conclusions to be deduced from it. The result arrived at in this paper is as follows: the Oedipus complex in male children receives its death-blow from the castration complex, that is to say, that both in the positive and the negative Oedipus attitude the boy has to fear castration by his father, whose strength is superior to his own. In the first case castration is the punishment for the inadmissible incest-wish and, in the second, it is the necessary condition of the boy's adopting the feminine role in relation to his father. Thus, in order to escape castration and to retain his genital he must renounce his love-relations with both parents. We see the peculiarly important part which this organ plays in boys and the enormous psychic significance it acquires in their mental life. Further, analytic experience has shown how extraordinarily difficult it is for a child to give up the possession of the mother, who has been his love-object since he was capable of object-love at all. This reflection leads us to wonder whether the victory of the castration complex over the Oedipus complex, together with the narcissistic interest in the highly-prized bodily organ, may not be due also to yet another factor, namely, the tenac-ity of the first love-relation. Possibly, too, the following train of thought may have some significance: If the boy gives up his ownership of the penis, it means that the possession of the mother (or mother-substitute) becomes for ever impossible to him. If, however, forced by the superior power of that far stronger rival, his father, he announces the fulfilment of his desire, the way remains open to him at some later period to fight his father with greater success and to return to his first love-object, or, more correctly, to her substitute. It seems not impossible that this knowledge of a future chance of fulfilling his wish (a knowledge probably phylo-genetically acquired and, of course, unconscious) may be a contributing motive in the boy's temporary renunciation of the prohibited love-craving. This would also explain why before, or just at the beginning of, the latency-period a little boy longs so intensely to be 'big' and 'grown-up'.

In this work, then, Freud largely explains the connections between the Oedipus and the castration-complex in little boys, but he does not tell us much that is new about the same processes in little girls. Hence his paper, published in 1925, 'Some Psychological Consequences of the Anatomical Distinction between the Sexes',[3] throws all the more light on the fate of the early infantile love-impulses of the little girl. Freud holds that in girls the Oedipus complex (he is speaking of the attitude which for the girl is positive: love for the father and rivalry with the mother) is a secondary formation, first introduced by the castration-complex; that is to say, that it arises after the little girl has become aware of the difference between the sexes and has accepted the fact of her own castration. This theory throws a new light on many hitherto obscure problems. By this assumption Freud explains many later developmental characteristics, various differences in the further vicissitudes of the Oedipus complex in girls and in boys, and in the super-ego formation in the two sexes, and so forth.

Nevertheless, even after this connection has been discovered, there are several problems which remain unsolved. Freud mentions that, when the castration-complex has become operative in the girl, that is, when she has accepted her lack of the penis and therewith become a victim of penis-envy, 'a loosening of the tender relation with the mother as love-object' begins to take place. He thinks that one possible reason for this may be the fact that the girl ultimately holds her mother responsible for her own lack of the penis and, further, quotes a historical factor in the case, namely, that often jealousy is conceived later on against a second child who is more beloved by the mother. But, Freud says, 'we do not very clearly understand the connection'. According to him another remarkable effect of penis-envy is the girl's struggle against onanism, which is more intense than that of the boy and which, in general, still makes itself felt at a later age. Freud's view is that the reason why the little girl revolts so strongly against phallic onanism is the blow dealt to her narcissism in connection with her penis-envy: she suspects that in this matter it is no use to compete with the boy and therefore it is best not to enter into rivalry with him. This statement gives rise to the invol-untary thought: How should the little girl who never possessed a penis and there-fore never knew its value from her own experience, regard it as so precious?

Why has the discovery of this lack in herself such far-reaching mental conse-quences and, above all, why should it begin to produce a mental effect at a certain moment, when it is probable that the bodily difference between herself and little boys has already been perceived countless times without any reaction? Probably the little girl produces pleasurable physical sensations in the clitoris in the same way and presumably with the same degree of intensity as the boy does in the penis, and perhaps she feels them in the vagina too. About this latter fact we received a communication by Josine Müller in the German Psycho-Analytical Society, and I have been told of it by an acquaintance, the mother of two little girls. Why, then, should there be this mental reaction in the girl to the discovery that her own member is smaller than the boy's or is lacking altogether? I should like to try whether the following considerations, which have been suggested to me by experiences in my analytic practice (to be narrated hereafter), may bring us a little nearer to answering these questions.

I think that several points will be clearer to us if we consider the previous history of the castration-complex or penis-envy in little girls. But, before doing so, it will be advisable to examine once more the analogous process in boys. As soon as the little boy is capable of an object-relation he takes as his first love-object the mother who feeds and tends him. As he passes through the pregenital phases of libidinal development he retains always the same object. When he reaches the phallic stage he adopts the typical Oedipus attitude, i.e. he loves his mother and desires to possess her and to get rid of his rival, the father. Throughout this development the love-object remains the same. An alternative in his love-attitude, an alteration characteristic of his sex, occurs at the moment when he accepts the possibility of castration as a punishment threatened by his powerful father for these libidinal desires of his. It is not impossible, indeed it is very probable, that the boy, even before he reaches the phallic stage and adopts the Oedipus attitude which coincides with it, has perceived the difference between the sexes by observing either a sister or a girl play-fellow. But we assume that this perception has no further significance to him. If, however, such a perception occurs when he is already in the Oedipus situation and has recognized the possibility of castration as a punishment with which he is threatened, we know how great its significance may be in his mind. The child's first reaction is an endeavour to deny the actuality of castration and to hold very tenaciously to his first love-object. After violent inward struggles, however, the little fellow makes a virtue of necessity; he renounces his love-object in order to retain his penis. Possibly he thus ensures for himself the chance of a renewed and more successful battle with his father at some later date – a possibility which I suggested earlier in this paper. For we know that, when the young man reaches maturity, he succeeds in wresting the victory from his father, normally in relation to a mother-substitute.

Now what happens in the little girl? She, too, takes as her first love-object the mother who feeds and tends her. She, too, retains the same object as she passes through the pregenital phases of libidinal evolution. She, too, enters upon the phallic stage of libido-development. Moreover, the little girl has a bodily organ analogous to the little boy's penis, namely, the clitoris, which gives her pleasurable feelings in masturbation. Physically she behaves exactly like the little boy. We may suppose that in the psychic realm also children of either sex develop up to this point in an entirely similar manner; that is to say, that girls as well as boys, when they reach the phallic stage enter into the Oedipus situation, i.e. that which for the girl is negative. She wants to conquer the mother for herself and to get rid of the father. Up to this point, too, a chance observation of the difference between the sexes may have been without significance; now, however, a perception of this sort is fraught with serious consequences for the little girl. It strikes her that the boy's genital is larger, stronger and more visible than her own and that he can use it actively in urinating, a process which for the child has a sexual significance. When she makes this comparison, the little girl must feel her own organ to be inferior. She imagines that hers was once like the boy's and that it has been taken from her as a punishment for her prohibited love-cravings in relation to the mother. At first the little girl tries, as does the boy, to deny the fact of castration or to comfort herself with the idea that she will still grow a genital. The acceptance of castration has for her the same consequences as for the boy. Not only does her narcissism suffer a blow on account of her physical inferiority, but she is forced to renounce the fulfilment of her first love-longings. Now at this point the difference in the psychic development of the two sexes sets in, in connection, that is, with the perception of the anatomical difference between male and female. To the boy castration was only a threat, which can be escaped by a suitable modification of behaviour. To the girl it is an accomplished fact, which is irrevocable, but the recognition of which compels her finally to renounce her first love-object and to taste to the full the bitterness of its loss. Normally, the female child is bound at some time to come to this recognition: she is forced thereby completely to abandon her negative Oedipus attitude, and with it the onanism which is its accompaniment. The object-libidinal relation to the mother is transformed into an identification with her; the father is chosen as a love-object, the enemy becomes the beloved. Now, too, there arises the desire for the child in the place of the wish for the penis. A child of her own acquires for the girl a similar narcissistic value to that which the penis possesses for the boy; for only a woman, and never a man, can have children.

The little girl, then, has now adopted the positive Oedipus attitude with the very far-reaching after-results of which we are so familiar. Freud has explained more than once that there is no motive for the shattering of the positive Oedipus complex in the female such as we have in the threat of castration in the case of the boy. Hence, the female Oedipus complex vanishes only gradually, is largely incorporated in the normal development of the woman, and explains many of the differences between the mental lite of women and of men.

We may now sum up by saying that the little girl's castration complex (or her discovery of the anatomical difference between the sexes) which, according to Freud, ushers in and renders possible her normal, positive Oedipus attitude, has its psychic correlative just as that of the boy, and it is only this correlative which lends it its enormous significance for the mental evolution of the female child. In the first years of her development as an individual (leaving out of account the phylogenetic influences which, of course, are undeniable) she behaves exactly like a boy not only in the matter of onanism but in other respects in her mental life: in her love-aim and object-choice she is actually a little man. When she has discovered and fully accepted the fact that castration has taken place, the little girl is forced once and for all to renounce her mother as love-object and therewith to give up the active, conquering tendency of her love-aim as well as the practice of clitoral onanism. Perhaps here, too, we have the explanation of a fact with which we have long been familiar, namely, that the woman who is wholly feminine does not know object-love in the true sense of the word: she can only 'let herself be loved'. Thus it is to the mental accompaniments of phallic onanism that we must ascribe the fact that the little girl normally represses this practice much more energetically and has to make a far more intense struggle against it than the boy. For she has to forget with it the first love-disappointment, the pain of the first loss of a love-object.

We know how often this repression of the little girl's negative Oedipus attitude is wholly or partly unsuccessful. For the female as well as for the male child it is very hard to give up the first love-object: in many cases the little girl clings to it for an abnormally long time. She tries to deny the punishment (castration) which would inevitably convince her of the forbidden nature of her desires. She firmly refuses to give up her masculine position. If later her love-longing is disappointed a second time, this time in relation to the father who does not give way to her passive wooing of his love, she often tries to return to her former situation and to resume a masculine attitude. In extreme cases this leads to the manifest homosexuality of which Freud gives so excellent and clear an account in 'A Case of Female Homosexuality'.[4] The patient about whom Freud tells us in this work made a faint effort on entering puberty to adopt a feminine love attitude but, later in the period of puberty, she behaved towards an elder woman whom she loved exactly like a young man in love. At the same time she was a pronounced feminist, denying the difference between man and woman; thus she had gone right back to the first, negative phase of the Oedipus complex.

There is another process which is perhaps commoner. The girl does not entirely deny the fact of castration, but she seeks overcompensation for her bodily inferiority on some plane other than the sexual (in her work, her profession). But in so doing she represses sexual desire altogether, that is, remains sexually unmoved. It is as if she wished to say: 'I may not and cannot love my mother, and so I must give up any further attempt to love at all'. Her belief in her possession of the penis has then been shifted to the intellectual sphere; there the woman can be masculine and compete with the man.

We may observe as a third possible outcome that a woman may form relationships with a man, and yet remain nevertheless inwardly attached to the first object of her love, her mother. She is obliged to be frigid in coitus because she does not really desire the father or his substitute, but the mother. Now these considerations place in a somewhat different light the phantasies of prostitution so common amongst women. According to this view they would be an act of revenge, not so much against the father as against the mother. The fact that prostitutes are so often manifest or disguised homosexuals might be explained in analogous fashion as follows: the prostitute turns to the man out of revenge against the mother, but her attitude is not that of passive feminine surrender but of masculine activity; she captures the man on the street, castrates him by taking his money and thus makes herself the masculine and him the feminine partner in the sexual act.

I think that in considering these disturbances in the woman's development to complete femininity we must keep two possibilities in view. Either the little girl has never been able wholly to give up her longing to possess her mother and thus has formed only a weak attachment to her father, or she has made an energetic attempt to substitute her father for her mother as love-object but, after suffering a fresh disappointment at his hands, has returned to her first position.

In the paper 'Some Psychological Consequences of the Anatomical Distinction between the Sexes', Freud draws attention to the fact that jealousy plays a far greater part in the mental life of women than in that of men. He thinks that the reason for this is that in the former jealousy is reinforced by deflected penis-envy. Perhaps one might add that a woman's jealousy is stronger than a man's because she can never succeed in securing her first love-object, while the man, when he grows up, has the possibility of doing so.

In another paragraph Freud traces the phantasy 'a child is being beaten' ultimately to the masturbation of the little girl when in the phallic phase. The child which is beaten or caressed is at bottom the clitoris (i.e. the penis); the being beaten is on one hand the punishment for the forbidden genital relation and on the other a regressive substitute for it. But in this phase the punishment for prohibited libidinal relations is precisely castration. Thus the formula 'a child is being beaten' means 'a child is being castrated'. In the phantasies in which the child beaten is a stranger the idea of its being castrated is intelligible at the first glance. It means: 'No one else shall have what I have not got'. Now we know that in the phantasies of puberty, which are often greatly metamorphosed and condensed, the child beaten by the father always represents as well the girl herself. Thus she is constantly subjecting herself to castration, for this is the necessary condition of being loved by the father; she is making a fresh effort to get clear of her old love-relations and reconcile herself to her womanhood. In spite of the many punishments, pains and tortures which the hero has to undergo, the phantasies always end happily'[5] i.e. the sacrifice having been made the passive, feminine love is victorious. Sometimes this immolation permits the return to masturbation, the first forbidden love-tendency having been duly expiated. Often, however, onanism remains none the less prohibited, or it becomes unconscious and is practised in some disguised form, sometimes accompanied by a deep sense of guilt. It seems as though the repeated submission to the punishment of castration signifies not only the expiation due to the feelings of guilt but also a form of wooing the father, whereby the subject experiences also masochistic pleasure.

To sum up what I have said above: In little boys who develop normally the positive Oedipus attitude is by far the more prevalent, for by adopting it the child through his temporary renunciation of the mother-object can retain his genital and perhaps ensure for himself thereby the possibility of winning later in life a mother-substitute; if he adopted the negative attitude, it would mean that he must renounce both from the outset. Little girls, however, normally pass through both situations in the Oedipus complex: first the negative, which occurs under precisely the same conditions as in boys, but which they are compelled finally to abandon when they discover and accept the fact of their castration. Now, the girl's attitude changes; she identifies herself with the lost love-object and puts in its place her former rival, the father, thus passing into the positive Oedipus situation. Thus, in female children the castration-complex deals a death-blow to the negative Oedipus attitude and ushers in the positive Oedipus complex.

This view confirms Freud's hypothesis that the (positive) Oedipus complex in women is made possible and ushered in by the castration-complex. But, in contradistinction to Freud, we are assuming that the castration-complex in female children is a secondary formation and that its precursor is the negative Oedipus situation. Further, that it is only from the latter that the castration-complex derives its greater psychic significance, and it is probably this negative attitude which enables us to explain in greater detail many peculiarities subsequently met with in the mental life of women.

I am afraid it will be objected that all this looks like speculation and is lacking in any empirical basis. I must reply that this objection may be just as regards part of what I have said, but that nevertheless the whole argument is built up on a foundation of practical experience, although unfortunately this is still but meagre. I shall now give a short account of the material which has led me to my conclusions.

Some time ago I was treating a young girl who had been handed over to me by a male colleague. He had analysed her for some years already, but there were certain difficulties connected with the transference which resisted solution. This girl had suffered from a somewhat severe hysterical neurosis. Her analysis had already been carried a good way. The normal, positive Oedipus complex, her rivalry with her sister and her envy of her younger brother's penis had been dealt with thoroughly, and the patient had understood and accepted them. Many of her symptoms had disappeared, but nevertheless she remained to her great regret unfit for work. When she came to me, the unresolved, ambivalent transference to the male analyst was playing a principal part in the situation. It was difficult to determine which was the stronger: her passionate love or her no less passionate hate. I knew this patient personally before she came to me for treatment, and the analysis began with a strong positive transference to me. Her attitude was rather that of a child who goes to its mother for protection. But after a short time a profound change began to take place. The patient's behaviour became first rebellious and hostile and soon, behind this attitude, there was revealed a very deep-seated and wholly active tendency to woo my love. She behaved just like a young man in love, displaying, for instance, a violent jealousy of a young man whom she suspected of being her rival in real life. One day she came to analysis with the idea that she would like to read all Freud's writings and become an analyst herself. The obvious interpretation which we tried first, namely, that she wanted to identify herself with me, proved inadequate. A series of dreams showed an unmistakable desire to get rid of my own analyst, to 'castrate' him and take his place, so as to be able to analyse (possess) me. In this connection the patient remembered various situations in her childhood when her parents quarrelled and she assumed a defensive and protective attitude towards her mother, and also times when they displayed mutual affection and she detested her father and wished to have her mother to herself. The analysis had long ago revealed a strong positive attachment to the father and also the experience which put an end to this. As a child the patient slept in a room next to her parents' and was in the habit of calling them at night when she had to urinate; of course, the intention was to disturb them. At first she generally demanded that her mother should come but, later on, her father.

She said that, when she was five years old, this once happened again and her father came to her and quite unexpectedly boxed her ears. From that moment the child resolved to hate him. The patient produced yet another recollection: when she was four years old she dreamt that she was lying in bed with her mother beside her and that she had a sense of supreme bliss. In her dream her mother said: 'That is right, that is how it ought to be'. The patient awoke and found that she had passed urine in bed; she was greatly disappointed and felt very unhappy.

She had various recollections of the time when she still slept in her parents' room. She said she used often to awake in the night and sit up in bed. These recollections are a fairly certain indication that she observed her parents' coitus. The dream she had as a child may very well have been dreamt after such an observation. It clearly represents coitus with her mother, accompanied by a sense of bliss. Even in later life urethral erotism played a particularly important part in this patient. Her disappointment on awaking showed that she was already conscious of her inability to possess her mother: she had long ago discovered the male genital in her younger brother. The bed-wetting can be construed either as a substitute for or a continuation of masturbation; the dream shows how intense must have been her emotional relation to her mother at that time. Hence it is clear that the patient, after the disappointment with her father (the box on the ears) tried to return to the earlier object, whom she had loved at the time of the dream, i.e. to her mother. When she grew up she made a similar attempt. After an unsuccessful love-affair with a younger brother of her father's she had for a short time a homosexual relation. This situation was repeated in her analysis when she came from the male analyst to me.

This patient stated that she had had a special form of the beating phantasy when she was from eight to ten years old. She described it as 'the hospital phantasy'. The gist of it was as follows: A large number of patients went to a hospital to get well. But they had to endure the most frightful pains and tortures. One of the most frequent practices was that they were flayed alive. The patient had a feeling of shuddering pleasure when she imagined their painful, bleeding wounds. Her associations brought recollections of how her younger brother sometimes pushed back the foreskin of his penis, whereupon she saw something red, which she thought of as a wound. The method of cure in her phantasy was therefore obviously a representation of castration. She identified herself on one occasion with the patients, who at the end always got well and left the hospital with great gratitude. But generally she had a different role. She was the protecting, compassionate Christ, who flew over the beds in the ward, in order to bring relief and comfort to the sick people. In this phantasy, which reveals its sexual-symbolic character in the detail of *flying*, the patient is the man who alone possesses his mother (for Christ was born without father), but who finally, in order to atone for the guilt and to be able to reach God the Father, offered the sacrifice of crucifixion (castration). After we broke off the analysis, which the patient gave up in a state of negative transference, a reaction to the disappointment of her love, she tried to translate this phantasy into reality by deciding to become a nurse. After a year, however, she abandoned this new profession for her earlier one, which was more masculine in character and much more suited to her temperament. Gradually, too, her feelings of hate towards me disappeared.

I had a second patient in whom I discovered similar processes with regard to the transference. In the first two months of treatment this patient produced very strong resistances. She acted the part of a naughty, defiant child and would utter nothing but monotonous complaints to the effect that she was forsaken and that her husband treated her badly. After we had succeeded in discovering that her resistance arose from feelings of hate towards me, due to envy and jealousy, the full, positive, feminine Oedipus attitude gradually developed in her – there entered into it both love for the father and the wish for a child. Soon, too, penis-envy began to show itself. She produced a recollection from her fifth or sixth year. She said that she had once put on her elder brother's clothes and displayed herself proudly to all and sundry. Besides this she had made repeated efforts to urinate like a boy. At a later period she always felt that she was very stupid and inferior and thought that the other members of her family treated her as if this were the case. During puberty she conceived a remarkably strong aversion from every sort of sexual interest. She would listen to none of the mysterious conversations in which her girl-friends joined. She was interested only in intellectual subjects, literature, etc. When she married she was frigid. During her analysis she experienced a desire to have some profession; this stood to her for being male. But her feelings of inferiority forbade any real attempt to compass this ambition. Up to this point the analysis had made splendid progress. The patient had one peculiarity: she remembered very little, but she enacted all the more in her behaviour. Envy and jealousy and the desire to do away with the mother were repeated in the most diverse guises in the transference. After this position had been worked through, a new resistance presented itself; we discovered behind it deep homosexual desires having reference to myself. The patient now began to woo my love in a thoroughly masculine manner. The times of these declarations of love, during which in her dreams and phantasies she always pictured herself with a male genital, invariably coincided with some active behaviour in real life. They alternated, however, with periods in which her behaviour was wholly passive. At such times the patient was once more incapable of anything; she failed in everything, suffered from her inferiority and was tortured with feelings of guilt. The meaning of this was that every time she conquered the mother, she was impelled to castrate herself in order to get free from her sense of guilt. Her attitude to masturbation also was noteworthy. Before analysis she had never consciously practised this habit; during the period when she was being treated she began clitoral masturbation. At first this onanism was accompanied by a strong sense of guilt; later, at times when her love-wishes in relation to her father were most vehemently manifested, the feelings of guilt abated. They were succeeded by the fear that the onanism might do her some physical harm: 'weaken her genitals'. At the stage when she was in love with me the sense of guilt reappeared and she gave up masturbating, because this fear became in her mind a certainty. Now this 'weak-ening' of the genital organs signified castration. Thus the patient constantly oscillated between a heterosexual and homosexual love. She had a tendency to regress to her first love-relation – with the mother – and at this stage tried to deny the fact of castration. To make up, however, she had to refrain from onanism and sexual gratification of any kind. She could not derive satisfaction from her husband, because she herself really wanted to be a man in order to be able to possess the mother.

Thus, in both the cases which I have quoted it was plain that behind the woman's positive Oedipus attitude there lay a negative attitude, with the mother as love-object, which revealed itself later in the analysis and therefore had been experienced at an earlier stage of development. Whether this evolution is typical cannot, of course, be asserted with any certainty from the observation of two cases. I should be inclined to believe that in other female patients the Oedipus complex has had a similar previous history, but I have not been able to gather enough material from their analyses to establish this beyond question. The phase of the negative Oedipus attitude, lying, as it does, so far back in the patient's mental history, cannot be reached until the analysis has made very considerable progress. Perhaps with a male analyst it may be very hard to bring this period to light at all. For it is difficult for a female patient to enter into rivalry with the father-analyst, so that possibly treatment under these conditions cannot get beyond the analysis of the positive Oedipus attitude. The homosexual tendency, which can hardly be missed in any analyses, may then merely give the impression of a later reaction to the disappointment experienced at the father's hands. In our cases, however, it was clearly a regression to an earlier phase – one which may help us to understand better the enormous psychic significance that the lack of a penis has in the erotic life of women. I do not know whether in the future it will turn out that my exposition in this paper explains only the development of these two patients of mine. I think it not impossible that it may be found to have a more general significance. Only the gathering of further material will enable us to decide this question.

NOTES

1. Abraham, 'Manifestations of the Female Castration Complex', 1920, *International Journal of Psycho-Analysis*, Vol. III, 1922. Alexander, 'The Castration Complex in the Formation of Character,' ibid., Vol. IV, 1923. Helene Deutsch, *Psychoanalyse der weiblichen Sexualfunktionen*, Neue Arbeiten zur ärztlichen Psychoanalyse, No. V. Horney, 'On the Genesis of the Castration Complex in Women', ibid., Vol. V, 1924; 'The Flight from Womanhood', ibid., Vol. VII, 1926. Van Ophuijsen, 'Contributions to the Masculinity Complex in Women' (1917), ibid., Vol. V, 1924.
2. *Collected Papers.*
3. *International Journal of Psycho-Analysis*, Vol. VIII, 1927.
4. *Collected Papers.*
5. Cf. Anna Freud, *Schlagephantasie und Tagtraum, Imago*, VIII, 1922.

5

Womanliness as a Masquerade

Joan Riviere

Every direction in which psycho-analytic research has pointed seems in its turn to have attracted the interest of Ernest Jones, and now that of recent years investigation has slowly spread to the development of the sexual life of women, we find as a matter of course one by him among the most important contributions to the subject. As always, he throws great light on his material, with his peculiar gift both clarifying the knowledge we had already and also adding to it fresh observations of his own.

In his paper on 'The Early Development of Female Sexuality'[1] he sketches out a rough scheme of types of female development, which he first divides into heterosexual and homosexual, subsequently subdividing the latter homosexual group into two types. He acknowledges the roughly schematic nature of his classification and postulates a number of intermediate types. It is with one of these intermediate types that I am today concerned. In daily life types of men and women are constantly met with who, while mainly heterosexual in their development, plainly display strong features of the other sex. This has been judged to be an expression of the bisexuality inherent in us all; and analysis has shown that what appears as homosexual or heterosexual character-traits, or sexual manifestations, is the end-result of the interplay of conflicts and not necessarily evidence of a radical or fundamental tendency. The difference between homosexual and heterosexual development results from differences in the degree of anxiety, with the corresponding effect this has on development. Ferenczi pointed out a similar reaction in behaviour,'[2] namely, that homosexual men exaggerate their heterosexuality as a 'defence' against their homosexuality. I shall attempt to show that women who wish for masculinity may put on a mask of womanliness to avert anxiety and the retribution feared from men.

It is with a particular type of intellectual woman that I have to deal. Not long ago intellectual pursuits for women were associated almost exclusively with an overtly masculine type of woman, who in pronounced cases made no secret of her wish or claim to be a man. This has now changed. Of all the women engaged in professional work today, it would be hard to say whether the greater number are more feminine than masculine in their mode of life and character. In University life, in scientific professions and in business, one constantly meets women who seem to fulfil every criterion of complete feminine development. They are excellent wives and mothers, capable housewives; they maintain social life and assist culture; they have no lack of feminine interests, e.g. in their personal appearance, and when called upon they can still find time to play the part of devoted and disinterested mother-substitutes among a wide circle of relatives and friends. At the same time they fulfil the duties of their profession at least as well as the average man. It is really a puzzle to know how to classify this type psychologically.

Some time ago, in the course of an analysis of a woman of this kind, I came upon some interesting discoveries. She conformed in almost every particular to the description just given; her excellent relations with her husband included a very intimate affectionate attachment between them and full and frequent sexual enjoyment; she prided herself on her proficiency as a housewife. She had followed her profession with marked success all her life. She had a high degree of adaptation to reality, and managed to sustain good and appropriate relations with almost everyone with whom she came in contact.

Certain reactions in her life showed, however, that her stability was not as flawless as it appeared; one of these will illustrate my theme. She was an American woman engaged in work of a propagandist nature, which consisted principally in speaking and writing. All her life a certain degree of anxiety, sometimes very severe, was experienced after every public performance, such as speaking to an audience. In spite of her unquestionable success and ability, both intellectual and practical, and her capacity for managing an audience and dealing with discussions, etc., she would be excited and apprehensive all night after, with misgivings whether she had done anything inappropriate, and obsessed by a need for reassurance. This need for reassurance led her compulsively on any such occasion to seek some attention or complimentary notice from a man or men at the close of the proceedings in which she had taken part or been the principal figure; and it soon became evident that the men chosen for the purpose were always unmistakable father-figures, although often not persons whose judgement on her performance would in reality carry much weight. There were clearly two types of reassurance sought from these father-figures: first, direct reassurance of the nature of compliments about her performance; secondly, and more important, indirect reassurance of the nature of sexual attentions from these men. To speak broadly, analysis of her behaviour after her performance showed that she was attempting to obtain sexual advances from the particular type of men by means of flirting and coquetting with them in a more or less veiled manner. The extraordinary incongruity of this attitude with her highly impersonal and objective attitude during her intellectual performance, which it succeeded so rapidly in time, was a problem.

Analysis showed that the Oedipus situation of rivalry with the mother was extremely acute and had never been satisfactorily solved. I shall come back to this later. But beside the conflict in regard to the mother, the rivalry with the father was also very great. Her intellectual work, which took the form of speaking and writing, was based on an evident identification with her father, who had first been a literary man and later had taken to political life; her adolescence had been characterized by conscious revolt against him, with rivalry and contempt of him. Dreams and phantasies of this nature, castrating the husband, were frequently uncovered by analysis. She had quite conscious feelings of rivalry and claims to superiority over many of the 'father-figures' whose favour she would then woo after her own performances! She bitterly resented any assumption that she was not equal to them, and (in private) would reject the idea of being subject to their judgement or criticism. In this she corresponded clearly to one type Ernest Jones has sketched: his first group of homosexual women who, while taking no interest in other women, wish for 'recognition' of their masculinity from men and claim to be the equals of men, or in other words, to be men themselves. Her resentment, however, was not openly expressed; publicly she acknowledged her condition of womanhood.

Analysis then revealed that the explanation of her compulsive ogling and coquetting – which actually she was herself hardly aware of till analysis made it manifest – was as follows: it was an unconscious attempt to ward off the anxiety which would ensue on account of the reprisals she anticipated from the father-figures after her intellectual performance. The exhibition in public of her intellectual proficiency, which was in itself carried through successfully, signified an exhibition of herself in possession of the father's penis, having castrated him. The display once over, she was seized by horrible dread of the retribution the father would then exact. Obviously it was a step towards propitiating the avenger to endeavour to offer herself to his sexually. This phantasy, it then appeared, had been very common in her childhood and youth, which had been spent in the Southern States of America; if a negro came to attack her, she planned to defend herself by making him kiss her and make love to her (ultimately so that she could then deliver him over to justice). But there was a further determinant of the obsessive behaviour. In a dream which had a rather similar content to this childhood phantasy, she was in terror alone in the house; then a negro came in and found her washing clothes, with her sleeves rolled up and arms exposed. She resisted him, with the secret intention of attracting him sexually, and he began to admire her arms and to caress them and her breasts. The meaning was that she had killed father and mother and obtained everything for herself (alone in the house), became terrified of their retribution (expected shots through the window), and defended herself by taking on a menial role (washing clothes) and by *washing off* dirt and sweat, guilt and blood, everything she had obtained by the deed, and 'disguising herself' as merely a castrated woman. In that guise the man found no stolen property on her which he need attack her to recover and, further, found her attractive as an object of love. Thus the aim of the compulsion was not merely to secure reassurance by evoking friendly feelings towards her in the man; it was chiefly to make sure of safety by masquerading as guiltless and innocent. It was a compulsive reversal of her intellectual performance; and the two together formed the 'double-action' of an obsessive act, just as her life as a whole consisted alternately of masculine and feminine activities.

Before this dream she had had dreams of people putting masks on their faces in order to avert disaster. One of these dreams was of a high tower on a hill being pushed over and falling down on the inhabitants of a village below, but the people put on masks and escaped injury!

Womanliness therefore could be assumed and worn as a mask, both to hide the possession of masculinity and to avert the reprisals expected if she was found to possess it – much as a thief will turn out his pockets and ask to be searched to prove that he has not the stolen goods. The reader may now ask how I define womanliness or where I draw the line between genuine womanliness and the 'masquerade'. My suggestion is not, however, that there is any such difference; whether radical or superficial, they are the same thing. The capacity for woman-liness was there in this woman – and one might even say it exists in the most completely homosexual woman – but owing to her conflicts it did not represent her main development, and was used far more as a device for avoiding anxiety than as a primary mode of sexual enjoyment.

I will give some brief particulars to illustrate this. She had married late, at twenty-nine; she had had great anxiety about defloration, and had had the hymen stretched or slit before the wedding by a woman doctor. Her attitude to sexual intercourse before marriage was a set determination to obtain and experience the enjoyment and pleasure which she knew some women have in it, and the orgasm. She was afraid of impotence in exactly the same way as a man. This was partly a determination to surpass certain mother-figures who were frigid, but on deeper levels it was a determination not to be beaten by the man.[3] In effect, sexual enjoy-ment was full and frequent, with complete orgasm; but the fact emerged that the gratification it brought was of the nature of a reassurance and restitution of some-thing lost, and not ultimately pure enjoyment. The man's love gave her back her self-esteem. During analysis, while the hostile castrating impulses towards the husband were in process of coming to light, the desire for intercourse very much abated, and she became for periods relatively frigid. The mask of womanliness was being peeled away, and she was revealed either as castrated (lifeless, inca-pable of pleasure), or was wishing to castrate (therefore afraid to receive the penis or welcome it by gratification). Once, while for a period her husband had had a love-affair with another woman, she had detected a very intense identification with him in regard to the rival woman. It is striking that she had had no homo-sexual experiences (since before puberty with a younger sister); but it appeared during analysis that this lack was compensated for by frequent homosexual dreams with intense orgasm.

In every-day life one may observe the mask of femininity taking curious forms. One capable housewife of my acquaintance is a woman of great ability, and can herself attend to typically masculine matters. But when, e.g. any builder or uphol-sterer is called in, she has a compulsion to hide all her technical knowledge from him and show deference to the workman, making her suggestions in an innocent and artless manner, as if they were 'lucky guesses'. She has confessed to me that even with the butcher and baker, whom she rules in reality with a rod of iron, she cannot openly take up a firm straightforward stand; she feels herself as it were 'acting a part', she puts on the semblance of a rather uneducated, foolish and bewildered woman, yet in the end always making her point. In all other relations in life this woman is a gracious, cultured lady, competent and well-informed, and can manage her affairs by sensible rational behaviour without any subterfuges. This woman is now aged fifty, but she tells me that as a young woman she had great anxiety in dealings with men such as porters, waiters, cabmen, tradesmen, or any other potentially hostile father-figures, such as doctors, builders and lawyers; moreover, she often quarrelled with such men and had altercations with them, accusing them of defrauding her and so forth.

Another case from every-day observation is that of a clever woman, wife and mother, a University lecturer in an abstruse subject which seldom attracts women. When lecturing, not to students but to colleagues, she chooses particularly feminine clothes. Her behaviour on these occasions is also marked by an inappropriate feature: she becomes flippant and joking, so much so that it has caused comment and rebuke. She has to treat the situation of displaying her masculinity to men as a 'game', as something *not real*, as a 'joke'. She cannot treat herself and her subject seriously, cannot seriously contemplate herself as on equal terms with men; moreover, the flippant attitude enables some of her sadism to escape, hence the offence it causes.

Many other instances could be quoted, and I have met with a similar mechanism in the analysis of manifest homosexual men. In one such man with severe inhibition and anxiety, homosexual activities really took second place, the source of greatest sexual gratification being actually masturbation under special conditions, namely, while looking at himself in a mirror dressed in a particular way. The excitation was produced by the sight of himself with hair parted in the centre, wearing a bow tie. These extraordinary 'fetishes' turned out to represent a *disguise of himself* as his sister; the hair and bow were taken from her. His conscious attitude was a desire to *be* a woman, but his manifest relations with men had never been stable. Unconsciously the homosexual relation proved to be entirely sadistic and based on masculine rivalry. Phantasies of sadism and *'possession of a penis'* could be indulged only while reassurance against anxiety was being obtained from the mirror that he was safely 'disguised as a woman'.

To return to the case I first described. Underneath her apparently satisfactory heterosexuality it is clear that this woman displayed well-known manifestations of the castration complex. Horney was the first among others to point out the sources of that complex in the Oedipus situation; my belief is that the fact that womanliness may be assumed as a mask may contribute further in this direction to the analysis of female development. With that in view I will now sketch the early libido-development in this case.

But before this I must give some account of her relations with women. She was conscious of rivalry of almost any woman who had either good looks or intellectual pretensions. She was conscious of flashes of hatred against almost any woman with whom she had much to do, but where permanent or close relations with women were concerned she was none the less able to establish a very satisfactory footing. Unconsciously she did this almost entirely by means of feeling herself superior in some way to them (her relations with her inferiors were uniformly excellent). Her proficiency as a housewife largely had its root in this. By it she surpassed her mother, won her approval and proved her superiority among rival 'feminine' women. Her intellectual attainments undoubtedly had in part the same object. They too proved her superiority to her mother; it seemed probable that since she reached womanhood her rivalry with women had been more acute in regard to intellectual things than in regard to beauty, since she could usually take refuge in her superior brains where beauty was concerned.

The analysis showed that the origin of all these reactions, both to men and women, lay in the reaction to the parents during the oral-biting sadistic phase. These reactions took the form of the phantasies sketched by Melanie Klein[4] in her Congress paper, 1927. In consequence of disappointment or frustration during sucking or weaning, coupled with experiences during the primal scene which is interpreted in oral terms, extremely intense sadism develops towards both parents.[5] The desire to bite off the nipple shifts, and desires to destroy, penetrate and disembowel the mother and devour her and the contents of her body succeed it. These contents include the father's penis, her fæces and her children – all her possessions and love-objects, imagined as within her body.[6] The desire to bite off the nipple is also shifted, as we know, on to the desire to castrate the father by biting off his penis. Both parents are rivals in this stage, both possess desired objects; the sadism is directed against both and the revenge of both is feared. But, as always with girls, the mother is the more hated, and consequently the more feared. She will execute the punishment that fits the crime – destroy the girl's body, her beauty, her children, her capacity for having children, mutilate her, devour her, torture her and kill her. In this appalling predicament the girl's only safety lies in placating the mother and atoning for her crime. She must retire from rivalry with the mother, and if she can, endeavour to restore to her what she has stolen. As we know, she identifies herself with the father; and then she uses the masculinity she thus obtains by *putting it at the service of the mother*. She becomes the father, and takes his place; so she can 'restore' him to the mother. This position was very clear in many typical situations in my patient's life. She delighted in using her great practical ability to aid or assist weaker and more helpless women, and could maintain this attitude successfully so long as rivalry did not emerge too strongly. But this restitution could be made on one condition only; it must procure her a lavish return in the form of gratitude and 'recognition'. The recognition desired was supposed by her to be owing for her self-sacrifices; more unconsciously what she claimed was recognition of her *supremacy* in *having* the penis to give back. If her supremacy were not acknowledged, then rivalry became at once acute; if gratitude and recognition were withheld, her sadism broke out in full force and she would be subject (in private) to paroxysms of oral-sadistic fury, exactly like a raging infant.

In regard to the father, resentment against him arose in two ways: (1) during the primal scene he took from the mother the milk, etc., which the child missed; (2) at the same time he gave to the mother the penis or children instead of to her. Therefore all that he had or took should be taken from him by her; he was castrated and reduced to nothingness, like the mother. Fear of him, though never so acute as of the mother, remained; partly, too, because his vengeance for the death and destruction of the mother was expected. So he too must be placated and appeased. This was done by masquerading in a feminine guise for him, thus showing him her 'love' and guiltlessness towards him. It is significant that this woman's mask, though transparent to other women, was successful with men, and served its purpose very well. Many men were attracted in this way, and gave her reassurance by showing her favour. Closer examination showed that these men were of the type who themselves fear the ultra-womanly woman. They prefer a woman who herself has male attributes, for to them her claims on them are less.

At the primal scene the talisman which both parents possess and which she lacks is the father's penis; hence her rage, also her dread and helplessness.[7] By depriving the father of it and possessing it herself she obtains the talisman – the invincible sword, the 'organ of sadism'; he becomes powerless and helpless (her gentle husband), but she still guards herself from attack by wearing towards him the mask of womanly subservience, and under that screen, performing many of his masculine functions herself – 'for him' – (her practical ability and management). Likewise with the mother: having robbed her of the penis, destroyed her and reduced her to pitiful inferiority, she triumphs over her, but again secretly; outwardly she acknowledges and admires the virtues of 'feminine' women. But the task of guarding herself against the woman's retribution is harder than with the man; her efforts to placate and make reparation by restoring and using the penis in the mother's service were never enough; this device was worked to death, and sometimes it almost worked her to death.

It appeared, therefore, that this woman had saved herself from the intolerable anxiety resulting from her sadistic fury against both parents by creating in phantasy a situation in which she became supreme and no harm could be done to her. The essence of the phantasy was her *supremacy* over the parent-objects; by it her sadism was gratified, she triumphed over them. By this same supremacy she also succeeded in averting their revenges; the means she adopted for this were reaction-formations and concealment of her hostility. Thus she could gratify her id-impulses, her narcissistic ego and her super-ego at one and the same time. The phantasy was the main-spring of her whole life and character, and she came within a narrow margin of carrying it through to complete perfection. But its weak point was the megalomanic character, under all the disguises, of the necessity for supremacy. When this supremacy was seriously disturbed during analysis, she fell into an abyss of anxiety, rage and abject depression; before the analysis, into illness.

I should like to say a word about Ernest Jones's type of homosexual woman whose aim is to obtain 'recognition' of her masculinity from men. The question arises whether the need for recognition in this type is connected with the mechanism of the same need, operating differently (recognition for services performed), in the case I have described. In my case direct recognition of the possession of the penis was not claimed openly; it was claimed for the reaction-formations, though only the possession of the penis made them possible. Indirectly, therefore, recognition was none the less claimed for the penis. This indirectness was due to apprehension lest her possession of a penis *should be* 'recognized', in other words 'found out'. One can see that with less anxiety my patient too would have openly claimed recognition from men for her possession of a penis, and in private she did in fact, like Ernest Jones's cases, bitterly resent any lack of this direct recognition. It is clear that in his cases the primary sadism obtains more gratification; the father has been castrated, and shall even acknowledge his defeat. But how then is the anxiety averted by these women? In regard to the mother, this is done of course by denying her existence. To judge from indications in analyses I have carried out, I conclude that, first, as Jones implies, this claim is simply a displacement of the original sadistic claim that the desired object, nipple, milk, penis, should be instantly surrendered; secondarily, the need for recognition is largely a need for absolution. Now the mother has been relegated to limbo; no relations with her are possible. Her existence appears to be denied, though in truth it is only too much feared. So the guilt of having triumphed over both can only be absolved by the father; if he sanctions her possession of the penis by acknowledging it, she is safe. By *giving* her recognition, he *gives* her the penis and to her instead of to the mother; then she has it, and she may have it, and all is well. 'Recognition' is always in part reassurance, sanction, love; further, it renders her supreme again. Little as he may know it, to her the man has admitted his defeat. Thus in its content such a woman's phantasy-relation to the father is similar to the normal Oedipus one; the difference is that it rests on a basis of sadism. The mother she has indeed killed, but she is thereby excluded from enjoying much that the mother had, and what she does obtain from the father she has still in great measure to extort and extract.

These conclusions compel one once more to face the question: what is the essential nature of fully-developed femininity? What is *das ewig Weibliche*? The conception of womanliness as a mask, behind which man suspects some hidden danger, throws a little light on the enigma. Fully-developed heterosexual womanhood is founded, as Helene Deutsch and Ernest Jones have stated, on the oral-sucking stage. The sole gratification of a primary order in it is that of receiving the (nipple, milk) penis, semen, child from the father. For the rest it depends upon reaction-formations. The acceptance of 'castration', the humility, the admiration of men, come partly from the over-estimation of the object on the oral-sucking plane; but chiefly from the renunciation (lesser intensity) of sadistic castration-wishes deriving from the later oral-biting level. 'I must not take, I must not even ask; it must be *given* me'. The capacity for self-sacrifice, devotion, self-abnegation expresses efforts to restore and make good, whether to mother or to father figures, what has been taken from them. It is also what Radó has called a 'narcissistic insurance' of the highest value.

It becomes clear how the attainment of full heterosexuality coincides with that of genitality. And once more we see, as Abraham first stated, that genitality implies attainment of a *post-ambivalent* state. Both the 'normal' woman and the homosexual desire the father's penis and rebel against frustration (or castration); but one of the differences between them lies in the difference in the degree of sadism and of the power of dealing both with it and with the anxiety it gives rise to in the two types of women.

NOTES

1. [*International Journal of Psycho-Analysis*], Vol. VIII, 1927.
2. 'The Nosology of Male Homosexuality', *Contributions to Psycho-Analysis* (1916).
3. I have found this attitude in several women analysands and the self-ordained defloration in nearly all of them (five cases). In the light of Freud's 'Taboo of Virginity', this latter symptomatic act is instructive.
4. 'Early Stages of the Oedipus Conflict', [*International Journal of Psycho-Analysis*], Vol. IX, 1928.
5. Ernest Jones, op. cit., ['The Early Development of Female Sexuality'] p. 469, regards an intensification of the oral-sadistic stage as the central feature of homosexual development in women.
6. As it was not essential to my argument, I have omitted all reference to the further development of the relation to children.
7. Cf. M. N. Searl, 'Danger Situations of the Immature Ego', Oxford Congress, 1929.

6

The Meaning of 'Penis Envy' in Women

Maria Torok

I

In the psychoanalysis of women there comes a period in which an envious desire for the male member and its symbolic equivalents appears. Episodic for some women, for others 'penis envy' constitutes the very centre of the therapeutic process. The exacerbated wish to possess that which women believe they are deprived of by fate – or by the mother – expresses a basic dissatisfaction some people have ascribed to the fact of being a woman. Surely, the conviction that their own privation is balanced by the enjoyment of others is common to patients of both sexes and is found in all analyses. Jealousy and demands, spite and despair, inhibition and anxiety, admiration and idealization, inner emptiness and depression: such are the diverse symptoms of this state of lack. Yet it is remarkable that, of men and women, only women should trace this state of lack to their very sex: 'It's because I'm a woman.' By which we should understand: I do not have a penis: hence my weakness, my inertia, my lack of intelligence, my dependency, and my ills.

> Ultimately, all women are like me and I cannot help feeling contempt for them, as I do for myself. It's they, the men, who possess all the qualities, all the attributes that make them worthy of admiration.

How is so radical a depreciation of one's own sex conceivable? Is it perhaps rooted in real biological inferiority? This idea came to seem inevitable to Freud following his unsuccessful attempts to cure the problem of desire for an inherently inaccessible object. We might as well 'preach to the fish' – as Freud's colorful phrase would put it – as overexert ourselves in the hopeless endeavour to make patients give up once and for all their childhood wish to acquire a penis. Given the failure of so many attempts, was it not inevitable for Freud to yield in the end, conceding some legitimacy to 'penis envy' and ascribing it to the nature of things: 'the biological inferiority of the female sex'? From another point of view, that of the child's affective development, Freud drew the same conclusion. So when he saw fit to insert an intermediary phallic phase between the anal and genital phases, he conceived the phallic phase as similar in both sexes, as wholly given to the male member. If it is true that the child at this stage knows one sex only, the male sex, then we should understand the little girl's frustration at being deprived of it. All her conjectures concerning her state of castration and the value of the opposite sex would spring from her frustration and from the phallic phase's inherent psycho-biological phallocentrism. That is why both 'penis envy' and the attempts to make women relinquish it are doomed to come to an *impasse* in Freud's psychoanalytic perspective. Yet, even if fantasies relating to the phallic stage may confirm Freud's thesis of its universality, it would seem that this state of affairs might still admit of a genuinely psychoanalytic explanation without our having to admit defeat by resorting to biology.

I understand Freud's exasperation on hearing: 'What's the use of continuing the analysis when you can't give me *that*.' But I also understand his patient's despair at being asked to *relinquish* a wish she holds so dear. And Freud would have been the first to agree that it is not the analyst's function to promote mourning for a desire, whatever it may be.

Now, precisely because it is envious, the woman's desire to have a 'penis' – to be a 'man' – can be exposed as a subterfuge through analysis. A desire can be satisfied, envy never. Envy can only breed more envy and destruction. It happens occasionally that envy disguised as desire achieves a semblance of satisfaction. Such is the so-called 'phallic' attitude of some women who are completely estranged through their imitation of the other sex or, at least, through their imitation of the image they have of it. The fragile structure thus constructed merely houses emptiness, anguish, and frustration. The task of analysis is to bring to light a genuine but forbidden desire lying buried beneath the guise of envy. Here as elsewhere, taking literally the analysand's protestations closes the door to analysis. One sure way to achieve this result would consist in legitimizing women's 'penis envy' by declaring that the supposed state of castration is a phylogenetically determined destiny. Another guaranteed means of falling short of analysis would be to posit extra-analytical motives – for instance the real inferiority of today's women as regards their social and cultural fulfilment – behind the demand to have a penis.

Analysts who do not recoil from 'penis envy', this 'stumbling block' of therapy, will want first of all to clarify the nature of the conflict giving rise to such a desperate compromise. They will also need to evaluate fairly the benefits this compromise solution of 'penis envy' nonetheless does provide the patient, ultimately taking advantage, for the purposes of treatment, of the painful contradictions into which 'penis envy' locks her.

Among post-Freudian authors, Ernest Jones and Melanie Klein have the signal distinction of no longer placing 'penis envy' beyond the scope of explanation. Both consider the quality of the initial relationship to the maternal Breast as decisive. As soon as analysis improves the initial maternal relation (by deconflictualizing the introjection of the Breast), envy in general and 'penis envy' in particular lose their reason for being.

It is perhaps useful to add and underscore the following: for the purposes of analysis object-things are mere *signs* of conscious or unconscious desires or fears, that is, they are reminders of the subjective moments that caused the subject to create them. In the libidinal economy of individuals, the object (and even the Object) is considered by Freud as a simple *mediator* towards attaining the aim of instinct: satisfaction. Admittedly, *object-things* have means and spatial dimensions and therefore are indeed *objective*: their being the same for everyone makes them apt for exchange, but also for disguising desires. Is it not the task of analysis to recover from behind the *thing* the desire it at once negates and fulfils? Analysing via the *things* an envious patient might desire, such as the 'penis' or the 'breast' (even if they are the analyst's), thus amounts to exacerbating the conditions that relate to objects (and Objects). Transcending these contradictions would involve, instead, the revelation (and hence dissolution) of the internal conflicts implied by the *satisfaction* of a vital desire. The fulfilment of desires is not a matter of objective realities; it is dependent on our capacity to satisfy ourselves and on our right to satisfaction, that is, on our freedom to accomplish the relational acts of our bodies. The objective realities, invoked as so many – usually inaccessible – objects of lack or desire, are traps in therapy; they are meant to mask (and therefore sustain) the inhibitions linked to relational acts. These traps – all too often – imprison desire for life.

For this reason I must exclude from this study on 'penis envy' the penis itself insofar as it is considered a thing, an objective, biological or social and cultural reality. Though a seeming paradox at first, the fact is that in 'penis envy' nothing matters less than the penis itself. This 'partial object' appears to me as a stop gap invented to camouflage a desire, as an artificially constructed obstacle thrown in the way of our becoming one with ourselves in the course of being liberated from inhibited acts. What is the purpose of this artifice? What does it protect against? This needs to be *understood* before it can be exposed.

However deformed or estranged from itself it may have become, the desire underlying 'penis envy' cannot fail to show through. As all others, this symptom deserves therefore our respect and attention. If through luck my analytic endeavour manages to reach the source of 'penis envy', rendering it superfluous, it will never exchange acquisition for renunciation. 'Penis envy' will disappear by itself the moment the painful state of lack responsible for it has ceased to exist.

II

The way is opened for a genuinely psychoanalytic approach, provided that we abandon objectivistic views about the coveted 'penis' and suspend all questions about the social and cultural legitimacy of the envy. For the psychoanalyst, 'penis envy' is not the symptom of an illness, but the symptom of a certain state of desire – the state of unfulfilled desire – no doubt due to contradictory demands. When the symptom is examined in this light, we will be surprised to find that such an examination, provided it does not stray from the analytic stance, is itself enough to reveal the general meaning of this phenomenon, the nature of the conflict it tends to resolve, and the manner in which it attempts to do so.

Freud's idea comes to mind: the little girl's discovery of the boy's genitals was sufficient reason to provoke envy and, concomitantly, hatred towards the mother, the person responsible, according to the girl's hypothesis, for her state of 'castra-tion'. And of course, 'penis envy' could not derive its *content*, that is its pretext, from anything but experience. A problem still remains: under what conditions must this experience take place for it to result in an insurmountable and lifelong envy? After all, we meet only what we are ready to meet. 'The polar bear and the whale . . . each confined to his element . . . cannot come together,' as Freud himself says. If indeed a decisive meeting occurs between the little girl and the boy, they meet not as different from each other but precisely as similar, namely as marked by sex. We may legitimately surmise that the girl's discovery of the boy's genitals occurs within the framework of the exploration of her own. The discovery of the penis must have come at a fitting moment for it to escape being reduced to a mere childhood incident. When the girl tells herself: 'My mother didn't give me *that*; that's why I hate her,' she takes advantage of a convenient pretext. Yet, in saying this, she merely gives voice to her hatred without in the least explaining it.

The association of 'penis envy' with conscious or unconscious hatred for the mother is a matter of common observation. But there is another no less remark-able clinical fact whose study allows us to understand the deep-seated motivation of this hatred. This clinically constant and highly significant fact is what I might call the *idealization* of the 'penis'. Many a woman has fantastic ideas about the male organ's extraordinary qualities: infinite power, good or bad, that guarantees for its owner absolute security and freedom as well as immunity to any form of anxiety or guilt; a power that brings him pleasure, love, and the fulfilment of all his wishes. *'Penis envy' is always envy of an idealized penis.*

> 'When you've got *that*' ["the penis"],' says Ida. 'you've got everything, you feel protected, nothing can harm you . . . You are what you are and others have no choice but to follow you and admire you . . . it represents absolute power; they [the men] can never sink into a state of need, of lack of love. Women? Incompleteness, perpetual dependency; they have the role of Vestal Virgins guarding the flame. It's no use speaking to me about the Virgin Mary . . . God the Father is a man! The word pure reminds me of puréed. . . . I've always held women in contempt.'
>
> 'I don't know why I have this feeling,' says Agnes, 'when it has nothing to

do with reality; but it's always been like that for me. It's as if men were the only ones made to be fulfilled, to have opinions, to develop themselves, to advance. And everything seems so easy to them . . . they're a force nothing at all opposes . . . they can do anything they want. And I simply stagnate, hesitate; I feel there's a wall in front of me . . . I've always had the feeling that I was not quite completed. Something like a statue waiting for its sculptor to make up his mind finally to shape its arms . . .'

When she was little, Yvonne always believed that boys 'succeed in everything . . . they are instantly fluent in several languages. . . . They could take all the candles in a church and no one would stop them. If ever they encounter an obstacle, they just naturally jump over it.'

These are eloquent descriptions of an *idealized* penis. It is clear that we are dealing with created meaning: 'the *thing*, whatever it may be, *that one does not have*'. Now, so vital a lack cannot be natural; it must be the effect of deprivation or renunciation. And so the question arises: how does it happen that one deprives oneself of so precious a part of oneself in exchange for an external 'object' that is inaccessible and, going by the patients' own words, even non-existent? For the time being let me limit myself to registering the fact. Its name is *repression*. Every idealization has a repression as its counterpart. But who benefits from this repression? The mother, of course, since the hatred is directed at her. In fact, though the idealized penis has no real existence at all, its counterpart for the subject – depression, self-depression, rage – does, and how! I will not believe for a second that affective states of such intensity could spring from an *idea* one fabricates about an object one has encountered. When the girls says to the mother living within her: 'I hate you because of that thing you never gave me,' she also says: 'My hatred is as legitimate as the absence of that thing in me is obvious. But rest assured, I do not consider legitimate the real hatred I feel because of the repression you force on my desire.'

What is this repression? It is surely no accident that precisely the penis – absent from the girl's anatomy – should have been invested with values from which the subject has had to divest herself. The genitals one does not have lend themselves famously to representing inaccessibility, especially since they are by nature alien to the experiences of one's own body. Here is then a marvellous way of symbolizing the prohibition affecting those very experiences of the body that relate to one's own genitals. In sum, the naming of an inaccessible thing as the coveted object masks the existence within the subject of a desire that has been refracted by an impassable barrier. The over-investment of the coveted thing merely demonstrates the primary value attached to the desire renounced. Women tend to overlook the agency responsible for repression, the faceless prosecutor dwelling within them. To unmask it would imply coming face to face with shadowy areas where hate and aggression smoulder against the Object one cannot help but love.

A complex unconscious speech, directed at the maternal imago, condenses in 'penis envy'. It can be made explicit in the following statements:

1. 'You see, it is in a *thing* and *not in myself* that I look for what I am deprived of.'
2. 'My attempts are *useless* since the thing cannot be acquired. The obvious futility of my efforts should guarantee my final renunciation of the desires you disapprove of.'
3. 'I want to insist on the value of this inaccessible thing so that you may see the extent of my sacrifice in allowing myself to be stripped of what I desire.'
4. 'I should accuse you and strip you in turn, but that is exactly what I want to avoid, deny, overlook, since I need your love.'
5. 'In short, idealizing the penis so as to covet it all the more is a way of reassuring you by showing you that I will never be at one with myself, that I will never attain that in myself. It is, I tell you, as impossible as changing into another body.'

This is the pledge of allegiance on which 'penis envy' affixes its seal.

The forbidden part of herself – which corresponds to 'penis' in the little girl's imagoic speech – is in fact her own sex, struck by repression.

An astonishing statement. It seems to mean that the girl's actual lived sex can be symbolized through the boy's penis *thing* or, put another way, through an anal understanding of the penis. In point of fact, a link is missing in the genesis of this symbolization: the anal relation to the mother. The idea of an accessible or inaccessible, condoned or forbidden 'thing' clearly alludes to this. The girl speaks to the Mother through her appeal: 'I want that *thing*.' Yet the demand's futility, both as regards its form and substance, implies reassurance towards the Mother. Her prerogatives will remain intact. It is quite remarkable that the Mother's authority or superiority in fact concerns less the 'things' that 'belong' to her than the acts of sphincter control, acts she claims to command at will. Hence the difficulty of the child, and later of the adult, in accepting these acts without first passing through the agency of the imago. 'Penis envy' needs to be situated in this context. It can be understood then that what is coveted is not the 'thing' but the acts allowing for mastery of 'things' in general. Coveting a *thing* amounts to displaying for the imago the renunciation of *acts*. In the anal relation the child will have transferred its acts of sphincter control to the Mother. The result is incredible aggression towards her. Let us consider the following process. The child cannot interpret the mother's exercise of control otherwise than as a show of her interest in possessing the child's faeces, even while they are still inside the body. The result: *the body's interior falls under the sway of maternal control.* The child can free herself from this domination only by a reversal of the relation: hence the birth of killer fantasies such as evisceration, evacuation of the maternal body's insides, as well as destruction of the place and function of the Mother's control.

This is why the Mother has to be reassured. The fact that the show of desire for the penis-thing – inaccessible anyhow – can perform this role of reassurance marvellously is now abundantly clear.

Let us return to the final question: What motivates this specific choice? Why precisely the 'penis'?

I shall use another, complementary way of examining symptoms in order to define the problem more precisely. In addition to my previous attempt to reconstruct the symptom's *retrospective* genesis, I now want to consider another equally crucial aspect, the symptom's *prospective* dimension. This examination will perhaps reward us along the way with some insight into the question of genesis itself.

I understand by the prospective dimension of a symptom (as well as of its underlying conflict) its genuinely negative aspect, one that provides no solution to any problem whatever and is solely defined by something not yet realized, not yet existent. The prospective dimension is the step ahead that was thwarted. At the same time, the prospective moment gives repression all of its dynamic features. The obstructed stages of affective maturation demand their realization. Even though a hint of these stages does shine through the repression blocking them, the symptom's prospective aspect is not articulated in the imagoic speech. The little girl could not, even unconsciously, state the following to her imago: 'Though I can tell you that I covet the penis-thing for my possession so that I can become a boy, what I cannot even feel is my aborted desire *to experience pleasure with* the penis as women do and as it is *preordinated* in the destiny of my own sex.' This very fact of genital non-attainment should put us on the road to identifying the repressive prohibitions. At stake is the experience that should have *prepared and set forth the girl's genital project and identification*, an experience obviously related to the 'precious part' of herself that underwent repression.

We have seen that this 'precious part' is a *set of acts* transferred to the anal Mother as her prerogative. The little girl had at her disposal, nonetheless, an indirect means of reclaiming what was taken from her: *identification* with the Mother, sovereign in her powers. And yet what we observe is a lack of identification, a lack 'penis envy' richly bespeaks. Thus I am led to incriminate not only the repression of pregenital anal conflicts but also a specific inhibition: the total or partial inhibition to masturbate, to have orgasm, and to engage in attendant phantasmic activities. 'Penis envy' emerges then as a disguised demand not for the genitals and attributes of the opposite sex, but for *one's own masturbatory and self-developmental desires realized through encounters with oneself in a combination of orgasmic and identificatory experiences.* This is the first conclusion we may draw regarding the general significance of 'penis envy' considered as a symptom in the Freudian sense of the term.

III

M. Klein, E. Jones, K. Horney, J. Müller have already indicated the early discovery and repression of vaginal sensations. As for me, I have observed that encounters with the other sex always entail a reminder or occasion for becoming aware of one's own. Clinically speaking, 'penis envy,' i.e., the discovery of the boy's genitals, is often associated with the repressed memory of an orgasmic experience.

> For a few sessions Martha had wild fits of laughter and crying. Her emotions gradually found their content: when she was a little girl, she met some boys in a swimming pool. Since then she has often repeated the sentence: 'I can't live *like that.*' In the course of her analysis this sentence would reappear when she was deeply depressed. 'Like that' means consciously: 'deprived of the penis'. But I came to understand with her that at the same time she 'pressed her thighs together', 'pushed part of her swimming suit inside', and felt something like a 'palpable wave'. The combination of laughter and tears (joy combined with guilt) refers to the idea: if I am 'like that' (feeling 'this wave'), 'will they still have me at home?' At puberty the same patient felt such intense guilt towards her mother that she kept her ignorant of the onset of her periods – the mark of her genital attainment – for an entire year.

Far from being neglected, her own genitals were a constant source of latent preoccupation since the need to please the mother triumphed at that time over the pleasure of orgasm. During the session, however, the desire for orgasm came to the fore through fits of laughter; previously it had had to stay repressed, precisely by means of 'penis envy'. At first there had been an 'inexpressible joy', 'tremendous hope'. But then, she does not know how, she came to be convinced: There is, not in me, but out there, not in my body, but in an *object*, something infinitely desirable, though entirely inaccessible. Note the contradiction: 'the palpable and infinitely good wave' makes the little girl lose her sense of *being good* for her environment. The 'penis' is perceived in this case as the 'good' sex organ, the one providing pleasure to its owner without any guilt. This sex organ is not linked to guilty acts of masturbation and incorporation; it combines pleasure for oneself and harmony with one's environment, resulting in conditions of truly perfect harmony. To feel 'this wave' must appear arrogant and evil to others. So this 'good' is relinquished in exchange for an external object, the idealized penis. The emptiness thus created within the subject fills with sadness, bitterness, and jealousy. Yet smouldering aggression cannot replace what has been missed: the progressive and sensuous awakening to maturity. Only analytic therapy can perform the reawakening by freeing the instruments needed to accomplish it.

The joy of maturational awakenings reaches beyond instant gratification. It signifies for the subject a sudden opening towards the future. It is the joy of great discoveries, of 'Yes! I understand.' 'So, that's how I can become *myself*, an adult. I acquire my value through the joy that turns me into myself.' (J. Müller notes aptly that the free play of infantile sexuality guarantees self-esteem.) True enough, the orgasmic joys of early childhood constitute the means whereby genital sex, and therefore the budding personality itself, are foreshadowed and developed. What do we discover on the way to orgasm? The power to fantasize our identity with our parents and the power to picture ourselves in all the positions of the primal scene, in accordance with the various levels at which it is apprehended. *The completed orgasm actually functions as verification: the fantasy is valid since it 'provoked' the climax.* Clearly, every inhibition of such a self-to-self encounter leaves a gap within the subject in place of a vital identification. The result is an incomplete 'body of one's own' (some might say Body Image) that has as its corollary a world peopled with fragmentary realities.[1]

There are dreams which aptly call to mind the meaning of orgasmic experience, its joyous sense of opening toward the future.

This is how Agnes recalls the memory and excitement of her early orgasmic experiences. She first dreamed of an 'incredible joy' turning into despair. At the seashore, she was waiting. An excited crowd thronged about her (= she awaits an orgasm). Behind her there were restrooms (= memory of a place where she masturbated). She was seated: all of a sudden, a wonderful animal, soft and silky to the touch, landed on her taut skirt. She is breathing heavily, extending her arms, caressing the animal. The admiring crowd vibrates with her. Everything was 'so full', so 'wonderful'. That moment, she says, *gathered together everything, all that I've been, all that I will be.* As when you say to yourself: I want to be in a beautiful place, I want it badly, and you've hardly thought it when you find you're already there.

As the dream also shows us, the repressed fantasy of orgasm concerns the incorporation of the penis in its instinctual function as the *generator of orgasm.* This same patient felt that her body was incomplete, and wished that a 'sculptor' would 'make her *arms*'. Barred from masturbatory activity, she was limited in the use of her hands, whose fundamental phantasmic function is that of being the *penis for the vagina.*

Ferenczi taught us that masturbation brings with it a doubling of the subject; s/he identifies at once with both parties in the couple, performing intercourse self-sufficiently. Let me add that this doubling – touching oneself, the 'I-me' experience authenticated by orgasm – also means: 'Since I can do it to myself all alone, I am liberated from those who, up to now, have provided or forbidden pleasure at will.' From a maternal relationship of dependence the child moves to autonomy through masturbation, though self-touching in both the literal and specifically reflexive sense of fantasy. In the process, the child sets up an independent maternal imago, which is seen as capable of having pleasure otherwise than with it.

This possibility is clearly lacking when the maternal imago prohibits masturbation. The imago develops in this case during excessive or premature anal training and carries over its despotism to all other analogical realms. An excessively demanding mother will produce a jealous, empty, and unsatisfied maternal imago. How could she be self-sufficient when her control over the child is her only satisfaction? Of course, she is jealous and irritable when she sees the child escape her grip during its masturbation. The effect of forbidding the child to masturbate is precisely to chain the child to the mother's body, hindering the child's own life project. Patients often express this situation by saying:

> A part of my body stayed in my mother (hand, penis, faeces, etc.). How can I take it back? She needs it so very much. This is her only pleasure.

The hand that 'belongs to Mother' cannot symbolize for the patient what the Mother forbids to herself; the hand will resist penile representation.[2] The road towards the Father is thereby blocked, and the relation of dependency on the Mother becomes permanent. The little girl experiences an insoluble dilemma: her only choices are either to identify with a mother deprived of value and dangerously aggressive, who needs to supplement herself by means of possession, or else to remain the futile appendage of an incomplete body. Women are likely to repeat these two positions in their relationship to their spouses. In analysis the aim is thus precisely to open the spellbinding circle of being and possessing. No, surely it is not a penis-appendage that is to be conferred; the 'arms' Agnes recovers correspond to the penis as complement, which represents, beyond being or possessing, *the right to act and to become.* When the 'penis-appendage envy' no longer masks the wish for a penis-complement, closeness to the Father need not falter on a sense of having too dangerous a body for the penis. This means at the same time that masturbation, as well as the (maturational) identifications, are no longer perceived as destructive of the Mother.

During analysis a sense of power always accompanies the removal of orgasmic inhibition. Analysis could not lead a woman towards genital maturity without first resolving the 'penis envy' that disguises the underlying anal conflict. It is especially inconceivable that 'penis envy' could be turned directly into a 'wish to have a child from the Father'. In fact, if the child is considered as playing the part of a coveted penis-object that fills a prior lack, the Mother – who without the child would lapse once again into bitterness and envy – will never be able to accept, desire, or encourage the evolution and fulfilment of the child's life project. Such a Mother has only one wish: to keep the child-penis in a state of perpetual appendage, as the illusory guarantee of her own plenitude.

To the extent that 'penis envy' is based on repression and shields the child from the return of *pregenital* anxieties, it is an obstacle to genitality and in no way can lead to it. The road going from 'penis envy' to genitality must go through an intermediary stage, the stage of tolerated fantasy. The child that is desired will no longer carry the meaning of what one *has*, but will represent something that is integrated into life's very becoming.

IV

Arrested in her genital attainment, the woman who suffers from 'penis envy' lives with a feeling of frustration whose core she barely suspects. She has only an external idea of what orgasmic genital fullness might be. In any case, she cannot achieve it as long as the repression remains.

As we have seen, the symptom consists in idealizing the penis, in investing it with all that one has lost hope of for oneself: one's own life project, that is, genital maturity. This is what fulfilment means for the child, since she does not yet have it. Surely, desire springs eternal, it never relents, yet it is forced to 'run on empty' or to fix itself to conventional images. Meeting a man in full orgasmic fusion is both the deepest wish of a woman suffering from 'penis envy' and the thing she most avoids. Daily clinical observation shows us women yearning for the penis-complement – for the means of feminine fulfilment – only to see them grappling with a threatening and jealous imago. This is how envy emerges, envy of the idealized penis along with hatred for its supposed owner. Thus disappointment triumphs over love and frustration over fullness.

The passage to the so-called genital phase goes hand in hand with the feeling: I am no longer 'castrated' since 'I can'. This means first and foremost the removal of inhibition from masturbatory acts and fantasies, which otherwise would block the analytic process itself. Repression being equivalent to a gap in the ego, to a restriction of one's power and worth, the removal of repression brings with it strength, self-esteem, and especially *confidence* in one's power and becoming.

'I don't know how to put it,' says Olga, 'the feeling your words left me with. I can't get over it. It's as if you had *transferred* power to me. Even though, I was very depressed the other day. But after leaving here, I repeated what you told me. All my anxiety melted away. I have rarely cried as I did this week . . . It's like a sudden source of light . . . And last night, I . . . no, I've never talked to anyone about those things. Anyway, it was like an *awakening*, I felt pleasure. Now I feel like trying things out and I've been flashing smiles at men and, you know, they respond nicely: I just can't get over it, people pay me compliments!'

During the previous session the two of us had understood how, by means of idealization, she forbade herself access to a reality within her reach and also to what extent this refusal was in full agreement with her mother's prohibition against approaching her father's virility. The rejection of the imago opened the road to the heart of the problem, masturbation. Olga came back a few sessions later with '*one* utterly cold hand', so cold that it seemed not to be hers. We talked about this in connection with all the objects her mother would not let her touch, including her own genitals. The 'utterly cold' hand was simply a show of compliance with the forbidding maternal imago.

Tracing the idealization of the 'penis' to the repression of masturbation frees up energy and clearly empowers one with one's own sex. This power, once taken from the child and now reclaimed, is the capacity to identify with the characters in the primal scene of each successive stage of development and the capacity to verify the transient accuracy of these identifications through the orgasmic pleasure produced by them.[3]

[. . .]

NOTES

[The notes have been renumbered for this volume.]

1. Masturbation might, of course, reappear later with a fantasy content corresponding to a different level, but the previous repression will have imprinted its negative mark on the personality as it develops subsequently.
2. It is surprising to note that, as an instrument for introjecting the primal scene, the hand always represents the genitals of the opposite sex.
3. This is so true that even the identification with the castrating prohibitor of 'auto-eroticism' entails masturbation fantasies. In the absence of such an identification – paradoxical and distressing though it may be – the prohibition acts as an effectual castration and manifests itself through a state of shock and great tension. Psychotic self-castration has this meaning of attempting to effect a lethal identification in despair so as to remove a no less lethal inhibition.

   There are two ways of endangering the child's maturational identifications, either by forbidding the orgasm that would confirm the validity of the child's attempts at self-elaboration, or by annihilating fantasy life through the substitution of objectal reality in the form of seduction. In the latter case, the process of identification through fantasy is short-circuited by an effective but premature realization. The crippling effects of the inhibition resulting from this traumatism are in all respects comparable to those that derive from the other extreme. This is why women suffering from masturbatory inhibition can at times reach for mythomaniac fantasies of rape, whereas those who suffered rape early behave as if they were inhibited orgasmically.

Suggested Further Reading

Useful further reading on Freud's views of female sexuality includes:

'Some Psychical Consequences of the Anatomical Distinction Between the Sexes' (1925), SE XIX; PFL 7.

'Fragment of an Analysis of a case of Hysteria' [Dora's Case], (1905), SE VII; PFL 8.

'Three Essays on the Theory Of Sexuality' (1905), SE VII; PFL 7.

Freud's 1926 essay 'The Question of Lay Analysis' is an extremely clear and programmatic outline of the theory, development and practice of psychoanalysis. SE XX; PFL 15.

Freud's Women by Lisa Appignanesi and John Forrester (1993) discusses the relationships between Freud and many of his female colleagues, followers and analysands and illuminates the significance of their contribution to Freud's own theories.

Further work by 'Freud's women' is indicated in the Bibliography below. Of these, the following may be of particular interest:

Karen Horney, 'On the Genesis of the Castration Complex in Women' (1923), 'The Denial of the Vagina' (1933) and 'The Dread of Woman' (1932), all of which are collected in Karen Horney, *Feminine Psychology* (1967).

Helene Deutsch, 'On Female Homosexuality' (1933) and 'The Psychology of Women in Relation to the Functions of Reproduction' (1925), collected in P. Roazen, *The Therapeutic Process, The Self and Female Psychology: Collected Psychoanalytic Papers* (1992).

Further essays by Helene Deutsch, Jeanne Lampl de Groot and others are collected in *The Psycho-Analytic Reader*, edited by Richard Fliess (1950).

An interesting response to Joan Riviere's essay is Stephen Heath's 'Joan Riviere and the Masquerade' collected (with Riviere's essay) in *Formations of Fantasy*, edited by Victor Burgin, James Donald and Cora Kaplan (1986).

The 'Translator's Introduction' to Maria Torok's and Nicolas Abraham's *The Wolf Man's Magic Word: A Cryptonomy* by Nicholas Rand (1986) contextualizes their work and explains their extension of Freud's psychoanalytic theory to their own 'cryptonomic analysis'.

An indispensable resource for students of Freud and Lacan, as a glossary and bibliographical cross-reference, is *The Language of Psychoanalysis* by L. Laplanche and J. B. Pontalis (1988).

PART 2: KLEIN AND OBJECT RELATIONS

Melanie Klein's 1928 paper, 'Early Stages of the Oedipus Complex', is included here to show both the manner of her allegiance to Freud, and her independence and innovativeness. The essay comes relatively early in Klein's career and corpus of work. Her autonomy became more pronounced as her work progressed, although she always continued to acknowledge a loyalty and intellectual debt to Freud.

If Freud's most shocking theory was that of infant sexuality, Klein's most startling must be her extension of this to an emphasis on infantile aggression. Powerful feelings of envy, guilt and hatred (manifest in cannibalistic and sadistic complexities of desiring to devour, cut and destroy, and then of fearing the same in retaliation) are pre-verbal and pre-Oedipal, and, in Klein's eventual opinion, may be innate. She is clear, even in this early essay, that these powerful and 'tainted' feelings are being developed before, rather than by, the Oedipus conflict as such. The development, too, of the child's super-ego is established in pre-genital phases which pre-date castration anxiety or penis envy. Strategies or 'defences' for dealing with these traumas include splitting what one apprehends into good or bad objects and projecting or introjecting them. These are concepts which Klein elaborated variously, and which are referred to and more thoroughly explicated in the essays which follow Klein's own.

Klein's analytical approach focused primarily, though not exclusively, on the analysis of children. She was thus led to place great importance on witnessing and interpreting children's play. We see in her essay here that Klein's emphasis is on the paramount significance of the mother – for children of both sexes. Freud discussed the valorization of the penis, Klein, the breast, showing its impact in respect of the child's earliest desires and frustrations. The first incidence of envy is not for the penis that is the father's, and which the unfortunate mother lacks, but rather, as Juliet Mitchell points out in her essay here, for a mother who 'has everything' – and who has the power to take (her) everything away.

Freud's theories and techniques have been seen as far-fetched, obsessive and discomforting, whereas Klein's may seem shocking indeed, not least for the ways in which the adult analyst provides for the child itself an interpretative narrative of the symbolism of the child's play. In *The Psychoanalysis of Children*, Klein describes a session with a particular child, the three-year-old Trude:

This child was very neurotic and unusually strongly fixated on her mother . . .
soon she had given me an idea of the nature of her complexes. She insisted upon
the flowers in a vase being removed; she threw a little toy man out of a cart into
which she had previously put him and heaped abuse on him; she wanted a
certain man with a high hat that figured in a picture-book she had brought with
her to be taken out of it; and she declared that the cushions in the room had been
thrown into disorder by a dog. My immediate interpretation of these utterances
in the sense that she desired to do away with her father's penis, because it was
playing havoc with her mother (as represented by the vase, the cart, the picture-
book and the cushion), at once diminished her anxiety . . . .[1]

Julia Segal, with reference to the extract above, acknowledges the reader's probable alarm upon approaching Klein's analysis of young children:

Reading such a description the reader may be astonished at the audacity of
Klein's interpretations: it probably did not occur to the reader that the vase, the
cart, the picture-book and cushion all represented the child's mother or the
contents of her body thrown into disorder. Nor may it be immediately obvious
why or that they should. What is astonishing is that it obviously did make
some kind of sense to the child. It seems in the cold light of day that this kind
of interpretation would be more likely to make the child run from a mad-
woman; in fact, she stayed and she wanted to come back.[2]

Whether the apparent efficacy of this approach – or, more particularly, of Klein's
specific abilities in a clinical situation – legitimates a 'school' of theory and practice is, however, a moot discussion point.[3] In the essay reprinted here, Klein's
interest is in the development of the super-ego through a number of phases and at
an earlier stage than Freud had suggested. She is also at pains to emphasize the
'epistemophilic impulse' in the child's development and the ways in which lack
of knowledge, limited perception and misinformation create an incipient tangle of
dreads and defences.

Kleinian 'object relations theory' has had, and continues to have, a significant
influence, and is often incorporated, to varying degrees, into more eclectic,
psychotherapeutic approaches: the essays which follow are a testament to this.
Even the deeply critical assessment by Noreen O'Connor and Joanna Ryan has to
begin by acknowledging the impact (for women in particular) of Klein's difference of emphasis in psychoanalytic theory:

Many feminists have been impressed by Melanie Klein's emphasis on the
centrality of the mother in the infant's early development. It has signified a
move from Freud's phallocentrism . . . for Klein, the baby's unconscious phantasies in relation to the breast initiate and underpin her relationship to others.

Nancy Chodorow, whose extract is taken from *The Reproduction of Mothering* (1978), also announces her debt to, and interest in, object relations theory: 'I apply object-relations theory and the theory of the personal ego to our understanding of masculine and feminine development.'[4] This very development is 'systemic, an outcome of family structures in which women mother'[5] and is manifest in what Chodorow calls 'Oedipal asymmetries'. Hers is an investigation into the sociological – and therefore culturally arbitrary – reproduction of gendered roles where fathers, for all their 'presence' are largely absent in the home and where mothers tend to be intensely present. She refers for the most part to heterosexual developments, and consequently, in this regard, to 'most women' or 'most often':

> Most women emerge from their oedipus complex oriented to their father and men as primary *erotic* objects, but it is clear that men tend to remain *emotionally* secondary, or at most, emotionally equal, compared to the primacy and exclusivity of an oedipal boy's emotional tie to his mother and women . . . [B]ecause the father is an additional important love object, who becomes important in the context of a relational triangle, the feminine inner object world is more complex than the masculine. [see p. 110 below]

The ways in which mothering is reproduced is attendant, for Chodorow, on these Oedipal object-relational differences. Women, who are not so exclusive in their attachments, and who experience themselves relationally, require the triangulation that a child provides. Here, the Freudian notion that the child is the surrogate for the missing penis has been modified, so that the child is the substitute which completes and re-enacts the girl's triangular Oedipal experience. For a man, the child is an interruption and an interference; *his* completion is found in the dyadic relation which has its foundation in his love-object relation to woman alone (first the mother and then her substitute). Chodorow aims to show that the asymmetries and inequalities in a male-dominated society have their origin in the Oedipal relation to the mother, a relation which is culturally specific and therefore not inevitable. Roles pertaining to human reproduction thus become thoroughly normatized by the far-reaching implications of their own complex 'reproduction'.

The extract from Juliet Mitchell's essay, 'The Question of Femininity and the Theory of Psychoanalysis', begins with Freud's notion of hysteria: 'the most Oedipal neurosis, the one that most utilizes bisexuality'. The very 'question of sexual difference – femininity and masculinity' is integral to hysteria, asserts Mitchell, and the 'repudiation of femininity' is the 'bedrock of psychoanalysis both as theory and therapy'. In tracing the 'compulsory' repudiation of femininity, Mitchell surmises that human subjectivity itself demands sexual categorization: 'one cannot be no sex', she states. While Virginia Woolf's *Orlando*, which she cites, may be an example in support of this premise, Jeanette Winterson's *Written on the Body* may now refute the claim that a novelist 'never writes of anyone of no sex, or in the middle of the dividing line'. Mitchell's essay is difficult and, as she herself acknowledges in a later preface not collected here, speculative: 'it represents work-in-progress; incomplete, uncertain'.[6] It is included here for, among other things, its attention to Klein, and particularly for its consideration of 'motherhood' and the complexity of a continuum of 'femininity', which must also be thoroughly repudiated. The mother *is not* feminine, but in her primal resplendence she belies the loss that femininity covers: she impels the hysteric, caught in the (bisexual) middle, simultaneously to reminisce and renounce.

Finally, a chapter specifically on Klein has been selected from Noreen O'Connor's and Joanna Ryan's more comprehensive, *Wild Desires and Mistaken Identities: Lesbianism and Psychoanalysis.* While the authors acknowledge those ground-breaking elements of Klein's 'genius' noted earlier, at the same time, they chart and lament the intransigence of her universalizing and normatizing notions of 'heterosexuality, potency, monogamy and absence of perversion'. O'Connor and Ryan contest this a priori refusal to consider homosexual relationships as anything other than problematical and predicated on failure.

NOTES

1. M. Klein, *The Psychoanalysis of Children* (London: Hogarth Press and the Institute o Psychoanalysis, 1975), pp. 21–2.
2. J. Segal, *Melanie Klein* (London: Sage, 1993), p. 59.
3. Julia Segal's introduction to Klein, cited above, provides an excellent overview, not just of Klein's own work, but also of those who have been influenced by or have been critical of it. See Segal's chapters, 'Criticisms and Rebuttals' and 'The Overall Influence of Melanie Klein'.
4. N. Chodorow, *The Reproduction of Mothering* (Berkeley, Los Angeles, London: University of California Press, 1978), p. 54.
5. Ibid.
6. Juliet Mitchell, preface to 'The Question of Femininity and the Theory of Psychoanalysis', *Women: The Longest Revolution* (London: Virago, 1984), p. 295.

7

Early Stages of the Oedipus Conflict[1]

Melanie Klein

In my analyses of children, especially of children between the ages of three and six, I have come to a number of conclusions of which I shall here present a summary.

I have repeatedly alluded to the conclusion that the Oedipus complex comes into operation earlier than is usually supposed. In my last paper, 'The Psychological Principles of Infant Analysis',[2] I discussed this subject in greater detail. The conclusion which I reached there was that the Oedipus tendencies are released in consequence of the frustration which the child experiences at weaning, and that they make their appearance at the end of the first and the beginning of the second year of life; they receive reinforcement through the anal frustrations undergone during training in cleanliness. The next determining influence upon the mental processes is that of the anatomical difference between the sexes.

The boy, when he finds himself impelled to abandon the oral and anal positions for the genital, passes on to the aim of *penetration* associated with possession of the penis. Thus he changes not only his libido-position, but its *aim*, and this enables him to retain his original love-object. In the girl, on the other hand, the *receptive* aim is carried over from the oral to the genital position: she changes her libido-position, but retains its aim, which has already led to disappointment in relation to her mother. In this way receptivity for the penis is induced in the girl, who then turns to the father as her love-object.

The very onset of the Oedipus wishes, however, already becomes associated with incipient dread of castration and feelings of guilt.

The analysis of adults, as well as of children, has familiarized us with the fact that the pregenital instinctual impulses carry with them a sense of guilt, and it was thought at first that the feelings of guilt were of subsequent growth, displaced back on to these tendencies, though not originally associated with them. Ferenczi assumes that, connected with the urethral and anal impulses, there is a 'kind of physiological forerunner of the super-ego', which he terms 'sphincter-morality'. According to Abraham, anxiety makes its appearance on the cannibalistic level, while the sense of guilt arises in the succeeding early anal-sadistic phase.

My findings lead rather further. They shew that the sense of guilt associated with pregenital fixation is already the direct effect of the Oedipus conflict. And this seems to account satisfactorily for the genesis of such feelings, for we know the sense of guilt to be simply a result of the introjection (already accomplished or, as I would add, in process of being accomplished) of the Oedipus love-objects: that is, a sense of guilt is a product of the formation of the super-ego.

The analysis of little children reveals the structure of the super-ego as built up of identifications dating from very different periods and strata in the mental life. These identifications are surprisingly contradictory in character, over-indulgence and excessive severity existing side by side. We find in them, too, an explanation of the severity of the super-ego, which comes out specially plainly in these infant analyses. It does not seem clear why a child of, say, four years old should set up in his mind an unreal, phantastic image of parents who devour, cut and bite. But is *is* clear why in a child of about *one year* old the anxiety caused by the beginning of the Oedipus conflict takes the form of a dread of being devoured and destroyed. The child himself desires to destroy the libidinal object by biting, devouring and cutting it, which leads to anxiety, since awakening of the Oedipus tendencies is followed by introjection of the object, which then becomes one from which punishment is to be expected. The child then dreads a punishment corresponding to the offence: the super-ego becomes something which bites, devours and cuts.

The connection between the formation of the super-ego and the pregenital phases of development is very important from two points of view. On the one hand, the sense of guilt attaches itself to the oral and anal-sadistic phases, which as yet predominate; and, on the other, the super-ego comes into being while these phases are in the ascendant, which accounts for its sadistic severity.

These conclusions open up a new perspective. Only by strong repression can the still very feeble ego defend itself against a super-ego so menacing. Since the Oedipus tendencies are at first chiefly expressed in the form of oral and anal impulses, the question of which fixations will predominate in the Oedipus development will be mainly determined by the degree of the repression which takes place at this early stage.

Another reason why the direct connection between the pregenital phase of development and the sense of guilt is so important is that the oral and anal frustrations, which are the prototypes of all later frustrations in life, at the same time signify *punishment* and give rise to anxiety. This circumstance makes the frustration more acutely felt, and this bitterness contributes largely to the hardship of all subsequent frustrations.

We find that important consequences ensue from the fact that the ego is still so little developed when it is assailed by the onset of the Oedipus tendencies and the incipient sexual curiosity associated with them. Still quite undeveloped intellectually, it is exposed to an onrush of problems and questions. One of the most bitter grievances which we come upon in the unconscious is that this tremendous questioning impulse, which is apparently only partly conscious and even so far as it is cannot yet be expressed in words, remains unanswered. Another reproach follows hard upon this, namely, that the child could not understand words and speech. Thus his first questions go back beyond the beginnings of his under-standing of speech.

In analysis both these grievances give rise to an extraordinary amount of hate. Singly or in conjunction they are the cause of numerous inhibitions of the episte-mophilic impulse: for instance, the incapacity to learn foreign languages, and, further, hatred of those who speak a different tongue. They are also responsible for direct disturbances in speech, etc. The curiosity which shews itself plainly later on, mostly in the fourth or fifth year of life, is not the beginning, but the climax and termination, of this phase of development, which I have also found to be true of the Oedipus conflict in general.

The early feeling of *not knowing* has manifold connections. It unites with the feeling of being incapable, impotent, which soon results from the Oedipus situa-tion. The child also feels this frustration the more acutely because he *knows noth-ing* definite about sexual processes. In both sexes the castration complex is accentuated by this feeling of ignorance.

The early connection between the epistemophilic impulse and sadism is very important for the whole mental development. This instinct, roused by the striving of the Oedipus tendencies, at first mainly concerns itself with the mother's womb, which is assumed to be the scene of all sexual processes and developments. The child is still dominated by the anal-sadistic libido-position which impels him to wish to *appropriate* the contents of the womb. He thus begins to be curious about what it contains, what it is like, etc. So the epistemophilic instinct and the desire to take possession come quite early to be most intimately connected with one another and at the same time with the sense of guilt aroused by the incipient Oedipus conflict. This significant connection ushers in a phase of development in both sexes which is of vital importance, hitherto not sufficiently recognized. It consists of a very early identification with the mother.

The course run by this 'femininity' phase must be examined separately in boys and in girls, but, before I proceed to this, I will show its connection with the previous phase, which is common to both sexes.

In the early anal-sadistic stage the child sustains his second severe trauma, which strengthens his tendency to turn away from the mother. She has frustrated his oral desires, and now she also interferes with his anal pleasures. It seems as though at this point the anal deprivations cause the anal tendencies to amalgamate with the sadistic tendencies. The child desires to get possession of the mother's faeces, by penetrating into her body, cutting it to pieces, devouring and destroy-ing it. Under the influence of his genital impulses, the boy is beginning to turn to his mother as love-object. But his sadistic impulses are in full activity, and the hate originating in earlier frustrations is powerfully opposed to his object-love on the genital level. A still greater obstacle to his love is his dread of castration by the father, which arises with the Oedipus impulses. The degree in which he attains to the genital position will partly depend on his capacity for tolerating this anxiety. Here the intensity of the oral-sadistic and anal-sadistic fixations is an important factor. It affects the degree of hatred which the boy feels towards the mother; and this, in its turn, hinders him to a greater or lesser extent in attaining a positive relation to her. The sadistic fixations exercise also a decisive influence upon the formation of the super-ego, which is coming into being whilst these phases are in the ascendant. The more cruel the super-ego the more terrifying will be the father as castrator, and the more tenaciously in the child's flight from his genital impulses will he cling to the sadistic levels, from which his Oedipus tendencies in the first instance then also take their colour.

In these early stages all the positions in the Oedipus development are cathected in rapid succession. This, however, is not noticeable, because the picture is dominated by the pregenital impulses. Moreover, no rigid line can be drawn between the active heterosexual attitude which finds expression on the anal level and the further stage of identification with the mother.

We have now reached that phase of development of which I spoke before under the name of the 'femininity-phase'. It has its basis on the anal-sadistic level and imparts to that level a new content, for faeces are now equated with the child that is longed for, and the desire to rob the mother now applies to the child as well as to faeces. Here we can discern two aims which merge with one another. The one is directed by the desire for children, the intention being to appropriate them, while the other aim is motivated by jealousy of the future brothers and sisters whose appearance is expected and by the wish to destroy them in the womb. A third object of the boy's oral-sadistic tendencies in the mother's womb is the father's penis.

As in the castration-complex of girls, so in the femininity-complex of the male, there is at bottom the frustrated desire for a special organ. The tendencies to steal and destroy are concerned with the organs of conception, pregnancy and parturition, which the boy assumes to exist in the womb, and further with the vagina and the breasts, the fountain of milk, which are coveted as organs of receptivity and bounty from the time when the libidinal position is purely oral.

The boy fears punishment for his destruction of his mother's body, but, besides this, his fear is of a more general nature, and here we have an analogy to the anxiety associated with the castration-wishes of the girl. He fears that his body will be mutilated and dismembered, and amongst other things castrated. Here we have a direct contribution to the castration-complex. In this early period of development the mother who takes away the child's faeces signifies also a mother who dismembers and castrates him. Not only by means of the anal frustrations which she inflicts does she pave the way for the castration-complex: in terms of psychic reality she *is* also already the *castrator*.

This dread of the mother is so overwhelming because there is combined with it an intense dread of castration by the father. The destructive tendencies whose object is the womb are also directed with their full oral- and anal-sadistic intensity against the father's penis, which is supposed to be located there. It is upon his penis that the dread of castration by the father is focused in this phase. Thus the femininity-phase is characterized by anxiety relating to the womb and the father's penis, and this anxiety subjects the boy to the tyranny of a super-ego which devours, dismembers and castrates and is formed from the image of father and mother alike.

The aims of the incipient genital libido-positions are thus crisscrossed by and intermingled with the manifold pregenital tendencies. The greater the preponderance of sadistic fixations the more does the boy's identification with his mother correspond to an attitude of rivalry towards the woman, with its blending of envy and hatred; for on account of his wish for a child he feels himself at a disadvantage and inferior to the mother.

Let us now consider why the femininity-complex of men seems so much more obscure than the castration-complex in women, with which it is equally important.

The amalgamation of the desire for a child with the epistemophilic impulse enables a boy to effect a displacement on to the intellectual plane; his sense of being at a disadvantage is then concealed and over-compensated by the superiority he deduces from his possession of a penis, which is also acknowledged by girls. This exaggeration of the masculine position results in excessive protestations of masculinity. In her paper entitled 'Notes on Curiosity',[3] Mary Chadwick, too, has traced the man's narcissistic over-estimation of the penis and his attitude of intellectual rivalry towards women to the frustration of his wish for a child and the displacement of this desire on to the intellectual plane.

A tendency to excess in the direction of aggression, which very frequently occurs, has its source in the femininity-complex. It goes with an attitude of contempt and 'knowing better', and is highly asocial and sadistic; it is partly conditioned as an attempt to mask the anxiety and ignorance which lie behind it. In part it coincides with the boy's protest (originating in his fear of castration) against the feminine role, but it is rooted also in his dread of his mother, whom he intended to rob of the father's penis, her children and her female sexual organs. This excessive aggression unites with the pleasure in attack which proceeds from the direct, genital Oedipus situation, but it represents that part of the situation which is by far the more asocial factor in character-formation. This is why a man's rivalry with women will be far more asocial than his rivalry with his fellow-men, which is largely prompted through the genital position. Of course the quantity of sadistic fixations will also determine the relationship of a man to other men when they are rivals. If, on the contrary, the identification with the mother is based on a more securely established genital position, on the one hand his relation to women will be positive in character, and on the other the desire for a child and the feminine component, which play so essential a part in men's work, will find more favourable opportunities for sublimation.

In both sexes one of the principal roots of inhibitions in work is the anxiety and sense of guilt associated with the femininity-phase. Experience has taught me, however, that a thorough analysis of this phase is, for other reasons as well, important from a therapeutic point of view, and should be of help in some obsessional cases which seem to have reached a point where nothing more could be resolved.

In the boy's development the femininity-phase is succeeded by a prolonged struggle between the pregenital and the genital positions of the libido. When at its height, in the third to the fifth year of life, this struggle is plainly recognizable as the Oedipus conflict. The anxiety associated with the femininity-phase drives the boy back to identification with the father; but this stimulus in itself does not provide a firm foundation for the genital position, since it leads mainly to repression and over-compensation of the anal-sadistic instincts, and not to overcoming them. The dread of castration by the father strengthens the fixation to the anal-sadistic levels. The degree of constitutional genitality also plays an important part as regards a favourable issue, i.e. the attainment of the genital level. Often the outcome of the struggle remains undecided, and this gives rise to neurotic troubles and disturbances of potency.[4] Thus the attainment of complete potency and reaching the genital position will in part depend upon the favourable issue of the femininity-phase.

I will now turn to the development of girls. As a result of the process of weaning, the girl-child has turned from the mother, being impelled more strongly to do so by the anal deprivations she has undergone. The genital now begins to influence her mental development.

I entirely agree with Helene Deutsch,[5] who holds that the genital development of the woman finds its completion in the successful displacement of oral libido on to the genital. Only, my results lead me to believe that this displacement begins with the first stirrings of the genital impulses and that the oral, receptive aim of the genital exercises a determining influence in the *girl's turning to the father*. Also I am led to conclude that not only an unconscious awareness of the vagina, but also sensations in that organ and the rest of the genital apparatus, are aroused as soon as the Oedipus impulses make their appearance. In girls, however, onanism does not afford anything like so adequate an outlet for these quantities of excitation as it does in boys. Hence the accumulated lack of satisfaction provides yet another reason for more complications and disturbances of female sexual development. The difficulty of obtaining complete gratification by onanism may be another cause, besides those indicated by Freud, for the girl's repudiation of the practice, and may partly explain why, during her struggle to give it up, manual masturbation is generally replaced by pressing the legs together.

Besides the receptive quality of the genital organ, which is brought into play by the intense desire for a new source of gratification, envy and hatred of the mother who possesses the father's penis seem, at the period when these first

Oedipus impulses are stirring, to be a further motive for the little girl's turning to the father. His caresses have now the effect of a seduction and are felt as 'the attraction of the opposite sex'.[6]

In the girl identification with the mother results directly from the Oedipus impulses: the whole struggle caused in the boy by his castration-anxiety is absent in her. In girls as well as boys this identification coincides with the anal-sadistic tendencies to rob and destroy the mother. If identification with the mother takes place at a stage at which the oral- and anal-sadistic tendencies predominate, dread of a primitive maternal super-ego will lead to the repression and fixation of this phase and interfere with further genital development. Dread of the mother, too, impels the little girl to give up identification with her, and identification with the father begins.

The little girl's epistemophilic impulse is first roused by the Oedipus complex; the result is that she discovers her lack of a penis. She feels this lack to be a fresh cause of hatred of the mother, but at the same time her sense of guilt makes her regard it as a punishment. This embitters her frustration in this direction, and it, in its turn, exercises a profound influence on the whole castration-complex.

This early grievance about the lack of a penis is greatly magnified later on, when the phallic phase and the castration-complex are in full swing. Freud has stated that the discovery of the lack of a penis causes the turning from the mother to the father. My findings show, however, that this discovery operates only as a reinforcement in this direction, since it follows on a very early stage in the Oedipus conflict, and is succeeded by the wish for a child, by which it is actually replaced in later development. I regard the deprivation of the breast as the most fundamental cause of the turning to the father.

Identification with the father is less charged with anxiety than that with the mother; moreover, the sense of guilt towards her impels to over-compensation through a fresh love-relation with her. Against this new love-relation with her there operates the castration-complex which makes a masculine attitude difficult, and also the hatred of her which sprang from the earlier situations. Hate and rivalry of the mother, however, again lead to abandoning the identification with the father and turning to him as the object to be secured and loved.

The little girl's relation with her mother causes that to her father to take both a positive and a negative direction. The frustration undergone at his hands has as its very deepest basis the disappointment already suffered in relation to the mother; a powerful motive in the desire to possess him springs from the hatred and envy against the mother. If the sadistic fixations remain predominant, this hatred and its over-compensation will also materially affect the woman's relation to men. On the other hand, if there is a more positive relation to the mother, built up on the genital position, not only will the woman be freer from a sense of guilt in her relation to her children, but her love for her husband will be strongly reinforced, since for the woman he always stands at one and the same time for the mother who gives what is desired and for the beloved child. On this very significant foundation is built up that part of the relation which is connected exclusively with the father. At first it is focused on the act of the penis in coitus. This act, which also promises gratification of the desires that are now displaced on to the genital, seems to the little girl a most consummate performance.

Her admiration is, indeed, shaken by the Oedipus frustration, but unless it is converted into hate, it constitutes one of the fundamental features of the woman's relation to the man. Later, when full satisfaction of the love-impulses is obtained, there is joined with this admiration the great gratitude ensuing from the long-pent-up deprivation. This gratitude finds expression in the greater feminine capacity for complete and lasting surrender to a love-object, especially to the 'first love'.

One way in which the little girl's development is greatly handicapped is the following. Whilst the boy does in reality *possess* the penis, in respect of which he enters into rivalry with the father, the little girl has only the *unsatisfied* desire for motherhood, and of this, too, she has but a dim and uncertain, though a very intense, awareness.

It is not merely this uncertainty which disturbs her hope of future motherhood. It is weakened far more by anxiety and sense of guilt, and these may seriously and permanently damage the maternal capacity of a woman. Because of the destructive tendencies once directed by her against the mother's body (or certain organs in it) and against the children in the womb, the girl anticipates retribution in the form of destruction of her own capacity for motherhood or of the organs connected with this function and of her own children. Here we have also one root of the constant concern of women (often so excessive) for their personal beauty, for they dread that this too will be destroyed by the mother. At the bottom of the impulse to deck and beautify themselves there is always the motive of *restoring* damaged comeliness, and this has its origin in anxiety and sense of guilt.[7]

It is probable that this deep dread of the destruction of internal organs may be the psychic cause of the greater susceptibility of women, as compared with men, to conversion-hysteria and organic diseases.

It is this anxiety and sense of guilt which is the chief cause of the repression of feelings of pride and joy in the feminine role, which are originally very strong. This repression results in depreciation of the capacity for motherhood, at the outset so highly prized. Thus the girl lacks the powerful support which the boy derives from his possession of the penis, and which she herself might find in the anticipation of motherhood.

The girl's very intense anxiety about her womanhood can be shewn to be analogous to the boy's dread of castration, for it certainly contributes to the checking of her Oedipus impulses. The course run by the boy's castration-anxiety concerning the penis which *visibly* exists is, however, different; it might be termed more *acute* than the more chronic anxiety of the girl concerning her internal organs, with which she is necessarily less familiar. Moreover, it is bound to make a difference that the boy's anxiety is determined by the paternal and the girl's by the maternal super-ego.

Freud has said that the girl's super-ego develops on different lines from that of the boy. We constantly find confirmation of the fact that jealousy plays a greater part in women's lives than in men's, because it is reinforced by deflected envy of the male on account of the penis. On the other hand, however, women especially possess a great capacity, which is not based merely on an over-compensation, for disregarding their own wishes and devoting themselves with self-sacrifice to ethical and social tasks. We cannot account for this capacity by the blending of masculine and feminine traits which, because of the human being's bisexual disposition, does in individual cases influence the formation of character, for this capacity is so plainly maternal in nature. I think that, in order to explain how women can run so wide a gamut from the most petty jealousy to the most self-forgetful loving-kindness, we have to take into consideration the peculiar conditions of the formation of the feminine super-ego. From the early identification with the mother in which the anal-sadistic level so largely preponderates, the little girl derives jealousy and hatred and forms a cruel super-ego after the maternal imago. The super-ego which develops at this stage from a father-identification can also be menacing and cause anxiety, but it seems never to reach the same proportions as that derived from the mother-identification. But the more the identification with the mother becomes stabilized on the genital basis, the more will it be characterized by the devoted kindness of an indulgent mother-ideal. Thus this positive affective attitude depends on the extent to which the maternal mother-ideal bears the characteristics of the pregenital or of the genital stage. But when it comes to the active conversion of the emotional attitude into social or other activities, it would seem that it is the paternal ego-ideal which is at work. The deep admiration felt by the little girl for the father's genital activity leads to the formation of a paternal super-ego which sets before her active aims to which she can never fully attain. If, owing to certain factors in her development, the incentive to accomplish these aims is strong enough, their very impossibility of attainment may lend an impetus to her efforts which, combined with the capacity for self-sacrifice which she derives from the maternal super-ego, gives a woman, in individual instances, the capacity for very exceptional achievements on the intuitive plane and in specific fields.

The boy, too, derives from the feminine phase a maternal super-ego which causes him, like the girl, to make both cruelly primitive and kindly identifications. But he passes through this phase to resume (it is true, in varying degrees) identification with the father. However much the maternal side makes itself felt in the formation of the super-ego, it is yet the *paternal* super-ego which from the beginning is the decisive influence for the man. He too sets before himself a figure of an exalted character upon which to model himself, but, because the boy *is* 'made in the image of' his ideal, it is not unattainable. This circumstance contributes to the more sustained and objective creative work of the male.

The dread of injury to her womanhood exercises a profound influence on the castration-complex of the little girl, for it causes her to over-estimate the penis which she herself lacks; this exaggeration is then much more obvious than is the underlying anxiety about her own womanhood. I would remind you here of the work of Karen Horney, who was the first to examine the sources of the castration-complex in women in so far as those sources lie in the Oedipus situation.

In this connection I must speak of the importance for sexual development of certain early experiences in childhood. In the paper which I read at the Salzburg Congress in 1924, I mentioned that when observations of coitus take place at a later stage of development they assume the character of traumata, but that if such experiences occur at an early age they become fixated and form part of the sexual development. I must now add that a fixation of this sort may hold in its grip not only that particular stage of development, but also the super-ego which is then in process of formation, and may thus injure its further development. For the more completely the super-ego reaches its zenith in the genital stage the less prominent will the sadistic identifications be in its structure and the more surely will an ethically fine personality be developed and greater possibilities of mental health be secured.

There is another kind of experience in early childhood which strikes me as typical and exceedingly important. These experiences often follow closely in time upon the observations of coitus and are induced or fostered by the excitations set up thereby. I refer to the sexual relations of little children with one another, between brothers and sisters or playmates, which consist in the most varied acts: looking, touching, performing excretion in common, fellatio, cunnilingus and often direct attempts at coitus. They are deeply repressed and have a cathexis of profound feelings of guilt. These feelings are mainly due to the fact that this love-object, chosen under the pressure of the excitation due to the Oedipus conflict, is felt by the child to be a substitute for the father or mother or both. Thus these relations, which seem so insignificant and which apparently no child under the stimulus of the Oedipus development escapes, take on the character of an Oedipus relation actually realized, and exercise a determining influence upon the formation of the Oedipus complex, the subject's detachment from that complex and upon his later sexual relations. Moreover, an experience of this sort forms an important fixation-point in the development of the super-ego. In consequence of the need for punishment and the repetition-compulsion, these experiences often cause the child to subject himself to sexual traumata. In this connection I would refer you to Abraham,[8] who showed that experiencing sexual traumata is one part of the sexual development of children. The analytic investigation of these experiences, during the analysis of adults as well as of children, to a great extent clears up the Oedipus situation in its connection with early fixations and is therefore important from the therapeutic point of view.

To sum up my conclusions: I wish above all to point out that they do not, in my opinion, contradict the statements of Professor Freud. I think that the essential point in the additional considerations which I have advanced is that I date these processes earlier and that the different phases (especially in the initial stages) merge more freely in one another than was hitherto supposed.

The early stages of the Oedipus conflict are so largely dominated by pregenital phases of development that the genital phase, when it begins to be active, is at first heavily shrouded and only later, between the third and fifth years of life, becomes clearly recognizable. At this age the Oedipus complex and the formation of the super-ego reach their climax. But the fact that the Oedipus tendencies begin so much earlier than we supposed, the pressure of the sense of guilt which therefore falls upon the pregenital levels, the determining influence thus exercised so early upon the Oedipus development on the one hand and that of the super-ego on the other, and accordingly upon character-formation, sexuality and all the rest of the subject's development – all these things seem to me of great and hitherto unrecognized importance. I found out the therapeutic value of this knowledge in the analyses of children, but it is not confined to these. I have been able to test the resulting conclusions in the analysis of adults and have found not only that their theoretical correctness was confirmed, but that their therapeutic importance was established.

NOTES

1. Read at the Tenth International Psycho-Analytical Congress, Innsbruck, 3 September 1927.
2. [*International Journal of Psycho-Analysis*], Vol. VIII, 1927.
3. *Internationale Zeitschrift für Psychoanalyse*, Bd. XI, 1925.
4. Cf. here Reich, *Die Funktion des Orgasmus*, Internationaler Psychoanalytischer Verlag.
5. H. Deutsch, *Psychoanalyse der weiblichen Sexualfunktion*.
6. We regularly come across the unconscious reproach that the mother has seduced the child whilst tending it. The explanation is that at the period when she had to minister to its bodily needs the Oedipus tendencies were awakening.
7. Cf. Hárnik's paper at the Innsbruck Psycho-Analytical Congress, 'Die ökonomischen Beziehungen zwischen dem Schuldgefühl und dem weiblichen Narzissmus'.
8. Karl Abraham, *Selected Papers*, International Psycho-Analytical Library, No. 13.

8

The Psychodynamics of the Family

Nancy Chodorow

Let us recall that we left the pubescent girl in a triangular situation and expressed the hope that later she would dissolve the sexually mixed triangle . . . in favor of heterosexuality. This formulation was made for the sake of simplication. Actually, whether a constitutional bisexual factor contributes to the creation of such a triangle or not, this triangle can never be given up completely. The deepest and most ineradicable emotional relations with both parents share in its formation. It succeeds another relation, even older and more enduring – the relationship between mother and child, which every man or woman preserves from his birth to his death. It is erroneous to say that the little girl gives up her first mother relation in favor of the father. She only gradually draws him into the alliance, develops from the mother-child exclusiveness toward the triangular parent-child relation and continues the latter, just as she does the former, although in a weaker and less elemental form, all her life. Only the principal part changes; now the mother, now the father plays it. The ineradicability of affective constellations manifests itself in later repetitions.

Helene Deutsch,
The Psychology of Women

A woman *is* her mother
That's the main thing

Anne Sexton,
'Housewife'

OEDIPAL ASYMMETRIES AND HETEROSEXUAL KNOTS[1]

The same Oedipally produced ideology and psychology of male dominance, repression, and denial of dependence that propel men into the nonfamilial competitive work world place structural strains on marriage and family life. Because women mother, the development and meaning of heterosexual object-choice differ for men and women. The traditional psychoanalytic account of femininity and masculinity begins from this perception. In our society, marriage has assumed a larger and larger emotional weight, supposedly offsetting the strains of increasingly alienated and bureaucratized work in the paid economy. It no longer has the economic and political basis it once had, and the family has collapsed in upon its psychological and personal functions as production, education, religion, and care for the sick and aged have left the home. In this context, the contradictions between women's and men's heterosexuality that result from women's performing mothering functions stand out clearly.

According to psychoanalytic theory, heterosexual erotic orientation is a primary outcome of the Oedipus complex for both sexes. Boys and girls differ in this, however. Boys retain one primary love object throughout their boyhood. For this reason, the development of masculine heterosexual object choice is relatively continuous: 'In males the path of this development is straightforward, and the advance from the "phallic" phase does not take place in consequence of a complicated "wave of repression" but is based upon a ratification of that which already exists. . . .'[2] In theory, a boy resolves his Oedipus complex by repressing his attachment to his mother. He is therefore ready in adulthood to find a primary relationship with someone *like* his mother. When he does, the relationship is given meaning from its psychological reactivation of what was originally an intense and exclusive relationship – first an identity, then a 'dual-unity', finally a two-person relationship.

Things are not so simple for girls: 'Psychoanalytic research discovered at the very outset that the development of the infantile libido to the normal heterosexual object-choice is in women rendered difficult by certain peculiar circumstances.'[3] These 'peculiar circumstances' are universal facts of family organization. Because her first love object is a woman, a girl, in order to attain her proper heterosexual orientation, must transfer her primary object choice to her father and men. This creates asymmetry in the feminine and masculine Oedipus complex, and difficulties in the development of female sexuality, given heterosexuality as a developmental goal.

For girls, just as for boys, mothers are primary love objects. As a result, the structural inner object setting of female heterosexuality differs from that of males. When a girl's father does become an important primary person, it is in the context of a bisexual relational triangle. A girl's relation to him is emotionally in reaction to, interwoven and competing for primacy with, her relation to her mother. A girl usually turns to her father as an object of primary interest from the exclusivity of the relationship to her mother, but this libidinal turning to her father does not substitute for her attachment to her mother. Instead, a girl retains her pre-Oedipal tie to her mother (an intense tie involved with issues of primary identification, primary love, dependence, and separation) and builds Oedipal attachments to both her mother and her father upon it. These attachments are characterized by eroticized demands for exclusivity, feelings of competition, and jealousy. She retains the internalized early relationship, including its implications for the nature of her definition of self, and internalizes these other relationships in addition to and not as replacements for it.

For girls, then, there is no absolute change of object, nor exclusive attachment to their fathers. Moreover, a father's behavior and family role, and a girl's relationship to him are crucial to the development of heterosexual orientation in her. But fathers are comparatively unavailable physically and emotionally. They are not present as much and are not primary caretakers, and their own training for masculinity may have led them to deny emotionality. Because of the father's lack of availability to his daughter, and because of the intensity of the mother–daughter relationship in which she participates, girls tend not to make a total transfer of affection to their fathers but to remain also involved with their mothers, and to oscillate emotionally between mother and father.

The implications of this are twofold. First, the nature of the heterosexual relationship differs for boys and girls. Most women emerge from their Oedipus complex oriented to their father and men as primary *erotic* objects, but it is clear that men tend to remain *emotionally* secondary, or at most emotionally equal, compared to the primacy and exclusivity of an Oedipal boy's emotional tie to his mother and women. Second, because the father is an additional important love object, who becomes important in the context of a relational triangle, the feminine inner object world is more complex than the masculine. This internal situation continues into adulthood and affects adult women's participation in relationships. Women, according to Deutsch, experience heterosexual relationships in a triangular context, in which men are not exclusive objects for them. The implication of her statement is confirmed by cross-cultural examination of family structure and relations between the sexes, which suggests that conjugal closeness is the exception and not the rule.[4]

Because mother and father are not the same *kind* of parent, the nature and intensity of a child's relationship to them differ as does the relationship's degree of exclusiveness. Because children first experience the social and cognitive world as continuous with themselves and do not differentiate objects, their mother, as first caretaking figure, is not a separate person and has no separate interests. In addition, this lack of separateness is in the context of the infant's total dependence on its mother for physical and psychological survival. The internalized experience of self in the original mother-relation remains seductive and frightening: Unity was bliss, yet meant the loss of self and absolute dependence. By contrast, a child has always differentiated itself from its father and known him as a separate person with separate interests. And the child has never been totally dependent on him. Her father has not posed the original narcissistic threat (the threat to basic ego integrity and boundaries) nor provided the original narcissistic unity (the original experience of oneness) to a girl. Oedipal love for the mother, then, contains both a threat to selfhood and a promise of primal unity which love for the father never does. A girl's love for her father and women's attachment to men reflect all aspects of these asymmetries.

Men cannot provide the kind of return to oneness that women can. Michael Balint argues that the return to the experience of primary love – the possibility of regressing to the infantile stage of a sense of oneness, no reality testing, and a tranquil sense of well-being in which all needs are satisfied – is a main goal of adult sexual relationship: 'This primary tendency, I shall be loved always, everywhere, in every way, my whole body, my whole being – without any criticism, without the slightest effort on my part – is the final aim of all erotic striving.'[5] He implies, though, that women can fulfil this need better than men, because a sexual relationship with a woman reproduces the early situation more completely and is more completely a return to the mother. Thus, males in coitus come nearest to the experience of refusion with the mother – 'The male comes nearest to achieving this regression during coitus: with his semen in reality, with his penis symbolically, with his whole self in phantasy.'[6]

Women's participation here is dual. (Balint is presuming women's heterosexuality.) First, a woman identifies with the man penetrating her and thus experiences through identification refusion with a woman (mother). Second, she *becomes* the mother (phylogenetically the all-embracing sea, ontogenetically the womb). Thus, a woman in a heterosexual relationship cannot, like a man, recapture *as herself* her own experience of merging. She can do so only by identifying with someone who can, on the one hand, and by identifying with the person with whom she was merged on the other. The 'regressive restitution' (Balint's term) which coitus brings, then, is not complete for a woman in the way that it is for a man.

Freud speaks to the way that women seek to recapture their relationship with their mother in heterosexual relationships.[7] He suggests that as women 'change object' from mother to father, the mother remains their primary internal object, so that they often impose on the relation to their father, and later to men, the issues which preoccupy them in their internal relation to their mother. They look in relations to men for gratifications that they want from a woman. Freud points to the common clinical discovery of a woman who has apparently taken her father as a model for her choice of husband, but whose marriage in fact repeats the conflicts and feelings of her relationship with her mother. For instance, a woman who remains ambivalently dependent on her mother, or preoccupied internally with the question of whether she is separate or not, is likely to transfer this stance and sense of self to a relationship with her husband.[8] Or she may identify herself as a part-object of her male partner, as an extension of her father and men, rather than an extension of her mother and women.*

But children seek to escape from their mother as well as return to her. Fathers serve in part to break a daughter's primary unity with and dependence on her

---

* This is obviously only one side of the psychological matter. Chasseguet-Smirgel, who points this out, notes that men also gain satisfaction and security from turning their all-powerful mother into a part-object attachment.

mother. For this and a number of other reasons, fathers and men are idealized.[9] A girl's father provides a last ditch escape from maternal omnipotence, so a girl cannot risk driving him away. At the same time, occupying a position of distance and ideological authority in the family, a father may be a remote figure understood to a large extent through her mother's interpretation of his role. This makes the development of a relationship based on his real strengths and weaknesses difficult. Finally, the girl herself has not received the same kind of love from her mother as a boy has. Mothers experience daughters as one with themselves; their relationships to daughters are 'narcissistic', while those with their sons are more 'anaclitic'.

Thus, a daughter looks to her father for a sense of separateness and for the same confirmation of her specialness that her brother receives from her mother. She (and the woman she becomes), is willing to deny her father's limitations (and those of her lover or husband) as long as she feels loved.[10] She is more able to do this because his distance means that she does not really know him. The relationship, then, because of the father's distance and importance to her, occurs largely as fantasy and idealization, and lacks the grounded reality which a boy's relation to his mother has.

These differences in the experience of self in relation to father and mother are reinforced by the different stages at which boys and girls are likely to enter the Oedipal situation. Girls remain longer in the pre-Oedipal relationship, enter the Oedipus situation later than boys, and their modes of Oedipal resolution differ. Bibring, Slater, and John Whiting have suggested that in the absence of men, a mother sexualizes her relationship with her son early, so that 'Oedipal' issues of sexual attraction and connection, competition and jealousy, become fused with 'pre-Oedipal' issues of primary love and oneness. By contrast, since the girl's relationship to her father develops later, her sense of self is more firmly established. If Oedipal and pre-Oedipal issues are fused for her, this fusion is more likely to occur in relation to her mother, and not to her father. Because her sense of self is firmer, and because Oedipal love for her father is not so threatening, a girl does not 'resolve' her Oedipus complex to the same extent as a boy. This means that she grows up more concerned with both internalized and external object-relationships, while men tend to repress their Oedipal needs for love and relationship. At the same time, men often become intolerant and disparaging of those who can express needs for love, as they attempt to deny their own needs.[*11]

Men defend themselves against the threat posed by love, but needs for love do not disappear through repression. Their training for masculinity and repression of affective relational needs, and their primarily non-emotional and impersonal relationship in the public world make deep primary relationships with other men hard

---

* Chasseguet-Smirgel argues that what Freud and Brunswick call the boy's 'normal contempt' for women, and consider a standard outcome of the Oedipus complex, is a pathological and defensive reaction to the sense of inescapable maternal omnipotence rather than a direct outcome of genital differences.

to come by.[12] Given this, it is not surprising that men tend to find themselves in heterosexual relationships.

These relationships to women derive a large part of their meaning and dynamics from the men's relation to their mothers. But the maternal treatment described by Bibring, Slater and Whiting creates relational problems in sons. When a boy's mother has treated him as an extension of herself and at the same time as a sexual object, he learns to use his masculinity and possession of a penis as a narcissistic defense. In adulthood, he will look to relationships with women for narcissistic-phallic reassurance rather than for mutual affirmation and love. Because their sexualized pre-Oedipal attachment was encouraged, while their Oedipal-genital wishes were thwarted and threatened with punishment, men may defensively invest more exclusively in the instinctual gratifications to be gained in a sexual relationship in order to avoid risking rejection of love.

Women have not repressed affective needs. They still want love and narcissistic confirmation and may be willing to put up with limitations in their masculine lover or husband in exchange for evidence of caring and love. This can lead to the denial of more immediately felt aggressive and erotic drives. Chasseguet-Smirgel suggests that a strong sexuality requires the expression of aggressive, demanding impulses fused with erotic love impulses and idealization. To the extent that women feel conflict and fear punishment especially over all impulses they define as aggressive, their sexuality suffers.*

As a result of the social organization of parenting, then, men operate on two levels in women's psyche. On one level, they are emotionally secondary and not exclusively loved – are not primary love objects like mothers. On another, they are idealized and experienced as needed, but are unable either to express their emotional needs or respond to those of women. As Grunberger puts it. 'The tragedy of this situation is that the person who could give [a woman] this confirmation, her sexual partner, is precisely the one who, as we have just seen, has come to despise narcissistic needs in an effort to disengage himself from them.'[13]

This situation is illuminated by sociological and clinical findings. Conventional wisdom has it, and much of our everyday observation confirms, that women are the romantic ones in our society, the ones for whom love, marriage, and relationships matter. However, several studies point out that men love and fall in love romantically, women sensibly and rationally.[14] Most of these studies argue that in the current situation, where women are economically dependent on men, women must make rational calculations for the provision of themselves and their (future) children. This view suggests that women's apparent romanticism is an emotional and ideological response to their very real economic dependence. On the social

---

* She suggests that this reaction, in which aggressive and erotic drives opposed to idealization are counter-cathected and repressed, better explains feminine frigidity and what Marie Bonaparte and Deutsch consider to be the 'normal' feminine spiritualization of sex. Bonaparte explains these in terms of women's lesser libidinal energy, and Deutsch explains them as constitutional inhibition.

level, especially given economic inequity, men are exceedingly important to women. The recent tendency for women to initiate divorce and separation more than men as income becomes more available to them (and as the feminist movement begins to remove the stigma of 'divorcée') further confirms this.

Adult women are objectively dependent on men economically, just as in childhood girls are objectively dependent on their fathers to escape from maternal domination. Their developed ability to romanticize rational decisions (to ignore or even idealize the failings of their father and men because of their dependence) stands women in good stead in this adult situation.

There is another side to this situation, however. Women have acquired a real capacity for rationality and distance in heterosexual relationships, qualities built into their earliest relationship with a man. Direct evidence for the psychological primacy of this latter stance comes from findings about the experience of loss itself. George Goethals reports the clinical finding that men's loss of at least the first adult relationship 'throws them into a turmoil and a depression of the most extreme kind'[15] – a melancholic reaction to object-loss of the type Freud describes in 'Mourning and Melancholia' – in which they withdraw and are unable to look elsewhere for new relationships. He implies, by contrast, that first adult loss may not result in as severe a depression for a woman, and claims that his women patients did not withdraw to the same extent and were more able to look elsewhere for new relationships. Zick Rubin reports similar findings.[16] The women he studied more frequently broke up relationships, and the men, whether or not they initiated the break-up, were more depressed and lonely afterward. Jessie Bernard, discussing older people, reports that the frequency of psychological distress, death and suicide is much higher among recently widowed men than women, and indicates that the same difference can be found in a comparison of divorced men and women.[17]

These studies imply that women have other resources and a certain distance from their relationships to men. My account stresses that women have a richer, ongoing inner world to fall back on, and that the men in their lives do not represent the intensity and exclusivity that women represent to men. Externally, they also retain and develop more relationships. It seems that, developmentally, men do not become as emotionally important to women as women do to men.

Because women care for children, then, heterosexual symbiosis has a different 'meaning' for men and women. Freud originally noted that 'a man's love and a woman's are a phase apart psychologically'.[18] He and psychoanalytic thinkers after him point to ways in which women and men, though usually looking for intimacy with each other, do not fulfil each other's needs because of the social organization of parenting. Differences in female and male Oedipal experiences, all growing out of women's mothering, create this situation. Girls enter adulthood with a complex layering of affective ties and a rich, ongoing inner object world. Boys have a simpler Oedipal situation and more direct affective relationships, and this situation is repressed in a way that the girl's is not. The mother remains a primary internal object to the girl, so that heterosexual relationships are on the model of a non-exclusive, second relationship for her, whereas for the boy they recreate an exclusive, primary relationship.

As a result of being parented by a woman, both sexes look for a return to this emotional and physical union. A man achieves this directly through the heterosexual bond, which replicates the early mother–infant exclusivity. He is supported in this endeavor by women, who, through their own development, have remained open to relational needs, have retained an ongoing inner affective life, and have learned to deny the limitations of masculine lovers for both psychological and practical reasons.

Men both look for and fear exclusivity. Throughout their development, they have tended to repress their affective relational needs, and to develop ties based more on categorical and abstract role expectations, particularly with other males. They are likely to participate in an intimate heterosexual relationship with the ambivalence created by an intensity which one both wants and fears – demanding from women what men are at the same time afraid of receiving.

As a result of being parented by a woman and growing up heterosexual, women have different and more complex relational needs in which an exclusive relationship to a man is not enough. As noted previously, this is because women situate themselves psychologically as part of a relational triangle in which their father and men are emotionally secondary or, at most, equal to their mother and women. In addition, the relation to the man itself has difficulties. Idealization, growing out of a girl's relation to her father, involves denial of real feelings and to a certain extent an unreal relationship to men. The contradictions in women's heterosexual relationships, though, are due as much to men's problems with intimacy as to outcomes of early childhood relationships. Men grow up rejecting their own needs for love, and therefore find it difficult and threatening to meet women's emotional needs. As a result, they collude in maintaining distance from women.

THE CYCLE COMPLETED: MOTHERS AND CHILDREN

Families create children gendered, heterosexual, and ready to marry. But families organized around women's mothering and male dominance create incompatibilities in women's and men's relational needs. In particular, relationships to men are unlikely to provide for women satisfaction of the relational needs that their mothering by women and the social organization of gender have produced. The less men participate in the domestic sphere, and especially in parenting, the more this will be the case.

Women try to fulfil their need to be loved, try to complete the relational triangle, and try to re-experience the sense of dual unity they had with their mother, which the heterosexual relationship tends to fulfil for men. This situation daily reinforces what women first experienced developmentally and intrapsychically in relation to men. While they are likely to become and remain erotically hetero-sexual, they are encouraged both by men's difficulties with love by their own rela-tional history with their mothers to look elsewhere for love and emotional gratification.

One way that women fulfil these needs is through the creation and mainte-nance of important personal relations with other women. Cross-culturally, segre-gation by gender is the rule: Women tend to have closer personal ties with each other than men have, and to spend more time in the company of women than they do with men. In our society, there is some sociological evidence that women's friendships are affectively richer than men's.[19] In other societies, and in most sub-cultures of our own, women remain involved with female relatives in adulthood.[20] Deutsch suggests further that adult female relationships sometimes express a woman's psychological participation in the relational triangle. Some women, she suggests, always need a woman rival in their relationship to a man; others need a best friend with whom they share all confidences about their heterosexual rela-tionships. These relationships are one way of resolving and recreating the mother–daughter bond and are an expression of women's general relational capacities and definitions of self in relationship.

However, deep affective relationships to women are hard to come by on a routine, daily, ongoing basis for many women. Lesbian relationships do tend to recreate mother–daughter emotions and connections,[21] but most women are heterosexual. This heterosexual preference and taboos against homosexuality, in addition to objective economic dependence on men, make the option of primary sexual bonds with other women unlikely – though more prevalent in recent years. In an earlier period, women tended to remain physically close to their own mother and sisters after marriage, and could find relationships with other women in their daily work and community. The development of industrial capitalism, however – and the increasingly physically isolated nuclear family it has produced – has made these primary relationships more rare and has turned women (and men) increasingly and exclusively to conjugal family relationships for emotional support and love.[22]

There is a second alternative, made all the more significant by the elimination of the first, which also builds both upon the nature of women's self-definition in a heterosexual relationship and upon the primary mother–child bond. As Deutsch makes clear, women's psyche consists in a layering of relational constellations. The pre-Oedipal mother–child relation and the Oedipal triangle have lasted until late in a woman's childhood, in fact throughout her development. To the extent that relations with a man gain significance for a woman, this experience is incom-plete. Given the triangular situation and emotional asymmetry of her own parent-ing a woman's relation to a man *requires* on the level of psychic structure a third person, since it was originally established in a triangle. A man's relation to women does not. His relation to his mother was originally established first as an identity, then as a dual unity, then as a two-person relationship, before his father ever entered the picture.

On the level of psychic structure, then, a child completes the relational triangle for a woman. Having a child, and experiencing her relation to a man in this context, enables her to reimpose intrapsychic relational structure on the social world, while at the same time resolving the generational component of her Oedipus complex as she takes a new place in the triangle – a maternal place in relation to her own child.

The mother–child relationship also recreates an even more basic relational constellation. The exclusive symbiotic mother–child relationship of a mother's own infancy reappears, a relationship which all people who have been mothered want basically to recreate. This contrasts to the situation of a man. A man often wants a child through his role-based, positional identification with his father, or his primary or personal identification with his mother. Similarly, a woman has been involved in relational identification processes with her mother, which include identifying with a mother who has come to stand to both sexes as someone with unique capacities for mothering. Yet on a less conscious, object-relational level, having a child recreates the desired mother–child exclusivity for a woman and interrupts it for a man, just as the man's father intruded into his relation to his mother. Accordingly, as Benedek, Zilboorg, and Bakan suggest, men often feel extremely jealous toward children.[*] These differences hold also on the level of sexual and biological fantasy and symbolism. A woman, as I have suggested, cannot return to the mother in coitus as directly as can a man. Symbolically her identification with the man can help. However, a much more straightforward symbolic return occurs through her identification with the child who is in her womb: 'Ferenczi's "maternal regression" is realized for the woman in equating coitus with the situation of sucking. The last act of this regression (return into the uterus) which the man accomplishes by the act of introjection in coitus, is realized by the woman in pregnancy in the complete identification between mother and child.'[23]

For all these reasons, it seems psychologically logical to a woman to turn her marriage into a family, and to be more involved with these children (this child) than her husband. By doing so, she recreates for herself the exclusive intense primary unit which a heterosexual relationship tends to recreate for men. She recreates also her internalized asymmetrical relational triangle. These relational issues and needs predate and underlie her identifications, and come out of normal family structure regardless of explicit role training. Usually, however, this training intensifies their effects. In mothering, a woman acts also on her personal identification with a mother who parents and her own training for women's role.

---

[*] This is not to deny the conflicts and resentments which women may feel about their children.

This account indicates a larger structural issue regarding the way in which a woman's relation to her children recreates the psychic situation of the relationship to her mother. This relationship is recreated on two levels: most deeply and unconsciously, that of the primary mother–infant tie; and upon this, the relationship of the bisexual triangle. Because the primary mother–infant unit is exclusive, and because oscillation in the bisexual triangle includes a constant pull back to the mother attachment, there may be a psychological contradiction for a woman between interest in and commitment to children and that to men. Insofar as a woman experiences her relationship to her child on the level of intrapsychic structure as exclusive, her relationship to a man may therefore be superfluous.

Freud points tentatively to this (to him, unwelcome) situation, in contrasting men's and women's object-love. In his essay 'On Narcissism', he claims that 'complete object-love of the attachment type is, properly speaking, characteristic of the male'.[24] Women, by contrast, tend to love narcissistically – on one level, to want to be loved or to be largely self-sufficient; on another, to love someone as an extension of their self rather than a differentiated object. He implies here that the necessary mode of relating to infants is the normal way women love. Yet he also claims that women do attain true object-love, but only in relation to their children – who are both part of them and separate. Freud's stance here seems to be that of the excluded man viewing women's potential psychological self-sufficiency vis-à-vis *men*. This situation may be the basis of the early psychoanalytic claim that women are more narcissistic than men, since clinically it is clear that men have just as many and as serious problems of fundamental object-relatedness as do women.[25]

Clinical accounts reveal this contradiction between male–female and mother–child love. Fliess and Deutsch point to the extreme case where children are an exclusively mother–daughter affair.[26] Some women fantasize giving their mother a baby, or even having one from her. These are often teenage girls with extreme problems of attachment and separation in relation to their mothers, whose fathers were more or less irrelevant in the home. Often a girl expresses this fantasy through either not knowing who the father of her baby is, or knowing and not caring. Her main object is to take her baby home to her mother.

Deutsch points out that in women's fantasies and dreams, sexuality and erotism are often opposed to motherhood and reproduction.[27] She reports clinical and literary cases of women who choose either sexuality or motherhood exclusively, mothers for whom sexual satisfactions become insignificant, women with parthenogenic fantasies. Benedek and Winnicott observe that the experience of pregnancy, and the anticipation of motherhood, often entail a withdrawal of a woman's interest from other primary commitments to her own body and developing child. As Benedek puts it, 'The woman's interest shifts from extraverted activities to her body and its welfare. Expressed in psychodynamic terms: the libido is withdrawn from external, heterosexual objects, becomes concentrated upon the self.'[28]

This libidinal shift may continue after birth. Psychological and libidinal gratifications from the nursing relationship may substitute for psychological and libidinal gratifications formerly found in heterosexual involvements.[29] The clinical findings and theoretical claims of Bakan, Benedek and Zilboorg concerning men's jealousy of their children confirm this as a possibility.

On the level of the relational triangle also, there can be a contradiction between women's interest in children and in men. This is evident in Freud's suggestion that women oscillate psychologically between a pre-Oedipal and Oedipal stance (he says between periods of 'masculinity' and femininity') and that women's and men's love is a phase apart psychologically (that a woman is more likely to love her son than her husband). Deutsch points out that a man may or may not be psychologically necessary or desirable to the mother–child exclusivity. When she is oriented to the man, a woman's fantasy of having children is 'I want a child by him, *with him*'; when men are emotionally in the background, it is 'I want a *child*'.[30]

Women come to want and need primary relationships to children. These wants and needs result from wanting intense primary relationships, which men tend not to provide both because of their place in women's Oedipal constellation and because of their difficulties with intimacy. Women's desires for intense primary relationships tend not to be with other women, both because of internal and external taboos on homosexuality, and because of women's isolation from their primary female kin (especially mothers) and other women.

As they develop these wants and needs, women also develop the capacities for participating in parent–child relationships. They develop capacities for mothering. Because of the structural situation of parenting, women remain in a primary, pre-Oedipal relationship with their mother longer than men. They do not feel the need to repress or cut off the capacity for experiencing the primary identification and primary love which are the basis of parental empathy. Also, their development and Oedipal resolution do not require the ego defense against either regression or relation which characterizes masculine development. Woman also tend to remain bound up in pre-Oedipal issues in relation to their own mother, so that they in fact have some unconscious investment in reactivating them. When they have a child, they are more liable than a man to do so. In each critical period of their child's development, the parent's own development conflicts and experiences of that period affect their attitudes and behavior.[31] The pre-Oedipal relational stance, latent in women's normal relationship to the world and experience of self, is activated in their coming to care for an infant, encouraging their empathic identification with this infant which is the basis of maternal care.

Mothering, moreover, involves a double identification for women, both as mother *and* as child. The whole pro-Oedipal relationship has been internalized and perpetuated in a more ongoing way for women than for men. Women take both parts in it. Women have capacities for primary identification with their child through regression to primary love and empathy. Through their mother identification, they have ego capacities and the sense of responsibility which go into caring for children. In addition, women have an investment in mothering in order to make reparation to their own mother (or to get back at her). Throughout their development, moreover, women have been building layers of identification with their mothers upon the primary internalized mother–child relationship.[32]

Women develop capacities for mothering from their object-relational stance. This stance grows out of the special nature and length of their pre-Oedipal relationship to their mother; the non-absolute repression of Oedipal relationships; and their general ongoing mother–daughter preoccupation as they are growing up. It also develops because they have not formed the same defenses against relationships as men. Related to this, they develop wants and needs to be mothers from their Oedipal experience and the contradictions in heterosexual love that result.

The *wants and needs* which lead women to become mothers put them in situations where their mothering *capacities* can be expressed. At the same time, women remain in conflict with their internal mother and often their real mother as well. The preoccupation with issues of separation and primary identification, the ability to recall their early relationship to their mother – precisely those capacities which enable mothering – are also those which may lead to over-identification and pseudoempathy based on maternal projection rather than any real perception or understanding of their infant's needs.[33] Similarly, the need for primary relationships becomes more prominent and weighted as relationships to other women become less possible and as father/husband absence grows. Though women come to mother, and to be mothers, the very capacities and commitments for mothering can be in contradiction one with the other and within themselves. Capacities which enable mothering are also precisely those which can make mothering problematic.

GENDER PERSONALITY AND THE REPRODUCTION
OF MOTHERING

In spite of the apparently close tie between women's capacities for childbearing and lactation on the one hand and their responsibilities for child-care on the other, and in spite of the probable prehistoric convenience (and perhaps survival necessity) of a sexual division of labor in which women mothered, biology and instinct do not provide adequate explanations for how women come to mother. Women's mothering as a feature of social structure requires an explanation in terms of social structure. Conventional feminist and social psychological explanations for the genesis of gender roles – girls and boys are 'taught' appropriate behaviors and 'learn' appropriate feelings – are insufficient both empirically and methodologically to account for how women become mothers.

Methodologically, socialization theories rely inappropriately on individual intention. Ongoing social structures include the means for their own reproduction – in the regularized repetition of social processes, in the perpetuation of conditions which require members' participation, in the genesis of legitimating ideologies and institutions, and in the psychological as well as physical reproduction of people to perform necessary roles. Accounts of socialization help to explain the perpetuation of ideologies about gender roles. However, notions of appropriate behavior, like coercion, cannot in themselves produce parenting. Psychological capacities and a particular object-relational stance are central and definitional to parenting in a way that they are not to many other roles and activities.

Women's mothering includes the capacities for its own reproduction. This reproduction consists in the production of women with, and men without, the particular psychological capacities and stance which go into primary parenting. Psychoanalytic theory provides us with a theory of social reproduction that explains major features of personality development and the development of psychic structure, and the differential development of gender personality in particular. Psychoanalysts argue that personality both results from and consists in the ways a child appropriates, internalizes, and organizes early experiences in their family – from the fantasies they have, the defenses they use, the ways they channel and redirect drives in this object-relational context. A person subsequently imposes this intrapsychic structure, and the fantasies, defenses, and relational modes and preoccupations which go with it, onto external social situations. This re-externalization (or mutual re-externalization) is a major constituting feature of social and interpersonal situations themselves.

Psychoanalysis, however, has not had an adequate theory of the reproduction of mothering. Because of the teleological assumption that anatomy is destiny, and that women's destiny includes primary parenting, the ontogenesis of women's mothering has been largely ignored, even while the genesis of a wide variety of related disturbances and problems has been accorded widespread clinical attention. Most psychoanalysts agree that the basis for parenting is laid for both genders in the early relationship to a primary caretaker. Beyond that, in order to explain why *women* mother, they tend to rely on vague notions of a girl's subsequent identification with her mother, which makes her and not her brother a primary parent, or on an unspecified and uninvestigated innate femaleness in girls, or on logical leaps from lactation or early vaginal sensations to caretaking abilities and commitments.

The psychoanalytic account of male and female development, when reinterpreted, gives us a developmental theory of the reproduction of women's mothering. Women's mothering reproduces itself through differing object-relational experiences and differing psychic outcomes in women and men. As a result of having been parented by a woman, women are more likely than men to seek to be mothers, that is, to relocate themselves in a primary mother–child relationship, to get gratification from the mothering relationship, and to have psychological and relational capacities for mothering.

The early relation to a primary caretaker provides in children of both genders both the basic capacity to participate in a relationship with the features of the early parent–child one, and the desire to create this intimacy. However, because women mother, the early experience and pre-Oedipal relationship differ for boys and girls. Girls retain more concern with early childhood issues in relation to their mother, and a sense of self involved with these issues. Their attachments therefore retain more pre-Oedipal aspects. The greater length and different nature of their pre-Oedipal experience, and their continuing preoccupation with the issues of this period, mean that women's sense of self is continuous with others and that they retain capacities for primary identification, both of which enable them to experience the empathy and lack of reality sense needed by a cared-for infant. In men, these qualities have been curtailed, both because they are early treated as an opposite by their mother and because their later attachment to her must be repressed. The relational basis for mothering is thus extended in women, and inhibited in men, who experience themselves as more separate and distinct from others.

The different structure of the feminine and masculine Oedipal triangle and process of Oedipal experience that results from women's mothering contributes further to gender personality differentiation and the reproduction of women's mothering. As a result of this experience, women's inner object world, and the affects and issues associated with it, are more actively sustained and more complex than men's. This means that women define and experience themselves relationally. Their heterosexual orientation is always in internal dialogue with both Oedipal and pre-Oedipal mother–child relational issues. Thus, women's heterosexuality is triangular and requires a third person – a child – for its structural and emotional completion. For men, by contrast, the heterosexual relationship alone recreates the early bond to their mother; a child interrupts it. Men, moreover, do not define themselves in relationship and have come to suppress relational capacities and repress relational needs. This prepares them to participate in the affect-denying world of alienated work, but not to fulfil women's needs for intimacy and primary relationships.

The Oedipus complex, as it emerges from the asymmetrical organization of parenting, secures a psychological taboo on parent–child incest and pushes boys and girls in the direction of extrafamilial heterosexual relationships. This is one step toward the reproduction of parenting. The creation and maintenance of the incest taboo and of heterosexuality in girls and boys are different, however. For boys, super-ego formation and identification with their father, rewarded by the superiority of masculinity, maintain the taboo on incest with their mother, while heterosexual orientation continues from their earliest love relation with her. For girls, creating them as heterosexual in the first place maintains the taboo. However, women's heterosexuality is not so exclusive as men's. This makes it easier for them to accept or seek a male substitute for their fathers. At the same time, in a male-dominant society, women's exclusive emotional heterosexuality is not so necessary, nor is her repression of love for her father. Men are more likely to initiate relationships, and women's economic dependence on men pushes them anyway into heterosexual marriage.

Male dominance in heterosexual couples and marriage solves the problem of women's lack of heterosexual commitment and lack of satisfaction by making women more reactive in the sexual bonding process. At the same time, contradictions in heterosexuality help to perpetuate families and parenting by ensuring that women will seek relations to children and will not find heterosexual relationships alone satisfactory. Thus, men's lack of emotional availability and women's less exclusive heterosexual commitment help ensure women's mothering.

Women's mothering, then, produces psychological self-definition and capacities appropriate to mothering in women, and curtails and inhibits these capacities and this self-definition in men. The early experience of being cared for by a woman produces a fundamental structure of expectations in women and men concerning mothers' lack of separate interests from their infants and total concern for their infants' welfare. Daughters grow up identifying with these mothers, about whom they have such expectations. This set of expectations is generalized to the assumption that women naturally take care of children of all ages and the belief that women's 'maternal' qualities can and should be extended to the non-mothering work that they do. All these results of women's mothering have ensured that women will mother infants and will take continuing responsibility for children.

The reproduction of women's mothering is the basis for the reproduction of women's location and responsibilities in the domestic sphere. This mothering, and its generalization to women's structural location in the domestic sphere, links the contemporary social organization of gender and social organization of production and contributes to the reproduction of each. That women mother is a fundamental organizational feature of the sex-gender system: it is basic to the sexual division of labor and generates a psychology and ideology of male dominance as well as an ideology about women's capacities and nature. Women, as wives and mothers, contribute as well to the daily and generational reproduction, both physical and psychological, of male workers and thus to the reproduction of capitalist production.

Women's mothering also reproduces the family as it is constituted in male-dominant society. The sexual and familial division of labor in which women mother creates a sexual division of psychic organization and orientation. It produces socially gendered women and men who enter into asymmetrical heterosexual relationships: it produces men who react to, fear, and act superior to women, and who put most of their energies into the non-familial work and do not parent. Finally, it produces women who turn their energies toward nurturing and caring for children – in turn reproducing the sexual and familial division of labor in which women mother.

Social reproduction is thus asymmetrical. Women in their domestic role reproduce men and children physically, psychologically, and emotionally. Women in their domestic role as houseworkers reconstitute themselves physically on a daily basis and reproduce themselves as mothers, emotionally and psychologically, in the next generation. They thus contribute to the perpetuation of their own social roles and position in the hierarchy of gender.

Institutionalized features of family structure and the social relations of reproduction reproduce themselves. A psychoanalytic investigation shows that women's mothering capacities and commitments, and the general psychological capacities and wants which are the basis of women's emotion work, are built developmentally into feminine personality. Because women are themselves mothered by women, they grow up with the relational capacities and needs, and psychological definition of self-in-relationship, which commits them to mothering. Men, because they are mothered by women, do not. Women mother daughters who, when they become women, mother.

NOTES

1. Some of the material in this section appeared previously in Nancy Chodorow, 1976, 'Oedipal Asymmetries and Heterosexual Knots,' *Social Problems*, 23, #4, pp. 454–68.
2. Deutsch, 1925, 'The Psychology of Woman', p. 165.
3. Ibid.
4. This claim comes from my reading of ethnographic literature and is confirmed by anthropologist Michelle Z. Rosaldo (personal communication).
5. Michael Balint, 1935, 'Critical Notes on the Theory', p. 50.
6. Michael Balint, 1956a, 'Perversions and Genitality', in *Primary Love and Psycho-Analytic Technique*, p. 141. Balint follows Sandor Ferenczi here (1924, *Thalassa: A Theory of Genitality*).
7. Freud, 1931, 'Female Sexuality'.
8. See Freedman, 1961, 'On Women Who Hate', for an excellent clinical account of this.
9. See Chasseguet-Smirgel, 1964, 'Feminine Guilt', and Grunberger, 1964, 'Outline for a Study'.
10. For sociological confirmation of this, see William M. Kephart, 1967, 'Some Correlates of Romantic Love', *Journal of Marriage and the Family*, 29, pp. 470–4, and Zick Rubin, 1970, 'Measurement of Romantic Love', *Journal of Personality and Social Psychology*, 6, pp. 265–73.
11. Chasseguet-Smirgel, 1964, 'Feminine Guilt', and Grunberger, 1964, 'Outline for a Study'.
12. Alan Booth (1972, 'Sex and Social Participation', *American Sociological Review*, 37, pp. 183–93) reports that women's friendships in our society are affectively richer than men's. Along the same lines, Mirra Komarovsky (1974, 'Patterns of Self-Disclosure of Male Undergraduates', *Journal of Marriage and the Family*, 36, #4, pp. 677–86) found that men students confided more in a special women friend and that they maintained a front of strength with men. Moreover, these men felt at a disadvantage vis-à-vis their woman confidante, because she tended to have a number of other persons in whom she could confide.
13. Grunberger, 1964, 'Outline for a Study', p. 74.
14. See Martha Baum, 1971, 'Love, Marriage and the Division of Labor', *Sociological Inquiry*, 41, #1, pp. 107–17; Arlie Russell Hochschild, 1975a, 'Attending to,

Codifying, and Managing Feelings'; Kephart, 1967, 'Some Correlates'; Zick Rubin, 1975, 'Loving and Leaving'.
15. Goethals, 1974, 'Symbiosis', p. 96.
16. Zick Rubin, 1975, 'Loving and Leaving'.
17. Jessie Bernard, 1972, *The Future of Marriage*.
18. Freud, 1933, *New Introductory Lectures*, p. 134.
19. Booth, 1972, 'Sex and Social Participation'; this is a finding certainly confirmed by most writing from the men's liberation movement.
20. See, for cross-cultural confirmation, most ethnographies and also Rosaldo and Lamphere, 1974, *Women, Culture and Society*. For contemporary capitalist society, see Booth, 1972, 'Sex and Social Participation', and for concrete illustration, Elizabeth Bott, 1957, *Family and Social Network: Roles, Norms and External Relationships in Ordinary Urban Families*; Herbert Gans, 1967, *The Levittowners*; Mirra Komarovsky, 1962, *Blue-Collar Marriage*; Carol B. Stack, 1974, *All Our Kin*; Young and Willmott, 1957, *Family and Kinship*.
21. See Deutsch, 1944, *Psychology of Women*; Charlotte Wolff, 1971, *Love Between Women*; Adrienne Rich, 1976, *Of Woman Born: Motherhood as Experience and Institution*.
22. For a contemporary account of exactly this transition, see Young and Willmott, 1957, *Family and Kinship*.
23. Deutsch, 1925, 'The Psychology of Woman', p. 171.
24. Freud, 1914, 'On Narcissism', p. 88.
25. See Heinz Kohut, 1971, *Analysis of Self: A Systematic Approach to the Psychoanalytic Treatment of Narcissistic Personality Disorders. Psychoanalytic Study of the Child*, monograph #4. New York, International Universities Press; Otto Kernberg, 1975, *Borderline Conditions and Pathological Narcissism*.
26. Fliess, 1961, *Ego and Body Ego*; Deutsch, 1944, *Psychology of Women*.
27. Deutsch, 1944. *Psychology of Women*.
28. Benedek, 1949, 'Psychosomatic Implications', p. 643.
29. On this, see Alice Balint, 1939, 'Love for the Mother'; Fliess, 1961, *Ego and Body Ego*; Whiting et al., 1958, 'The Function of Male Initiation Rites'; Newton, 1955, *Maternal Emotions*, and 1973, 'Interrelationships between Sexual Responsiveness'.
30. Deutsch, 1944, *Psychology of Women*, p. 205.
31. Benedek, 1959, 'Parenthood as Developmental Phase'.
32. See Klein, 1937, 'Love, Guilt and Reparation'. Barbara Deck (personal communication) pointed out to me that Klein's interpretation of a woman's participation in mothering is homologous to that described by Ferenczi and Balint in coitus. A woman's gratification in mothering comes from becoming her mother and from identifying with her mothered infant. Similarly, she is both the receiving mother (womb) and identifies with the male penetrating her in coitus.
33 The mothers I describe in Chapter 6 [*The Reproduction of Mothering*] are cases in point.

REFERENCES

[Edited for the present volume.]
Balint, A., 'Love for the Mother and Mother Love', *International Journal of Psycho-Analysis*, XXX, 1949 and collected in M. Balint (ed.), *Primary Love and Psycho-Analytic Technique* (New York: Liveright Publishing, 1965).
Balint, M., 'Critical Notes on the Theory of the Pregenital Organizations of the Libido'

(1935) in M. Balint (ed.), *Primary Love and Psycho-Analytic Technique* (New York: Liveright Publishing, 1965).

Balint, M., 'Perversions and Genitality' in *Primary Love and Psycho-Analytic Technique* (1965).

Benedek, T., 'Psychosomatic Implications of the Primary Unit, Mother–Child', *American Journal of Ortho-Psychiatry*, 19, #4, 1949.

Benedek, T., 'Parenthood as a Developmental Phase: A Contribution to the Libido Theory', *Journal of the American Psychoanalytic Association*, 7, #3, 1959.

Bernard, J., *The Future of Marriage* (New York: Bantam, 1972).

Booth, A., 'Sex and Social Participation', *American Sociological Review*, 37, 1972.

Bott, E., *Family and Social Network: Roles, Norms and External Relationships in Ordinary Urban Families* (London: Tavistock, 1957).

Chasseguet-Smirgel, J., 'Feminine Guilt and the Oedipus Complex' (1964), in J. Chasseguet-Smirgel (ed.), *Female Sexuality* (Ann Arbor: University of Michigan Press, 1970).

Deutsch. H., *Psychology of Women* Vols 1 and 2 (New York: Grune and Stratton, 1944 and 1945).

Deutsch, H., 'The Psychology of Women in Relation to the Functions of Reproduction', *International Journal of Psycho-Analysis*, VI, 1925.

Ferenczi, S., *Thalassa: A Theory of Genitality* (New York: Norton, [1924] 1968).

Fliess, R., *Ego and Body Ego: Contributions to Their Psychoanalytic Psychology* (New York: International Universities Press, [1961] 1970).

Freedman, D., 'On Women Who Hate Their Husbands' (1961), in Hendrick M. Ruitenbeek (ed.), *Psychoanalysis and Female Sexuality* (New Haven: College and University Press Services, 1966).

Freud, S., *New Introductory Lectures on Psychoanalysis*, SE XXII.

Freud, S., 'On Narcissism: An Introduction' (1914), SE XIV.

Gans, H., *The Levittowners* (New York: Vintage, 1967).

Goethals, G. W., 'Symbiosis and the Life Cycle', *British Journal of Medical Psychology*, 46, 1973.

Grunberger, B., 'Outline for a Study of Narcissism in Female Sexuality' (1964) in J. Chasseguet-Smirgel (ed.), *Female Sexuality* (Ann Arbor: University of Michigan Press, 1970).

Hochschild, A. R., 'Attending to, Codifying, and Managing Feelings: Sex Differences in Love', paper presented to the American Sociological Association Meetings, San Francisco, 29 August, 1975.

Kephart, W. M., 'Some Correlatives of Romantic Love', *Journal of Marriage and the Family*, 29, 1967.

Kernberg, O., *Borderline Conditions and Pathological Narcissism* (New York: Jason Aronson, 1975).

Kohut, H., 'Analysis of Self: A Systematic Approach to the Psychoanalytic Treatment of Narcissistic Personality Disorders', *Psychoanalytic Study of the Child*, monograph 4 (New York: International Universities Press, 1971).

Komarovsky, M., *Blue-Collar Marriage* (New York: Vintage, 1967).

Newton, N., *Maternal Emotions: A Study of Women's Feelings Toward Menstruation, Pregnancy, Childbirth, Breastfeeding, Infant Care, and Other Aspects of Their Femininity*, Psychosomatic Medicine Monograph (New York: Paul Hoeber, Harper & Brothers, 1955).

Newton, N., 'Interrelationships Between Sexual Responsiveness, Birth, and Breastfeeding', in Zubin, J. and Money, J. (eds), *Contemporary Sexual Behavior: Critical Issues in the 1970s* (Baltimore: John Hopkins University Press, 1973).

Rich, A., *Of Women Born: Motherhood as Experience and Institution* (New York: Norton, 1976).

Rosaldo, M. Z. and Lamphere, L. (eds), *Women, Culture and Society* (Stanford: Stanford University Press, 1974).

Rubin, Z., 'Loving and Leaving' (1975). Unpublished paper.

Stack, C. B., *All Our Kin* (New York: Harper & Row, 1974).

Whiting, J. W. M., Kluckhohn, R. and Anthony, A., 'The Function of Male Initiation Rites at Puberty' in Maccoby, E. E., Newcomb, T. M. and Hartley, E. L. (eds), *Readings in Social Psychology* (New York: Holt, 1958).

Wolff, C., *Love Between Women* (New York: Harper & Row, 1971).

Young, M. and Wilmott, P., *Family and Kinship in East London* (London: Penguin, 1966).

Zilboorg, G., 'Masculine and Feminine: Some Biological and Cultural Aspects' (1944) in J. B. Miller (ed.), *Psychoanalysis and Women* (1973).

9

The Question of Femininity and the Theory of Psychoanalysis

Juliet Mitchell

This talk is not about psychoanalytic concepts of femininity; it is about the connection between the question of femininity and the construction of psychoanalytic theory. I suggest that for Freud, 'femininity' sets the limits – the starting- and the end-point – of his theory, just as its repudiation marked the limits of the possibility of psychotherapeutic cure:

> We often have the impression that with the wish for a penis and the masculine protest we have penetrated through all the psychological strata and have reached bedrock, and that thus our activities are at an end. This is probably true . . . The repudiation of femininity can be nothing else than a biological fact . . .[1]

This intimate relationship between the problem of femininity and the creation of theory has not characterized other psychoanalytic work. This is largely to do with the shifting orientation: from neuroses to their underlying psychoses; from Oedipal to pre-Oedipal. In part it is to do with a difference in the nature of the theoretical constructions. After Freud the theoretical concepts belonging to psychoanalysis were there to be added to, repudiated, confirmed. By and large, alterations and alternatives emanate directly from the clinical work. But Freud had a different task: it was to make *other* concepts psychoanalytical.

For Freud the notion of the unconscious is there, an idea waiting in the circum-ambient literature; it is transformed into a theory by his application of it to the material he observed. Freud's patients, correct, repudiate or confirm his concepts which remain always larger, wider in application than their particularity in the clinical setting. But if we take Melanie Klein as an example we can see a different intellectual process. When she starts her work the theory and practice of psychoanalysis is already established. Immersed in her practice she comes to question specific aspects of the existent psychoanalytic theory. Her patients do not lead her back into an overarching theory but forward to a new description which relates only to what is observed and experienced. There is no preoccupation with the nature of theory as such, or with the nature of science, or with making psycho-analysis scientific. This is assumed. Not so for Freud.

What did Freud consider to be the nature of theory? I am going to give two quotations which will mark the framework. First, from the *New Introductory Lectures*:

> We cannot do justice to the characteristics of the mind by linear outlines like those in a drawing or in a primitive painting, but rather by areas of colour melting into one another as they are represented by modern artists. After making the separation we must allow what we have separated to merge together once more.[2]

and in 'Why War?', his address to Einstein:

> It may perhaps seem to you as though our theories are a kind of mythology and, in the present case, not even an agreeable one. But does not every science come in the end to be a kind of mythology like this? Cannot the same be said today of your own Physics?[3]

Lines drawn to communicate what we know is only a blurred merging. Myths – symbolical stories set up to explain other stories.

When he first used hypnosis with patients, Freud (like others) was aware that the treatment echoed an important hypnoid state within the hysterical attack itself. At least within Freud's psychoanalytic theory, there remains, I believe, always this homologous structure: a characteristic element of the illness is taken up and repeated in the treatment and then, in its turn, finds a place at the centre of the theoretical construction. The famous reflection at the end of the Shreber case is an indication:

> Since I neither fear the criticism of others nor shrink from criticizing myself, I have no motive for avoiding the mention of a similarity which may possibly damage our libido theory in the estimation of many of my readers. Schreber's 'rays of God' which are made up of a condensation of the sun's rays, of nerve fibres, and of spermatozoa, are in reality nothing else than a concrete representation and projection outwards of libidinal cathexes, and they thus lend his delusions a striking conformity with our theory . . . It remains for the future to decide whether there is more delusion in my theory than I should like to admit, or whether there is more truth in Schreber's delusion than other people are as yet prepared to believe.[4]

And later:

> I have not been able to resist the seduction of an analogy. The delusions of patients appear to me to be the equivalent of the constructions which we

build up in the course of analytic treatment – attempts at explanations and cure . . .[5]

If for Freud a scientific theory was a myth (there is nothing pejorative in this), then we should remember both how his case histories read like *romans à clef* and how, if uneasily, he was well aware of this:

> I have not always been a psychotherapist. Like other neuropathologists, I was trained to employ local diagnosis and electro-prognosis, and it still strikes me myself as strange that the case histories I write should read like short stories and that, as one might say, they lack the serious stamp of science.[6]

If the theory is a myth, the case history a short story, then of course the essence of the illness is in some way a story too. As one commentator has put it: 'Charcot sees, Freud will hear. Perhaps the whole of psychoanalysis is in that shift.'[7] I don't believe that this particular transition is the whole of psychoanalysis; but I do feel that it is important. Rather than stress language, the talking cure, I would emphasize here the listening treatment. Hysterics are creative artists, they suffer from reminiscences, they have heard something that has made them ill:

> The point that escaped me in the solution of hysteria lies in the discovery of a new source from which a new element of unconscious production arises. What I have in mind are hysterical phantasies, which regularly, as it seems to me, *go back to things heard* by children at an early age and only understood later. The age at which they take in information of this kind is very remarkable – from the age of six to seven months onwards.[8]

In these early papers – before *The Interpretation of Dreams* and an interest once more in the visual and in perception – the stress is on the aural and its connection with the formation of unconscious phantasies. Charcot saw and classified and dismissed what he heard:

> You see how hysterics shout. Much ado about nothing . . . [She is said to talk] of someone with a beard, man or woman . . . Whether man or woman is not without importance, but let us slide over that mystery.[9]

But Freud decided that these tales of sound and fury did signify something. The move from seeing to hearing, from Charcot to Freud, is the move away from observation and the attendant blindness of the seeing eye.

Stories have two dimensions: what they are about and who tells them. Freud first believed that the stories were true and then that they were true as stories. Hysterics tell tales and fabricate stories – particularly for doctors who will listen. At first Freud was over-credulous. He thought they were about what they said they were about on a realistic plane, he then realized his patients were telling stories. The stories were about psychic reality: the object of psychoanalysis. What they are about then, is first seduction and then phantasy; who tells them – this is the beginning of psychoanalysis as a theory and therapy of subjectivity.

Social historians of western Europe and America consider that hysteria reached epidemic proportions during the nineteenth century. It was primarily a disease of women. Alice James, sister of the novelist Henry and philosopher William James, will do to illustrate my theme here. Like Dora, Alice's conversion symptoms seem mainly to have been constructed from an identification with her father: an hysterical paralysis of the leg for his amputation. No one doubted that Alice was as able as her brothers; but she made her illness into her career, writing her diaries to parallel the communications of her body. She described her own feelings:

> As I used to sit immovable reading in the library with waves of violent inclination suddenly invading my muscles taking some one of their myriad forms such as throwing myself out of the window, or knocking off the head of the benignant pater as he sat with silver locks, writing at his table, it used to seem to me that the only difference between me and the insane was that I had all the horrors and suffering of insanity but the duties of doctor, nurse and straitjacket imposed upon me too. Conceive of never being without the sense that if you let yourself go for a moment you must abandon all, let the dykes break and the flood sweep in, acknowledging yourself abjectly impotent before immutable laws.[10]

She also commented:

> When I am gone pray don't think of me simply as a creature who might have been something else, had neurotic science been born.[11]

Many nineteenth-century doctors got furious with their hysterical patients, finding themselves locked in a power struggle in which their opponent's best weapon was the refusal to be cured. Freud and subsequent analysts are familiar with the problem. Freud's understanding of this – in characteristic fashion – moved from the notion of a social gain in illness (removal of middle-class women from intolerable situations) to a psychological one where it bifurcated. It became on the one hand, the theories of resistance, the negative therapeutic reaction, and, particularly, after the case of Dora, of transference and counter-transference. On the other hand, after a difficult trajectory which I am going to try to trace here, it led to the concept of a fundamental human repudiation of femininity – a repudiation which, for Freud, was the bedrock of psychoanalysis both as theory and therapy.

I think – and I want to be tentative here – that psychoanalysis had to start from an understanding of hysteria. It could not have developed – or certainly not in the same way – from one of the other neuroses or psychoses. Hysteria led Freud to what is universal in psychic construction and it led him there in a particular way – by the route of a prolonged and central preoccupation with the difference between the sexes. The sexual aetiology of hysteria spoke to Freud from the symptoms, stories and associations of his parents and the otherwise unattended to, accidental comments of his colleagues. But the question of sexual difference – femininity and masculinity – was built into the very structure of the illness.

There are two aspects to Freud's interest in Charcot's work that I think should be stressed. They are separate, but I suggest Freud brought them together. Charcot emphasized the existence of male hysteria. He also organized the disease. When Freud returned from Paris to Vienna the first paper he presented was on male hysteria. In his report, he commented of Charcot's work:

> Hysteria was lifted out of the chaos of the neuroses, was differentiated from other conditions with a similar appearance, and was provided with a symptomatology which, though sufficiently multifarious, nevertheless makes it impossible any longer to doubt the rule of law and order.[12]

At the same time, when Freud's friendship with Fliess was at its height, he wrote to him congratulating him on his work on menstruation with these words: '[Fliess had] stemmed the power of the female sex so that it bears its share of obedience to the law.'[13] The search for laws, lines to sort out the blurred picture; laws that in the end are anyway only myths.

The laws about the human psyche will be one and the same thing as the laws about sexual difference. Hysteria was the woman's disease: a man could have it. In Freud's hands hysteria ceases to be a category pertaining to any given sector of the population, it becomes a general human possibility. And a possibility not only in the sense that anyone can have it, but in that it provides the clues to the human psyche itself.

We can see Freud stumbling from the specificity of hysteria to the construction of subjectivity in the general human condition in these early writings from the 1880s and 1890s. Always it is via the dilemma of sexual difference.

> Conditions related *functionally* to sexual life play a great part in the aetiology of hysteria . . . and they do so on account of the high psychical significance of this function especially in the female sex.[14]

> Hysteria necessarily presupposes a primary experience of unpleasure – that is, of a passive nature. The natural sexual passivity of women explains their being more inclined to hysteria. Where I have found hysteria in men, I have been able to prove the presence of abundant sexual passivity in their anamnesis.[15]

Her hysteria can therefore be described as an acquired one, and it presupposed nothing more than the possession of what is probably a very widespread proclivity – the proclivity to acquire hysteria.[16]

Freud tried all sorts of explanations as to why an illness so clearly found predominantly in women, should also occur in men. But it was a cry of Eureka! when he wrote enthusiastically to Fliess: 'Bisexuality! I'm sure you are right!' Bisexuality was a postulate of something universal in the human psyche. But while bisexuality explained why men and women could be hysterics it did not account for why it was their femininity that was called into play.

At the level of the story, the tale Freud heard was of paternal seduction. After holding on to this information with conviction he writes to Fliess that something is hindering his work. The obstacle has something to do with Freud's relationship to Fliess – the relationship of a man to a man which, by 1937, was to be the other expression of the bedrock of psychoanalytic theory and therapy, once more, a repudiation – this time, on the man's side – of femininity, of passivity in relation to a man.

Many commentators, including Freud himself, have observed that it was Freud's femininity that predominated in this relationship with Fliess; it is possible that it was his femininity that rendered that friendship eventually untenable. Freud referred on several occasions to his own neurosis as 'my mild hysteria'. He did so frequently at the time when he was blocked in his work on hysteria. He has a breakthrough: 'I no longer believe in my neurotica'. Hysterics are not suffering the trauma of paternal seduction, they are expressing the phantasy of infantile desire. Is this true of hysterics or of everyone? Freud's clinical listening and his self-analysis come together:

One single thought of general value has been revealed to me. I have found, in my own case too, falling in love with the mother and jealousy of the father, and I regard it as a universal event of early childhood, even if not so early as in children who have been made hysterical . . . If that is so, we can understand the riveting power of *Oedipus Rex* . . .[17]

Hysteria, the Oedipal illness; source of the concept of the Oedipus complex, discovered through the hysteria of Freud, a male analyst. Universal bisexuality; universal Oedipus complex; hysteria the most Oedipal neurosis, the one that most utilizes bisexuality. Women more Oedipal, more bisexual, more hysterical. These connections were to remain for many years in search of a theory that explained them. What was universal, what specific to hysteria, what to femininity?

Something else that came to be connected was going on with Freud's investigations. These early texts are preoccupied with two aspects of hysteria: the absences or gaps in consciousness and the splitting of consciousness. Anna O's illness reveals the absences, Miss Lucy R's the splitting.

[The] idea is not annihilated by a repudiation of this kind, but merely repressed into the unconscious. When this process occurs for the first time there comes into being a nucleus and centre of crystallization for the formation of a psychical group divorced from the ego – a group around which everything which would imply an acceptance of the incompatible idea subsequently collects. The splitting of consciousness in these cases of acquired hysteria is accordingly a deliberate and intentional one. At least it is often *introduced* by an act of volition; for the actual outcome is something different from what the subject intended. What he wanted was to do away with an idea, as though it had never appeared, but all he succeeds in doing is to isolate it psychically.[18]

The splitting of consciousness, the disappearance of meaning, the unconscious – these cease to be confined as characteristics of hysteria and again become universalised. Freud finally distinguishes his theory of hysteria from Pierre Janet's on the grounds that Janet argues that hysteria's defining feature was splitting and Freud that it was conversion. For Freud, splitting was a general condition. Freud came back to the question at the end of his life. In the fragmentary paper on 'Splitting of the Ego in the Process of Defence' he is uncertain whether, in 1938, he is on to something new or merely saying again what he has said before. It is a return to the preoccupation with splitting that had marked his work on hysteria fifty to sixty years before. I shall argue that what he says at the end is both old and new. What is new is that by the end of the 1930s he has brought it into line with the problem of sexual difference. In the early days, it went only side by side with that question – he had not yet established the point of their connection.

Not yet connected with splitting, then, in the early work on hysteria there remained the problem of the diversion into masculinity and femininity. In the 1890s Freud came very close to sexualizing repression. Fliess offered one version of this argument, the other was to be Adler's mistake. In a draft entitled 'The Architecture of Hysteria', Freud wrote: 'It is to be expected that the essentially repressed element is always what is feminine. What men essentially repress is the paederastic element.'[19] How close and yet how different is this to the repudiation of femininity as the bedrock of psychoanalysis in *Analysis Terminable and Interminable* in 1937. But sexualizing repression was not an idea that Freud held on to for long. Six months later, in the letter to Fliess in which he tells of the hold-up in his self-analysis, he comments: 'I have also given up the idea of explaining libido as the masculine factor and repression as the feminine one . . .'[20] And yet – with all the difference in the world – in Freud's theory libido remains 'masculine' and it is not that repression is feminine, but that femininity is repudiated.

The concept that brought together Freud's observation of splitting and the dilemma of sexual difference as it was posed in hysteria, was the castration complex. I don't want to go into details of the concept here – merely to note whence it arose, what it explained and how forcefully it was (and maybe still is), rejected by other analysts. It came from Freud's pursuit of the internal logic of what he needed to describe. He used both Fliess's biological and Adler's socio-logical accounts as buffers from which his theory needed to bump away. In a fascinating two pages at the end of the paper on 'A Child is being Beaten', he explains why these accounts fail. The concept of castration arose, too, from a listening ear tuned to the problem in the case histories, in particular, in that of Little Hans. What it explained was briefly this: how the formation of the human psyche was inextricably linked with the construction of a psychological notion of sexual difference.

For Freud, the child's first question is hypothesized as 'where do babies come from?' The second (or maybe chronologically the other way round for girls) is: 'what is the difference between the sexes?' The theoretician in Freud reformu-lated his own hypothesis – the child's imagined questions – as the myth (or theory) of the Oedipus complex and the myth (or theory) of the castration complex: lines around blurred fields of colour.

The splitting that set up the unconscious is repeated in a split that sets up the division between the sexes. For this reason, the 1938 paper on the splitting of the ego uses as its exemplary instance the conscious acceptance of the castration complex and the simultaneous unconscious repudiation of the possibility of its implications (femininity) as expressed in the setting up of a fetish object.

For Freud the final formation of the human psyche is coincident with the psychological acquisition of the meaning of sexual difference. In Freud's theory this is not there from the beginning, it has to be acquired:

> If we could divest ourselves of our corporeal existence, and could view the things of this earth with a fresh eye as purely thinking beings, from another planet for instance, nothing perhaps would strike our attention more forcibly than the fact of the existence of two sexes among human beings, who, though so much alike in other respects, yet mark the difference between them with such obvious external signs. But it does not seem that children choose this fundamental fact in the same way as the starting-point of their researches into sexual problems . . . A child's desire for knowledge on this point does not in fact awaken spontaneously, prompted perhaps by some inborn need for estab-lished causes.[21]

The story told is about the acquisition and repudiation of this knowledge.

Sexual difference – but why should it be femininity that is repudiated? Before Freud, many doctors and commentators thought that hysterics were women trying to escape or protest their female role; Freud toyed with the possibility that all that was feminine was repressed, the repressed feminine would thus have been the content of the unconscious itself. We are all familiar with how often women are thought to be more in touch with the unconscious, more intuitive, nearer the roots of nature – in Ezra Pound's words:

> . . . the female
> Is an element, the female
> Is a chaos
> An octopus
> A biological process

Freud's answer was: no, 'we must keep psychoanalysis separate from biology';
repression must not be sexualized. But femininity *does* come to represent this
point where meaning and consciousness vanish. Because this point is chaos, that
which has been made to stand in for it – made to indicate the gap – is unbearable
and will be repudiated. In the loss of balance, something to fill the gap will be
hallucinated, a breast; produced as fetish, envied – a penis. The clinical experience of splitting and of castration is horror – penis-envy, hallucination, fetishism
are quick relief.

It is commonly held that castration rests on deprivation – what is taken
away from one, as, for instance, in weaning. I would suggest, however, that
what it rests on and organizes into its sexual meanings is, on the contrary, splitting. It only then 'subsequently' uses deprivation. One cannot experience
absence, a gap – mankind, like nature, abhors a vacuum – one can only experience this unexperienceable as something taken away. One *uses* deprivation to
describe the indescribable – the indescribable are splitting and the castration
complex.

Freud talks of splitting where Klein perceives 'split off parts' which can be
communicated to the analyst by projection. The similarity of vocabulary conceals
essential differences. I am not sure that the splitting of which Freud talks could
be experienced in the transference. It can be witnessed in fetishism, but on the
other side of the fetish object there is nothing there: no object, therefore, no
subject. In my limited experience all the analyst can do is bear witness; all the
patient can do is experience the most intense horror, a horror that is about absence
but which can become filled with phantasmagoria. The emptiness of chaos made
carnate, a plethora of unorganized feelings and objects.

In splitting, the subjectivity of the subject disappears. The horror is about the
loss of oneself into one's own unconscious – into the gap. But because human
subjectivity cannot ultimately exist outside a division into one of two sexes, then
it is castration that finally comes to symbolize this split. The feminine comes to
stand over the point of disappearance, the loss. In popular imagery, castration is
usually thought of as something cut off, missing, absent, a wound, a scar.
Analytically, I believe it is experienced not only in these pallid indicators of
absence but as something appallingly out of place: something there which should
not be there. The trauma captured in splitting is that one isn't there; the same
trauma that castration comes to symbolize is that one is incomplete; the trauma
that can be lived over and over again in the endless by-ways of life's failures and
imperfections. The loss can only be filled up:

If one of the ordinary symbols for a penis occurs in a dream doubled or multiplied, it is to be regarded as a warding off of castration.[22]

Because human subjectivity cannot ultimately exist outside a division between the sexes – one cannot be no sex – then castration organizes the loss of subjecthood into its sexual meanings. Something with which the subject has identified, felt to be his or herself (something that satisfies the mother, the phallic phase – *being* the phallus for the mother – completing her), disappears, is missing. Castration is 'discovered' in the mother who is no longer perceived as whole, complete – something is missing, the baby has left her. The baby goes absent – vanishes from the mirror. Bisexuality is a movement across a line, it is *not* androgyny. For Freud there is no sexual distinction symbolized before the castration complex has done its organizing of the desires expressed within the Oedipal situation. There are male and female, active and passive, multifarious *behavioural* distinctions between boy and girl infants, but no notion in the psyche that one is not complete; that something can be missing.

The castration complex is not about women, nor men, but a danger, a horror to both – a gap that has to be filled in differently by each. In the fictional ideal type this will be for the boy by the illusion that a future regaining of phallic potency will replace his totality; for a girl this will be achieved by something psychically the same: a baby. Phallic potency and maternity – for men and women – come to stand for wholeness.

Hysteria was, and is – whatever the age or generational status of the man or woman who expresses it – the daughter's disease: a child's phantasy about her parents: the 'daughter' in the man or woman has not found a solution in homosexuality, maternity, or a career. To 'her' femininity really seems to equal the gap indicated by castration or, in Joan Riviere's words, it is enacted as 'a masquerade' to cover it. She is good at this but it cannot satisfy.

In the 1920s some important developments took place culminating on the one hand in ego psychology and on the other in object-relations theory, both Kleinian and non-Kleinian. There was a series of important and unresolved disagreements about the nature of female sexuality, but my point here is that despite an insistence on the problem, the question of femininity ceases to be what motivates the theoretical constructions. I propose to single out a few trends within Melanie Klein's work to indicate the implications of this.

In deciphering phantasy, Freud heard the child in his adult patients. Klein worked with children and found the infant in their phantasies. But there is a difference: the child and infant merge in Klein's way of thinking – their phantasies cope with the inner and outer realities in the present. For Freud, too, through his notion of the repetition compulsion, the child is alive in the adult's present. But for Freud the present always contains a construction of the past: the subject from birth to death is first and foremost, indeed, entirely, an historical subject, nothing other than what he makes of him or herself. This sense of history is not there in Klein's theory nor in her practice. Right until the end of his life, Freud's theory emphasized the analytic task of reconstruction of a history; Klein's highlighted interpretation and the analysis of the transference experience in which the task is to understand (largely through projection and introjection) what is being communicated between two people within the analytical session. Experience of psychic mechanism elicits the story which is no longer a tale told, but something revealed, discovered in process.

Where phantasy to Freud was the story – conscious or unconscious – that the subject tells about himself, for Klein it is the mental representation of the instinct and, simultaneously, a capacity to deal with inner and outer worlds. It joins instinct to object: primitively the oral drive phantasizes an object; a breast or some substitute that can be sucked, a penis. And in turn, the object alters the inner ego; what is taken in from outside transforms the inside:

> The analysis of early projective and introjective object relationships revealed phantasies of objects introjected into the ego from earliest infancy, starting with the ideal of the persecutory breast. To begin with part-objects were intro- jected, like the breast and, later, the penis; then whole objects like the mother, the father, the parental couples.[23]

The boy and the girl have both the same and different drives: where their biology is different, their urges must differ. For Klein, the instinct is biological; for Freud it is 'our main mythology'. The boy and girl have the same objects. In Klein's theory, the object they first take in is predominantly part of the mother, then the whole mother; this gives them both in Klein's theory a 'primary femininity'. There is a shift of emphasis which, I believe, is crucial. For Klein, what you have got you transform by your phantasies and then take it in and it becomes you. For Freud, it is the attachment to what you have had to abandon that you take in. Freud's subject is constituted by filling the interstices where something is miss- ing: one hallucinates, has delusions, tells stories. Klein's person becomes him or herself by taking in what is present. Psychically the mother in Freud's scheme is important when she goes away (the fort/da game), the penis when it is not there (penis-envy). Klein's concept of envy (interestingly enough also the bedrock of her theory and therapy) is for a mother who has everything.

For Klein the theory sets up a situation in which the ego phantasizes directly out of its instincts and body feelings onto an object. Whereas Freud's 'body-ego' is always an homunculus standing on its head, for Klein, the objects (despite the accreted confusing phantasies) are, in essence, taken for what they are biologi- cally and socially. The mother is a woman, feminine. The penis, even when inside the mother, is a masculine attribute. So, for instance, when the object of the oral phase moves from breast to penis, for the girl this becomes the heterosexual moment. The projecting penis is masculine where the breast is not. The gendered object gives meaning:

For the little girl, this first oral turning to the penis is a heterosexual move paving the way to the genital situation and the wish to incorporate the penis in her vagina. But at the same time it contributes to her homosexual trends in that . . . the oral desire is linked with incorporation and identification, and the wish to be fed by the penis is accompanied by a wish to possess a penis of her own.[24]

Freud listens to a story, constructs a myth. The unconscious shows they are only stories, myths. It is the gap, the point where the story vanishes, the subject disappears. (Ego psychologists believe the story is the whole truth and nothing but the truth – the story is all.) But, what we are witnessing in Klein's description is not the unconscious as another scene, that gap which has its own laws, but an unconscious that is filled, replete with a chaos of phantasmagoria, an unconscious as full as the external world seems to be. Her theory is about such an unconscious.

Perhaps I can give another analogy, tentative; a thought-in-flight. Freud's theory is a myth, a story of a story – the subject's narrative structuring of him or herself. It stops, it fails, it needs re-telling another way. Though a novelist writes of characters of different sexes, he or she never writes of anyone of no sex or in the middle of the dividing line – Virgina Woolf's *Orlando*, whose hero/heroine must change sides, highlights this. In Freudian theory, masculinity and femininity are only their difference from each other. Difference is articulated by something imagined to be missing. From the position of something missing, each sex can be imagined as having what the other has not. In essence this is what a novelist's story is all about.

But there is another literary analogy that could act as a possibility for theory. Not a myth, but a symbolist poem. This is what Klein's theory suggests. The wish to bite indicates the oral drive; the oral drive, aggression; aggression is Klein's (not Freud's) death drive. Physical impulse becomes a conception, the conception a theory. In a symbolist poem, the symbol shapes the product. The task is not to produce hypothetical lines around blurred fields of colour but to let the image produce its own shape. The poem, however, does not speak to sexual differentiation. As Adrienne Rich writes:

> If they ask me my identity
> what can I say but
> I am the androgyne
> I am the living mind
> you fail to describe
> In your dead language,
> the lost noun, the verb surviving
> only in the infinitive.

As far as femininity is concerned, we have moved from the hysteric whose femininity, being about nothing, had nothing she wanted, to the feminine boy and girl who, in imaginatively taking in their mother, have everything. But I believe there is a confusion in the conceptualization here. This mother who has everything is not 'feminine'; she is complete. The poem is not, as many people including Klein in her theory of primary femininity argue, feminine, even if it partakes of the mother. Of course, the mother is where femininity in its positive filling in of a gap has landed and the association must retrospectively be made. But this poem and this mother are about notions of plenitude, fullness, completeness. Nothing is missing. The verb is in the infinitive. There is no 'I' nor 'other'. In the story sexual difference is symbolized around absence – the abandoned object cathexis, the envy of what is missing that once, imaginatively, was there. Here in the poem, the envy is for what is there and it is everything – milk, breast, faeces, babies, penises. What Klein is describing here is the raw material, the plenitude of objects and feelings which the story relies on when it comes to construct itself, to fill in its gaps. It is perhaps poetic justice that the hysteric who must repudiate her femininity which is about nothing comes to rest on a mother who has all. But we must allow the story to tell us something about the poem as well. In describing what he calls the deployment of sexuality in the nineteenth century Michel Foucault argues that there took place:

> A hysterization of women's bodies: a threefold process whereby the feminine body was analysed – qualified and disqualified– as being thoroughly saturated with sexuality; whereby it was integrated into the sphere of medical practices, by reason of a pathology intrinsic to it; whereby, finally, it was placed in organic communication with the social body (whose regulated fecundity it was supposed to ensure), the family space (of which it had to be a substantial and functional element), and the life of children (which it produced and had to guarantee, by virtue of a biologico-moral responsibility lasting through the entire period of the children's education): *the Mother, with her negative image of 'nervous woman', constituted the most visible form of this hysterization.* (My italics.)[25]

Motherhood purports to fill in the absence which femininity covers over and which hysteria tries not to acknowledge. From their positions along a continuum, motherhood and hysteria, to have or to have not, to be or not to be, constantly question each other.

NOTES

1. Freud, *Standard Edition*, XXIII, 1937, p. 252.
2. Freud, *Standard Edition*, XXII, 1933, p. 79.
3. Ibid., p. 211.
4. Freud, *Standard Edition*, XII, 1911, pp. 78–9.
5. Freud, *Standard Edition*, XXIII, 1937, p. 268.

6. Freud, *Standard Edition*, I, 1893 [1888–1893], p. 160.
7. Stephen Heath, *The Sexual Fix*, 1982, p. 38.
8. Freud, *Standard Edition*, I, 1897, pp. 244–5.
9. Quoted in Heath, op. cit., p. 38.
10. Quoted in Jean Strouse, *Alice James*, 1989, p. 118.
11. Ibid., p. IX.
12. Freud, *Standard Edition*, I, 1956 [1886], p. 12.
13. Quoted in Heath, op. cit., p. 46.
14. Freud, *Standard Edition*, I, 1888, p. 51.
15. Ibid., p. 228.
16. Freud, *Standard Edition*, II, 1893–1895, p. 122.
17. Freud, *Standard Edition*, I, 1897, p. 265.
18. Freud, *Standard Edition*, II, 1893–1895, p. 123.
19. Freud, *Standard Edition*, I, 1897, p. 251.
20. Ibid., p. 271.
21. Freud, *Standard Edition*, IX, 1908, pp. 211–12.
22. Freud, *Standard Edition*, V, 1900, p. 357.
23. Hanna Segal, *Introduction to the Work of Melanie Klein*, 1964, p. 8.
24. Ibid., p. 97.
25. [This note is missing in the original edition.]

10

Klein:
The Phantasy that Anatomy
is Destiny

Noreen O'Connor and Joanna Ryan

Many feminists have been impressed by Melanie Klein's emphasis on the centrality of the mother in the infant's early development. It has signified a move from Freud's phallocentrism, and the language of instincts and their satisfaction. For Klein, the baby's unconscious phantasies in relation to the breast initiate and underpin her relationship to others. These are initially 'part-objects' identified in relations of anxiety and satisfaction from oral, anal and genital positions; if development proceeds 'normally', relationships to whole objects are established in which both 'good' and 'bad' feelings towards the object can be sustained together.

Susie Orbach and Luise Eichenbaum, feminist psychotherapists and founder members of the Women's Therapy Centre in London, praise Dorothy Dinnerstein for showing us how Kleinian theory explains the misogynist nature of 'all our psychologies'.[1] Dinnerstein (1978) uses Klein's concept of envy to argue that women are the objects of oppression, hatred and destructiveness because of the power of the baby's earliest feelings towards the mother:

> who was half human, half nature – we feel torn between two impulses: the impulse, on the one hand, to give free rein to the nursling's angry greed, its wild yearning to own, control, suck dry the source of good, its wish to avenge deprivation; and the impulse, on the other hand, to make reparation for these feelings, which threaten to destroy what is most precious and deeply needed.[2]

This reading of Klein recognizes that psychoanalysis is not only a theory of individual suffering and development but also a social theory which has moral and political effects. However, these feminist psychotherapists and psychologists have failed to discuss Klein's specification of female homosexuality as oral-sadistic, destructive, fixated at the paranoid-schizoid position. There is no critique of the normativeness of Klein's metapsychology, notably her privileging of hetero-sexual dynamics.

It is relevant and important to analyse Klein's metapsychology, the way in which she constructs her theories, in order to highlight its implicit and explicit value judgements regarding psychic health and illness. Such value judgements can generate social and political judgements regarding morally correct behaviour and relationships. On this issue Teresa Brennan succinctly distinguishes Klein from Freud by pointing out that for Klein and ego-psychoanalysts:

> heterosexuality, potency, monogamy, and absence of perversion are listed as desirable outcomes of psychoanalysis. This would have been foreign to Freud, who recognized the force of social sanctions in causing unhappiness, but did not think it was the analyst's task to induce conformity.[3]

Like any social theory – and this holds true of those theories we have already described – Klein's theory of psychoanalysis embodies certain notions of truth, reality and value from a value-laden perspective. Klein claims to present the 'objective' truth of human development without sufficiently addressing the issue of her own inevitable historical, cultural and psychic biases. Often what is regarded as the truth of the patient's intrapsychic relationships results from an analyst's own strongly held views of the normal, which remain unquestioned for her/him.

Klein, unlike some of her followers, does not provide specific clinical exam-ples of lesbianism. Instead, references to the 'female homosexual attitude' are intertwined with her accounts of the progress and vicissitudes of early male and female relationships to the mother/breast and father/penis. Thus it is not possible to extricate her position on solely the aetiology – the family background – of lesbianism. For this reason we present a general outline of her position on the Oedipus complex and the pre–Oedipal psyche in order to set the context for understanding her position on homosexuality and lesbianism. Our exposition illustrates how Klein – along with earlier psychoanalysts, as we have shown – retains stereotypical gender descriptions which she assumes to be present from earlier infancy. Sexuality is theorized as intrinsic to gender differences. There is an assumption of a natural causality connecting sex, gender and desire, such that sexuality and desire are presented as the 'natural' expression of a given gender. In every scenario, as we will show, female homosexuality is regarded as 'oral-sadis-tic', pregenital and immature.

Klein (1950) specifies 'heterosexuality' as a major criterion for the termination of an analysis – that is to say, heterosexuality is a criterion of being psychically healthy, 'cured' of pathology. Thus in 'On the Criteria for the Termination of a Psycho-Analysis' she writes:

The question arises how far the approach I am suggesting is related to some of the well-known criteria, such as an established potency and heterosexuality, capacity for love, object-relations and work, and certain characteristics of the ego which make for mental stability and are bound up with adequate defences.[4]

Although Klein differs from Freud's emphasis on the role of instincts at the pre-Oedipal developmental stage she does, nevertheless, retain Freud's alignment of gender and sexuality. As well as arguing in favour of two distinct gender 'identities', masculine and feminine, whose characteristics are knowable and natural, she attributes appropriate – normal – sexual desires to each gender. In fact, sexual desire is postulated as intrinsic to gender identity. She maintains (1928):

The next determining influence upon the mental processes is that of the anatomical difference between the sexes.

The boy, when he finds himself impelled to abandon the oral and anal positions for the genital, passes on to the aim of penetration associated with the possession of the penis. Thus he changes not only his libido-position, but its *aim*, and this enables him to retain his original love-object. In the girl, on the other hand, the *receptive* aim is carried over from the oral to the genital position: she changes her libido-position, but retains its aim, which has already led to a disappointment in relation to her mother.[5]

Thirty years of clinical practice did not alter Klein's alignment of gender and sexuality:

There are great differences in the Oedipus complex of the girl and of the boy, which I shall characterize only by saying that whereas the boy in his genital development returns to his original object, the mother, and therefore seeks female objects, with some consequent jealousy of the father and men in general, the girl to some extent has to turn away from the mother and find the object of her desires in the father and later on in other men. (1959)[6]

As in Freud, homosexuality is designated as a negative choice and results from a failure adequately to negotiate Oedipal conflicts. Klein does not question the fundamental assumptions of her developmental theory but bases changes and variations in her theories on 'empirical' clinical practice.

Klein, like Freud, bases her metapsychology on the assumption of 'life' and 'death' instincts. She (1958) criticizes Freud for not giving sufficient weight to the importance of aggression in emotional life.[7] She argues that from the beginning of life the two instincts attach themselves to objects, primarily the mother's breast, and thus initiate the various processes constitutive of psychic development. The primal process of projection results from deflecting the death instinct outwards. Klein stresses the importance in every analysis of considering the internal processes in relation to constitutional and relational factors – that is to say, 'external' factors.

SPLITTING OF INTERNAL AND EXTERNAL

For Klein, female homosexuality is to be understood in terms of its cause or causes. It occurs because of unresolved difficulties at the paranoid-schizoid position. Preceding the depressive position, when the baby becomes able to relate to whole objects, this position (at age three to four months) is characterized by part-object relations involving processes of splitting, denial and idealization. According to Klein, female homosexuality can therefore be only a relationship of part objects.

Introjection of the mother's feeding breast is foundational for all internalization processes. This relation to the mother determines the emotional and sexual development for both sexes.[8] Gratifying experiences of the breast allow the child to internalize a good object. When bad experiences are felt, they are projected on to the breast as a bad object. Klein emphasizes the 'fact' that, from the beginning, the libido is fused with aggressiveness; this generates anxiety. To master the persecution anxiety derived from phantasies of the breast as destructive, the baby splits breast and mother internally and externally into a loved and, on the other hand, a hated object. This splitting of the breast into a good and a bad object is, Klein argues, the expression of the innate conflict between love and hate, and the anxieties generated by this.[9] Furthermore, this splitting is a precondition of the infant's relative stability because the ego (the self), which is initially unstable, gets rid of its destructive impulses and persecutory anxieties.

The infant achieves relative stability by turning a 'good' object into an 'ideal' one as a protection from the 'bad', 'persecuting' object. It is in phantasy that the infant splits object from its 'self'. As a result of this phantasized split, feelings and relations are cut off from one another.[10] These early processes are also the origin of transferences. Klein maintains that the life and death instincts are closely interconnected and so, therefore, are love and hatred. Negative and positive transferences are thus closely connected, and both require analysis 'in depth'.[11]

The paranoid-schizoid position is characterized by oral desires. Satisfaction from the breast allows the infant to find other gratifying objects, the secondary primary object being the father's penis. The penis is also the focus of the conflicting 'good' and 'bad' attitudes to the breast. According to Klein (1945), oral libido allows for the establishment of images of mother's breast and father's penis in the ego, and these form the nucleus of the super-ego.[12] Along with the anxiety, guilt and depression of libidinal development an urge towards reparation is also operative. This urge lessens persecutory anxiety towards the object, and is linked to gratitude and love.

Klein argues that the child expects to find the father's penis, excrement and children as edible substances within the mother's body. The infant phantasizes excreta as dangerous weapons. This is in line with her assumption that the Oedipus complex originates at an early stage of development dominated by sadism. In fact the first relation to reality is constituted by sadistic phantasies directed against the inside of the mother. This sadism activates anxieties regarding excrement, organs, objects, and things which are equated with one another. Anxiety is not an exclusively negative concept but, argues Klein, a sufficient 'quantity' of anxiety is necessary for symbol formation and phantasy – that is, for the subject's relation to reality. The satisfactory resolution of this developmental stage or position depends on an adequate capacity to tolerate these anxieties.

FEMALE DEVELOPMENT

Klein maintains that the girl's wish to possess her father's penis, stolen from the hated mother, is a fundamental factor in female sexual development. She assumes that the girl wants a penis as an object of oral satisfaction rather than as an attribute of masculinity,[13] as Freud had proposed. Klein argues that this desire for the penis is not the result of the castration complex, but expresses Oedipal desires. The girl is directly influenced by Oedipal impulses as a result of her feminine instincts rather than indirectly through her masculine tendencies. She unconsciously believes that her mother has incorporated her father's penis, and she envies this. The equation of penis and breast activates oral-receptive qualities in the girl, and is the foundation of her sexual development in that it prepares the vagina to receive the penis. Girls' Oedipal impulses are much more dominated by oral desires than boys'. The girl's sadistic omnipotence over her parents produces phantasies of destroying the inside of the mother's body and its contents, including the penis. Feminine masochism is based on fear of the bad objects the girl has internalized; she turns her sadistic instincts against these.

Sensations are felt in the vagina as soon as Oedipal impulses emerge. The girl identifies with her father shortly after identifying with her mother, and because of this her masturbatory phantasies constitute her clitoris as a penis. Klein claims that 'onanism' in girls does not provide as adequate an outlet for excitations as it does in boys. The girl experiences greater lack of gratification, which can cause complications and disturbances of her sexual development.[14] The girl's development is disturbed by the fact that while the boy actually possesses the penis which allows him to rival his father, the girl 'has only' the unqualified desire for motherhood. This is why Klein concludes that jealousy is more common in women than in men; it is reinforced by deflected penis-envy.

Klein's theories rely heavily on anatomical similarity and difference. She argues that the girl has more problems in the formation of her super-ego because of her anatomical difference from the father and she has difficulty in identifying

with her mother because the internal organs of sexual functioning and the possession of children are not open to reality testing.[15] Klein concludes that in men the
ego and relations based on reality are psychically dominant; men, therefore, have
the capacity for objectivity. In women the unconscious, with its sadistic and
masochistic elements as well as maternal wishes, dominates. This is the basis for
her claim that women are closer to children than men are, and that adult women
have a stronger desire for children than for a sexual partner.

FEMALE HOMOSEXUALITY AS A DEFENCE AGAINST PSYCHOSIS

Because Klein characterizes female homosexuality as originating from the paranoid-schizoid position, the implication is that lesbians have not achieved
adequate ego development: their relationship to reality therefore, is that of the
psychotic. Their relationships are part-object relationships, driven by envious
destructive phantasies arising from their failure to achieve the depressive position
and the capacity for whole-object relationships.

In *Envy and Gratitude* Klein discusses female homosexuality in the context of
her discussion of penis-envy and its oral origin.[16] She specifies envy as the angry
feeling that another person possesses something which is desirable, and the envious impulse is to destroy or spoil it. While she maintains that it is rooted in the
earliest relation to the mother, the feeding breast, Klein praises Freud's 'discovery' of penis-envy in women and his emphasis on the analysis of the girl's attitude to her mother as determining her subsequent relationships with men. Since,
according to Klein, full oral gratification resulting from a satisfactory relation to
the mother forms the basis for full genital (heterosexual) orgasm, envy interferes
with this.

Three specific scenarios involving the 'female homosexual attitude' emerge in
Klein's account. In one, the father's penis becomes the target of envy originally
experienced at the breast. This is a defensive move, an attempt to assuage the
anxieties which would allow for the depressive position, whole-object relations,
and subsequent reparation:

> Freud has shown how vital is the attitude of the girl to her mother in her subse-
> quent relations to men. When envy of the mother's breast has been strongly
> transferred to the father's penis, the outcome may be a reinforcing of her
> homosexual attitude.[17]

In the second scenario, restitutive tendencies can also reinforce female homosexuality. In *The Psycho-Analysis of Children*, Klein claims that where the girl has
focused her sadistic phantasies on the destruction of the mother by identifying
with her father's dangerous penis, 'she will feel urged to restore her mother by

means of a penis with healing powers and thus her homosexual trends will become reinforced'.[18]

In the third scenario, Klein claims that if envy of the mother's breast is not so strong, idealization of the father's penis can offer women the possibility of combining envy of the mother with love for the father, and consequently for other men. Disappointment with the mother's breast, however, may lead to the search for a 'mother substitute'. She concludes that 'Friendship with women and homosexuality may then be based on the need to find a good object instead of the avoided primal object.'[19] She warns that expressions of good object relations in homosexual women are 'deceptive', and that 'the underlying envy toward the primal object is split off but remains operative and is liable to disturb any relations'.[20]

KLEIN'S CURE

Klein emphasizes the necessity for the patient to 'co-operate' with the analyst, and to be determined 'to discover the truth about himself if he is to accept and assimilate the analyst's interpretations relating to these early layers of the mind'.[21] Every utterance of the patient is interpreted in terms of early pre-linguistic phantasies related to the breast. Her metapsychology presents these interpretations as ahistorical 'psychic' facts. Lesbians in emotionally fulfilling relationships are thus in flight from the truth, the facts of the schisms in their psyches. Klein stresses the impossibility in every psyche of ever achieving complete and permanent integration: there are always residues of paranoid and schizoid feelings and mechanisms. This, however, does not imply that homosexuality is any the less pathological within her schema.

In her focus on the infant's early relationship with the mother's breast, Klein assumes the existence of an 'inner world' that lies outside language. Analysis of the patient's positive and negative transference in relation to the analyst revives these earliest object relations. Through the processes of projection and introjection the ego becomes strengthened, and this allows for the retention of a good inner object. The introjection of the analyst as a good object, not idealized, can provide a good inner object where one had earlier been lacking. Klein points out that a strong positive transference can be deceptive, since it is based on idealization, which denies anxieties related to hate and envy. She found that patients often experience depression following recognition of an interpretation which heals splits in the self, but these depressive feelings involve relating to a whole object, and are thus a necessary step towards integration and cure.

In assuming the existence of an 'inner world' Klein ignores all twentieth-century advances in hermeneutic theory which 'systematically criticize divisions between thought and language, and spatial metaphors of "inside" and "outside" arising from that dualistic split'.[22] Wittgenstein's critique of Freud's analysis of dreams[23] can be fruitfully related to Klein's arguments on 'early' psychotic positions which, as it were, 'remain' in the psyche and are triggered off by later adult experiences. This is an analysis of intentionality which relies on a later reaction caused in daily life by a later situation. The implication is that the later reaction not only points to the original desire or meaning but is a logically necessary and sufficient condition of the truth of the statement that the person originally desired or meant such a thing. In separating thought and language, Klein postulates an 'inner' world of mechanisms without language, but mysteriously available to 'knowledge'. This is in line with many essentialist, universalist, foundational theories.

Klein's genius was to have charted the desolate hinterland of psychosis; going beyond discrete conceptions of the life and death instinct, she explores the somatic/psychic territory of anxieties, persecution, splitting, loss, disintegration, phantasy. By thematizing psychotic states or 'positions' she developed psychoanalytic technique in such a way that it has seriously challenged psychiatry's pretension to total 'expertise' in this area; she also challenges the primacy of pharmacological treatments of psychosis.[24] The paradox of such psychoanalytic theorizing is that while it claims to be attentive to the individuality of each person's speaking, it simultaneously vitiates singularity. This is operative in Klein's *a priori* refusal to consider that two men or two women in sexual relationships can have happy, fulfilled lives and, furthermore, may be happier than many of those struggling in apparently 'successful' heterosexual relationships.

NOTES

1. L. Eichenbaum and S. Orbach, *Outside In . . . Inside Out* (Harmondsworth: Penguin, 1982), p. 111.
2. D. Dinnerstein, *The Rocking of the Cradle and the Ruling of the World* (London: Souvenir Press, 1978), p. 100.
3. T. Brennan (ed.), *Between Feminism and Psychoanalysis* (London: Routledge, 1989), p. 19.
4. M. Klein, 'On the Criteria for the Termination of a Psycho-Analysis', in *Envy and Gratitude and Other Works 1946–1963* (London: Hogarth, 1984), p. 45.
5. Klein, 'Early Stages of the Oedipus Conflict', in *Contributions to Psycho-Analysis 1921–1945* (London: Hogarth, 1984), p. 202.
6. Klein, 'Our Adult World and Its Roots in Infancy', in *Envy and Gratitude*, p. 252.
7. Klein, 'The Development of Mental Functioning', in ibid., p. 245.
8. Klein, 'The Oedipus Complex in the Light of Early Anxieties', in *Contributions to Psycho-Analysis*, p. 378.
9. Klein, *Envy and Gratitude*, p. 191.
10. Klein, 'The Emotional Life of the Infant', in *Envy and Gratitude*, p. 67.
11. Klein, 'The Origins of Transference', in ibid., p. 54.
12. Klein, 'The Oedipus Complex in the Light of Early Anxieties', p. 379.
13. Klein, *The Psycho-Analysis of Children* (London: Virago, 1989), p. 196.
14. Klein, 'Early Stages of the Oedipus Conflict', p. 208.

15. Klein, *The Psycho-Analysis of Children*, p. 235.
16. Klein, *Envy and Gratitude*, pp. 191–201.
17. Ibid., p. 199.
18. Klein, *The Psycho-Analysis of Children*, p. 216.
19. Klein, *Envy and Gratitude*, p. 200.
20. Ibid.
21. Ibid.
22. N. O'Connor, 'Is Melanie Klein the One Who Knows Who You Really Are?', *Women: A Cultural Review*, vol. 1, no. 2, Oxford: Oxford University Press, Summer 1990, p. 188.
23. C. Barrett and L. Wittgenstein (eds), *Lectures and Conversations on Aesthetics, Psychology and Religious Belief* (Oxford: Basil Blackwell, 1978), pp. 41–3.
24. O'Connor, 'Is Melanie Klein the One . . .?', p. 180.

Suggested Further Reading

There are some excellent introductions to the work of Melanie Klein available, including, most notably:

Hanna Segal, *Introduction to the Work of Melanie Klein* (1964);
Juliet Mitchell, *The Selected Melanie Klein* (1986);
Julia Segal, *Melanie Klein* (1993).

Klein's own *The Psycho-Analysis of Children* (1989) is also extremely useful as an introduction to her distinctive approach.

A collection of essays, edited by J. Phillips and L. Stonebridge, *Reading Melanie Klein* (1998), with contributors such as Juliet Mitchell, Hanna Segal, Jacqueline Rose, Maria Torok and Judith Butler among others, provides contemporary critiques and applications of Klein's tenets.

R.D. Hinshelwood's *A Dictionary of Kleinian Thought* (1989) will also prove helpful.

Those interested in Nancy Chodorow's work should read *The Reproduction of Mothering: Psychoanalysis and the Sociology of Gender* (1978), from which the extract collected here is taken, as well as her more recent work:

Nancy Chodorow, *Feminism and Psychoanalysis* (1989);
Nancy Chodorow, *Femininities, Masculinities, Sexualities* (1994).

A special issue of *Women: A Cultural Review* (vol. 1, no. 2, Summer 1990) is also dedicated to Klein's work.

PART 3: JUNG AND THE JUNGIANS

The four essays collected here represent Jungian thought on the nature of 'the feminine'. The section necessarily begins with an essay by Jung which elaborates his fundamental premises of a psychical 'feminine' inner figure for men (he names it 'the anima') and a correlative 'masculine' one for women, 'the animus'. The animus, woman's masculine inner figure, is much less thoroughly explicated by Jung than the man's feminine anima. Paradoxically, the 'feminine' is less of a problem when manifest as the man's inner woman but the woman's inner man is too much of an enigma. Whether it is her femininity or her masculine aspects which are under discussion, Jung finds woman too difficult to explain:

> The anima, being of feminine gender, is exclusively a figure that compensates the masculine consciousness. In woman the compensating figure is of a masculine character, and can therefore appropriately be termed the *animus*. If it was no easy task to describe what is meant by the anima, the difficulties become almost insuperable when we set out to describe the psychology of the animus.

The animus has received consistently less explication by Jungians until relatively recently. Esther Harding makes an early contribution in her chapter, 'The Ghostly Lover', in *The Way of All Women* (1933). In the extract reprinted here, she discusses the issue of women's 'projection'[1] of typological animus figures (here, The Ghostly Lover and Prince Charming) onto men. As with anima-projections for the man, they are – while unconscious – distorting, destructive and compulsively serial in aspect. At the end of this chapter, included below p. 185, she makes a claim for redeeming the negative and unconscious aspects of the effects of the animus:

> Psychologically it is . . . true that the spiritual animus comes to dwell within the psyche only after the projection of the animus, the incarnation of the Ghostly Lover, has been overcome. Thus it is that the Ghostly Lover disappears and in his stead is born a new spiritual power transforming the life of the individual. Through this redeemed animus the woman gains a relation to the

masculine principle within herself. This masculine principle is the Logos, or wisdom. When she is identified with the animus she is possessed by opinions and rationalizations and so-called principles which do not represent true wisdom at all. These are the work of the Ghostly Lover. True wisdom can be known only through the spiritual, or redeemed animus, who is a mediator between conscious and unconscious.[2]

Of course, 'true wisdom' can be seen as a very relative term ('true wisdom' according to whose criteria?) and a particularly problematic one for women within a patriarchal culture. The progress of this release from treacherous animus to 'redeemed animus' raises many questions, but it is pointedly significant that the 'masculine in women's minds' – as unredeemed animus – seems to be so thoroughly negative, whereas the anima, while problematic in terms of 'projection', appears to be fundamentally positive.

Esther Harding and Marie-Louise von Franz, consciously writing from a complementary or corrective 'woman's perspective', nevertheless do little to revise Jung's view of the woman's animus. Significantly, however, they do acknowledge that most representations of the archetypal feminine – in myth, literature and art, for example – have been depicted from a male perspective, and are thus comprised of masculine 'anima projections'. This does at least free the concept of the archetype from stereotype, since, rather than being inherent and unchanging, it is inherited and an affect. There is a telling phrase in Marie-Louise von Franz's lecture: in describing the reciprocal effects of a man's anima-projection onto a real woman, and the real-woman's 'reflection' of this, she states that the real woman can have a transforming effect on the man and his 'eros-side' 'if she can stand up for her rights without animus'. 'Animus' in this context seems to slip inevitably towards 'animosity', thus being further inflected with the notion that a woman's animus is almost always negative. There is no suggestion that the man should ever be, or strive to be, 'without anima', for 'she' is innately his 'soul'. There is less an emphasis on the anima figure becoming a 'redeemed anima' than on an estimation that 'she' is the man's redeemer simply by virtue of being the anima (however 'acquired' *her* image might be).

As late as 1986, the editors of *A Critical Dictionary of Jungian Analysis* could write:

> There is no up-to-date work of corresponding depth on the animus. Moreover, because of the unfortunate connotations of animus possession that may have characterized pioneering women in a male-dominated society, very little attention has been given to the psychic interventions of the so-called positive or natural animus in contrast to the negative and acquired animus.[3]

A recent development in attention to the animus is revealed in Marion Woodman's essay, from her book *The Pregnant Virgin: The Process of*

Psychological Transformation (1985). Another of Woodman's works, *The Ravaged Bridegroom* (1990), is entirely devoted to considering 'masculinity in women'. In a postscript to the chapter, 'Lover, Can You Spare a Dime' in the latter work, she exhorts a residual 'frail masculine rebel energy' to move to healthy 'masculinity', which is divorced from a destructive patriarchy:

> The world as it has been is crumbling. We in our comfortable nests are too often deaf to our own soul and do not realize that the dictators out there are being mirrored by the dictators in our own dreams . . . Instead of soaring out of our prisons, we gobble alcohol or drugs or whatever poison suits our particular paralysis. We rape our souls. We kill our imaginations. Then we opt out, 'There's nothing I can do about it.' But if we trust our frail masculine rebel energy to stand up for our soul values, we *can* do something about it. We can contact the inner images that will show us what to do and where the future lies. Patriarchy is self-destructing.[4]

Yet another of her books, *Leaving My Father's House*, is dedicated to the consideration of conscious femininity which 'is not bound to gender. It belongs to both men and women.'[5] She continues:

> Although in the *history of the arts [my emphasis]*, men have articulated their femininity far more than women, women are now becoming custodians of their own feminine consciousness. For centuries, men have projected their inner image of femininity, raising it to a consciousness that left women who accepted the projection separated from their own reality. They became artifacts rather than people.[6]

The difficulty in perceiving – or describing – the animus, then, has everything to do with patriarchy, as the extract by Woodman which follows below reveals. At an earlier stage in its history, patriarchy had a vested interest in women not having access to those attributes labelled 'masculine'. Now, many 'masculine' aspects are falling under severe criticism and positive masculine images are not so easy to identify, internally or externally. In Woodman's terms, however, a positive masculinity is crucial for everyone:

> We are all the children of patriarchy. While our culture depends upon three thousand years of cultural process focused through masculine eyes, it has been won at high cost. What began as masculine values has degenerated into lust for control. Power has bludgeoned both our femininity and our masculinity. We all function with these two different energies.[7]

Although Jung first introduced his notion of 'the anima' in 1920, 'Anima and Animus', the essay of his collected here which most fully elaborates this theory, dates from 1953. Esther Harding's 1933 text, *The Way of All Women*, from which the extract presented here is taken, is therefore chronologically prior to Jung's essay, and was introduced (and thus endorsed) by Jung himself. Other women who were engaged alongside Jung in such developments (and to whom, it has been argued, he was indebted)[8] include his wife, Emma Jung (whose 1931 essay 'On the Nature of the Animus' might have been included here but for the fact that it echoes too closely Jung's own), Toni Wolff,[9] Sabina Spielrein[10] and, of course, Marie-Louise von Franz.[11]

Jung's essay on 'Anima and Animus' reveals both his relation to, and divergence from, Freudian thought. Predicated initially on Freud's views, Jung's own theories are extended to discussions of 'archetypes' and 'the collective unconscious'. The history of the gulf which emerged between the thinking of the two has been chronicled variously (and often with more attention to their relationship and rivalry than to their theoretical differences). To generalize: Jung's theories developed to take more account of religions and religiosity, mysticism, alchemy and magic, acausal phenomena (such as synchronicity) and paranormal occurrences. Again in summary: Jung's emphasis was on the 'transformative', as opposed to the 'archaeological';[12] on the 'prospective',[13] rather than the recuperative. He emphasized an archetypal process known as 'individuation' – more to do with 'rebirth' (transformation) and the awareness of a collectively and archetypally integrated Self than ego-consciousness or 'development' – while Freud was more interested in the fundamental motive force of the pleasure principle and the individual's *ad hoc* strategies and negotiations for diminishing 'unpleasure'.[14] It is these particular aspects of Jung's work which have been taken up in the recent proliferation of material which is broadly 'Jungian'. One recent commentator notes 'the widespread presence of works on Jungian psychology in occult bookshops, amid the amulets, crystals and New Age music',[15] while the influx and extensive presence in all bookshops of material broadly described as 'self-help' or 'self-development' also evinces a strong Jungian influence or inflection. This popularity, with all its extension – and, in many cases, dilution – of Jungian thought, helps to explain why Jung is so rarely included on academic syllabuses. There is, of course, a 'school' of Jungian literary criticism (and, as we see in the essays included here, Jung and his followers themselves make frequent references to such literary texts as Rider Haggard's *She* and to other narratives from the Bible to the Brothers Grimm), but its ahistorical approach and tendency to a programmatic attention to archetypes perhaps keep it marginal.

To a reader of the 1990s, Jung's own writing can seem chillingly biased, and yet in Marion Woodman's work, for example, we see that his tenets of the 'anima' and 'animus' are retained as useful and meaningful. Rather, as Woodman insists, it is the lens of patriarchy, through which both men and women have been looking, which needs to be changed. And this will, in turn, change the nature and character of those internal psychical figures which are so bound up in 'projections', often with drastic consequences for relationships – particularly, in most Jungian thought – for those between men and women.

NOTES

1. The extracts which follow this one make clear some of the complexities of the concept of 'projection' in Jungian terms. See also the entry under 'Projection' in Andrew Samuels, Bani Shorter and Fred Plaut (eds), *A Critical Dictionary of Jungian Analysis*, (London and New York: Routledge & Kegan Paul, 1986), pp. 113–14.
2. M. Esther Harding, *The Way of All Women* (London: Rider, 1983 [1933]), pp. 63–4.
3. A. Samuels, B. Shorter and F. Plaut (eds), op. cit., p. 25.
4. M. Woodman, *The Ravaged Bridegroom: Masculinity in Women* (Toronto: Inner City Books, 1990) p. 127.
5. M. Woodman, *Leaving My Father's House: A journey to conscious femininity* (London: Rider, 1993), p. 1.
6. Ibid.
7. Ibid., p. 2.
8. A. Carotenuto, *A Secret Symmetry: Sabina Spielrein Between Freud and Jung* (New York: Pantheon, 1982), J. Kerr *A Most Dangerous Method: The Story of Jung, Freud & Sabrina Spielrein* (London: Sinclair-Stevenson, 1994), and L. Appignanesi and J. Forrester, *Freud's Women* (London: Virago, 1993), all discuss the contribution made by Jung's female colleagues to the development of his ideas – contributions largely unacknowledged, underemphasized, or misattributed.
9. See Kerr, ibid., for example, p. 372: 'It is known that Toni Wolff, the "discovery" who had attended the Weimar congress, did some research work in Jung's library for "Transformations" . . .'
10. At time of writing, Sabina Spielrein's work has not yet been translated.
11. Marie-Louise von Franz worked with Jung from 1934 until the latter's death in 1961, and was a founder of the C. G. Jung Institute in Zurich.
12. In his Prefatory Remarks to Dora's case history, Freud likens the analyst to an 'archae-ologist'. See S. Freud, PFL 8, p. 41.
13. Appignanesi and Forrester (op. cit.) use the term 'prospective' in describing Jung's break with Freud, outlining their respective relationships with Sabina Spielrein and their relation to her own theoretical position: 'In presenting her work . . . Freud ignored the "transformative" principle, perhaps seeing it as too akin to the prospective, future oriented tendencies of Jung's interpretation of dreams and myth dating from the period of their break, in 1912–13, and after. Perhaps Freud was right to sense that Spielrein's emphasis on transformation was linked to Jung's heresies. However, although the prospective and the occult had been themes in Jung's earliest work, in 1902, it is highly probable that when he returned to them, in 1908 and 1909, he was doing so in part under Spielrein's influence,' p. 220.
14. In Freud's theory: 'The whole of psychical activity is aimed at avoiding unpleasure and procuring pleasure'; see J. Laplanche and J. B. Pontalis, *The Language of Psychoanalysis* (London: Karnac, 1988), p. 322.
15. S. Shamdasani, 'Jung, gifted and blackened', *Times Higher Education Supplement*, 6 March 1998, p. 23.

11

Anima and Animus

Carl G. Jung

Among all possible spirits the spirits of the parents are in practice the most important; hence the universal incidence of the ancestor cult. In its original form it served to conciliate the *revenants*, but on a higher level of culture it became an essentially moral and educational institution, as in China. For the child, the parents are his closest and most influential relations. But as he grows older this influence is split off; consequently the parental imagos become increasingly shut away from consciousness, and on account of the restrictive influence they sometimes continue to exert, they easily acquire a negative aspect. In this way the parental imagos remain as alien elements somewhere 'outside' the psyche. In place of the parents, woman now takes up her position as the most immediate environmental influence in the life of the adult man. She becomes his companion, she belongs to him in so far as she shares his life and is more or less of the same age. She is not of a superior order, either by virtue of age, authority, or physical strength. She is, however, a very influential factor and, like the parents, she produces an imago of a relatively autonomous nature – not an imago to be split off like that of the parents, but one that has to be kept associated with consciousness. Woman, with her very dissimilar psychology, is and always has been a source of information about things for which a man has no eyes. She can be his inspiration; her intuitive capacity, often superior to man's, can give him timely warning, and her feeling, always directed towards the personal, can show him ways which his own less personally accented feeling would never have discovered. What Tacitus says about the Germanic women is exactly to the point in this respect.[1]

Here, without a doubt, is one of the main sources for the feminine quality of the soul. But it does not seem to be the only source. No man is so entirely masculine that he has nothing feminine in him. The fact is, rather, that very masculine men have – carefully guarded and hidden – a very soft emotional life, often incorrectly described as 'feminine'. A man counts it a virtue to repress his feminine traits as much as possible, just as a woman, at least until recently, considered it unbecoming to be 'mannish'. The repression of feminine traits and inclinations naturally causes these contrasexual demands to accumulate in the unconscious.

No less naturally, the imago of woman (the soul-image) becomes a receptacle for these demands, which is why a man, in his love-choice, is strongly tempted to win the woman who best corresponds to his own unconscious femininity – a woman, in short, who can unhesitatingly receive the projection of his soul. Although such a choice is often regarded and felt as altogether ideal, it may turn out that the man has manifestly married his own worst weakness. This would explain some highly remarkable conjunctions.

It seems to me, therefore, that apart from the influence of woman there is also the man's own femininity to explain the feminine nature of the soul-complex. There is no question here of any linguistic 'accident', of the kind that makes the sun feminine in German and masculine in other languages. We have, in this matter, the testimony of art from all ages, and besides that the famous question: *habet mulier animam?* Most men, probably, who have any psychological insight at all will know what Rider Haggard means by 'She-who-must-be-obeyed', and will also recognize the chord that is struck when they read Benoît's description of Antinéa.[2] Moreover they know at once the kind of woman who most readily embodies this mysterious factor, of which they have so vivid a premonition.

The wide recognition accorded to such books shows that there must be some supra-individual quality in this image of the anima,[3] something that does not owe a fleeting existence simply to its individual uniqueness, but is far more typical, with roots that go deeper than the obvious surface attachments I have pointed out. Both Rider Haggard and Benoît give unmistakable utterance to this supposition in the *historical* aspect of their anima figures.

As we know, there is no human experience, nor would experience be possible at all, without the intervention of a subjective aptitude. What is this subjective aptitude? Ultimately it consists in an innate psychic structure which allows man to have experiences of this kind. Thus the whole nature of man presupposes woman, both physically and spiritually. His system is tuned in to woman from the start, just as it is prepared for a quite definite world where there is water, light, air, salt, carbohydrates, etc. The form of the world into which he is born is already inborn in him as a virtual image. Likewise parents, wife, children, birth, and death are inborn in him as virtual images, as psychic aptitudes. These *a priori* categories have by nature a collective character; they are images of parents, wife, and children in general, and are not individual predestinations. We must therefore think of these images as lacking in solid content, hence as unconscious. They only acquire solidity, influence, and eventual consciousness in the encounter with empirical facts, which touch the unconscious aptitude and quicken it to life. They are in a sense the deposits of all our ancestral experiences, but they are not the experiences themselves. So at least it seems to us, in the present limited state of our knowledge. (I must confess that I have never yet found infallible evidence for the inheritance of memory images, but I do not regard it as positively precluded that in addition to these collective deposits which contain nothing specifically individual, there may also be inherited memories that are individually determined.)

An inherited collective image of woman exists in a man's unconscious, with the help of which he apprehends the nature of woman. This inherited image is the third important source for the femininity of the soul.

As the reader will have grasped, we are not concerned here with a philosophical, much less a religious, concept of the soul, but with the psychological recognition of the existence of a semiconscious psychic complex, having partial autonomy of function. Clearly, this recognition has as much or as little to do with philosophical or religious conceptions of the soul, as psychology has as much or as little to do with philosophy or religion. I have no wish to embark here on a 'battle of the faculties', nor do I seek to demonstrate either to the philosopher or to the theologian what exactly he means by 'soul'. I must, however, restrain both of them from prescribing what the psychologist *ought* to mean by 'soul'. The quality of personal immortality so fondly attributed to the soul by religion is, for science, no more than a psychological *indicium* which is already included in the idea of autonomy. The quality of personal immortality is by no means a constant attribute of the soul as the primitive sees it, nor even immortality as such. But setting this view aside as altogether inaccessible to science, the immediate meaning of 'immortality' is simply a psychic activity that transcends the limits of consciousness. 'Beyond the grave' or 'on the other side of death' means, psychologically, 'beyond consciousness'. There is positively nothing else it could mean, since statements about immortality can only be made by the living, who, as such, are not exactly in a position to pontificate about conditions 'beyond the grave'.

The autonomy of the soul-complex naturally lends support to the notion of an invisible, personal entity that apparently lives in a world very different from ours. Consequently, once the activity of the soul is felt to be that of an autonomous entity having no ties with our mortal substance, it is but a step to imagining that this entity must lead an entirely independent existence, perhaps in a world of invisible things. Yet it is not immediately clear why the *invisibility* of this independent entity should simultaneously imply its *immortality*. The quality of immortality might easily derive from another fact to which I have already alluded, namely the characteristically historical aspect of the soul. Rider Haggard has given one of the best descriptions of this in *She*. When the Buddhists say that progressive perfection through meditation awakens memories of former incarnations, they are no doubt referring to the same psychological reality, the only difference being that they ascribe the historical factor not to the soul but to the Self (*atman*). It is altogether in keeping with the thoroughly extraverted attitude of the Western mind so far, that immortality should be ascribed, both by feeling and by tradition, to a soul which we distinguish more or less from our ego, and which also differs from the ego on account of its feminine qualities. It would be entirely logical if, by deepening that neglected, introverted side of our spiritual culture, there were to take place in us a transformation more akin to the Eastern frame of mind, where the quality of immortality would transfer itself from the ambiguous figure of the soul (*anima*) to the self. For it is essentially the overvaluation of the material object without that constellates a spiritual and immortal figure within (obviously for the purpose of compensation and self-regulation). Fundamentally, the historical factor does not attach only to the archetype of the feminine, but to all archetypes whatsoever, i.e., to every inherited unit, mental as well as physical. Our life is indeed the same as it ever was. At all events, in our sense of the word it is not transitory; for the same physiological and psychological processes that have been man's for hundreds of thousands of years still endure, instilling into our inmost hearts this profound intuition of the 'eternal' continuity of the living. But the self, as an inclusive term that embraces our whole living organism, not only contains the deposit and totality of all past life, but is also a point of departure, the fertile soil from which all future life will spring. This premonition of futurity is as clearly impressed upon our innermost feelings as is the historical aspect. The idea of immortality follows legitimately from these psychological premises.

In the Eastern view the concept of the anima, as we have stated it here, is lacking, and so, logically, is the concept of a persona. This is certainly no accident, for, as I have already indicated, a compensatory relationship exists between persona and anima.

The persona is a complicated system of relations between the individual consciousness and society, fittingly enough a kind of mask, designed on the one hand to make a definite impression upon others, and, on the other, to conceal the true nature of the individual. That the latter function is superfluous could be maintained only by one who is so identified with his persona that he no longer knows himself; and that the former is unnecessary could only occur to one who is quite unconscious of the true nature of his fellows. Society expects, and indeed must expect, every individual to play the part assigned to him as perfectly as possible, so that a man who is a parson must not only carry out his official functions objectively, but must at all times and in all circumstances play the role of parson in a flawless manner. Society demands this as a kind of surety; each must stand at his post, here a cobbler, there a poet. No man is expected to be both. Nor is it advisable to be both, for that would be 'odd'. Such a man would be 'different' from other people, not quite reliable. In the academic world he would be a dilettante, in politics an 'unpredictable' quantity, in religion a free-thinker – in short, he would always be suspected of unreliability and incompetence, because society is persuaded that only the cobbler who is not a poet can supply workmanlike shoes. To present an unequivocal face to the world is a matter of practical importance: the average man – the only kind society knows anything about – must keep his nose to one thing in order to achieve anything worthwhile, two would be too much. Our society is undoubtedly set on such an ideal. It is therefore not surprising that everyone who wants to get on must take these expectations into account. Obviously no one could completely submerge his individuality in these expectations; hence the construction of an artificial personality becomes an unavoidable necessity. The demands of propriety and good manners are an added inducement to assume a becoming mask. What goes on behind the mask is then called 'private life'. This painfully familiar division of consciousness into two figures, often preposterously different, is an incisive psychological operation that is bound to have a repercussions on the unconscious.

The construction of a collectively suitable persona means a formidable concession to the external world, a genuine self-sacrifice which drives the ego straight into identification with the persona, so that people really do exist who believe they are what they pretend to be. The 'soullessness' of such an attitude is, however, only apparent, for under no circumstances will the unconscious tolerate this shifting of the centre of gravity. When we examine such cases critically, we find that the excellence of the mask is compensated by the 'private life' going on behind it. The pious Drummond once lamented that 'bad temper is the vice of the virtuous'. Whoever builds up too good a persona for himself naturally has to pay for it with irritability. Bismarck had hysterical weeping fits, Wagner indulged in correspondence about the belts of silk dressing-gowns, Nietzsche wrote letters to his 'dear lama', Goethe held conversations with Eckermann, etc. But there are subtler things than the banal lapses of heroes. I once made the acquaintance of a very venerable personage – in fact, one might easily call him a saint. I stalked round him for three whole days, but never a mortal failing did I find in him. My feeling of inferiority grew ominous, and I was beginning to think seriously of how I might better myself. Then, on the fourth day, his wife came to consult me . . . Well, nothing of the sort has ever happened to me since. But this I did learn: that any man who becomes one with his persona can cheerfully let all disturbances manifest themselves through his wife without her noticing it, though she pays for her self-sacrifice with a bad neurosis.

These identifications with a social role are a very fruitful source of neuroses. A man cannot get rid of himself in favour of an artificial personality without punishment. Even the attempt to do so brings on, in all ordinary cases, unconscious reactions in the form of bad moods, affects, phobias, obsessive ideas, backslidings, vice, etc. The social 'strong man' is in his private life often a mere child where his own states of feeling are concerned; his discipline in public (which he demands quite particularly of others) goes miserably to pieces in private. His 'happiness in his work' assumes a woeful countenance at home; his 'spotless' public morality looks strange indeed behind the mask – we will not mention deeds, but only fantasies, and the wives of such men would have a pretty tale to tell. As to his selfless altruism, his children have decided views about that.

To the degree that the world invites the individual to identify with the mask, he is delivered over to influences from within 'High rests on low,' says Lao-tzu. An opposite forces its way up from inside; it is exactly as though the unconscious suppressed the ego with the very same power which drew the ego into the persona. The absence of resistance outwardly against the lure of the persona means a similar weakness inwardly against the influence of the unconscious. Outwardly an effective and powerful role is played, while inwardly an effeminate weakness develops in the face of every influence coming from the unconscious. Moods, vagaries, timidity, even a limp sexuality (culminating in impotence) gradually gain the upper hand.

The persona, the ideal picture of a man as he should be, is inwardly compensated by feminine weakness, and as the individual outwardly plays the strong man, so he becomes inwardly a woman, i.e., the anima, for it is the anima that reacts to the persona. But because the inner world is dark and invisible to the extraverted consciousness, and because a man is all the less capable of conceiving his weakness the more he is identified with the persona, the persona's counterpart, the anima, remains completely in the dark and is at once projected, so that our hero comes under the heel of his wife's slipper. If this results in a considerable increase of her power, she will acquit herself none too well. She becomes inferior, thus providing her husband with the welcome proof that it is not he, the hero, who is inferior in private, but his wife. In return the wife can cherish the illusion, so attractive to many, that at least she has married a hero, unperturbed by her own uselessness. This little game of illusion is often taken to be the whole meaning of life.

Just as, for the purpose of individuation, or self-realization, it is essential for a man to distinguish between what he is and how he appears to himself and to others, so it is also necessary for the same purpose that he should become conscious of his invisible system of relations to the unconscious, and especially of the anima, so as to be able to distinguish himself from her. One cannot of course distinguish oneself from something unconscious. In the matter of the persona it is easy enough to make it clear to a man that he and his office are two different things. But it is very difficult for a man to distinguish himself from his anima, the more so because she is invisible. Indeed, he has first to contend with the prejudice that everything coming from inside him springs from the truest depths of his being. The 'strong man' will perhaps concede that in private life he is singularly undisciplined, but that, he says, is just his 'weakness' with which, as it were, he proclaims his solidarity. Now there is in this tendency a cultural legacy that is not to be despised; for when a man recognizes that his ideal persona is responsible for his anything but ideal anima, his ideals are shattered, the world becomes ambiguous, he becomes ambiguous even to himself. He is seized by doubts about goodness, and what is worse, he doubts his own good intentions. When one considers how much our private idea of good intentions is bound up with vast historical assumptions, it will readily be understood that it is pleasanter and more in keeping with our present view of the world to deplore a personal weakness than to shatter ideals.

But since the unconscious factors act as determinants no less than the factors that regulate the life of society, and are no less collective, I might just as well learn to distinguish between what *I* want and what the unconscious thrusts upon me, as to see what my office demands of me and what I myself desire. At first the only thing that is at all clear is the incompatibility of the demands coming from without and from within, with the ego standing between them, as between hammer and anvil. But over against this ego, tossed like a shuttlecock between the outer and inner demands, there stands some scarcely definable arbiter, which I would on no account label with the deceptive name 'conscience', although, taken in its best sense, the word fits that arbiter very aptly indeed. What we have made of this 'conscience' Spitteler has described with unsurpassable humour.[4] Hence we should strenuously avoid this particular signification. We should do far better to realize that the tragic counterplay between inside and outside (depicted in Job and *Faust* as the wager with God) represents, at bottom, the energetics of the life process, the polar tension that is necessary for self-regulation. However different, to all intents and purposes, these opposing forces may be, their fundamental meaning and desire is the life of the individual: they always fluctuate round this centre of balance. Just because they are inseparably related through opposition, they also unite in a mediatory meaning, which, willingly or unwillingly, is born out of the individual and is therefore divined by him. He has a strong feeling of what should be and what could be. To depart from this divination means error, aberration, illness.

It is probably no accident that our modern notions of 'personal' and 'personality' derive from the word *persona*. I can assert that my ego is personal or a personality, and in exactly the same sense I can say that my persona is a personality with which I identify myself more or less. The fact that I then possess two personalities is not so remarkable, since every autonomous or even relatively autonomous complex has the peculiarity of appearing as a personality, i.e., of being personified. This can be observed most readily in the so-called spiritualistic manifestations of automatic writing and the like. The sentences produced are always personal statements and are propounded in the first person singular, as though behind every utterance there stood an actual personality. A naïve intelligence at once thinks of spirits. The same sort of thing is also observable in the hallucinations of the insane, although these, more clearly than the first, can often be recognized as mere thoughts or fragments of thoughts whose connection with the conscious personality is immediately apparent to everyone.

The tendency of the relatively autonomous complex to direct personification also explains why the persona exercises such a 'personal' effect that the ego is all too easily deceived as to which is the 'true' personality.

Now, everything that is true of the persona and of all autonomous complexes in general also holds true of the anima. She likewise is a personality, and this is why she is so easily projected upon a woman. So long as the anima is unconscious she is always projected, for everything unconscious is projected. The first bearer of the soul-image is always the mother; later it is borne by those women who arouse the man's feelings, whether in a positive or a negative sense. Because the mother is the first bearer of the soul-image, separation from her is a delicate and important matter of the greatest educational significance. Accordingly among primitives we find a large number of rites designed to organize this separation.

The mere fact of becoming adult, and of outward separation, is not enough; impressive initiations into the 'men's house' and ceremonies of rebirth are still needed in order to make the separation from the mother (and hence from childhood) entirely effective.

Just as the father acts as a protection against the dangers of the external world and thus serves his son as a model persona, so the mother protects him against the dangers that threaten from the darkness of his psyche. In the puberty rites, therefore, the initiate receives instruction about these things of 'the other side', so that he is put in a position to dispense with his mother's protection.

The modern civilized man has to forgo this primitive but nonetheless admirable system of education. The consequence is that the anima, in the form of the mother-imago, is transferred to the wife; and the man, as soon as he marries, becomes childish, sentimental, dependent, and subservient, or else truculent, tyrannical, hypersensitive, always thinking about the prestige of his superior masculinity. The last is of course merely the reverse of the first. The safeguard against the unconscious, which is what his mother meant to him, is not replaced by anything in the modern man's education; unconsciously, therefore, his ideal of marriage is so arranged that his wife has to take over the magical role of the mother. Under the cloak of the ideally exclusive marriage he is really seeking his mother's protection, and thus he plays into the hands of his wife's possessive instincts. His fear of the dark incalculable power of the unconscious gives his wife an illegitimate authority over him, and forges such a dangerously close union that the marriage is permanently on the brink of explosion from internal tension – or else, out of protest, he flies to the other extreme, with the same results.

I am of the opinion that it is absolutely essential for a certain type of modern man to recognize his distinction not only from the persona, but from the anima as well. For the most part our consciousness, in true Western style, looks outwards, and the inner world remains in darkness. But this difficulty can be overcome easily enough, if only we will make the effort to apply the same concentration and criticism to the psychic material which manifests itself, not outside, but in our private lives. So accustomed are we to keep a shamefaced silence about this other side – we even tremble before our wives, lest they betray us! – and, if found out, to make rueful confessions of 'weakness', that there would seem to be only one method of education, namely, to crush or repress the weaknesses as much as possible or at least hide them from the public. But that gets us nowhere.

Perhaps I can best explain what has to be done if I use the persona as an example. Here everything is plain and straightforward, whereas with the anima all is dark, to Western eyes anyway. When the anima continually thwarts the good intentions of the conscious mind, by contriving a private life that stands in sorry contrast to the dazzling persona, it is exactly the same as when a naïve individual, who has not the ghost of a persona, encounters the most painful difficulties in his passage through the world. There are indeed people who lack a developed persona – 'Canadians who know not Europe's sham politeness' –

blundering from one social solecism to the next, perfectly harmless and innocent, soulful bores or appealing children, or, if they are women, spectral
Cassandras dreaded for their tactlessness, eternally misunderstood, never knowing what they are about, always taking forgiveness for granted, blind to the
world, hopeless dreamers. From them we can see how a neglected persona
works, and what one must do to remedy the evil. Such people can avoid disappointments and an infinity of sufferings, scenes, and social catastrophes only by
learning to see how men behave in the world. They must learn to understand
what society expects of them; they must realize that there are factors and persons
in the world far above them; they must know that what they do has a meaning
for others, and so forth. Naturally all this is child's play for one who has a properly developed persona. But if we reverse the picture and confront the man who
possesses a brilliant persona with the anima, and, for the sake of comparison, set
him beside the man with no persona, then we shall see that the latter is just as
well informed about the anima and her affairs as the former is about the world.
The use which either makes of his knowledge can just as easily be abused, in fact
it is more than likely that it will be.

The man with the persona is blind to the existence of inner realities, just as the
other is blind to the reality of the world, which for him has merely the value of
an amusing or fantastic playground. But the fact of inner realities and their
unqualified recognition is obviously the *sine qua non* for a serious consideration
of the anima problem. If the external world is, for me, simply a phantasm, how
should I take the trouble to establish a complicated system of relationship and
adaptation to it? Equally, the 'nothing but fantasy' attitude will never persuade me
to regard my anima manifestations as anything more than fatuous weakness. If,
however, I take the line that the world is outside *and* inside, that reality falls to
the share of both, I must logically accept the upsets and annoyances that come to
me from inside as symptoms of faulty adaptation to the conditions of that inner
world. No more than the blows rained on the innocent abroad can be healed by
moral repression will it help him resignedly to catalogue his 'weaknesses'. Here
are reasons, intentions, consequences, which can be tackled by will and understanding. Take, for example, the 'spotless' man of honour and public benefactor,
whose trantrums and explosive moodiness terrify his wife and children. What is
the anima doing here?

We can see it at once if we just allow things to take their natural course. Wife
and children will become estranged; a vacuum will form about him. At first, he
will bewail the hardheartedness of his family, and will behave if possible even
more vilely than before. That will make the estrangement absolute. If the good
spirits have not utterly forsaken him, he will after a time notice his isolation, and
in his loneliness he will begin to understand how he caused the estrangement.
Perhaps, aghast at himself, he will ask, 'What sort of devil has got into me?' –
without of course seeing the meaning of this metaphor. Then follow remorse,
reconciliation, oblivion, repression, and, in next to no time, a new explosion.

Clearly, the anima is trying to enforce a separation. This tendency is in nobody's interest. The anima comes between them like a jealous mistress who tries to alienate the man from his family. An official post or any other advantageous social position can do the same thing, but there we can understand the force of the attraction. Whence does the anima obtain the power to wield such enchantment? On the analogy with the persona there must be values or some other important and influential factors lying in the background like seductive promises. In such matters we must guard against rationalizations. Our first thought is that the man of honour is on the lookout for another woman. That might be – it might even be arranged by the anima as the most effective means to the desired end. Such an arrangement should not be misconstrued as an end in itself, for the blameless gentleman who is correctly married according to the law can be just as correctly divorced according to the law, which does not alter his fundamental attitude one iota. The old picture has merely received a new frame.

As a matter of fact, this arrangement is a very common method of implementing a separation – and of hampering a final solution. Therefore it is more reasonable not to assume that such an obvious possibility is the end-purpose of the separation. We would be better advised to investigate what is behind the tendencies of the anima. The first step is what I would call the objectivation of the anima, that is, the strict refusal to regard the trend towards separation as a weakness of one's own. Only when this has been done can one face the anima with the question, 'Why do you want this separation?' To put the question in this personal way has the great advantage of recognizing the anima as a personality, and of making a relationship possible. The more personally she is taken the better.

To anyone accustomed to proceed purely intellectually and rationally, this may seem altogether too ridiculous. It would indeed be the height of absurdity if a man tried to have a conversation with his persona, which he recognized merely as a psychological means of relationship. But it is absurd only for the man who *has* a persona. If he has none, he is in this point no different from the primitive who, as we know, has only one foot in what we commonly call reality. With the other foot he stands in a world of spirits, which is quite real to him. Our model case behaves, in the world, like a modern European; but in the world of spirits he is the child of a troglodyte. He must therefore submit to living in a kind of prehistoric kindergarten until he has got the right idea of the powers and factors which rule that other world. Hence he is quite right to treat the anima as an autonomous personality and to address personal questions to her.

I mean this as an actual technique. We know that practically every one has not only the peculiarity, but also the faculty, of holding a conversation with himself. Whenever we are in a predicament we ask ourselves (or whom else?), 'What shall I do?' either aloud or beneath our breath, and we (or who else?) supply the answer. Since it is our intention to learn what we can about the foundations of our being, this little matter of living in a metaphor should not bother us. We have to accept it as a symbol of our primitive backwardness (or of such naturalness as is still, mercifully, left to us) that we can, like the Negro, discourse personally with our 'snake'. The psyche not being a unity but a contradictory multiplicity of complexes, the dissociation required for our dialectics with the anima is not so terribly difficult. The art of it consists only in allowing our invisible partner to make herself heard, in putting the mechanism of expression momentarily at her disposal, without being overcome by the distaste one naturally feels at playing such an apparently ludicrous game with oneself, or by doubts as to the genuineness of the voice of one's interlocutor. This latter point is technically very important: we are so in the habit of identifying ourselves with the thoughts that come to us that we invariably assume we have made them. Curiously enough, it is precisely the most impossible thoughts for which we feel the greatest subjective responsibility. If we were more conscious of the inflexible universal laws that govern even the wildest and most wanton fantasy, we might perhaps be in a better position to see these thoughts above all others as objective occurrences, just as we see dreams, which nobody supposes to be deliberate or arbitrary inventions. It certainly requires the greatest objectivity and absence of prejudice to give the 'other side' the opportunity for perceptible psychic activity. As a result of the repressive attitude of the conscious mind, the other side is driven into indirect and purely symptomatic manifestations, mostly of an emotional kind, and only in moments of overwhelming affectivity can fragments of the unconscious come to the surface in the form of thoughts or images. The inevitable accompanying symptom is that the ego momentarily identifies with these utterances, only to revoke them in the same breath. And, indeed, the things one says when in the grip of an affect sometimes seem very strange and daring. But they are easily forgotten, or wholly denied. This mechanism of depreciation and denial naturally has to be reckoned with if one wants to adopt an objective attitude. The habit of rushing in to correct and criticize is already strong enough in our tradition, and it is as a rule further reinforced by fear – a fear that can be confessed neither to oneself nor to others, a fear of insidious truths, of dangerous knowledge, of disagreeable verifications, in a word, fear of all those things that cause so many of us to flee from being alone with ourselves as from the plague. We say that it is egoistic or 'morbid' to be preoccupied with oneself; one's own company is the worst, 'it makes you melancholy' – such are the glowing testimonials accorded to our human make-up. They are evidently deeply ingrained in our Western minds. Whoever thinks in this way has obviously never asked himself what possible pleasure other people could find in the company of such a miserable coward. Starting from the fact that in a state of affect one often surrenders involuntarily to the truths of the other side, would it not be far better to make use of an affect so as to give the other side an opportunity to speak? It could therefore be said just as truly that one should cultivate the art of conversing with oneself in the setting provided by an affect, as though the affect itself were speaking without regard to our rational criticism. So long as the affect is speaking, criticism must be withheld. But once it has presented its case, we should begin criticizing as conscientiously as though a real person closely connected with us were our interlocutor. Nor should the matter rest there, but statement and answer must follow one another until a satisfactory end to the discussion is reached. Whether the result is satisfactory or not, only subjective feeling can decide. Any humbug is of course quite useless. Scrupulous honesty with oneself and no rash anticipation of what the other side might conceivably say are the indispensable conditions of this technique for educating the anima.

There is, however, something to be said for this characteristically Western fear of the other side. It is not entirely without justification, quite apart from the fact that it is real. We can understand at once the fear that the child and the primitive have of the great unknown. We have the same childish fear of our inner side, where we likewise touch upon a great unknown world. All we have is the affect, the fear, without knowing that this is a world-fear – for the world of affects is invisible. We have either purely theoretical prejudices against it, or superstitious ideas. One cannot even talk about the unconscious before many educated people without being accused of mysticism. The fear is legitimate in so far as our rational *Weltanschauung* with its scientific and moral certitudes – so hotly believed in because so deeply questionable – is shattered by the facts of the other side. If only one could avoid them, then the emphatic advice of the Philistine to 'let sleeping dogs lie' would be the only truth worth advocating. And here I would expressly point out that I am not recommending the above technique as either necessary or even useful to any person not driven to it by necessity. The stages, as I said, are many, and there are greybeards who die as innocent as babes in arms, and in this year of grace troglodytes are still being born. There are truths which belong to the future, truths which belong to the past, and truths which belong to no time.

I can imagine someone using this technique out of a kind of holy inquisitiveness, some youth, perhaps, who would like to set wings to his feet, not because of lameness, but because he yearns for the sun. But a grown man, with too many illusions dissipated, will submit to this inner humiliation and surrender only if forced, for why should he let the terrors of childhood again have their way with him? It is no light matter to stand between a day-world of exploded ideals and discredited values, and a night-world of apparently senseless fantasy. The weirdness of this standpoint is in fact so great that there is probably nobody who does not reach out for security, even though it be a reaching back to the mother who shielded his childhood from the terrors of night. Whoever is afraid must needs be dependent; a weak thing needs support. That is why the primitive mind, from deep psychological necessity, begot religious instruction and embodied it in magician and priest. *Extra ecclesiam nulla salus* is still a valid truth today – for those who can go back to it. For the few who cannot, there is only dependence upon a human being, a humbler and a prouder dependence, a weaker and a stronger support, so it seems to me, than any other. What can one say of the Protestant? He has neither church nor priest, but only God – and even God becomes doubtful.

The reader may ask in some consternation, 'But what on earth does the anima do, that such double insurances are needed before one can come to terms with her?' I would recommend my reader to study the comparative history of religion so intently as to fill these dead chronicles with the emotional life of those who lived these religions. Then he will get some idea of what lives on the other side. The old religions with their sublime and ridiculous, their friendly and fiendish symbols did not drop from the blue, but were born of this human soul that dwells within us at this moment. All those things, their primal forms, live on in us and may at any time burst in upon us with annihilating force, in the guise of mass-suggestions against which the individual is defenceless. Our fearsome gods have only changed their names: they now rhyme with *ism*. Or has anyone the nerve to claim that the World War or Bolshevism was an ingenious invention? Just as outwardly we live in a world where a whole continent may be submerged at any moment, or a pole be shifted, or a new pestilence break out, so inwardly we live in a world where at any moment something similar may occur, albeit in the form of an idea, but no less dangerous and untrustworthy for that. Failure to adapt to this inner world is a negligence entailing just as serious consequences as ignorance and ineptitude in the outer world. It is after all only a tiny fraction of humanity, living mainly on that thickly populated peninsula of Asia which juts out into the Atlantic Ocean, and calling themselves 'cultured', who, because they lack all contact with nature, have hit upon the idea that religion is a peculiar kind of mental disturbance of undiscoverable purport. Viewed from a safe distance, say from central Africa or Tibet, it would certainly look as if this fraction had projected its own unconscious mental derangements upon nations still possessed of healthy instincts.

Because the things of the inner world influence us all the more powerfully for being unconscious, it is essential for anyone who intends to make progress in self-culture (and does not all culture begin with the individual?) to objectivate the effects of the anima and then try to understand what contents underlie those effects. In this way he adapts to, and is protected against, the invisible. No adaptation can result without concessions to both worlds. From a consideration of the claims of the inner and outer worlds, or rather, from the conflict between them, the possible and the necessary follows. Unfortunately our Western mind, lacking all culture in this respect, has never yet devised a concept, nor even a name, for the *union of opposites through the middle path*, that most fundamental item of inward experience, which could respectably be set against the Chinese concept of Tao. It is at once the most individual act and the most universal, the most legitimate fulfilment of the meaning of the individual's life.

In the course of my exposition so far, I have kept exclusively to *masculine* psychology. The anima, being of feminine gender, is exclusively a figure that compensates the masculine consciousness. In woman the compensating figure is of a masculine character, and can therefore appropriately be termed the *animus*. If it was no easy task to describe what is meant by the anima, the difficulties become almost insuperable when we set out to describe the psychology of the animus.

The fact that a man naïvely ascribes his anima reaction to himself, without seeing that he really cannot identify himself with an autonomous complex, is repeated in feminine psychology, though if possible in even more marked form. This identification with an autonomous complex is the essential reason why it is so difficult to understand and describe the problem, quite apart from its inherent obscurity and strangeness. We always start with the naïve assumption that we are masters in our own house. Hence we must first accustom ourselves to the thought that, in our most intimate psychic life as well, we live in a kind of house which has doors and windows to the world, but that, although the objects or contents of this world act upon us, they do not belong to us. For many people this hypothesis is by no means easy to conceive, just as they do not find it at all easy to understand and to accept the fact that their neighbour's psychology is not necessarily identical with their own. My reader may think that the last remark is something of an exaggeration, since in general one is aware of individual differences. But it must be remembered that our individual conscious psychology develops out of an original state of unconsciousness and therefore of non-differentiation (termed by Lévy-Bruhl *participation mystique*). Consequently, consciousness of differentiation is a relatively late achievement of mankind, and presumably but a relatively small sector of the indefinitely large field of original identity. Differentiation is the essence, the *sine qua non* of consciousness. Everything unconscious is undifferentiated, and everything that happens unconsciously proceeds on the basis of non-differentiation – that is to say, there is no determining whether it belongs or does not belong to oneself. It cannot be established *a priori* whether it concerns me, or another, or both. Nor does feeling give us any clues in this respect.

An inferior consciousness cannot *eo ipso* be ascribed to women; it is merely different from masculine consciousness. But, just as a woman is often clearly conscious of things which a man is still groping for in the dark, so there are naturally fields of experience in a man which, for woman, are still wrapped in the shadows of non-differentiation, chiefly things in which she has little interest. Personal relations are as a rule more important and interesting to her than objective facts and their inter-connections. The wide fields of commerce, politics, technology, and science, the whole realm of the applied masculine mind, she relegates to the penumbra of consciousness; while, on the other hand, she develops a minute consciousness of personal relationships, the infinite nuances of which usually escape the man entirely.

We must therefore expect the unconscious of woman to show aspects essentially different from those found in man. If I were to attempt to put in a nutshell the difference between man and woman in this respect, i.e., what it is that characterizes the animus as opposed to the anima, I could only say this: as the anima produces *moods*, so the animus produces *opinions*; and as the moods of a man issue from a shadowy background, so the opinions of a woman rest on equally unconscious prior assumptions. Animus opinions very often have the character of solid convictions that are not lightly shaken, or of principles whose validity is seemingly unassailable. If we analyse these opinions, we immediately come upon unconscious assumptions whose existence must first be inferred; that is to say, the opinions are apparently conceived *as though* such assumptions existed. But in reality the opinions are not thought out at all; they exist ready made, and they are held so positively and with so much conviction that the woman never has the shadow of a doubt about them.

One would be inclined to suppose that the animus, like the anima, personifies itself in a single figure. But this, as experience shows, is true only up to a point, because another factor unexpectedly makes its appearance, which brings about an essentially different situation from that existing in a man. The animus does not appear as one person, but as a plurality of persons. In H. G. Wells's novel *Christina Alberta's Father*, the heroine, in all that she does or does not do, is constantly under the surveillance of a supreme moral authority, which tells her with remorseless precision and dry matter-of-factness what she is doing and for what motives. Wells calls this authority a 'Court of Conscience'. This collection of condemnatory judges, a sort of College of Preceptors, corresponds to a personification of the animus. The animus is rather like an assembly of fathers or dignitaries of some kind who lay down incontestable, 'rational', *ex cathedra* judgements. On closer examination these exacting judgements turn out to be largely sayings and opinions scraped together more or less unconsciously from childhood on, and compressed into a canon of average truth, justice, and reasonableness, a compendium of preconceptions which, whenever a conscious and competent judgement is lacking (as not infrequently happens), instantly obliges with an opinion. Sometimes these opinions take the form of so-called sound common sense, sometimes they appear as principles which are like a travesty of education: 'People have always done it like this,' or 'Everybody says it is like that.'

It goes without saying that the animus is just as often projected as the anima. The men who are particularly suited to these projections are either walking replicas of God himself, who know all about everything, or else they are misunderstood word-addicts with a vast and windy vocabulary at their command, who translate common or garden reality into the terminology of the sublime. It would be insufficient to characterize the animus merely as a conservative, collective conscience; he is also a neologist who, in flagrant contradiction to his correct opinions, has an extraordinary weakness for difficult and unfamiliar words which act as a pleasant substitute for the odious task of reflection.

Like the anima, the animus is a jealous lover. He is an adept at putting, in place of the real man, an opinion about him, the exceedingly disputable grounds for which are never submitted to criticism. Animus opinions are invariably collective, and they override individuals and individual judgements in exactly the same way as the anima thrusts her emotional anticipations and projections between man and wife. If the woman happens to be pretty, these animus opinions have for the man something rather touching and childlike about them, which makes him adopt a benevolent, fatherly, professorial manner. But if the woman does not stir his sentimental side, and competence is expected of her rather than appealing helplessness and stupidity, then her animus opinions irritate the man to death, chiefly because they are based on nothing but opinion for opinion's sake, and 'everybody has a right to his own opinions'. Men can be pretty venomous here, for it is an inescapable fact that the animus always plays up the anima and *vice versa*, of course – so that all further discussion becomes pointless.

In intellectual women the animus encourages a critical disputatiousness and would-be highbrowism, which, however, consists essentially in harping on some irrelevant weak point and nonsensically making it the main one. Or a perfectly lucid discussion gets tangled up in the most maddening way through the introduction of a quite different and if possible perverse point of view. Without knowing it, such women are solely intent upon exasperating the man and are, in consequence, the more completely at the mercy of the animus. 'Unfortunately I am always right,' one of these creatures once confessed to me.

However, all these traits, as familiar as they are unsavoury, are simply and solely due to the extraversion of the animus. The animus does not belong to the function of conscious relationship; his function is rather to facilitate relations with the unconscious. Instead of the woman merely associating opinions with external situations – situations which she ought to think about consciously – the animus, as an associative function, should be directed inwards, where it could associate the contents of the unconscious. The technique of coming to terms with the animus is the same in principle as in the case of the anima; only here the woman must learn to criticize and hold her opinions at a distance; not in order to repress them, but, by investigating their origins, to penetrate more deeply into the background, where she will then discover the primordial images, just as the man does in his dealings with the anima. The animus is the deposit, as it were, of all woman's ancestral experiences of man – and not only that, he is also a creative and procreative being, not in the sense of masculine creativity, but in the sense that he brings forth something we might call the λόγος σπερματικός, the spermatic word. Just as a man brings forth his work as a complete creation out of his inner feminine nature, so the inner masculine side of a woman brings forth creative seeds which have the power to fertilize the feminine side of the man. This would be the *femme inspiratrice* who, if falsely cultivated, can turn into the worst kind of dogmatist and high-handed pedagogue – a regular 'animus hound', as one of my women patients aptly expressed it.

A woman possessed by the animus is always in danger of losing her femininity, her adapted feminine persona, just as a man in like circumstances runs the risk of effeminacy. These psychic changes of sex are due entirely to the fact that a function which belongs inside has been turned outside. The reason for this perversion is clearly the failure to give adequate recognition to an inner world which stands autonomously opposed to the outer world, and makes just as serious demands on our capacity for adaptation.

With regard to the plurality of the animus as distinguished from what we might call the 'uni-personality' of the anima, this remarkable fact seems to me to be a correlate of the conscious attitude. The conscious attitude of woman is in general far more exclusively personal than that of man. Her world is made up of fathers and mothers, brothers and sisters, husbands and children. The rest of the world consists likewise of families, who nod to each other but are, in the main, interested essentially in themselves. The man's world is the nation, the state, business concerns, etc. His family is simply a means to an end, one of the foundations of the state, and his wife is not necessarily *the* woman for him (at any rate not as the woman means it when she says ('my man'). The general means more to him than the personal; his world consists of a multitude of co-ordinated factors, whereas her world, outside her husband, terminates in a sort of cosmic mist. A passionate exclusiveness therefore attaches to the man's anima, and an indefinite variety to the woman's animus. Whereas the man has, floating before him, in clear outlines, the alluring form of a Circe or a Calypso, the animus is better expressed as a bevy of Flying Dutchmen or unknown wanderers from over the sea, never quite clearly grasped, protean, given to persistent and violent motion. These personifications appear especially in dreams, though in concrete reality they can be famous tenors, boxing champions, or great men in far-away, unknown cities.

These two crepuscular figures from the dark hinterland of the psyche – truly the semi-grotesque 'guardians of the threshold', to use the pompous jargon of theosophy – can assume an almost inexhaustible number of shapes, enough to fill whole volumes. Their complicated transformations are as rich and strange as the world itself, as manifold as the limitless variety of their conscious correlate, the persona. They inhabit the twilight sphere, and we can just make out that the autonomous complex of anima and animus is essentially a psychological function that has usurped, or rather retained, a 'personality' only because this function is itself autonomous and undeveloped. But already we can see how it is possible to break up the personifications, since by making them conscious we convert them into bridges to the unconscious. It is because we are not using them purposefully as functions that they remain personified complexes. So long as they are in this state they must be accepted as relatively independent personalities. They cannot be integrated into consciousness while their contents remain unknown. The purpose of the dialectical process is to bring these contents into the light; and only when this task has been completed, and the conscious mind has become sufficiently familiar with the unconscious processes reflected in the anima, will the anima be felt simply as a function.

I do not expect every reader to grasp right away what is meant by animus and anima. But I hope he will at least have gained the impression that it is not a question of anything 'metaphysical', but far rather of empirical facts which could equally well be expressed in rational and abstract language. I have purposely avoided too abstract a terminology because, in matters of this kind, which hitherto have been so inaccessible to our experience, it is useless to present the reader with an intellectual formulation. It is far more to the point to give him some conception of what the actual possibilities of experience are. Nobody can really understand these things unless he has experienced them himself. I am therefore much more interested in pointing out the possible ways to such experience than in devising intellectual formulae which, for lack of experience, must necessarily remain an empty web of words. Unfortunately there are all too many who learn the words by heart and add the experiences in their heads, thereafter abandoning themselves, according to temperament, either to credulity or to criticism. We are concerned here with a new questioning, a new – and yet age-old – field of psychological experience. We shall be able to establish relatively valid theories about it only when the corresponding psychological facts are known to a sufficient number of people. The first things to be discovered are always facts, not theories. Theory-building is the outcome of discussion among many.

NOTES

1. *Germania* (Loeb edn), pars 18, 19.
2. Cf. Rider Haggard, *She*; Benoît, *L'Atlantide*.
3. Cf. *Psychological Types*, Def. 48, 'Soul'. [Also 'Concerning the Archetypes, with Special References to the Anima Concept' and 'The Psychological Aspects of the Kore'.]
4. *Psychological Types,* pars 282ff.

12

The Ghostly Lover

Esther Harding

To be 'in love' with a man is more than to 'love' him. The state of being in love carries with it a certain element of compulsion, and one who is in love, however enraptured he may be, is certainly not free. Love is proverbially blind. Indeed a girl may be in love with a man whom, in the absence of the glamour resulting from her state of mind, she might find not even likeable or attractive. The glamour and attraction are effects produced by forces in her unconscious which have been stirred to activity through her contact with the man. She projects on to him some important element from her unconscious and then is attracted or repelled by that which she sees in him, quite unaware that it has originated deep within her own psyche. It is her masculine soul, her *animus*, which she has projected. This mechanism is the exact equivalent of the projection of the man's feminine soul, or anima, which formed the subject of the last chapter. When a woman is in love we can either say that she *loves*, that is, she is active, or we can put it the other way round and say that she is attracted, that is, she is passive. In other words her animus, projected to the outside world, draws her irresistibly. Regardless of whether the man loves her or not, the fascination makes it appear as though he were the active party – as though *he* loved her. From her subjective point of view it seems to her that she is attracted from without, while in reality the thing which attracts her is from *within* – in her unconscious.

The possibility of this occurrence is occasionally shown in a play or novel where the girl is portrayed as having a lover who is not of this world but belongs, instead, to the spirit or ghost world. This was the case in the old Jewish legend of the dybbuk, which was made the subject of a drama by Solomon Rappaport and performed both in Yiddish and English.

In this legend the lover who lures his beloved away from reality into union with himself is shown quite objectively as the ghost of a dead youth with whom the heroine was in love. In certain scenes in the play the girl is represented as possessed by the ghost; he enters into her and takes possession of her and she is shown to be temporarily insane, which is to say she is suffering from a psychological illness. In these scenes the ghost has no objective reality but lives none the less in a subjective reality in the girl's psyche. She is entirely absorbed in him and by him. She is lost to the real world about her, for she is living only in her own subjective world with her ghostly lover.

In Eugene O'Neill's *Strange Interlude* the same subject is dwelt upon. But here the ghost does not appear at all; his presence must be inferred from the effects he has upon his lover-victim; that is, he appears *only* as a subjective factor in the girl's psychology. The heroine had been in love with a young soldier, an airman, and when he is killed in the war, she, as it were, loses her soul, and as a result, can give nothing of her real self to her life. She marries and is loved by many men, but her devotion always goes to her lost lover.

In both instances the lover is portrayed as the ghost or as the still-living influence of an actual man with whom the heroine had had a real relationship, however slender and frustrated it may have been. This influence which affects the woman as though it came from the action or desire of a man, when the truth is he is inactive or perhaps dead or may never have existed as an objective reality, must be a subjective effect within the woman's psyche – hence the term, *Ghostly Lover*. Manifestations of a ghostly lover may occur not only as the ghost of a real man but also in cases where an actual flesh-and-blood lover has never been in the picture. We may see instances of this in real life as well as in plays and novels. Barrie has shown the situation very clearly in his play *Mary Rose*, in which strange music lures Mary Rose away from her husband and child to the Island-that-wants-to-be-visited. This is a not unusual retreat which one frequently comes upon in the subjective life of real people. I have known many individuals who have built up an elaborate fantasy island or castle to which they retire when life is dull or difficult. Here they often spend endless time and energy constructing in fantasy a world more to their liking than the humdrum one to which they find it so hard to adapt. They 'rebuild the world nearer to the Heart's desire'. A fantasy world where everything is as one wishes is enormously alluring and exerts a fascination calling one away from reality; it becomes increasingly hard to resist, the more it is indulged in. This also is the work of the Ghostly Lover.

In talking about the Ghostly Lover we are not dealing with something which is remote or unusual or which occurs only in abnormal or pathological conditions. On the contrary the Ghostly Lover, in his psychological or subjective aspect, is a living reality to every woman. He holds his power and exerts his lure because he is a psychological entity, part of that conglomerate of autonomous, or relatively autonomous, factors which make up her psyche. As he is a part of her so she is bound to him; she *must* find him and consciously assimilate him if she is not to suffer the pain and distress of disintegration. For he is her soul mate, her 'other half', the invisible companion who accompanies her throughout life. Jung has named this soul-figure of the woman *animus*. The animus is the equivalent of the man's anima, but the two figures differ markedly in their characteristics and in their manifestations.[1]

The term Ghostly Lover has been devised to denote the destructive aspect of the animus, but it must be borne in mind that this is only one aspect, for he does not always function destructively. As *Ghostly Lover* he *always* acts as one who lures his victim away from reality by promises of bliss in another world. In the woman's psychology he is the counterpart of the siren in the man's. In the man's psychology, as in mythology, the siren by her music and charm lures the man to a watery grave. The Ghostly Lover, by the promise of untold bliss, entices the woman to seek his arms in the air.

The Ghostly Lover, however, is not merely an abstraction of the psychologist; he is manifested in actual, everyday life. In the first two of the plays mentioned above, the Ghostly Lover is personified and acts his part, a dominating one, as do the other persons in the play. He appears as a reality with power to act independently and autonomously. His psychological connection with the woman whose animus he represents is clearly shown by the curious and almost magical bond between them. In this way is expressed the autonomy of the animus, composed as he is of psychological contents of which the woman is unaware or over which her conscious ego exerts no control, for they belong to her unconscious. If she should become aware of these psychological contents, she would be in a position to dissolve the personification of the animus and thus to divest it of its power while she would be released from the 'magical' influence which the Ghostly Lover previously wielded.

The form of presentation in the plays is the result of the intuitive perception of the artist, who actually perceives the various psychological tendencies of his characters in personified form, as though they were separate people. In his artistic product he shares with us, the audience, the fruits of his insight, but – and here is a strange fact – he may not know himself that the characters he depicts are psychological tendencies and complexes. He himself may take the play as being a simple narration of objective fact. In much the same way, in real life the Ghostly Lover is occasionally personified in the memory of a dead or absent lover. More often it happens that in consciousness he is not personified; the woman victim herself does not know it is a ghostly lover who calls her away from reality to an unreal world, although in these cases her unconscious material, her dreams and daytime fantasies show clearly the real situation. In either case, however, when the Ghostly Lover calls and the woman follows she disappears, as it were, from reality, much as Mary Rose did. To those about here she becomes vague, falls into a brown study, is perhaps cross or irritable; or she may wear a baffling or propitiatory smile. To herself it seems that she has become absorbed in an inner experience of great beauty and value which she cannot by any means share with another. At a moment when she is actually trying to share her inner experience with a friend such a mood may overtake her; and not realizing how vague and meaningless her remarks have become it may seem to her that her friend is unsympathetic or wilfully misunderstands.

Sometimes such a mood is associated with thoughts of an actual, absent or dead friend. I recall a woman who wore black for twenty years for a man to whom she had refused to become engaged while he was living. She used this man as an absolute shield between herself and all reality. On the anniversary of his death her friends sent her flowers. Because of the grief she was still supposedly suffering for his loss, she managed to get herself excused from making even the ordinary efforts towards friendship that society demands. Her attitude to life asserted that she was sad, bereaved and must be carried by her circle of acquaintances for the rest of her life.

In another instance a woman suddenly widowed refused to weep for her husband. She felt that he had merely disappeared for a moment and was not really dead. She felt too that this attitude was in some way very noble and brave, and her friends sustained her in it by their comments on her wonderful courage. She did what was necessary towards readjusting to the outer world, but she held secretly to her fantasy that her husband was still alive and made no inner readjustment. Her attitude influenced her children who lost their old ability to make friends. Gradually their lives began to sink into emptiness, a kind of vacuum in which their mother existed. Meantime, she lived in the thought of her husband; her eyes held a curiously vacant yet expectant, look, for to her he was still alive and might appear at any moment. One day, when she was half-asleep, she thought he was standing by her. Throughout the rest of the day she went through the motions of living, but she wore a strange smile and was apparently far away. Again he came to her, and again and again. Sometimes she caught a glimpse of him, but more often she was merely overwhelmingly aware of his nearness. Gradually he seemed to grow bolder, until she came to have the feeling, when she looked up suddenly at almost any time, that he had only that instant stepped out of sight. At this point she became frightened, began to wonder if she were going insane or were really seeing a ghost. On psychological investigation the 'ghost' proved to be 'Ghostly Lover', that is, the appearance arose from the projection of the woman's animus, which in the absence of her dearly loved husband had become personified, as it were, in space. The condition cleared up completely under psychological treatment.

The idea of the Ghostly or Spiritual Lover is not a new one. Religious mystics of all ages and creeds – the Sufis, the Shaktas, the Christian mystics – have all sought for union with a Divine Lover. Rabia, the Islamic woman mystic, knew God as the Divine Lover; the Beloved of her Soul, as did St Bernard of Clairvaux, while many women saints of medieval Christianity tell us that their religious experience was of God as a Lover. Even today when a nun takes the veil, she is dedicated to this Divine Lover. She wears the bridal veil and is given a ring, as the Bride of Christ.

Religious experiences of this sort have been highly valued not only among Christians, but also with peoples of other religions, such as Mohammedans, Buddhists and Hindus. Individuals having them have been regarded as saints, possessing a wisdom different in character from the wisdom to be gained by knowledge of the world and having achieved a development of character which makes them in very truth superior human beings.

We can hardly dismiss as hysterical nonsense all the evidence concerned with these religious experiences, nor can we say that it is entirely in the nature of unreal fantasy, as in the case of Mary Rose. How much of it is of that nature, it is hard to say. Undoubtedly there are many who 'have professed religion' as a means of escaping from the burdens and difficulties of life in the world. The inner experience of such people would, in all probability, be of a lover who lured them away from the world of reality into a dream world. In other words, if anyone chooses a life of seclusion and introversion as an escape from the difficulties of life, he must expect to get lost in that inner world where as many difficulties and dangers await the adventurer as beset the explorer of the outer world. Indeed, the outer world is safe and protected compared with the inner world of the unconscious. But the pseudo-adventurers do not represent all who have explored the inner world.

[. . .]

When a woman finds herself in love with a man on to whom she has projected the Ghostly Lover, she can release herself from the dominance of her animus if she can work through the transference element in her love and make a real relationship with the man. This outcome is naturally more feasible if the involvement is mutual. There is obviously no possibility of relationship where the hero is adored by thousands of woman, as in the case of Rudolph Valentino, but in an ordinary social situation when a man and woman are attracted to each other, on account of a mutual anima–animus projection, it is possible to redeem the values which have been projected, by building up a relationship based on reality, in place of the illusion of the transferred values. The problem of the Ghostly Lover is most frequently resolved in this way. When a man and woman marry there is almost invariably some element of an animus–anima projection in their love. After the first glamour has worn off, each begins to realize that his partner does not see him as he is, but that in some strange way he is distorted in the other's eyes, for in certain ways each is glorified and in others depreciated. But the whole mechanism is subtle and may not come clearly into conscious focus. There is, moreover, a great tendency to let things slide and not to make an issue of slight misunderstandings. After a few protests and a more or less prolonged conflict, the young couple generally settle down to the business of life and allow these misconceptions to go on practically unchallenged. In such a case the projections of anima and animus persists and no real relatedness can develop.

One might think this was an ideal solution of the situation, were it not that the garment of the projected animus or anima, so docilely accepted in the early days of marriage, becomes increasingly hard to throw off, and the man and woman find themselves progressively forced to wear the mask which was not repudiated at first. Such a situation formed the theme of Eugene O'Neill's play *The Great God Brown*. The mask so slightly assumed by Dion in order that he might fufil his fiancée's ideal gradually hardens on him, crushing out his spontaneity and initiative. The second danger point now arises. The partner who has been submerged by the weight of the animus or the anima projection rebels and refuses to carry it any longer but forcibly reveals himself for what he is. If the whole situation does not disintegrate from the effects of the explosion, another opportunity is offered for building up something of reality-relatedness. But, once again, this outcome is, in the sense used above, historical; only the sequence of events brings the opportunity, and that generally not for many years. The obligation, in such a case, to work on the problem of relationships is the work of fate; it is not the free choice of the individuals concerned. If, however, instead of merely living along, carried by the energy and desire created by the projected animus or anima values, this man and woman had sought out the intimations from the unconscious, it would have been possible to discover where the animus or anima projections obscured the situation. By this means they could have established at each point a small measure of relatedness to each other in their own true persons. As a result there would have been built up gradually through the years a reality in place of the illusion based on projection. Dealing with the problems of life in this way has a double value for not only is reality substituted for illusion, but the anima or animus values, dissolved from their projection in the outer world, are also realized in the character and personality of the man or woman. The maturity which may sometimes be seen in a couple who have lived together for a lifetime, learning to know and accept each other, comes in no small measure from this assimilation of the anima and animus.

In other instances the values of the Ghostly Lover may be realized through the creation of a work of art, although here I speak with more reservation. For the production of a work of art, even when it embodies the values made available through the anima or the animus, does not always mean that these values are really incorporated into the personality of the artist. If this were so, every great artist and every great poet would be a great individuality, a really developed human being. We should like to believe this, but unfortunately we cannot. For, lamentable as it is, a great poet or artist is frequently an all-too-human personality. It seems as though some poets have paid, with their characters, the price of their genius. The work of art is often but another way in which the values of the animus are projected to the external world. Instead, however, of their being found in a loved object, they are projected in the form of an image of the inner drama. By this means something is gained; the world is richer in art; and the artist, through making actual the vision of his inner fantasy, has submitted himself to the discipline of hard work and to the appraisal of his fellowmen. He is no idle dreamer; he has made good on the reality side. Nevertheless, if he does not assimilate the psychological significance of his own work, he cannot obtain for his own personal development the values of the soul image which have inspired his creation. He has seen his vision as a vision only. He does not realize that it is the drama of his own inner life, and so he gains no development from his 'artist's' insight.

And here we come to what is perhaps the most important part of the whole subject, namely the assimilation of the values of the Ghostly Lover. At first when these values are unconscious they are completely unavailable for development. Then they are projected, and the individual becomes aware of them, but they are outside the personality. The problem is: How can they be brought back within the psyche in such a form that their energy may be available for conscious life-development?

If a woman whose animus values are constellated in a projection on to a man is analysed, a moment comes when the projection is broken. The psychological energy, or libido, formerly occupied with the projection is released and sinks down into the unconscious where it begins to activate the primordial images that lie hidden there. At this moment it sometimes happens that she begins to produce spontaneous fantasies and visions, which represent the transformations which the libido is undergoing in the unconscious. If the woman takes these fantasies seriously as representing a certain kind of reality, she can begin to take a part in the fantasy, that is, she can 'get into' the fantasy and participate in its development, instead of merely being obsessed by the mood of unhappiness into which such a disappointment is only too apt to throw her. Jung has described this method in his *Two Essays*. He says:

> Now this is the direct opposite of succumbing to a mood, which is so typical of neurosis. It is no weakness, no spineless surrender, but a hard achievement, the essence of which consists in keeping your objectivity despite the temptations of the mood, and in making the mood your object, instead of allowing it to become in you the dominating subject. So the patient must try to get his mood to speak to him; his mood must tell him all about itself and show him through what kind of fantastic analogies it is expressing itself.[2]

Through allowing the mood to unfold itself in this fashion a picture of the situation in the unconscious is revealed in which the subject can come to participate. If this participation can be achieved, a gradual development of the fantasy material takes place in such a way that the values, previously caught in the projection, are assimilated and serve to create a new centre for the personality which, as Jung says, 'ensures for the personality a new and more solid foundation'.[3] In the *Two Essays* he gives a most striking instance of this use of the fantasy as a means of so getting in touch with the images of the unconscious as to wrest their energy from them for utilization in the building up of the personality. In the following piece of fantasy material, something of the same sort is taking place. A woman who had projected her animus on to a man with whom she had fallen in love did not recognize that her involvement was due to an animus transference, but the man was apparently aware of danger. She met with a rebuff which threw her back upon herself. She was undergoing analysis at the time, hence, instead of falling into a depression, she tried to get her mood to talk to her and to show her in fantasy the movement of the images of the unconscious, hoping by this to understand the significance of the frustration of her love. This was the fantasy or waking vision that came to her. I quote it in her own words.

Out of the woods into a sunny field I came. Fresh cool breezes from the surrounding mountains blew across the stretch of green sunlit meadow. I seemed to be in a shallow bowl held high to heaven. I was alone. There was only the sound of the long grass swaying in the breeze.

Suddenly from the woods behind me galloped four horses, two black and two white. On them rode four knights in armour, each bearing a lance from which streamed a silken pennant. A knight in black armour with a dragon in rubies on his breast rode one white horse and carried a golden lance with a flaming red pennant that curled and twisted in the breeze like a tongue of flame. On the other white horse rode a knight in steel armour, with a blazing sun of sapphires on his breast, carrying a lance of steel, from which streamed a tongue of blue flame. A knight in gold armour with a topaz heart on his breast and a golden lance in his hand from which curled a tongue of yellow flame, rode one black horse. On the other rode a knight in silver armour with a crescent of emeralds on his breast and in his hand a silver lance with a long narrow pointed green flame streaming far behind.

The four horsemen galloped to the centre of the field. They dismounted and, leaving their horses, paced off one hundred paces in opposite directions: the knight of the dragon one hundred paces to the north; the golden knight one hundred paces to the east; the knight of the emerald crescent one hundred paces to the south; and the knight of the sapphire sun one hundred paces to the west. They drove their lances into the earth, called the horses to them, mounted and drew their swords of flaming steel from their scabbards. At a shout, brandishing their swords in the sunlight, they spurred their horses and dashed headlong to meet their opponents. I fell to the earth and covered my eyes. I heard the heavy impact of the horses' bodies, heard the ring of steel and got on my knees to pray. I must have fainted as I knelt. When I regained consciousness I opened my eyes and there before me in the centre of the field was an altar. On it was a shallow bowl of silver studded with rubies and emeralds and sapphires and topaz, in which burned a clear flame which shot to heaven. I staggered to my feet and drew near to the altar, and fell on my knees and bowed my head in prayer. Suddenly I heard a voice. I looked up and there in the flame, poised as if for flight, was a magnificent eagle.

To give anything like a full interpretation of such a fantasy is far beyond the scope of this book; the psychological problems that are touched upon would lead too far afield. But a general interpretation will show something of the course which the libido takes in its transformation.

The woman is in a bowl of the mountains, in a sort of earth-womb where she has drawn back in deep introversion. This drawing back into the womb of nature is a typical movement whenever the libido, which was streaming out forcefully towards an outer object, is suddenly checked. Here in the inner world she sees the heroes, the glorious personifications of the animus, come galloping. They are four in number and are related to the four fundamental colours and to the four points of the horizon. They represent the four divisions of the microcosm no less than of the macrocosm. We might speak to them as the four functions[4] of the psyche. They appear here as figures of chivalry. Their jewels and regal appearance indicate how important are the values that have been stirred to activity by a situation which, judged from external standards, is relatively trivial. This woman has made many animus transferences before, but this is the first time she has realized what she was doing *while she was doing it*. The annihilation of the unconscious figures in the conflict is the result of that realization.

Within the circle of the hills the knights trace out a square, one hundred paces each way. This is related to the age-old problem of the attempt to square the circle, to measure the incommensurable. The knights delimit a portion of the field which is measurable and, therefore, knowable. Psychologically this means that the animus projections measure off a segment of the illimitable cosmos which should rightly belong to the human psyche of the woman. When the animus is not dealt with and is not brought to consciousness he functions as the Ghostly Lover who lures the woman away from known and knowable reality to limitless regions. Therefore this delimiting activity of the four knights is very important. It means that while the human psyche is still incommensurable, by virtue of its contact with the unconscious, yet, in this instance, the animus figures delimit it and make it, as it were, available for experience through the function of relating the human being to the world of the collective unconscious.

Thus the patterns of this fantasy form a kind of diagram of the psyche. The similarity of such diagrams to the mandalas or magic circles of China, Tibet, and India has been discussed by Jung in *The Secret of the Golden Flower* and in *The Archetypes of the Collective Unconscious*. The pattern drawn here is a mandala. In the Orient such mandalas are used in meditation and other religious practices, in order to find the central point of the personality, which is not the ego, but is non-personal. And here through a psychological process the woman is doing a similar thing.

After the knights clash the woman finds that they have disappeared. What remains is a central altar with a bowl upon it, ornamented with the jewels previously worn by the knights; that is to say, the animus values are transferred to the bowl on the altar. Within the bowl is a flame (energy), the energy which was manifested before in the conflict of the knights, and, on the objective plane, in the intensity of the woman's involvement with the man on to whom she had made the animus projection. From the bowl arises, phoenix-like, an eagle, the bird of long flights, who soars up to the sun.

During the transformation the woman loses consciousness, an evidence that such a change cannot be understood or grasped by the conscious intellect. It is and will always remain a mystery – one of the miracles of life. This unconsciousness is also a kind of death. It signifies that the conscious ego is being displaced as the centre of the personality. It is a kind of death of the ego.

The bowl on the altar is like the bowl of the hills. Here within the four-square area which the knights measured off and delimited from the unknown circle in the hills, another circle appears, suggesting that this new centre of the microcosm has a certain similarity to the macrocosm. It too is a bowl or circle, not to be measured by our rule of measure. (Note that the area of a circle πr^2 is unknowable, except as an imaginary figure owing to the nature, of π, which cannot be worked out exactly.) This means that this new centre of the psyche is beyond complete comprehension by the conscious. It partakes of the nature of the cosmos. It is as though a fragment of the cosmos became crystallized in the very centre of the human psyche. And just as a drop of water is the ocean in miniature, so this central crystallization is the cosmos in miniature. In terms of religion it is God within the human being. Such a concept has been the central mystery of many great religions, and we meet the same idea coming directly from the unconscious in the fantasy of a modern American woman. The form of the fantasy shows plainly that the bowl and its contents carry for this woman the values of a religious object, for at sight of them she falls on her knees to pray.

The eagle which rises from the flame is, like the phoenix, the promise of the renewal of life. It is analogous to the dove, the Holy Spirit, which descended upon the disciples in tongues of flame. In the Christian story the Holy Spirit, which was to bring God to dwell within the hearts of the believers, descended only after Christ, the incarnation of God as Hero, had departed from the world. Psychologically it is also true that the spiritual animus comes to dwell within the psyche only after the projection of the animus, the incarnation of the Ghostly Lover, has been overcome. Thus it is that the Ghostly Lover disappears and in his stead is born a new spiritual power transforming the life of the individual. Through this redeemed animus the woman gains a relation to the masculine principle within herself. This masculine principle is the Logos, or wisdom. When she is identified with the animus she is possessed by opinions and rationalizations and so-called principles which do not represent true wisdom at all. These are the work of the Ghostly Lover. True wisdom can be known only through the spiritual, or redeemed animus, who is a mediator between conscious and unconscious. He brings the values of the creative sources of the unconscious within reach of that human being who has had the courage and the strength to overcome the Ghostly Lover.

NOTES

1. For a further discussion of this subject the reader is referred to C. G. Jung's essay 'Anima and Animus' in *Two Essays on Analytical Psychology.*
2. *Two Essays.* par. 348.
3. Ibid., para. 365.
4. See Jung, *Psychological Types*, pp. 412–517.

13

The Feminine in Fairy Tales

Marie-Louise von Franz

Women in the Western world nowadays seem to seek images which could define their identity. This search is motivated by a kind of disorientation and a deep uncertainty in modern women. In the West, this uncertainty is due to the fact, as Jung has pointed out, that women have no metaphysical representant in the Christian God-image. Protestantism must accept the blame of being a pure men's religion. Catholicism has at least the Virgin Mary as an archetypal representation of femininity, but this feminine archetypal image is incomplete because it encompasses only the sublime and light aspects of the divine feminine principle and therefore does not express the *whole* feminine principle. In studying fairy tales, I first came across feminine images which seem to me to complement this lack in the Christian religion. Fairy tales express the creative fantasies of the rural and less educated layers of the population. They have the great advantage of being naive (not 'literary') and of having been worked out in collective groups, with the result that they contain purely archetypal material unobscured by personal problems. Until about the seventeenth century, it was the adult population that was interested in fairy tales. Their allocation to the nursery is a late development, which probably has to do with the rejection of the irrational, and development of the rational outlook, so that they came to be regarded as nonsense and old wives' tales and good enough for children. It is only today that we rediscover their immense psychological value.[1]

If we look for feminine archetypal models of behavior, we at once stumble over the problem that the feminine figures in fairy tales might have been formed by a man, and therefore do not represent a woman's idea of femininity but rather what Jung called the anima – that is, man's femininity. Recent studies which concentrated on the question of who the storyteller is have brought to light that popular storytellers are sometimes men and sometimes women. The originator of the tale can therefore be of either sex. A feminine figure in a fairy tale with the whole story circling around it does not necessarily prove that the tale has to do with a woman's psychology. Many long stories of the sufferings of a woman have been written by men and are the projection of their anima problem. This is particularly the case in the theme of the rejected woman, who has to go a long way in suffering in order to find the right bridegroom, as, for instance, in the story of Amor and Psyche within the *Golden Ass* by Apuleius.[2] Also in various antique gnostic teachings there appears the figure of Sophia, a feminine personification of the divine wisdom, about whom the most amazing stories are told: that she was the youngest daughter of the Godhead, that she wanted to know the unknown Father, called Abyss, and by this bold wish got herself into a lot of trouble and suffering, fell into matter, and begged for redemption. This motif of the Sophia lost in matter is not only a theme in late antiquity; it appears also as the idea of the lost Shekhinah in the Jewish kabbalistic tradition. The authors of these religious writings were men. Under such circumstances, we can say that the figure of Sophia represents certain aspects of the man's anima. At other times, however, we could just as well say that the figure represents feminine psychology. The whole problem becomes in one way more, in another less, complicated if we try to concentrate on how the psychology of the feminine and the psychology of the anima are intertwined.

The real woman has an effect upon the anima and the anima upon the real woman. A woman has an educative and transforming influence on the man's eros. A man, especially if very much engaged in mental activities, tends to be a little bit coarse or undifferentiated on the eros side. He comes home tired, reads his newspaper, and then goes to bed (particularly if he is a Swiss). He does not think it necessary to demonstrate any feeling for this wife. He does not see the feminine person and her needs. Here the woman can have a transforming effect. If she can stand for her human rights without animus, and if she has a good relationship with the man she loves, she can tell him things about feminine psychology which will help him to differentiate his feelings. Since the anima of the man will have many characteristics of his mother, his first experience of woman, women in general will have a strong influence in forming and building up the man's relationship with his eros function.

On the other hand, women are influenced by the man's anima projections. For instance, they behave in a certain way and then notice that the man reacts in a bewildered or a shocked manner, because their behavior does not fit in with his anima image. Even small girls find out that if they play the part of the father's anima, put their arms round his neck, etc., they can get a lot out of their father. Fathers' daughters push aside the mother who insists on clean fingernails and going to school. They say 'Daddy' in a charming way and he falls for the trick; thus they learn to use the man's anima by adapting to it. Women who behave in this way we call 'anima women'. Such women simply play the role intimated to them by the man in whom they are at the moment interested. They are conscious of themselves only as mirrors of the man's reaction. Their lover will tell them they are wonderful, but if there is no man around, they feel as if they were nobody. It is only the man's reaction to them which makes them aware of their feminine personality.

Thus some women give in entirely to the anima projection. A woman I know had very small and rather weak feet, but her husband liked her to wear very high heels. She tortured herself by wearing these shoes, though doctors told her she should not. Such a woman is afraid of losing the man's affection. If he only likes her as an anima figure, she is forced to play the role of the anima. This interreaction can be positive or negative, but the woman is very much affected by the man's anima figure, which brings us to a very primitive and simple and collective level where we cannot separate the features of anima and real woman. Frequently they are mixed to some extent and react upon each other.

In our Christian civilization, as I mentioned, the image of the woman is incompletely represented. As Jung has said, she has no representative in the Upper Parliament. One could say that the anima is neglected and the real woman is uncertain as to her own essence, her own being, of what she is, or could be. So either she regresses to a primitive instinctive pattern and clings to that, which protects her from the projection that civilization exerts on her, or she falls into the animus and builds up a picture of herself to compensate the uncertainty within her. In a matriarchal structure, such as in South India, women have natural confidence in their own womanhood. They know their importance and that they are different from men in a special way, and that this does not imply any inferiority. Therefore they can assert their human existence and being in a natural way.

On a primitive level, the image of the real woman and the image of the anima of man is more or less the same thing and in our civilization underwent certain slow, secular processes of transformation which took about three to four hundred years. This slow movement of development is probably the sum of thousands of individual reactions, which in the course of centuries have surfaced and suddenly broken out as a movement in time. Possibly the bitterness resulting from being rejected and insufficiently appreciated, experienced by many thousands of women, brought forth the collective outburst of women's emancipation in the early 1900s. It slowly developed in many individuals, and then suddenly appeared on the surface so that people became aware of it. Previously reactions had taken place underground. Thus there are movements which have a psychological background and are the sum of many individual experiences.

We have thus to start with a paradox: feminine figures in fairy tales are neither the pattern of the anima nor of the real woman, but of both, because sometimes it is one, and sometimes another. But it is a fairly good guess to say that some fairy tales illustrate more the real woman and others more the man's anima, according to the sex of the last person who wrote down the story, thereby giving it a slightly different nuance. A friend of mine, a schoolteacher, taught drawing and painting and gave as a theme for painting a scene out of the fairy tale entitled 'Faithful John'. In my view, the story mirrors masculine psychology; there is only one pale anima figure in it. The teacher gave it to a mixed class of boys and girls, who might choose any scene. All the children were enthusiastic, and the boys naturally chose heroic and dramatic scenes, while the girls picked on the one feminine figure in the tale, identifying with that as the boys identified with the male figures, so that the pictures gave quite different aspects of the story.

Thus obviously different characteristics are emphasized according to the sex of the person retelling the story. We therefore may make the hypothesis that in some fairy tales the feminine formative influence has been greater and in others the male, but one can never be sure whether the woman or the anima is represented. A good approach is to interpret the tale both ways. Then it can be seen that some, when interpreted from the feminine angle, give a lot of rich material, but from the man's angle seem not so revealing. Following these impressions, I have selected a few of Grimm's stories which can be interpreted from the feminine angle, but I do not assert that they have nothing to do with the anima problem.

As to the figures in the story, it has been said, wrongly I think, that the myth is the story of the gods and the fairy tale the story of ordinary people, that the heroes and participants in fairy tales are ordinary beings while in myths they are gods and semigods. A problem with this theory, however, is that in some fairy tales the names point to gods. For instance, I shall discuss 'Sleeping Beauty', or 'Briar Rose', in which, in many versions, the children are called Sun and Moon. Now, the mother of the Sun and the Moon is not an ordinary human being, so you could say it is a symbol. But if the children are called Sun and Moon, or Day and Dawn, as in other versions, you are away again in the realm of what we normally call the world of the gods. So you cannot build up a theory on the basis of this difference. From a psychological angle, we know that they are archetypal figures and have, in their essence, nothing to do with ordinary human beings and human personalities as we deal with them in human psychology. For this reason, I will assume that there is no difference between fairy tales and myth, but rather that they both deal with archetypal figures.

If we really want to get the feeling of what this concept means, we have to ask ourselves how it is possible that people tell each other stories in which, in one case, the figures have the names of gods whom they worship in their national religion, in their *représentations collectives* and, in other stories the figures do not refer to the *représentations collectives*. The difference lies in historical reasons which I cannot discuss here. Let us assume that, drawing upon their dreams and waking visions, people are able to project into empty space certain figures of their unconscious and can speak of these figures.

I have a case of a very simple woman. She is the daughter of a carpenter and grew up in a primitive country and is very poor. She is a very severe schizophrenic borderline case, if not an actual schizophrenic. She has the most amazing voices, visions, and dreams and archetypal material. Though she had learned to be a hairdresser, she could not carry on because of her many fantasies, so she is a charwoman, but so quarrelsome and crazy and difficult that she has to clean up empty factories and work when there is nobody else around. She has been thrown out to the borders of human society, but she is a really religious person who might be compared with the German mystic Theresa von Konnersreuth – except that she is so swallowed up by her visions that she cannot function outwardly. She wanted to get into contact with me, but was not able to function for the first sixty minutes of the analytical hour. Her ego complex is too weak. First she had to get the feeling of the place, and of me, and she said that one could not talk about such subjects as God right away. I think that is true, for the atmosphere needs intimacy and friendship to be able to share a tremendous secret. So, in this special case, I agreed that we would see each other less often and for that I would give her a whole afternoon. Also I do not see her in my consulting room. We go to an inn and drink something together, or go elsewhere. She either does not talk or only on foolish subjects for about an hour and a half, which is exhausting, and then generally I either begin nervously to look at my watch or remark that I have to be back at seven o'clock, to call her back to reality. Then she suddenly starts to talk about her inner experiences, usually with a jump, and very often tells me a dream as though it were real. To strengthen her consciousness and keep her out of the archetypal world, I say, 'Yes, but it was a dream,' and to this she always agrees; she is not too confused to realize that. But then I notice that she cannot go on, for she is disturbed like an artist when you intrude upon his or her work. If you are artistically inspired and in the full swing of a new inspiration, you can be lamed by such an interruption and lose the thread. The first welling up of a creative idea must not be disturbed. One should never talk about such ideas before they have taken definite shape, for they are as delicate as newborn babies.

Creative people are generally very easily disturbed, and I noticed the same thing in this woman, so that usually I kept my comments for the end, at which time I thought I ought to get her more into reality, thereby following the pattern of the fairy tale, where very often a remark that comes at the end kicks you right out of the story – but only at the end!

This woman told me the most amazing archetypal stories and treated them as real, and there you have, *in flagrante*, an example of the possible origin of the fairy tale. Here someone tells you a classic literary dramatic story, and at the end he remarks that it was a dream! In such a case there is complete identity, but in the process of retelling the stories get changed and personal motifs left out. The remark at the end is likely to run: '*Et le coq chanta ki-keri-ki, l'aube est venu et mon conte est fini*' (The cock crowed *ki-keri-ki*, the dawn has come, and my tale is ended) – so it is time to wake up! As the cock crows you must get out of bed! Or, it might be: 'There was a wonderful wedding and a marvelous feast, and I,' the fairy tale teller says, 'I was in the kitchen, but I got nothing, because the cook gave me a kick in the bottom, and here I am telling you the story'; that is, he flies back into reality. The gypsies say: 'They married and were happy ever after, but we, poor devils, are so hungry that we are sucking our teeth,' and then they start begging for money.

So the listeners are reminded that the fairy tale is not about ordinary people. They are quite aware that the participants and events take place in another sphere, which we call the dimension of the unconscious; they feel it to be the other world and in strong contrast to their conscious reality. In this way, on a primitive level, there is a kind of shifting contact with the unconscious. The scene shifts without definite demarcations, but there is more emphasis on the feeling level. Fairy tales actually tell us about figures of the unconscious, of the other world. One could say that in myth the figures are confused with the gods of religion; they correspond to what Lucien Lévy-Bruhl calls *représentations collectives*. Fairy tales, on the contrary, migrate and cannot be linked up with a national collective consciousness. They rather contain a tremendous amount of compensatory material and usually contradict or compensate collective conscious ideas.

My schizophrenic charwoman sometimes brings dreams full of Christian traditions. God the Father appears and speaks to her, and then what appears corresponds with what she has learned in her Christian education. There is no difficulty in calling one figure the Father and the other the Holy Ghost. Once she had a vision of a beautiful male figure whose voice was heard and who stood beside her on a mountain and said: 'You have to paint this green to redeem yourself and mankind.' She said that she was not capable of that, and the voice said: 'I will help you.' She seemed then to have done it somehow and was therefore allowed to come down the mountain. Next she was at a hotel and waking up. I asked her whose voice it was, and she said that it was the Holy Ghost; the man fitted the *représentation collective* of the Holy Ghost, and she had no difficulty in identifying it, although the voice did not.

In another religious system, the figure would have received a different name. If a figure turns up which is not within the domain of the *représentations collectives*, if there is nothing which fits a figure, you have to say that something appears which seems like So-and-So; you cannot pin it onto a collective idea. Supposing there is an experience of a feminine goddess who has all the features of the Earth Mother, but is as sexually extravagant as Baubo was in Grecian times. If you were brought up as a Catholic, you cannot call this figure the Virgin Mary. But since that is the only representative you have of the feminine numinous figure, you must continue to call her the Mother or give her a fantastic name, say 'Little Mother Evergreen'. But that is not an official name, and we do not worship such a personage. In this way, fairy tales are to a great extent built up by inner experiences which do not quite fit the *représentations collectives*. Therefore, figures usually have no names, or odd names, but not the names of religious symbols or known systems. They give us more information about what is going on in the compensatory function of the unconscious than myths do.

What does the collective side want to express which is not expressed in the *représentations collectives*? We get valuable information on this point. Fairy tales also take official names and tell abominable stories about religious personages. In one country a number are told about the Lord Jesus, who behaves outrageously – going about with Saint Peter, whom he tricks into getting the beating from the innkeeper, for Saint Peter has always been naive and is naturally the fitting person to get the beating. In a Czechoslovakian fairy tale there is a helpless old man sitting up in a tree who has to be helped down, and at the end of the story the jittery old man turns out to be God himself. Now, imagine God himself being a helpless old creature not able to climb down a tree! But that a nice girl has to help him down is a very useful compensation for our ideas of God.

My charwoman sometimes gets into a rage with God. She says he is awful – he runs after women, and sometimes she has to shut him out of her bedroom. She says, 'God has gotten too close again.' He is indecent and a trickster, and she has found out that sometimes she must trick him too. Then he leaves her alone for a while. But let her tell that to a parson! She used to tell parsons, and none of them wanted to listen! She is very uncomfortable when God gets too close; but that is the time when she has her visions. When he is not so close, she is more comfortable and normal and nearer reality. This case taught me how an uneducated, simple mind deals with the power images of the collective unconscious.

In a similar manner, in fairy tales the figures of the *représentations collectives* either are not used or are misused. Christ in the previous story is just a trickster hero, and God is a boring old man, or an old man sitting in a tree, but the implication of the story shows that it was God. The figures are anonymous because it would be much too shocking if they were given their own names, which leads to the most amazing discoveries, and to restoring their real meaning.

This seeming distortion is not what it appears to be, but has to do with the law of compensation, which, according to Jung's discovery, characterizes the products of the unconscious. Dreams either compensate for the lopsidedness of our conscious view or complement its lacunae. Fairy tales, because they are also mostly unsophisticated products of the storyteller's unconscious, do the same. Like dreams, they help to keep our conscious attitude in a healthy balance, and have therefore a healing function.

As the conscious religious views of Western Europe in the past two thousand years have not given enough expression of the feminine principle, we can expect to find an especially rich crop of archetypal feminine figures in fairy tales giving expression to the neglected feminine principle. We can also expect to retrieve from them quite a few lost goddesses of pagan antiquity.

THE SLEEPING BEAUTY, OR BRIAR ROSE[3]

The fairy tale I want to discuss is called in the English translation either 'Briar Rose' or, more generally, 'The Sleeping Beauty'. It is the translation of a German fairy tale collected by the Brothers Grimm. Taking fairy tales from a literary angle, as first done by the Brothers Grimm, became a kind of modern movement and many collections appeared. In the Anglo-Saxon world our story is known only through translation. It was not well known even in Germany until the Grimm Brothers unearthed it through a woman living in Cassel, who was one of their main sources. The story immediately had an enormous effect. Poets used it in their writings and it had a sort of literary revival. It was naturally well suited to carry the projection of the poet's anima.

It is amusing that the fairy tale underwent the same fate as the Sleeping Beauty herself, for the tale faded out of people's memories, then suddenly became alive again and very popular. There were two versions of it, an Italian and a French one, which are romances or novels of the fourteenth century. The story is the same, however, with only slight variations, so we can conclude that it is very old and was suddenly revived. In the French fourteenth-century novel, the hero who wakes the princess bears the name of Perceforet, thus linking the tale with Parsifal and the Holy Grail legend. In that cycle the story was told as one of the many adventures of the chevalier hero. In the Italian variation the hero is called the Brother of Joy, and the heroine, the Sister of Pleasure. Both are allegoric novels written at the time of the Renaissance. In the Perceforet version, three goddesses are called to the girl's birth: one who carries the name of Lucina, the old Roman birth goddess Juno; Themis (a Greek name); and a fairy godmother who bears the name of Venus – thus going back to antique mythology. This is an interesting fact which throws some light on the feminine figure of the mother archetype in the late Middle Ages.

In the Renaissance they made the discovery, or mistake, of giving these figures antique names. Unfortunately, they thereby gave the fairy tales a historically regressive character in an unreal way because actually in the Renaissance people were Christian in their outlook on love and sex, so this play with antique names was half unreal. The use of antique names had been practised in the eleventh and twelfth centuries, but what they told of their heroes and gods was quite different from what was told of the original antique gods. In spite of this there has been a theory, about which there have been many quarrels in literary circles, that the Sleeping Beauty is an ancient theme from *Aetnae*, one of the last tragedies by the famous Greek poet Aeschylus, in which the following story was told: Talia, one of the goddesses of charm, a daughter of the smith god Hephaestus, was one of the many women whom Zeus loved and who was persecuted by the jealousy of Hera. Zeus hid Talia in the bowels of the earth until she gave birth to two boys, who were called Palikes.

It has been thought that this idea of a girl disappearing from the surface of reality and then reappearing at a certain time represented an earlier version of our 'Sleeping Beauty'. In the Italian version of 'Sleeping Beauty', the heroine is actually called Talia, which gives evidence for the theory. I think this is far-fetched, and could also be explained by archetypal kinship.

From the psychological angle, we cannot add to this literary quarrel. In general, we are more skeptical in regard to fantastic theories of survival and migration, because we know there is also the possibility of re-creating from the unconscious. On the other hand, it is astonishing how fairy tales do survive for hundreds of years. These are true facts but should not be exaggerated. I have not made up my mind what to believe, and I do not know what is more probable, but we certainly have to do with a very archaic and very archetypal motif, and you naturally see the idea of a feminine figure remaining dormant and reappearing after a time. For instance, there is the Demeter myth, in which Persephone disappears in winter and in spring returns to her mother on the surface of the earth – that is, of a girl goddess who disappears into death, or sleep, and returns at a certain time. That, as you know from Carl Kerényi's comments on the Kore myth, is an international myth, and our story is a special variation of it.[4]

Synopsis of the Tale

In olden times there lived a king and queen who lamented day by day that they had no children, and yet never a one was born. One day as the queen was bathing and thinking of her wish, a frog skipped out of the water and said to her, 'Your wish shall be fulfilled – before the year passes you shall have a daughter.'

As the frog had said, so it happened, and a little girl was born who was so beautiful that the king almost lost his senses, but he ordered a great feast to be held, to which he invited relatives, friends, and acquaintances, and all the wise women who are kind and affectionate to children. But as there were thirteen wise women in his dominions, and he had only twelve golden plates for them, one had to stay home.

As soon as the fête was over, the wise women presented the infant with their wonderful gifts – virtue, beauty, riches, and so on – but just as eleven had given their presents, the thirteenth old lady stepped in suddenly. She was in a tremendous passion because she had not been invited, and without greeting or looking at anybody, she exclaimed loudly, 'The princess shall prick herself with a spindle on her fifteenth birthday and die!'

All were terrified, but then the twelfth stepped up. Because she could not take away the evil wish, but only soften it, she said, 'She shall not die, but shall fall into a sleep of a hundred years' duration.'

The king, who naturally wished to protect his child, commanded that every spindle in the kingdom should be burned. But it happened that on the day when the princess was just fifteen years old, the king and queen were not at home, and she was left alone in the castle.

The maiden looked about in every place as she pleased. She came to an old tower and tripped up the narrow winding staircase, arriving at a door, in the lock of which was a rusty key. She turned the key and the door sprang open. There sat an old woman with a spindle, spinning flax. 'Good day, my good lady,' said the princess. 'What are you doing here?'

'I am spinning,' said the old woman, nodding her head.

'What thing is that which twists round so merrily?' inquired the maiden, and she took the spindle to try her hand at spinning. Scarcely had she done so when the prophecy was fulfilled, for she pricked her finger; and at the very same moment she fell back upon a bed which stood near, in a deep sleep.

This sleep extended over the whole palace. The king and queen fell asleep in the hall and all their courtiers with them. The horses in the stables, the doves under the eaves, the flies upon the wall, and even the fire upon the hearth, all ceased to stir. The meat which was cooking ceased to frizzle, and the cook at the instant of pulling the hair of the kitchen boy lost his hold and began to snore too. Even the wind ceased to blow.

Now around the palace a thick hedge of briars began growing which every year grew higher and higher, until the castle was quite hidden from view. Then there went through the land a legend of the beautiful maiden Briar Rose, and from time to time princes came endeavoring to penetrate the hedge into the castle; but it was not possible, for the thorns held them as if by hands. The youths, unable to free themselves, perished miserably.

After a lapse of many years, there came another king's son into the land who had heard the legend and of how many princes had tried to penetrate the hedge and had died. But the youth was not to be daunted, and however much people tried to dissuade him, he would not listen.

Just at that time came the last day of the hundred years, when Briar Rose was to awake again. As the young prince approached the hedge, the thorns turned to fine large flowers, which of their own accord made a way for him to pass through and again closed up behind him. He saw horses and dogs fast asleep and in the eaves the doves with their heads beneath their wings. The flies were asleep upon the wall, the cook still stood with his hand on the hair of the kitchen boy, the maid at the board with the unplucked fowl in her hand. The courtiers were asleep, and so were the king and queen. At last he came to the tower and opened the door of the little room where slept Briar Rose. He bent over and kissed her. Just as he did so, she opened her eyes and greeted him with a smile. They went downstairs together; the king and queen and the whole court awoke, and all stared at each other in wonder. The horses in the stables shook themselves, the dogs wagged their tails, the doves flew away, the flies began to crawl, the fire to burn brightly and cook the meat – the meat began to frizzle; the cook gave his lad a box upon the ear, which made him cry out; and the maid began to pluck the fowl furiously. The whole place was once more in motion.

By and by the wedding of the prince with Briar Rose was celebrated with great splendor, and to the end of their lives they lived happy and contented.

The parallel stories show certain variations.[5] The general motif always is that a certain number of fairy godmothers appear, and one is furious because there is no golden plate for her, but the number varies, sometimes between seven and eight, sometimes between two and three. According to Grimm, seven were invited and the eighth was left out. But also in Grimm it is said later that six were asked and the seventh omitted. There is uncertainty here, which should be noticed to prevent any hard and fast theories. A certain number appear, but one is left out, either because she has retired to a tower and has been forgotten, or because there were not enough golden plates or goblets; and, being female, she turns up infuriated and curses the child, usually with the death curse, which is then softened by a benevolent fairy godmother. In some versions those who attempt to penetrate the hedge of briar roses die miserable deaths, torn by the thorns; in other versions, they are caught in the hedge and fall asleep – it's a kind of infection of sleep. In another version a prince comes who has made up his mind to free the beautiful girl, and the hedge of thorns becomes a hedge of roses which opens before him and closes after him. According to a typical German version, he is merely the lucky one who comes on the day when the hundred years expire, so there is no question of merit. According to other versions, he heroically fights his way and then the charm is over, and everybody wakes up again – the cook gives the slap, and the whole court awakens and returns to life. The two marry and are happy ever after.

This is a rather quick solution for a fairy tale. Usually there are complications and difficulties afterward. A Russian, French, and Catalonian version is that the prince comes to the Sleeping Beauty and sleeps with her without waking her. She then gives birth to two children and has to find the father later. Another type of variation in the French story is that the prince has redeemed the Sleeping Beauty but does not tell the story in his kingdom, where they do not know that he is married and has a child. Only after the death of his father does he take his bride home, where his mother tries to kill her and the child. There is a typical fairy tale motif of the destructive mother-in-law who tries to destroy mother and child. Then the cook or the hunter saves them, and when the evil mother-in-law is punished, the couple reunite happily.

These variations are probably written with the feeling that the original tale was too simple, that things could not be as simple as all that. Just to go through a hedge of roses does not seem to be a heroic enough deed. This shows how fairy tales can be mixed up with different archetypal motifs. It is interesting to see how they are combined in different countries at different times. One may be a more redeeming variation than another. But if you examine them, all the variations are quite meaningful. There is always a definite and meaningful thread running through, for people's fancy runs along the right lines. If one follows one's spontaneous fantasies, one cannot go wrong unless there is conscious interference. These people are so unconscious that instinctively the right motifs are linked together.

The first motif is that of the miraculous birth, which often occurs in the case of the hero or heroine of the story. It is said that the central figure in the story has not come into reality in the ordinary way but that a mystery or miracle surrounds his birth.

That poses a very abstract and ticklish problem concerning how we should interpret the hero or heroine. What do they represent? The particular and obvious problem in interpreting mythological material, which even well-known Jungians stumble over, is whether the hero has to be treated as an ego or not. We tend to say the hero is the ego, the beautiful woman is his anima, and so on. This is not an interpretation but a pinning of Jungian concepts onto mythical images. However, there *is* a temptation to call the hero figure the ego. It is as if this figure would lure us into that idea. That has to do with the trickster nature of the unconscious. Dreams also sometimes have an insinuating tone which makes one feel that one knows what they mean, and then one is blinded. An analyst who has interpreted thousands of dreams of other people cannot interpret his own. I am not surprised when this happens, for I know that in my own dreams I cannot interpret the most simple facts. One has to say: 'What would you say if that was a patient's dream?' In a patient's dream one would have seen it at once. There is a kind of intimate feeling reaction which prevents one from having enough distance. If you wake up and think you know what the dreams mean, you are usually barking up the wrong tree – the trickster god has caught you. The unconscious loves to do that, especially with awkward, shadowy things. We would not have that particular dream if we could know its meaning as easily as that.

For instance, a married woman had a fairly harmless flirtation with a married man. It led nowhere, but she had felt it could go further than just talk. As she valued the man's wife very much, she interrupted the contact and retired from it. She forgot it, and it went underground. Then a tremendous creative problem emerged. The dreams showed that she should do something creative. Everything circled around this, so she made a step toward fulfilling the task of writing something – which she should have undertaken long before – and was interested to see what the unconscious would say. She dreamed that this other couple was divorced and that she was now somehow going to marry the man with whom she had flirted. Now suddenly there came up the thing she had avoided in reality. She thought that the unconscious was obviously rubbing her nose into the fact that she had had a sexual interest in the man. She was very much disturbed and would not even tell the dream. She thought the meaning was clear. But it meant something quite different, namely the divorce of animus and shadow.

If a woman keeps herself unconscious, there is a negative couple in her unconscious for which neighbors offer a good hook for projection. The secret interplay of this shadow tendency and her mental operations has been stopped, and she is now going to marry the man; that is, she is going consciously to make contact with her spiritual and mental side. In alchemical symbolism the feminine figure is often first married to the wrong kind of man, and it is the heroic deed to separate the couple. The hero has to win his partner and separate her from the wrong man. That was the kind of dynamism underlying that awkward business. Why did the unconscious pick on that? It is very obvious that if creative energy in a woman is not made conscious, it creates mischief – the overflow makes mischief. If you don't use your libido, you are bored to death and must start some kind of nonsense. The real thing is not done, but it is always expressed in some other form.

The woman's flirtation with the man was already the creative libido, the overflow of energy not satisfied in marriage and children and not parked in creative work. She realized that the flirtation was not the right thing, but the energy was again not invested; neither in the mischief nor creatively, which was why the dream used that theme. It was the first symptom that some energy wanted to overflow out of the marriage situation. The dream picked it up where the thing stopped. But when she woke up, she projected the conscious view and felt it to be a horrible and awful dream. My first thought was also – is it objective? But she was not repressing a wish for that flirtation. You have to watch the patient and see if there is still emotion, something which you cannot do for yourself. While you are telling the story you cannot look to see whether you are emotional. Then I ask myself – what is the motive in wishing to divorce? I had in mind all these archetypal and alchemical motifs which one must know and which give one a background on archaic processes. Then I referred the dream to the actual situation. What had happened the day before when she had made an attempt at marrying her mind? The ego had united with certain spiritual and mental impulses, but it needed a certain amount of detachment from the shadow.

Thus the unconscious is not really a trickster. That amount of energy which wanted to make mischief has now found its goal. The dream just states an actual fact, although consciousness, with its morality and prejudices, experiences it as if something awkward was insinuated. That is the difficulty in interpreting dreams and fairy tales. To identify with the hero or the heroine is so obvious that we are at once identical and cannot, with a certain amount of scientific objectiveness, ask the question as to who they are. In archetypal stories one must be able to see the images in a transpersonal way. There is nothing in the story to show that it tells about an actual human being; nothing is said about the girl's inner subjective life. She has been born miraculously, has fallen asleep, has woken up, and has married. It is an abstract pattern.

The folklorist Max Lüthi wrote that all figures in fairy tales are abstract.[6] We would rather say they are archetypal figures lacking human amplification. An abstract is something from which life has been abstracted, thus the archetype is transhuman. We would say that fairy-tale figures are not human individuals; they are not filled with actual life. The heroine is a feminine schematic figure – what shall we call it, an ego? A good way, and the way out taken by many psychological interpreters, is just to talk around it without pinning it down to what it is. Literary persons and those philosophically interested in Jungian psychology often do not use the Jungian terms. They avoid calling the figure the anima, or the Self, but talk around it. That I think is sheer cowardice. Why should we not make an attempt and admit that Jung has discovered such facts as the anima, ego, and Self? The difficulty, of course, is that Jung's terminology can lead one into thorny difficulties. We may go through the hedge which makes one fall asleep – it does not penetrate mentally anymore. Women love to talk about a concept brought out by a great man and forget to penetrate into it. They are mentally asleep, though this does not apply only to women!

If we try to penetrate that problem we must say that in one way, for instance in regard to the fairy godmother, it looks as though the girl would be a human being and the unconscious (the godmother) threatens her ego. If one amplifies mythologically and compares the figure with Persephone, or other such Spring figures, then you must say that the girl is an aspect of a goddess and ought to be called by the Jungian name of the Self. And what is collective and what individual? That the girl is not an individual feminine figure – Mary Miller or Ann Smith – is obvious. But why does she behave like an ego? And why do we assume that the ego is completely individual?

If you ask, 'What are you as an individual?,' most people point to their bodies. But put the question to yourself, 'What is individual in my ego?' The fact that I have an ego is not individual; it is the most common and most normal complex among human beings. That the ego helps in adaptation – 'I notice', 'I combine things', etc. – is not individual. One person does one thing less well and others better. Some have one faculty of association and some another. Functions which adapt to outer reality are usual for all individuals. The ego has such a tremendous number of general features that it is a puzzle to know what its individual essence is. This essence can only be discovered through a thorough analysis, which is not exactly what all egos go through. But there is an archetypal 'I', a collective disposition which is similar in everybody, and one aspect that occurs in some way in every human being.

How is this archetypal aspect of the ego related to the Self? If one has read Michael Fordham's writings on childhood problems[7] and Erich Neumann's *The Origins and History of Consciousness*[8] or has worked with a young analysand, one will have seen that many neuroses in early youth show an ego consciousness backward in its development. If one looks at the unconscious processes in children, one will see that there are play impulses, dreams, and fantasies that tend to bring forth the ego maturity the child should have. So we could say that it is the unconscious which wants the improvement in the ego. The infantile ego does not want it. It is the impulse from the unconscious that causes the neurotic disturbance in its attempts to get the child onto a higher level of consciousness, to build up a stronger ego complex. The school technique – being able to concentrate and overcome fatigue – is inadequate without the instinct from the unconscious, which expresses the tendency for building up such things. Therefore the urge is a general human disposition, i.e., archetype, which comes forth from the Self. Fordham discusses the dream symbolism in early childhood as a tendency to build up a stronger ego consciousness, a completely different role from that of the second half of life.

Young people in the bisexual phase of puberty sometimes develop a crush on an older person of the same sex. If one analyses them, the unconscious seems to support this admiration and imitation, this clinging to a person of the same sex. Looking at it superficially, one might interpret this figure in dreams either as indicating a homosexual tendency or as a symbol of the Self, for the older brother or uncle figure appears with magic qualities, as the saving factor or teacher. He is a projection of the Self. The natural reaction of the young admirer is that he would like to be like the object of his admiration. So the figure functions as a model of a more adult way of existence or behavior. It is a projection of the Self. As long as the ego complex is weak, this projection functions as a model to be copied and followed. It assists in building up a more adult ego complex. If you take all these practical facts into consideration, you can say that the ego has an archetypal foundation, and that it is the Self which builds up the ego complex. It is this aspect that is meant by the hero or heroine of a fairy tale: the archetypal foundation of the individual ego, or the pattern of an ego which functions in harmony with the Self.

NOTES

1. See Marie-Louise von Franz, *An Introduction to the Interpretation of Fairy Tales* (Dallas: Spring Publications, 1978).
2. See Marie-Louise von Franz, *The Golden Ass of Apuleius: The Liberation of the Feminine in Man* (Boston: Shambhala Publications, 1992).
3. C. G. Jung and Carl Kerényi, *Essays on a Science of Mythology* (New York: Pantheon Books, Bollingen Series XII, 1949), pp. 139ff.
4. *The Complete Grimm's Fairy Tales* (New York: Pantheon Books, 1972), pp. 237ff.
5. Cf. J. Bolte and G. Polivka, *Anmerkungen zu den Kinder- und Hausmärchen der Brüder Grimm*, 5 vols (Leipzig, 1913–1927), vol. 1, p. 434.
6. Max Lüthi, *Volksmärchen und Volkssage*, 2nd ed. (Bern & Munich: Francke Verlag, 1966).
7. Michael Fordham, *Children as Individuals* (New York: G. P. Putnam's Sons/C. G. Jung Foundation for Analytical Psychology, 1969).
8. Erich Neumann, *The Origins and History of Consciousness*, trans R. F. C. Hull (New York: Pantheon Books, Bollingen Series XLII, 1954).

14

'Taking it Like a Man': Abandonment in the Creative Woman

Marion Woodman

> Each night I am nailed into place
> and forget who I am.
> Daddy?
> That's another kind of prison.
>
> Anne Sexton, 'Sleeping Beauty'

For many women born and reared in a patriarchal culture, initiation into mature womanhood occurs through abandonment, actual or psychological. It is the identity-conferring experience that frees them from the father.

Some women can accept their destiny in a traditional, patriarchal relationship, finding within its obvious limitations – social, intellectual, spiritual – compensations that are important to them. Others who accept that destiny but nevertheless resist its limitations are forced for financial, political or social reasons to stay within its framework.

However, an increasing number of women whose psychic center has always radiated around the father, real or imagined, are determined to go through the initiation. These women are by inner necessity creators in the Keatsian sense of 'soul-makers';[1] that is, their quest for meaning drives them to find their own inner story. They reject collective masculine values as an intrusive imposition, but their search for a personal identity from within almost inevitably brings them into collision with the very forces they are struggling to integrate. In the effort to liberate themselves from the very real restrictions of a patriarchal culture, they ironically, even at a highly conscious level, tend to become its victims. The internal father, who in the soul-making process they sought to please, turns on them – or appears to – as soon as that father-image is projected onto a man, or they seek recognition and reward in those creative fields still largely dominated by men.

While this situation is now changing, there is still a long way to go. The psychic dynamics involved in the change are still far from understood. Men and woman caught up in those dynamics, and even consciously committed to so-called enlightened relationships, are still not getting through to each other despite their heroic efforts to do so, efforts that refuse to admit failure even when failure is all they experience. This can become vividly clear in the analytic relationship, often a microcosm of what is happening on the cultural level.

The word abandonment comes from the Old English verb *bannan*, meaning 'to summon' (OED). To be among those summoned was to relinquish oneself to service. Abandonment means literally 'to be uncalled', symbolically 'to be without a destiny'. If one's destiny has been dictated by the father, however, then to be uncalled may be a blessing rather than a curse. Free of the father, the daughter may then truly *abandon herself* to the process of her own soul-making. This rite of passage contains within itself the double meaning of abandonment. Emily Dickinson sums this up in her usual elliptical style:

> I'm ceded – I've stopped being Theirs –
> The name They dropped upon my face
> With water, in the country church
> Is finished using, now,
> And They can put it with my Dolls,
> My childhood, and the string of spools,
> I've finished threading – too –
>
> Baptized, before, without the choice,
> But this time, consciously, of Grace –
> Unto supremest name –
> Called to my Full – The Crescent dropped –
> Existence's whole Arc, filled up,
> With one small Diadem.
>
> My second Rank – too small the first –
> Crowned – Crowing – on my Father's breast –
> A half unconscious Queen –
> But this time – Adequate – Erect,
> With Will to choose, or to reject,
> And I choose, just a Crown –[2]

The 'half unconscious Queen', as I see her, is bonded, for better or for worse, to her creative imagination, a situation that originated in the psychological bonding to her father. Even in childhood such a woman is outside the ban (i.e., calling) that contains other children. In adolescence, while her sisters are conspiring about bangles, babies and bans of marriage, she is banished by her own decree. Her creativity is of a different nature: plays, canvasses, sonatas or chemical experiments. On some levels she always feels banned from life and yearns for what other people take for granted. Yet while part of her feels abandoned, part of her knows that were she to forsake her own creativity she would be abandoning her own soul.

Many variables are involved in defining the creative woman. Some women are creative in their homemaking, creating a loving, spontaneous environment for their husbands and children – a place to go out from, a place to go back to. Others are creating in an extraverted professional situation. Some are successfully doing both. In this discussion, however, I am thinking of the creative woman as one who is compelled from within to relate to her own creative imagination.

While the lights and shadows in individuals vary greatly, a basic pattern of such a woman's psychology can be outlined. As a little girl she loves and admires her father, or her image of what her absent father must be. And apparently for good reason. He is courageous, intelligent and sensitive, a man of high ideals, a man of vision committed to his own search, a man who in many cases never found his place in the patriarchy. His vision of the perfect woman quite naturally took him into marriage with a woman who loved his vision, usually a 'father's daughter' whose dream for herself was cut short by the reality of marriage and family. Thus the *puer* man typically finds his mate in the *puella* woman.[3]

In such a household there is no place for the chaos of unruly children, the 'filth' of the chthonic or earthy feminine, nor the energies of conscious sexuality. Ostensibly, the father may be 'the man around the house', but the wife and mother 'wears the pants'. Full of repressed sexuality and resentment, she deals stoically with a disappointing world and projects her unlived life onto her children.

The father, meanwhile, blessed with the comforting presence of his wife-mother, is then free to project his own unfulfilled feeling values – his young anima – onto his little girl. Together they build a Garden of Eden. The child is trapped in spiritual incest, even more dangerous than actual incest because neither he nor she has any reason to suspect that something is amiss. Called to be 'Daddy's little princess', the daughter is at once his spiritual mother, his beloved, his inspiratrice. With her he will have thoughts and feelings that never come up with anyone else. She instinctively knows how to act as buffer between him and a judgemental world; she instinctively knows how to connect him to his own inner reality. Indeed, this is the only world she really understands – this world where she acts as the connecting link between her father's ego and the collective unconscious. Feeding on his vision of Light, Beauty and Truth, her young psyche can plumb the depths of his anguish or soar to the heights of his dream. That dynamic interplay continues to be her life-source as a creative woman, and without it her life becomes empty.

If her father accepts her inner life, then they genuinely share the eternal world of the creative imagination. Its values become her reality. Quick to recognize the illusions of the temporal world, she sets her sights on what is authentic, often becoming a veritable Cassandra, outcast by both her peer group and her parents' friends. Her security lies in her commitment to *essence* (a commitment, incidentally, which may lead to anorexia because she either forgets to eat or her throat refuses to open to the food of a world of which she is not a part). Such a woman lives on the archetypal edge, where life is exciting, fraught with danger – all or nothing, perfect or impossible. She knows little about bread and butter living and does not suffer fools gladly.

If her father is not mature enough to value her for herself, but consciously or unconsciously, forces her into becoming his star performer, then her trap is a very different one because it involves his rejection of her reality. Unable to recognize her own responses, she simply relinquishes herself to trying to please Daddy.

Daughters of both types of men will be so-called anima women (good hooks for men's unconscious projections), though of a very different tempering. Both will have dreams where they appear, for instance, in well-lit glass solariums, in perfect blue apartments without kitchens, in plastic bags or coffins that threaten to suffocate them. Both will realize there is something between them and the world, something that cuts off their own feeling, a veil that is seldom penetrated. Both will strive to make life into a work of art, and vaguely realize they have not lived. Because of that primal relationship, the father's daughter walks a thin line precariously close to the collective unconscious, unable – like Rainer Maria Rilke, for example – to separate her personal angels and demons from the transpersonal.

And demons are as immediate to her as angels, because she lives so close to her father's shadow. Unless he has worked on himself, as in analysis, and gained some insight into his *puer* psychology, he is probably quite unaware of his ambivalence toward women. His bonding to his own mother may have created a Prince Charming, but a prince who is nevertheless dependent on women's approval. His chthonic shadow hates that dependence and hates the women who make him feel vulnerable. Unless he has worked hard on his own feeling values, he may function on a conscious level as an ascetic scholar, a priest, or even a carefree Don Juan, while his unconscious shadow is a cold, violent killer, intent on destroying any 'witch' who would seduce him into her power. Men who live close to the unconscious quite legitimately need to protect themselves from the seduction of the lamia as the Romantic artists, many of them dead before forty, make painfully clear. The *puer's* shadow, however, may murder not only witches but the femininity of his little daughter as well. On the one hand he may be mothering, nourishing, cherishing, while on the other creating a *femme fatale* whose attitude toward men is kill or be killed.

The *femme fatale* lives in an unconscious body: her femininity is unconscious, her sexuality is unconscious. Often promiscuous, she manipulates 'lovers' to prove her power as a woman, but her love is unrelated to her lust. Thus she may consciously love her father (or her father surrogate) and be committed to her own creativity through that incestuous bonding, and at the same time be lured into violent and dangerous adventures.

Her sexuality and femininity foundered on the reef of her primal relationship to her mother. The *puella* mother who has never taken up residence in her own body, and therefore fears her own chthonic nature, is not going to experience pregnancy as a quiet meditation with her unborn child, nor birth as a joyful bonding experience. Although she may go through the motions of natural childbirth, the psyche/soma split in her is so deep that physical bonding between her and her baby daughter does not take place. Her child lives with a profound sense of despair, a despair which becomes conscious if in later years she does active imagination with her body and releases waves of grief and terror that resonate with the initial, primal rejection.

The body that appears in dreams wrapped in wire, encircled by a black snake or encumbered by a fish tail from the waist down, may be holding a death-wish too deep for tears. The security of the mother's body world is not present for her in the original matrix, nor is there reinforcement for her maturing body as she moves toward puberty, attempting to differentiate her own boundaries from those of her mother and the external world. Unable to establish these fundamental physical demarcations, she often literally does not know where she begins or where she ends in relation to Mater (mother). During her developmental years, when she might otherwise be consolidating a sense of her physical identity, she is instead responding to the unconscious rejection by her mother.

The following is a recurring childhood dream which continued to haunt a fifty-year-old woman until it was worked through in analysis:

> I am four or five years old. I'm with my mother in a crowded building, probably a department store. My mother is wearing dark clothes, a coat and hat in brown or black, and throughout I see only her back. As we leave the building, I am slowed down by the crowd, and my mother, unknowing, moves ahead and disappears among the people. I try to call to her, but she doesn't hear me, nor does anyone else. I'm very frightened, not only at being lost but at my mother's not noticing we've been separated.
>
> I come out of the building onto a long flight of broad steps, rather like those outside the National Gallery in London, but higher. The steps lead down into a large square, empty of any objects, but with similar steps leading to buildings on the other sides. The square, the steps and the buildings are very clean and white. From my vantage point I look around the square, hoping to see my mother. She is nowhere to be seen. I am alone on the steps. There are other people in the square, but they are unaware of me. I know nothing I do will make them notice me.
>
> I am panic-stricken and overwhelmed with a sense of loss, of having been abandoned. It's as though I've ceased to exist for my mother, that she won't bother to come back for me, may even have forgotten about me, that in fact I can't make anyone aware that I exist.
>
> For a moment, and at the same time, I'm an adult observer across the square who sees the small child standing alone at the top of the steps, trying to call out. This is also I, a grown woman who feels enormous pity for this child,

longs to comfort and reassure her, but is unable to reach her. Something – the unconsciousness of the other people or the child's own panic – prevents communication between the child and the adult who cares and understands.

The woman associated this dream with Edvard Munch's painting *The Scream*, which evoked in her a similar panic. 'The background is dark and murky,' she said, 'while in my dream the environment is very clear, white and hard-edged, dotted with dark, ill-defined but equally hard-edged figures. The screamer is trying to escape from his environment; the child on the steps is trying to connect with hers.' Many men and women are trapped in lives of quiet desperation until they turn to help that child within.

The body's memory, stored in muscle and bone, fuses the desire to connect and the desire to escape so they are simultaneously present in an undifferentiated form. The result – an identity of opposites – manifests as despair: nothing can be done and everything must be endured.

The above dream, with its 'very clean and white' panorama of steps and square surrounded by buildings, while the dreamer is effectively alone and unable to 'make anyone aware that I exist', is a characteristic dream of an anorexic. (This woman was not anorexic, but her adolescent son suffered from a severe eating disorder.) It shows her inability to connect with the strangers in her own psyche. They are present but they cannot communicate. It is as if Mater is concretized outside the body because it cannot be incorporated: the baby could not assimilate milk and physical intimacy from a mother who 'won't bother to come back' and 'may even have forgotten' her.

Psychic intimacy and physical intimacy go together naturally, but, where they have been split apart at a pre-verbal level, the instinct is isolated. The emotional food that should be incorporated with the physical food is not present; thus the instinctual pole of what Jung called 'a psychoid process' receives a different message from the psychic pole.[4] Without the experience of the instincts, neither the feminine soul nor the masculine spirit is embodied; consequently in later life emotional intimacy, including love-making, may be undermined by a sense of betrayal. The body is not present. *She* is not there.

The woman who is whole resonates both physically and psychically. The soul, that is, is incarnate. Women who are robbed of that feminine birthright may have to experience physical acceptance by another woman, whether in dreams, in close friendship or in a lesbian relationship, before they can find security within themselves. (In rare cases, this can happen in relationship with a man, depending on the maturity of his anima.)

The distortion in the body/psyche relationship is compounded by the symbiotic relationship between father and daughter. There is a primal confusion between the spiritual and instinctual depths because the love she received from her father is the very energy which sustains her life. With such confusion between spirit and matter, she may experience her body as a prison to be lugged around while her spirit hovers somewhere above her head, at any moment ready to leap into 'the white radiance of eternity'.[5]

Her body becomes a prison because the symbiotic matrix – here more accurately termed the patrix – is the parent of the opposite sex. From her mother she has learned rejection of her body; from her father she has learned emotional withholding, for although she knows she is his beloved, and knows her mother is no real rival, she also senses there is a line she dare not cross. In her adult years, the gender confusion may manifest in the compulsion (or at least the preference) to be held by a man not as a lover but as a mother. She needs a 'cuddle bunny' because her sexuality is not sufficiently embodied to respond to mature masculine penetration.[6]

Such a woman's terror of abandonment, then, lies not only in the loss of a meaningful relationship, but also in the loss of the physical contact that grounds her in her body. Locked in her musculature, her feminine feelings are not available to her; thus, if she is threatened with abandonment, she may become virtually catatonic with unexpressed terror, and subject to strange physical symptoms. She is losing herself, physically and spiritually. Abandonment becomes annihilation because her body with its welter of undifferentiated feeling cannot provide the *temenos*, the safe place, to protect her ego. Nor can the collective world offer support. Her preoccupation with the world of the imagination makes her view the mundane world with scorn and fear. It is a cruel, illusory world in which unreal people clutter their lives with superfluous objects, and clutter is unendurable when the inner world is dismembered.

A woman whose survival is thus tied to the masculine spirit has unconsciously sacrificed her femininity to what she believes is the best in life. In relationship to a man she appears at first to relate superbly because she can so adroitly become what he is projecting onto her. She in turn loves what she projects onto him. Their relationship assumes suprahuman dimensions: loving father, loving mother, hardly less than god and goddess. When father/god fails to live up to the projection, or decides to reject it, he deals the 'imperial thunderbolt' that scalps her 'naked soul'.[7]

Cut off outwardly from her environment, cut off inwardly from her positive masculine guide, the woman identifies with the dark side of the father archetype – the demon lover. There is no one to mediate between her terrorized ego and the chaos through which it is falling. The abyss is bottomless. Her masculine solar consciousness asks questions for which there are no answers; her feminine lunar consciousness is not sufficiently mature to accept apparent meaninglessness.

She has done everything to make herself acceptable and she has failed; she is 'unlovable' and that verdict resonates right back to the primary abandonment. Life becomes a prison where the password is 'renunciation'; the animus-magician becomes the trickster with whom she has colluded in relinquishing herself. Describing this feeling of loss of soul, Emily Dickinson writes:

> And yet – Existence – some way back –
> Stopped – struck – my ticking – through – [8]

Suicide in that situation may become a fulfillment of her destiny. In Sylvia Plath's last 'Words':

> Years later I
> Encountered them on the road –
>
> Words dry and riderless,
> The indefatigable hoof-taps,
> While
> From the bottom of the pool, fixed stars
> Govern a life.[9]

Suicide is a final stroke of vengeance against the savage god who has abandoned her. Paradoxically, it is affirming what he has done to her ego: God has taken her out of life, so killing herself is affirming him. Suicide is a *Liebestod*, a death marriage in which she embraces the dark side of God – a negative mystical union. Psychologically, it is marriage to the demon lover. The relationship of the woman to the demon is sadomasochistic, and her battle with him fascinates because it has within it the elements of violent eroticism. As Shakespeare's Cleopatra says when she puts the asp to her breast:

> The stroke of death is as a lover's pinch,
> Which hurts, and is desir'd.[10]

Inherent in such a vision, however, is a sense of total defeat. One battles against a power which is inexorable. The father animus demands order, justice, meaning. However, the crucial events in her life – the loss of a lover, loss of a child or childlessness, the inability to create – may defy human comprehension. Without a compensating feminine consciousness, which would accept the deeper mysteries of Fate, life becomes a losing battle against meaningless suffering. The demon lover lures the woman into blind, egotistical pride that rejects the creative possibilities inherent in inner tension. Outwardly, she may perform as usual, but in the subterranean depths she knows the battle is being lost and yearns for release from despair. It is the last collision of the opposites – the desire to be a part of life, the desire to escape. The heart breaks, overwhelmed by rage against the inevitability of loss.

Suicide is the ultimate abandonment, and while few women have a conscious propensity for suicide, many are dealing with abysmal despair which may manifest unconsciously in a fatal accident or a terminal illness. They repeatedly go through the anguish of losing men onto whom they have projected their savior;

they fail to recognize that the passionate interaction of their relationships is based on narcissistic need; they will not sacrifice the complex and accept the 'boredom' of being human. They are forsaking their own souls and their own creativity – personified as the neglected little girls and boys who repeatedly appear in their dreams. Essentially, they are afraid to take responsibility for their own lives. If the object of loss is introjected and sealed off, it becomes, in Emily Dickinson's words:

> The Horror not to be surveyed –
> But skirted in the Dark –
> With Consciousness suspended –
> And Being under Lock –[11]

If, on the other hand, loneliness leads to insight and illumination, the ego may establish a creative relationship with the inner world and release its own destiny.

Martha, the middle-aged woman whose recurring childhood dream was quoted earlier, is a tall, stately woman with a studied air of confidence. Born into a professional family, she did all that was expected of her at university, married her high school sweetheart, had her family, divorced, and then held a careful balance between work, children and men for some twenty years. She would go out with men but nothing would last. She came into analysis to find out why the pattern of loss kept repeating itself.

Some time later she fell in love with a highly respected leader in her community; he fell in love with her, and soon marriage seemed inevitable. After one year things began to go wrong; after two years he left her. At that time, now in the habit of paying close attention to emotional events, Martha carefully articulated her feelings:

> I don't know where I've been. I am numb. I projected everything I ever wanted in a man onto him. And he left me for another – for an ordinary woman. All I want to be is ordinary. But I don't know how to be ordinary. I am a stranger to others, to myself.
>
> I think back to my childhood, to that terrible sense of abandonment. I was never at the center, the living center of anyone's life. That's all I want – to share my life in its deepest essentials with another. My parents didn't share their deepest core with me. My husband said he loved me, but the most important things of life he did not share. And he went off with a woman who could share the ordinary world with him. I don't know how to do that.
>
> I know what the man is projecting onto me. I become what he wants me to be, and at the time it feels natural and real to me. I feel totally alive. And then something goes dead in the relationship, usually in the sexuality. I feel he is manipulating, using power, forcing me to be what he wants me to be. He is making love to his image of me, not to me. I too am projecting. It is not he who

is making love to me. Everything swings into unreality. I hate myself for enduring it. I hate him for forcing me. It is intolerable. I go unconscious. Nothing has happened between us. We are both disappointed, resentful, confounded by the seeming intimacy which wasn't intimacy at all.

I know this lack of intimacy exists between me and my children. They too have developed magnificent personas – lively, efficient, able to cope with anything. Underneath there is grief; it comes out in their poems, their songs. That essential part of themselves they do not share with me. I feel there is a veil around me. When I write, when I am alone, the tragic side of myself surfaces, but I cannot share that with others.

I know in this situation I could go into my act. I could fly into activity, busy myself with any number of creative things, but that would be choosing the persona again. I won't do that. It's not quite as it was in the past. I'm not incapacitated. I'm not being swung helplessly around. I know something terrible has happened to me, but there is a quiet place at the center.

It's the ordinary things that hurt so much, the little human acts we shared together. I stumble along in my numbness. I see the plum blossoms and I'm overcome with slivers of pain. At least the pain is alive. At least I know I am somewhere feeling the reality of what I am going through. Behind the numbness is blind terror. It is the terror of the child within me – the child who knew everything was going wrong, that she was unacceptable, and frantically attempted to try to figure out what to do in order to be loved. It's the terrible aloneness of standing at the top of the stairs crying and no one pays any attention, of knowing that who I am is impossible to those around me. It is standing bereft, hearing mocking laughter in the empty corridor behind me, trying to contort myself into someone who could be loved. I have rejected that child, as everyone has rejected her. She's still standing there crying, 'What do you want me to be? I don't understand. I don't understand. I'll do anything you want, but don't reject me.'

Well, this time I won't build up my false persona. It can't relate because it can't feel. I know I have to stay with the feeling. I have to experience my vulnerability. I have to allow others to know how vulnerable I am. This is the loss of everything I ever wanted in a man. I am ashamed to be so naive. I respected and loved everything he was. He is gone. I am not young. I may never have such a relationship again. I do not trust that God has something new for me. I do not hope. Hope in me is an illusion. Honest despair is better than a fantasy of hope. This is the confrontation: the abandoning of all I hoped for.

Martha, like other women of her type, can be an enigma to men. Functioning without a strong feminine ego, she nevertheless gives an appearance of being, as she says, 'some kind of iron lady who can take anything, and take it alone'. And she *can* go on, but behind it all 'there's a black rock in the heart'.

The man who carries the positive projections of such a woman may feel himself quite unnecessary in the relationship, may even feel his masculine ego and his potency threatened. If he withdraws or leaves her, he may well be astonished to see her collapse. He probably had no idea of her dependence on him, her need for grounding. (As Martha put it, 'He thought my energy was all going into the analysis and I didn't care about the relationship. What does he think analysis is about?') If in addition to withdrawing he takes up with the opposite type of woman (a shadow sister of the first), the situation illustrated in Barbra Streisand's *Yentl* may arise, where the masculine-oriented Yentl projects her femininity onto her rival and sings, 'No wonder he loves her', thus passively surrendering what is crucial to her existence.

The projection of a woman's unconscious femininity onto a shadow sister is a typical trick of the magician animus. When he feels he is losing her to another man, he will do everything he can to destroy the possibility of authentic relationship. Once her shadow energy is projected onto the other woman, her lover's anima may also split: he loves *her* for her strength, her shadow for her sexual vulnerability.

Instead of acknowledging her appropriate rage and jealously, such a woman may retreat into her abandoned child, harangued by her negative animus: 'This is the way it always ends, will always end. When the chips are down, never trust a man. You can stand alone. You always have. You're a better man than he. You're not sweet and feminine like she is. If only you hadn't stood your ground in discussions. If only you'd pretended the issues didn't matter. If only you hadn't tried to make him more conscious. If only you had been more sensitive to his needs. If only . . . if only . . . if only. Never mind. Take it like a man.'

If she were to withdraw her projections, she might be able to look the man straight in the eye, honoring his manhood and her womanhood, and say, 'What the hell is going on here?' Instead, she is helplessly crippled by self-recriminations. She looks at the situation with rational understanding, thus ignoring her true feeling. She does not fly into a 'childish' tantrum. She does not whimper and cry. She knows she's not dead because she's still standing up. She plays the role of 'the perfect gentleman'.[12]

ANALYSING DADDY'S LITTLE PRINCESS

While many women attempt to work out their destiny through their own creative work or their own life experience, others enter analysis when they see a destructive pattern undermining their relationships with men. Sometimes they are shocked by their own *femme fatale*; sometimes they are grieved when the sexual relationship with a husband they love has failed, although it may have been fine *until* they married. Often they are driven into analysis by mysterious body problems which medical science has termed psychosomatic but can do nothing to relieve. Sometimes they are despairing in their separation from life; sometimes they are stricken because their creativity is blocked; sometimes they are terrified of madness.

Working with such a woman is like working with anyone else except that the ambushes are more immediate, precipitous and treacherous because the unconscious is her home and native land. The analyst must take full cognizance of the power of her imagination, her capacity to abandon herself to the archetypal world, and her lack of relationship to her own body.

The analyst, whether man or woman, will become her inspiratrice, her connecting link to the unconscious. If her father was her companion rather than her guide on the inner journey, then the analyst is treated as a partner, a *frater* or *soror*, daring the dangers and sharing the triumphs. Together they explore a world of imagination, rich with imagery and insights. She makes an exciting analysand because she is not afraid to enter the underworld and she regularly brings back to the analyst riches, both personal and transpersonal. She understands Silence, and if the analyst can endure the intensity of her world, every session becomes a happening.

If she is an Ariadne, betrothed to the god before her birth, but sidetracked by her love for the sun-hero Theseus, then, like Ariadne when she was eventually abandoned, she may give herself up to death. She may surrender to deep depression, and, at the nadir of that experience, recognize the light in the darkness. She may in fact find her true destiny: surrender to the god. Not many modern women want to face the nun in themselves, but not a few in analysis are forced to put the archetypal projections where they belong; they must separate personal relationships from archetypal, and work out their own salvation in harmony with the inner god and goddess without the support of a church or the containment of nunnery walls. The woman who knows she has a 'calling', artistically or spiritually, may sometimes question her commitment to her inner marriage, but essentially she *knows* she dare not betray that inner reality.

The woman who has carried the idealized projection of her father all her life, however, may question whether she is called or whether she is trapped in an illusion – an inner marriage that is itself unfruitful, yet forces her to seek the perfect marriage in the outer world. 'Called or uncalled' can be an anguished decision, but if the woman concludes she is not called then she needs to look carefully lest she abandon herself to an illusion of perfect union in the human world, an illusion that repeatedly lures her into inevitable abandonment in her relationships with men. Then she may recognize that her problem lies in falling in love with her own projection and attempting to create herself in an image which is being projected onto her, thus abandoning her own Being. As human intimacy develops, she herself rejects that image and cannot continue the pretense. As she reveals more and more of herself, the man experiences *her* as the betrayer because she had withheld so much of her true nature in order to win him. Unconsciously, her rage toward the man and toward herself (as self-betrayer) unites with his rage, creating the bomb which must inevitably explode.

The two shadow figures will have their revenge. If healing is to take place, she must not act like a gentleman; she must not try to understand why he is abandoning her. She is angry and her rage is killer-rage and killer-jealousy that needs an acceptable channel. The pent-up fury of a lifetime has to be released from the body to make room for the healing love. That personal rage has to be acknowledged and experienced before the transpersonal understanding and compassion can flow in.

Somewhere in that anguish and anger, the woman will realize that she has *not* been abandoned by the man she loves. The man she loves does not exist in human form. He never did. She has been projecting an inner image of her own. Her mirror has shattered, and now she can either die or accept reality. And the reality is that she does not grieve for that actual man. She grieves both for her perfect lover and for the beautiful woman she was when she was in love. Taken to her naked truth, she grieves for her own child, the child she herself abandoned when she first set out to please Daddy.

That child in all its childish and childlike faith, hope and love is the one that cries out in its aloneness. In spite of its vulnerability, it has to trust life if the woman is ever to bring her essence to maturity.

The original abandonment by her mother and the creative relationship with her father may make her feel that women are a waste of time. She may know, however, that she does not want to go through 'the hassle' of falling in love with a male analyst, and therefore choose to work with a woman. In the transference the analyst then carries the projection of the loving mother the woman never had. Together they nurture and discipline the abandoned child, giving it a safe place to play and cherishing it into maturity. It is that child who has suffered outside the limits of society, yet is still holding to its own innate wisdom, refusing to die. Its vulnerability and strength, born of its aloneness, give it the detachment necessary to the artist and the clown. In my experience, that detachment, simultaneously personal and transpersonal, is the only energy strong enough to depotentiate the trickster.

[. . .]

NOTES

1. John Keats, letter to George and Georgiana Keats (April 21, 1819), quoted in David Perkins, ed., *English Romantic Writers* (New York: Harcourt Brace Jovanovich, 1967), p. 1225.
2. *The Complete Poems of Emily Dickinson*, ed. Thomas H. Johnson (Boston: Little, Brown and Company, 1960), number 508, p. 247.
3. The term *puer aeternus* (Latin, 'eternal youth') refers to the type of man who remains too long in adolescent psychology, generally associated with a strong unconscious attachment to the mother (actual or symbolic). His female counterpart is the *puella aeterna*, an 'eternal girl' with a corresponding attachment to the father world.

4. Jung, 'On the Nature of the Psyche', in *The Structure and Dynamics of the Psyche*, CW [*Collected Works*] 8, pars 367, 417. See also Marion Woodman, *The Owl Was a Baker's Daughter: Obesity, Anorexia Nervosa and the Repressed Feminine* (Toronto: Inner City Books, 1980), pp. 66–7.

5. Percy Bysshe Shelley, 'Adonais', line 463.

6. As this was being written (March 1985), the popular columnist Ann Landers revealed the massive response to the question she asked her female readers: 'Which would you prefer: to be simply held tenderly, or perform "the act"?' She received more than 90,000 answers; 72 per cent preferred to be held – and 70 per cent of these were women under 40.

7. Emily Dickinson, number 315, p. 148.

8. Ibid., number 443, p. 212.

9. Sylvia Plath, *Ariel* (London: Faber and Faber, 1965), p. 86.

10. Shakespeare, *Antony and Cleopatra*, Act 5, Scene 2, lines 297–8.

11. Emily Dickinson, number 777, p. 379.

12. I am indebted to Dr Anne Maguire, Jungian analyst in London, England, for this phrase that so aptly encapsulates the psychology of this type of woman.

Suggested Further Reading

The best introduction to Jung's work on 'the feminine' is to be found in the selection *Aspects of the Feminine* in which 'Anima and Animus' is also collected. See, in particular, 'Marriage as a Psychological Relationship' and 'Woman in Europe'.

For a feminist engagement with Jung's ideas – and one that is persuaded that Jung and feminism can be reconciled and generative – see D. S. Wehr, *Jung and Feminism: Liberating Archetypes* (1988).

The following glossary of Jungian terms will also be of assistance: *A Critical Dictionary of Jungian Analysis* edited by A. Samuels, B. Shorter, and F. Plaut (1986).

Further reading of work by Marie-Louise von Franz should include *The Feminine in Fairy Tales* (1972) (from which the extract here is taken) and *The Golden Ass of Apuleius: the Liberation of the Feminine in Man* (1992).

Marion Woodman's works are illustrative of the 'next generation' of Jungian women theorists to follow Harding and von Franz. A contemporary Jungian analyst, Woodman concentrates on the 'divine feminine' as a neglected or repressed force in Western institutions; *Dancing in the Flames: The Dark Goddess in the Transformation of Consciousness* (1996), co-written with clinical psychologist Elinor Dickson, exemplifies her approach.

Part 4: Lacan and New French Feminisms

Accounts of, or introductions to, the work of Jacques Lacan frequently acknowledge the difficulty and inaccessibility of his writings. David Lodge, in his editorial preface to Lacan's 'The insistence of the letter in the unconscious', provides a reassuring example of this for anyone who finds themselves struggling with Lacan's work:

> Lacan was a notoriously, wilfully difficult writer, and the present editor certainly does not claim fully to understand everything in this essay . . . designed to mystify and intimidate rather than to shed light.[1]

Rather than feeling intimidated, or mocked for their earnest efforts, the reader of Lacan's work should be encouraged to see that the endeavour 'to understand everything' is precisely what Lacan aims to subvert. In his terms, this is, anyway, an impossibility. We would do better as readers if we were to see that Lacan's practice, rather than being obfuscating and bogus, is true to his own theoretical premises. This is not the same as suggesting that Lacan has 'nothing to say' and that we should abandon the endeavour of reading him, but rather to acknowledge that Lacan has no-*one*-thing to say and that our reading practice must be adjusted accordingly. Juliet Mitchell, in her introduction to *Feminine Sexuality: Jacques Lacan and the École Freudienne*, provides a useful explanation of the validity of Lacan's difficult style:

> The preposterous difficulty of Lacan's style is a challenge to easy comprehension, to the popularization and secularization of psychoanalysis . . . Psychoanalysis should aim to show us that we do not know those things we think we do; it therefore cannot assault our popular conceptions by using the very idiom it is intended to confront; a challenge to ideology cannot rest on a linguistic appeal to that same ideology. The dominant ideology of today, as it was of the time and place when psychoanalysis was established, is humanism. Humanism believes that man is at the centre of his own history and of himself; he is a subject more or less in control of his own actions, exercising choice. Humanistic psychoanalytic practice is in danger of seeing the patient

as someone who has lost control and a sense of a real or true self (identity) and it aims to help regain these. The matter and manner of all Lacan's work challenges this notion of the human subject: there is none such. In the sentence structure of most of his public addresses and of his written style the grammatical subject is either absent or shifting or, at most, only passively constructed. At this level, the difficulty of Lacan's style could be said to mirror his theory.[2]

Lacan's return to, and re-reading of, Freud has contributed to a renewed discussion of the primacy of male paradigms. Whereas Freud saw the biological penis, its presence, absence (as in clitoral 'inferiority') and threatened loss, as the determining factor in any human subject's ontology, Lacan's emphasis was to be on the phallus as a signifier. As he explains in 'The Meaning of the Phallus', included here, he borrows and extends aspects of 'modern linguistic analysis', seeing this approach as 'necessary to any articulation of analytic phenomena'. In particular, the phallus will be important as the 'notion of the signifier, in the sense which is opposed to that of the signified in modern linguistic analysis'. Hence: '. . . the relation of the subject to the phallus is set up regardless of the anatomical difference between the sexes'. Lacan's move is from the penis, and female 'envy', to a transcendental signifying phallus which, it is claimed, holds both sexes in thrall.

Perhaps the fundamental premise, outlined in Lacan's essay here, and necessary to any understanding of Lacan's work generally, is the theory which rejects the notion of a human subject's autonomy and proficiency with language, since the subject's merest *intention* to speak is not free from 'the structure of language'. The subject does not speak, however, until loss, division, and specular misrecognition are experienced. Only then can 'he' speak of the (m)Other and the self. The lacking subject uses language in a fictional filling-in, but the very words he or she uses/is used by are in themselves not stable or 'full'. Not only does the signified slip from the signifier, so that meaning itself is subsumed by a system of signifiers, but a linguistic sign can only *be* by virtue of that which it is not. A sign, in all its own arbitrariness, is always referring to another – and another – and another – along a signifying chain, in a constant deferral of meaning. Jacques Derrida's concept of *différance* in language may help clarify this concept in terms of signifiers and subject – and may also illuminate the selection of excerpts which follows:

> . . . [it] is a structure and a movement no longer conceivable on the basis of the opposition presence/absence. *Différance* is the systematic play of differences, of the traces of differences, of the *spacing* by means of which elements are related to each other. The spacing is the simultaneously active and passive . . . production of the intervals without which the 'full' terms would not signify, would not function. It is also the becoming-space of the spoken chain . . . . It confirms that the subject . . . the conscious and speaking subject, depends upon

the system of differences and the movement of *différance*, that the subject is constituted only in being divided from itself, in becoming space, in temporizing, in deferral . . . .[3]

This is why Lacan is at pains to point out the gap between the signifier, the phallus and the penis[4] and to suggest further, not just that the penis is inadequate, but that the signifying phallus is, too. Subjects require the (fictive) notion of a stable, fully-present 'I' in the same way that language fallaciously presumes an originary, meaning-full signifier. Absolute categories of sexual difference are similarly posited and constructed: plenitude, stability, absolute difference – these are the fictions and fetishes which arise, says Lacan, out of the Oedipal awareness of castration and all its effects.

Hélène Cixous's 1981 essay which follows, 'Castration or Decapitation?', makes specific reference to the double-focus on psychoanalysis and speaking subjects. The piece is an interesting amalgam which includes references to myths and tales; familial structures and sociological reproductions; economics (including libidinal economies); female sexual pleasure; textual practice; linguistic systems (after Lacan); and the classic psychoanalytic premises of the unconscious, repression and the castration complex. Although echoes of Lacanian thought are to be found throughout the essay, Cixous moves her own analysis to a more thoroughgoing exploration of the woman's relation to the phallus and her place within the symbolic order. The effects of the intransigent dualism, or binary oppositionalism, of western metaphysics are elaborated and challenged by Cixous throughout her work, but particularly notable is the widely anthologized 'Sorties: Out and Out: Attacks/Ways Out/ Forays', from *The Newly Born Woman*. Cixous is at pains to deconstruct this binary insistence, although she is also dedicated to the celebration of those differences that make (most/many) woman not-'masculine'. It is here that she comes into full flow and valorizes the female libidinal economy (sexual and textual in particular) which *risks*, which 'lets the body talk' (although this is often taken for silence by 'man'), and which retrieves and passes on that which is 'cut out' by the syntactical, orderly, originary and teleological 'symbolic'. This 'outpouring', this 'excess' (all familiar terms used in the derision of women, but here terms of pride) includes 'the voice of the mother . . . what is most archaic'.

Although there is an apparent essentialism in Cixous's work, particularly in her exhortation to 'write the body' and *parler femme,* in a project often referred to as *l'écriture féminine*, she explains that 'masculine writing' can be written and signed by a woman and that, conversely, a man may write a 'feminine text': 'it's rare, but you can sometimes find femininity in writings signed by men . . .' . For the most part, however, the task outlined here is sex/gender specific, and is a very particular address to the silenced, the excluded, the Othered: 'the lack of Lack' – to 'woman'. A sister essay to 'Castration or Decapitation?', 'The Laugh of the Medusa' (1976), also exhorts women to valorize the hysteric, to memorialize loss in excess, to be the 'madwomen' history has named them – and with a vengeance: hence such language as 'sorties', 'attacks', 'forays'.

The extract from Julia Kristeva's 1974 text, *About Chinese Women*,[5] warns against the denial of one extreme, 'an ostensibly masculine, paternal identification', for the sake of another: 'a smug polymorphism where it is so easy and comfortable for a woman to remain'. She aims to show the ways in which western monotheism requires 'a cleavage or abyss' between the two sexes. The pre-Oedipal, and particularly, the pre-linguistic semiotic (a realm of equal participation for male and female children) becomes marginalized and repressed by the monotheistic symbolic order, and it is this which genders the two realms, Kristeva suggests, rather than there being anything inherently 'female' about the semiotic or inherently 'male' about the symbolic. However, *jouissance* (which can be translated only approximately as 'orgasmic bliss' and particularly the woman's – even more so, the mother's) goes beyond the phallic libidinal economy and the symbolic authority that patriarchal authority exploits so exclusively. *Jouissance* is vertiginous and liminal in its access to the pre-Oedipal and pre-linguistic, and it can be subversive – or – suicidal.

Luce Irigaray's punningly entitled, 'This Sex Which Is Not One' plays with two notions of 'woman' and her sex: on the one hand is the claim that woman has no legitimate sex and is, therefore, not one (an absence to male presence), and, on the other, that her sex is not one – but two, and more. Here, she implicitly expands on the notion of female *jouissance* in a discussion of the plurality and diffuseness of female sexuality: 'woman has sex organs more or less everywhere'. Irigaray further discusses woman's alienation from her own body, from her own desire, so that she is left unable to give expression to these. Indeed, she is unable to know what she really wants: 'she does not know, or no longer knows, what she wants . . . woman's desire has doubtless been submerged by the logic that has dominated the West since the time of the Greeks'.

Each of these theorists accepts that a symbolic order necessarily follows the pre-linguistic and pre-Oedipal imaginary. The logic and 'grammar' of the symbolic have been dominated by, and have privileged, monotheism, patriarchy, capitalism, the specular, and the visual display of possessions (wealth, property, penis) which have positioned its female subjects (also possessions) outside its 'order'. Disorder, which is seen as pertaining to the pre-symbolic imaginary (pulsional, fluctuating, polymorphous) and to the unconscious, thus becomes (too) firmly aligned with 'femaleness' – and further aligns women with perpetual infancy.

At times, the celebration of woman's difference, in some of the essays collected here, may seem to do little to dislodge the old stereotypes or to move her from her babbling marginality. The expression of this female polysomatic fluency has a tendency to culminate in an ef/fluency for which women have always been disdained. A battle between the sexes fought along these lines may, some would claim, lead only to further ghettoization of the female. On the other hand, the analyses and the exhortations continue to strike a chord with many women:

> By writing her self, woman will return to the body which has been more than confiscated from her, which has been turned into the uncanny stranger on display . . . which so often turns out to be the nasty companion, the cause and location of inhibitions. Censor the body and you censor breath and speech at the same time . . . . To write. An act which will not only 'realize' the decensored relation of woman to her sexuality, to her womanly being, giving her access to her native strength; it will give her back her goods, her pleasures, her organs . . . it will tear her away from the superegoized structure in which she has always occupied the place reserved for the guilty (guilty of everything . . . for having desires, for not having any. . .) . . . A woman without a body, dumb, blind, can't possibly be a good fighter.[6]

The woman who writes, fights – and recovers her-self. A problem, however, seems to remain in that her weapons and tools *must* be in a tongue that is 'foreign', and her strategies thoroughly informed by the logic of her oppressors. Writing, as she does, to be understood, can she really be said to have torn herself away from 'the superegoized structure' that condemns her – and would this ever be possible? Where can a woman's authenticity begin to be found and how would it be articulated? These remain persistent and unresolved questions.

NOTES

1. David Lodge (ed.), *Modern Criticism and Theory: A Reader* (London and New York: Longman, 1988), p. 79.
2. Juliet Mitchell, 'Introduction I', *Feminine Sexuality: Jacques Lacan and the École Freudienne* (London: Macmillan, 1985), p. 4.
3. Jacques Derrida, 'Semiology and Grammatology: Interview with Julia Kristeva' in Alan Bass (trans. and ed.), *Positions* (London: Athlone Press, 1981), pp. 27, 29.
4. Elizabeth Grosz, however, as noted in the Introduction here, counters Lacan's insistence that the phallus can be divorced from the penis; see also her *Jacques Lacan: A Feminist Introduction* (London: Routledge, 1990), pp. 122–3.
5. Within its wider remit, Gayatri Chakravorty Spivak's essay, 'French Feminism in an International Frame', *In Other Worlds* (New York and London: Routledge, 1987), contains a direct response to Kristeva's 'About Chinese Women' and should certainly be read in conjunction with it.
6. Hélène Cixous, 'The Laugh of the Medusa', *Signs*, Summer, 1976, collected in Elaine Marks and Isabelle de Courtivron (eds), *New French Feminisms: An Anthology* (Brighton: Harvester, 1981), p. 250.

15

The Meaning of the Phallus

Jacques Lacan

We know that the unconscious castration complex has the function of a knot:

(1) in the dynamic structuring of symptoms in the analytic sense of the term, meaning that which can be analysed in neuroses, perversions and psychoses;

(2) as the regulator of development giving its *ratio* to this first role: that is, by installing in the subject an unconscious position without which he would be unable to identify with the ideal type of his sex, or to respond without grave risk to the needs of his partner in the sexual relation, or even to receive adequately the needs of the child thus procreated.

What we are dealing with is an antinomy internal to the assumption by man (*Mensch*) of his sex: why must he take up its attributes only by means of a threat, or even in the guise of a privation? As we know, in *Civilisation and its Discontents*, Freud went so far as to suggest not a contingent, but an essential disturbance of human sexuality, and one of his last articles turns on the irreducibility for any finite (*endliche*) analysis of the effects following from the castration complex in the masculine unconscious and from *penisneid* [penis envy] in the unconscious of the woman.

This is not the only point of uncertainty, but it is the first that the Freudian experience and its resulting metapsychology introduced into our experience of man. It cannot be solved by any reduction to biological factors, as the mere necessity of the myth underlying the structuring of the Oedipus complex makes sufficiently clear.

Any recourse to an hereditary amnesic given would in this instance be mere artifice, not only because such a factor is in itself disputable, but because it leaves the problem untouched, namely, the link between the murder of the father and the pact of the primordial law, given that it is included in that law that castration should be the punishment for incest.

Only on the basis of the clinical facts can there be any fruitful discussion. These facts go to show that the relation of the subject to the phallus is set up regardless of the anatomical difference between the sexes, which is what makes its interpretation particularly intractable in the case of the woman and in relationship to her, specifically on the four following counts:

(1) as to why the little girl herself considers, if only for a moment, that she is castrated, in the sense of being deprived of the phallus, at the hand of someone who is in the first instance her mother, an important point, and who then becomes her father, but in such a way that we must recognize in this transition a transference in the analytic sense of the term;

(2) as to why, at a more primordial level, the mother is for both sexes considered as provided with a phallus, that is, as a phallic mother;

(3) as to why, correlatively, the meaning of castration only acquires its full (clinically manifest) weight as regards symptom formation when it is discovered as castration of the mother;

(4) these three problems culminate in the question of the reason for the phallic phase in development. We know that Freud used this term to specify the earliest genital maturation – as on the one hand characterized by the imaginary predominance of the phallic attribute and masturbatory pleasure, and on the other by a localizing of this pleasure for the women in the clitoris, which is thereby raised to the function of the phallus. This would seem to rule out for both sexes, until the end of this phase, that is, until the dissolution of the Oedipus complex, any instinctual awareness of the vagina as the place of genital penetration.

This ignorance smacks of mis-recognition [*méconnaissance*] in the technical sense of the term, especially as it is on occasions disproved. All it agrees with, surely, is Longus's fable in which he depicts the initiation of Daphnis and Chloë as dependent on the revelations of an old woman.

It is for this reason that certain authors have been led to regard the phallic phase as an effect of repression, and the function assumed in it by the phallic object as a symptom. The difficulty starts when we need to know *which* symptom? Phobia, according to one, perversion according to another – or, indeed, to the same one. In this last case, it's not worth speculating: not that interesting transmutations of the object from phobia into fetish do not occur, but their interest resides precisely in the different place which they occupy in the structure. There would be no point in asking these authors to formulate this difference from the perspective of object relations which is currently in favour. This being for lack of any reference on the matter other than the loose notion of the part object, uncriticized since Karl Abraham first introduced it, which is more the pity in view of the easy option which it provides today.

The fact remains that, if one goes back to the surviving texts of the years 1928–32, the now abandoned debate on the phallic phase is a refreshing example of a passion for doctrine, which has been given an additional note of nostalgia by the degradation of psychoanalysis consequent on its American transplantation.

A mere summary of the debate could only distort the genuine diversity of the positions taken by figures such as Helene Deutsch, Karen Horney and Ernest Jones, to mention only the most eminent.

The series of three articles which Jones devoted to the subject is especially suggestive: if only for the starting premise on which he constructs his argument, signalled by the term *aphanisis*, which he himself coined. For by correctly posing the problem of the relationship between castration and desire, he reveals such a proximity to what he cannot quite grasp that the term which will later provide us with the key to the problem seems to emerge out of his very failure.

The amusing thing is the way he manages, on the authority of the very letter of Freud's text, to formulate a position which is directly opposed to it: a true model in a difficult genre.

The problem, however, refuses to go away, seeming to subvert Jones's own case for a re-establishment of the equality of natural rights (which surely gets the better of him in the Biblical 'Man and woman God created them' with which he concludes). What does he actually gain by normalizing the function of the phallus as part object if he has to invoke its presence in the mother's body as internal object, a term which is a function of the fantasies uncovered by Melanie Klein, and if he cannot therefore separate himself from her doctrine which sees these fantasies as a recurrence of the Oedipal formation which is located right back in earliest infancy.

We will not go far wrong if we re-open the question by asking what could have imposed on Freud the obvious paradox of his position. For one has to allow that he was better guided than anyone else in his recognition of the order of unconscious phenomena, which order he had discovered, and that for want of an adequate articulation of the nature of these phenomena his followers were bound to go more or less astray.

It is on the basis of such a wager – laid down by me as the principle of a commentary of Freud's work which I have been pursuing for seven years – that I have been led to certain conclusions: above all, to argue, as necessary to any articulation of analytic phenomena, for the notion of the signifier, in the sense in which it is opposed to that of the signified in modern linguistic analysis. The latter, born since Freud, could not be taken into account by him, but it is my contention that Freud's discovery stands out precisely for having had to anticipate its formulas, even while setting out from a domain in which one could hardly expect to recognize its sway. Conversely, it is Freud's discovery that gives to the opposition of signifier to signified the full weight which it should imply: namely, that the signifier has an active function in determining the effects in which the signifiable appears as submitting to its mark, becoming through that passion the signified.

This passion of the signifier then becomes a new dimension of the human condition, in that it is not only man who speaks, but in man and through man that it [*ça*] speaks, that his nature is woven by effects in which we can find the structure of language, whose material he becomes, and that consequently there resounds in him, beyond anything ever conceived of by the psychology of ideas, the relation of speech.

It is in this sense that one can say that the consequences of the discovery of the unconscious have not been so much as glimpsed in the theory, although its repercussions have been felt in the praxis to a much greater extent than we are as yet aware of, even if only translated into effects of retreat.

Let me make clear that to argue for man's relation to the signifier as such has nothing to do with a 'culturalist' position in the ordinary sense of the term, such as that which Karen Horney found herself anticipating in the dispute over the phallus and which Freud himself characterized as feminist. The issue is not man's relation to language as a social phenomenon, since the question does not even arise of anything resembling that all too familiar ideological psychogenesis, not superseded by a peremptory recourse to the entirely metaphysical notion, underlying the mandatory appeal to the concrete, which is so pathetically conveyed by the term 'affect'.

It is a question of rediscovering in the laws governing that other scene (*eine andere Schauplatz*) which Freud designated, in relation to dreams, as that of the unconscious, the effects discovered at the level of the materially unstable elements which constitute the chain of language: effects determined by the double play of combination and substitution in the signifier, along the two axes of metaphor and metonymy which generate the signified; effects which are determinant in the institution of the subject. What emerges from this attempt is a topology in the mathematical sense of the term, without which, as soon becomes clear, it is impossible even to register the structure of a symptom in the analytic sense of the term.

It speaks in the Other, I say, designating by this Other the very place called upon by a recourse to speech in any relation where it intervenes. If it speaks in the Other, whether or not the subject hears it with his own ears, it is because it is there that the subject, according to a logic prior to any awakening of the signified, finds his signifying place. The discovery of what he articulates in that place, that is, in the unconscious, enables us to grasp the price of the division (*Spaltung*) through which he is thus constituted.

The phallus is elucidated in its function here. In Freudian doctrine, the phallus is not a fantasy, if what is understood by that is an imaginary effect. Nor is it as such an object (part, internal, good, bad, etc . . .) in so far as this term tends to accentuate the reality involved in a relationship. It is even less the organ, penis or clitoris, which it symbolizes. And it is not incidental that Freud took his reference for it from the simulacrum which it represented for the Ancients.

For the phallus is a signifier, a signifier whose function in the intrasubjective economy of analysis might lift the veil from that which it served in the mysteries. For it is to this signified that it is given to designate as a whole the effect of there being a signified, inasmuch as it conditions any such effect by its presence as signifier.

Let us examine, then, the effects of this presence. First they follow from the deviation of man's needs by the fact that he speaks, in the sense that as long as his needs are subjected to demand they return to him alienated. This is not the effect of his real dependency (one should not expect to find here the parasitic conception represented by the notion of dependency in the theory of neuroses) but precisely of the putting into signifying form as such and of the fact that it is from the place of the Other that his message is emitted.

What is thus alienated in needs constitutes an *Urverdrängung* (primal repression) because it cannot, by definition, be articulated in demand. But it reappears in a residue which then presents itself in man as desire (*das Begehren*). The phenomenology which emerges from analytic experience is certainly such as to demonstrate the paradoxical, deviant, erratic, excentric and even scandalous character by which desire is distinguished from need. A fact too strongly attested not to have always won the recognition of moralists worthy of the name. It does seem that early Freudianism had to give this fact its due status. Yet paradoxically psychoanalysis finds itself at the head of an age-old obscurantism, all the more wearisome for its denial of the fact through the ideal of a theoretical and practical reduction of desire to need.

Hence the necessity for us to articulate that status here, starting with demand whose proper characteristics are eluded in the notion of frustration (which was never employed by Freud).

Demand in itself bears on something other than the satisfactions which it calls for. It is demand for a presence or an absence. This is manifest in the primordial relation to the mother, pregnant as it is with that Other to be situated *some way short of* any needs which it might gratify. Demand constitutes this Other as already possessing the 'privilege' of satisfying needs, that is, the power to deprive them of the one thing by which they are satisfied. This privilege of the Other thus sketches out the radical form of the gift of something which it does not have, namely, what is called its love.

Hence it is that demand cancels out (*aufhebt*) the particularity of anything which might be granted by transmuting it into a proof of love, and the very satisfactions of need which it obtains are degraded (*sich erniedrigt*) as being no more than a crushing of the demand for love (all of which is palpable in the psychology of early child-care to which our nurse-analysts are so dedicated).

There is, then, a necessity for the particularity thus abolished to reappear *beyond* demand. Where it does indeed reappear, but preserving the structure harbouring within the unconditional character of the demand for love. In a reversal which is not a simple negation of negation, the force of pure loss arises from the relic of an obliteration. In place of the unconditional aspect of demand, desire substitutes the 'absolute' condition: in effect this condition releases that part of the proof of love which is resistant to the satisfaction of a need. Thus desire is neither the appetite for satisfaction, nor the demand for love, but the difference resulting from the subtraction of the first from the second, the very phenomenon of their splitting (*Spaltung*).

One can see how the sexual relation occupies this closed field of desire in which it will come to play out its fate. For this field is constituted so as to produce the enigma which this relation provokes in the subject, by 'signifying' it to him twice over: as a return of the demand it arouses in the form of a demand made on the subject of need, and as an ambiguity cast onto the Other who is involved, in the proof of love demanded. The gap in this enigma betrays what determines it, conveyed at its simplest in this formula: that for each partner in the relation, the subject and the Other, it is not enough to be the subjects of need, nor objects of love, but they must stand as the cause of desire.

This truth is at the heart of all the mishaps of sexual life which belong in the field of psychoanalysis.

It is also the precondition in analysis for the subject's happiness: and to disguise this gap by relying on the virtue of the 'genital' to resolve it through the maturation of tenderness (that is by a recourse to the Other solely as reality), however piously intended, is none the less a fraud. Admittedly it was French psychoanalysts with their hypocritical notion of genital oblativity who started up the moralizing trend which, to the tune of Salvationist choirs, is now followed everywhere.

In any case man cannot aim at being whole (the 'total personality' being another premise where modern psychotherapy goes off course) once the play of displacement and condensation, to which he is committed in the exercise of his functions, marks his relation as subject to the signifier.

The phallus is the privileged signifier of that mark where the share of the logos is wedded to the advent of desire. One might say that this signifier is chosen as what stands out as most easily seized upon in the real of sexual copulation, and also as the most symbolic in the literal (typographical) sense of the term, since it is the equivalent in that relation of the (logical) copula. One might also say that by virtue of its turgidity, it is the image of the vital flow as it is transmitted in generation.

All these propositions merely veil over the fact that the phallus can only play its role as veiled, that is, as in itself the sign of the latency with which everything signifiable is struck as soon as it is raised (*aufgehoben*) to the function of signifier.

The phallus is the signifier of this *Aufhebung* itself which it inaugurates (initiates) by its own disappearance. This is why the demon of Αἰδώς [*Scham*, shame] in the ancient mysteries rises up exactly at the moment when the phallus is unveiled (cf. the famous painting of the Villa of Pompei).

It then becomes the bar which, at the hands of this demon, strikes the signified, branding it as the bastard offspring of its signifying concatenation.

In this way a condition of complementarity is produced by the signifier in the founding of the subject: which explains his *Spaltung* as well as the intervening movement through which this is effected.

Namely:

(1) that the subject designates his being only by crossing through everything which it signifies, as can be seen in the fact that he wishes to be loved for

himself, a mirage not dispelled merely by being denounced as grammatical (since it abolishes discourse);

(2) that the living part of that being in the *urverdrängt* [primary repressed] finds its signifier by receiving the mark of the *Verdrängung* [repression] of the phallus (whereby the unconscious is language).

The phallus as signifier gives the ratio of desire (in the musical sense of the term as the 'mean and extreme' ratio of harmonic division).

It is, therefore, as an algorithm that I am going to use it now, relying – necessarily if I am to avoid drawing out my account indefinitely – on the echoes of the experience which unites us to give you the sense of this usage.

If the phallus is a signifier then it is in the place of the Other that the subject gains access to it. But in that the signifier is only there veiled and as the ratio of the Other's desire, so it is this desire of the Other as such which the subject has to recognize, meaning, the Other as itself a subject divided by the signifying *Spaltung*.

What can be seen to emerge in psychological genesis confirms this signifying function of the phallus.

Thus, to begin with, we can formulate more correctly the Kleinian fact that the child apprehends from the outset that the mother 'contains' the phallus.

But it is the dialectic of the demand for love and the test of desire which dictates the order of development.

The demand for love can only suffer from a desire whose signifier is alien to it. If the desire of the mother *is* the phallus, then the child wishes to be the phallus so as to satisfy this desire. Thus the division immanent to desire already makes itself felt in the desire of the Other, since it stops the subject from being satisfied with presenting to the Other anything real it might *have* which corresponds to this phallus – what he has being worth no more than what he does not have as far as his demand for love is concerned, which requires that he *be* the phallus.

Clinical practice demonstrates that this test of the desire of the Other is not decisive in the sense that the subject learns from it whether or not he has a real phallus, but inasmuch as he learns that the mother does not. This is the moment of experience without which no symptomatic or structural consequence (that is, phobia or *penisneid*) referring to the castration complex can take effect. It is here that the conjunction is signed between desire, in so far as the phallic signifier is its mark, and the threat or the nostalgia of lack-in-having.

It is, of course, the law introduced into this sequence by the father which will decide its future.

But simply by keeping to the function of the phallus, we can pinpoint the structures which will govern the relations between the sexes.

Let us say that these relations will revolve around a being and a having which, because they refer to a signifier, the phallus, have the contradictory effect of on the one hand lending reality to the subject in that signifier, and on the other making unreal the relations to be signified.

This follows from the intervention of an 'appearing' which gets substituted for the 'having' so as to protect it on one side and to mask its lack on the other, with the effect that the ideal or typical manifestations of behaviour in both sexes, up to and including the act of sexual copulation, are entirely propelled into comedy.

These ideals gain new strength from the demand which it is in their power to satisfy, which is always the demand for love, with its complement of reducing desire to demand.

Paradoxical as this formulation might seem, I would say that it is in order to be the phallus, that is to say, the signifier of the desire of the Other, that the woman will reject an essential part of her femininity, notably all its attributes through masquerade. It is for what she is not that she expects to be desired as well as loved. But she finds the signifier of her own desire in the body of the one to whom she addresses her demand for love. Certainly we should not forget that the organ actually invested with this signifying function takes on the value of a fetish. But for the woman the result is still a convergence onto the same object of an experience of love which as such (cf. above) ideally deprives her of that which it gives, and a desire which finds in that same experience its signifier. Which is why it can be observed that the lack of satisfaction proper to sexual need, in other words, frigidity, is relatively well tolerated in women, whereas the *Verdrängung* inherent to desire is lesser in her case than in the case of the man.

In men, on the other hand, the dialectic of demand and desire gives rise to effects, whose exact point of connection Freud situated with a sureness which we must once again admire, under the rubric of a specific depreciation (*Erniedrigung*) of love.

If it is the case that the man manages to satisfy his demand for love in his relationship to the woman to the extent that the signifier of the phallus constitutes her precisely as giving in love what she does not have – conversely, his own desire for the phallus will throw up its signifier in the form of a persistent divergence towards 'another woman' who can signify this phallus under various guises, whether as a virgin or a prostitute. The result is a centrifugal tendency of the genital drive in the sexual life of the man which makes impotence much harder for him to bear, at the same time as the *Verdrängung* inherent to desire is greater.

We should not, however, think that the type of infidelity which then appears to be constitutive of the masculine function is exclusive to the man. For if one looks more closely, the same redoubling is to be found in the woman, except that in her case, the Other of love as such, that is to say, the Other as deprived of that which he gives, is hard to perceive in the withdrawal whereby it is substituted for the being of the man whose attributes she cherishes.

One might add here that masculine homosexuality, in accordance with the phallic mark which constitutes desire, is constituted on its axis, whereas the orientation of feminine homo-sexuality, as observation shows, follows from a disappointment which reinforces the side of the demand for love. These remarks should be qualified by going back to the function of the mask inasmuch as this function dominates the identifications through which refusals of love are resolved.

The fact that femininity takes refuge in this mask, because of the *Verdrängung* inherent to the phallic mark of desire, has the strange consequence that, in the human being, virile display itself appears as feminine.

Correlatively, one can glimpse the reason for a feature which has never been elucidated and which again gives a measure of the depth of Freud's intuition: namely, why he advances the view that there is only one libido, his text clearly indicating that he conceives of it as masculine in nature. The function of the signifier here touches on its most profound relation: by way of which the Ancients embodied in it both the Νους [*Nous*, sense] and the Λογος [*Logos*, reason].

16

Castration or Decapitation?

Hélène Cixous

On sexual difference: Let's start with these small points. One day Zeus and Hera, the ultimate couple, in the course of one of their intermittent and thoroughgoing disagreements – which today would be of the greatest interest to psychoanalysts – called on Tiresias to arbitrate. Tiresias, the blind seer who had enjoyed the uncommon fortune of having lived seven years as a woman and seven years as a man.

He was gifted with second sight. Second sight in a sense other than we might usually understand it: it isn't simply that as a prophet he could see into the future. He could also see it from both sides: from the side of the male and from the side of the female.

The subject of the disagreement was the question of sexual pleasure: 'Of man and woman, who enjoys the greater pleasure?' Obviously neither Zeus nor Hera could answer this without giving their *own* answer, which they saw would be inadequate, since the ancients made fewer assumptions than we do about the possibility of making such identifications. So it came about that Tiresias was sought, as the only person who could know 'which of the two'. And Tiresias answered: 'If sexual pleasure could be divided up into ten parts, nine of them would be the woman's.' Nine. It's no coincidence that Tiresias makes another appearance in none other than the oedipal scene. It was Tiresias who, at Oedipus's command, reminded Oedipus that blindness was his master, and Tiresias who, so they say, 'made the scales fall from his eyes' and showed Oedipus who he really was. We should note that these things are all linked together and bear some relation to the question 'What is woman for man?'

It reminds me of a little Chinese story. Every detail of this story counts. I've borrowed it from a very serious text, Sun Tse's manual of strategy, which is a kind of handbook for the warrior. This is the anecdote. The king commanded General Sun Tse: 'You who are a great strategist and claim to be able to train anybody in the arts of war . . . take my wives (all one hundred and eighty of them!) and make soldiers out of them.' We don't know why the king conceived this desire – it's the one thing we don't know . . . it remains precisely 'un(re)countable' or unaccountable in the story. But it is a king's wish, after all.

So Sun Tse had the women arranged in two rows, each headed by one of the two favorite wives, and then taught them the language of the drumbeat. It was very simple: two beats – right, three beats – left, four beats – about turn or backward march. But instead of learning the code very quickly, the ladies started laughing and chattering and paying no attention to the lesson, and Sun Tse, the master, repeated the lesson several times over. But the more he spoke, the more the women fell about laughing, upon which Sun Tse put his code to the test. It is said in this code that should women fall about laughing instead of becoming soldiers, their actions might be deemed mutinous, and the code has ordained that cases of mutiny call for the death penalty. So the women were condemned to death. This bothered the king somewhat: a hundred and eighty wives are a lot to lose! He didn't want his wives put to death. But Sun Tse replied that since he was put in charge of making soldiers out of the women, he would carry out the order: Sun Tse was a man of absolute principle. And in any case there's an order even more 'royal' than that of the king himself: the Absolute Law . . . One does not go back on an order. He therefore acted according to the code and with his sabre beheaded the two women commanders. They were replaced and the exercise started again, and as if they had never done anything except practice the art of war, the women turned right, left, and about in silence and with never a single mistake.

It's hard to imagine a more perfect example of a particular relationship between two economies: a masculine economy and a feminine economy, in which the masculine is governed by a rule that keeps time with two beats, three beats, four beats, with pipe and drum, exactly as it should be. An order that works by inculcation, by education: it's always a question of education. An education that consists of trying to make a soldier of the feminine by force, the force history keeps reserved for woman, the 'capital' force that is effectively decapitation. Women have no choice other than to be decapitated, and in any case the moral is that if they don't actually lose their heads by the sword, *they only keep them on condition that they lose them* – lose them, that is, to complete silence, turned into automatons.

It's a question of submitting feminine disorder, its laughter, its inability to take the drumbeats seriously, to the threat of decapitation. If man operates under the threat of castration, if masculinity is culturally ordered by the castration complex, it might be said that the backlash, the return, on women of this castration anxiety is its displacement as decapitation, execution, of woman, as loss of her head.

We are led to pose the woman question to history in quite elementary forms like, 'Where is she? Is there any such thing as woman?' At worst, many women wonder whether they even exist. They feel they don't exist and wonder if there has ever been a place for them. I am speaking of woman's place, *from* women's place, if she takes (a) place.

In *La Jeune Née*[1] I made use of a story that seemed to me particularly expressive of woman's place: the story of Sleeping Beauty. Woman, if you look for her, has a strong chance of always being found in one position: in bed. In bed and asleep – 'laid (out)'. She is always to be found on or in a bed: Sleeping Beauty is lifted from her bed by a man because, as we all know, women don't wake up by themselves: man has to intervene, you understand. She is lifted up by the man who will lay her in her next bed so that she may be confined to bed ever after, just as the fairy tales say.

And so her trajectory is from bed to bed: one bed to another, where she can dream all the more. There are some extraordinary analyses by Kierkegaard on women's 'existence' – or that part of it set aside for her by culture – in which he says he sees her as sleeper. She sleeps, he says, and first love dreams her and then she dreams of love. From dream to dream, and always in second position. In some stories, though, she can be found standing up, but not for long. Take Little Red Riding Hood as an example: it will not, I imagine, be lost on you that the 'red riding hood' in question is a little clitoris. Little Red Riding Hood basically gets up to some mischief: she's the little female sex that tries to play a bit and sets out with her little pot of butter and her little jar of honey. What is interesting is that it's her mother who gives them to her and sends her on an excursion that's tempting precisely because it's forbidden: Little Red Riding Hood leaves one house, mommy's house, not to go out into the big wide world but to go from one house to another by the shortest route possible: to make haste, in other words, from the mother to the other. The other in this case is grandmother, whom we might imagine as taking the place of the 'Great Mother', because there are great men but no great women: there are Grand-Mothers instead. And grandmothers are always wicked: she is the bad mother who always shuts the daughter in whenever the daughter might by chance want to live or take pleasure. So she'll always be carrying her little pot of butter and her little jar of honey to grandmother, who is there as jealousy . . . the jealousy of the woman who can't let her daughter go.

But in spite of all this Little Red Riding Hood makes her little detour, does what women should never do, travels through her own forest. She allows herself the forbidden . . . and pays dearly for it: she goes back to bed, in grandmother's stomach. The Wolf is grandmother, and all women recognize the Big Bad Wolf! We know that always lying in wait for us somewhere in some big bed is a Big Bad Wolf. The Big Bad Wolf represents, with his big teeth, his big eyes, and his grandmother's looks, that great Superego that threatens all the little female red riding hoods who try to go out and explore their forest without the psychoanalyst's permission. So, between two houses, between two beds, she is laid, ever caught in her chain of metaphors, metaphors that organize culture . . . ever her moon to the masculine sun, nature to culture, concavity to masculine convexity, matter to form, immobility/inertia to the march of progress, terrain trod by the masculine footstep, vessel . . . While man is obviously the active, the upright, the productive . . . and besides, that's how it happens in History.

This opposition to woman cuts endlessly across all the oppositions that order culture. It's the classic opposition, dualist and hierarchical. Man/Woman automatically means great/small, superior/inferior . . . means high or low, means

Nature/History, means transformation/inertia. In fact, every theory of culture, every theory of society, the whole conglomeration of symbolic systems – everything, that is, that's spoken, everything that's organized as discourse, art, religion, the family, language, everything that seizes us, everything that acts on us – it is all ordered around hierarchical oppositions that come back to the man/woman opposition, an opposition that can only be sustained by means of a difference posed by cultural discourse as 'natural', the difference between activity and passivity. It always works this way, and the opposition is founded in the *couple*. A couple posed in opposition, in tension, in conflict . . . a couple engaged in a kind of war in which death is always at work – and I keep emphasizing the importance of the opposition as *couple*, because all this isn't just about one word; rather everything turns on the Word: everything is the Word and only the Word. To be aware of the couple, that it's the couple that makes it all work, is also to point to the fact that it's on the couple that we have to work if we are to deconstruct and transform culture. The couple as terrain, as space of cultural struggle, but also as terrain, as space demanding, insisting on, a complete transformation in the relation of one to the other. And so work still has to be done on the couple . . . on the question, for example, of what a completely different couple relationship would be like, what a love that was more than merely a cover for, a veil of, war would be like.

I said it turns on the Word: we must take culture at its word, as it takes us into its Word, into its tongue. You'll understand why I think that no political reflection can dispense with reflection on language, with work on language. For as soon as we exist, we are born into language and language speaks (to) us, dictates its law, a law of death: it lays down its familial model, lays down its conjugal model, and even at the moment of uttering a sentence, admitting a notion of 'being', a question of being, an ontology, we are already seized by a certain kind of masculine desire, the desire that moblizes philosophical discourse. As soon as the question 'What is it?' is posed, from the moment a question is put, as soon as a reply is sought, *we are already caught up in masculine interrogation*. I say 'masculine interrogation': as we say so-and-so was interrogated by the police. And this interrogation precisely involves the work of signification: 'What is it? Where is it?' A work of meaning. 'This means that,' the predicative distribution that always at the same time orders the constitution of meaning. And while meaning is being constituted, it only gets constituted in a movement in which one of the terms of the couple is destroyed in favor of the other.

'Look for the lady,' as they say in the stories . . . 'Cherchez la femme' – we always know that means: you'll find her in bed. Another question that's posed in History, rather a strange question, a typical male question, is: 'What do women want?' The Freudian question, of course. In his work on desire, Freud asks somewhere, or rather doesn't ask, leaves hanging in the air, the question 'What do women want?' Let's talk a bit about this desire and about why/how the question 'What do women want?' gets put, how it's both posed and left hanging in the air by philosophical discourse, by analytic discourse (analytic discourse being only one province of philosophical discourse), and how it is posed, let us say, by the Big Bad Wolf and the Grand-Mother.

'What does she want?' Little Red Riding Hood knew quite well what she wanted, but Freud's question is not what it seems: it's a rhetorical question. To pose the question 'What do women want?' is to pose it already as answer, as from a man who isn't expecting any answer, because the answer is 'She wants nothing.' . . . 'What does she want? . . . Nothing!' Nothing because she is passive. The only thing man can do is offer the question 'What could she want, she who wants nothing?' Or in other words: 'Without me, what could she want?'

Old Lacan takes up the slogan 'What does she want?' when he says, 'A woman cannot speak of her pleasure.' Most interesting! It's all there, a woman *cannot*, is unable, hasn't the power. Not to mention 'speaking': it's exactly this that she's forever deprived of. Unable to speak of pleasure = no pleasure, no desire: power, desire, speaking, pleasure, none of these is for woman. And as a quick reminder of how this works in theoretical discourse, one question: you are aware, of course, that for Freud/Lacan, woman is said to be 'outside the Symbolic': outside the Symbolic, that is outside language, the place of the Law, excluded from any possible relationship with culture and the cultural order. And she is outside the Symbolic because she lacks any relation to the phallus, because she does not enjoy what orders masculinity – the castration complex. Woman does not have the advantage of the castration complex – it's reserved solely for the little boy. The phallus, in Lacanian parlance also called the 'transcendental signifier', transcendental precisely as primary organizer of the structure of subjectivity, is what, for psychoanalysis, inscribes its effects, its effects of castration and resistance to castration and hence the very organization of language, as unconscious relations, and so it is the phallus that is said to constitute the *a priori* condition of all symbolic functioning. This has important implications as far as the body is concerned: the body is not sexed, does not recognize itself as, say, female or male without having gone through the castration complex.

What psychoanalysis points to as defining woman is that she lacks lack. She lacks lack? Curious to put it in so contradictory, so extremely paradoxical, a manner: she lacks lack. To say she lacks lack is also, after all, to say she doesn't miss lack . . . since she doesn't miss the lack of lack. Yes, they say, but the point is 'she lacks The Lack', The Lack, lack of the Phallus. And so, supposedly, she misses the great lack, so that without man she would be indefinite, indefinable, nonsexed, unable to recognize herself: outside the Symbolic. But fortunately there is man: he who comes . . . Prince Charming. And it's man who teaches woman (because man is always the Master as well), who teaches her to be aware of lack, to be aware of absence, aware of death. It's man who will finally order woman, 'set her to rights,' by teaching her that without man she could 'misrecognize'. He will teach her the Law of the Father. Something of the order of: 'Without me, without me – the Absolute – Father (the father is always that much more absolute the more he is improbable, dubious) – without me you wouldn't exist, I'll show you.' Without him she'd remain in a state of distressing and distressed undifferentiation, unbordered, unorganized, 'unpoliced' by the phallus . . . incoherent, chaotic, and embedded in the Imaginary in her ignorance of the Law of the Signifier. Without him she would in all probability not be contained by the threat of death, might even, perhaps, believe herself eternal, immortal. Without him she would be deprived of sexuality. And it might be said that man works very actively to produce 'his woman'. Take for example *Le Ravissement de Lol V. Stein*,[2] and you will witness the moment when man can finally say 'his' woman, 'my' woman. It is that moment when he has taught her to be aware of Death. So man *makes*, he makes (up) his woman, not without being himself seized up and drawn into the dialectical movement that this sort of thing sets in play. We might say that the Absolute Woman, in culture, the woman who really represents femininity most effectively . . . who is closest to femininity as *prey* to masculinity, is actually the hysteric . . . he makes her image for her!

The hysteric is a divine spirit that is always at the edge, the turning point, of making. She is one who does not make herself . . . she does not make herself but she does make the other. It is said that the hysteric 'makes-believe' the father, plays the father, 'makes-believe' the master. Plays, makes up, makes-believe: she makes-believe she is a woman, unmakes-believe too . . . plays at desire, plays the father . . . turns herself into him, unmakes him at the same time. Anyway, without the hysteric, there's no father . . . without the hysteric, no master, no analyst, no analysis! She's the *unorganizable* feminine construct, whose power of producing the other is a power that never returns to her. She is really a wellspring nourishing the other for eternity, yet not drawing back from the other . . . not recognizing herself in the images the other may or may not give her. She is given images that don't belong to her, and she forces herself, as we've all done, to resemble them.

And so in the face of this person who lacks lack, who does not miss lack of lack, we have the construct that is infinitely easier to analyse, to put in place – manhood, flaunting its metaphors like banners through history. You know those metaphors: they are most effective. It's always clearly a question of war, of battle. If there is no battle, it's replaced by the stake of battle: strategy. Man is strategy, is reckoning . . . 'how to win' with the least possible loss, at the lowest possible cost. Throughout literature masculine figures all say the same thing: 'I'm reckoning' what to do to win. Take Don Juan and you have the whole masculine economy getting together to 'give women just what it takes to keep them in bed' then swiftly taking back the investment, then reinvesting, etc., so that nothing ever gets given, everything gets taken back, while in the process the greatest possible dividend of pleasure is taken. Consumption without payment, of course.

Let's take an example other than Don Juan, one clearly pushed to the point of paroxysm . . . Kafka. It was Kafka who said there was one struggle that terrified him beyond all others (he was an embattled man, but his battle was with death –

in this sense he was a man greater than the rest): but in matters concerning women his was a struggle that terrified him (death did not). He said the struggle with women ended up in bed: this was his greatest fear. If you know a little about Kafka's life you should know that in his complete integrity, his absolute honesty, he attempted to live through this awful anguish in his relationships with women, in the struggle whose only outcome is bed, by working . . . finally to produce a neurosis of quite extraordinary beauty and terror consisting of a life-and-death relationship with a woman, but at the greatest possible distance. As close as possible and as distanced as possible. He would be betrothed, passionately desire a marriage which he feared above all else, and keep putting off the wedding by endless unconscious maneuvers . . . by a pattern of repeated breakups that took him right to his deathbed, the very deathbed he'd always wanted – a bed, that is, in which he could finally be alone with death. This work of keeping women at a distance while at the same time drawing them to him shows up strikingly in his diary, again because Kafka was honest enough to reveal everything, to say everything. He wrote in little columns, putting debits on the left and credits on the right . . . all the reasons I absolutely must marry, all the reasons I absolutely must not. This tension points to the spirit of male/female relationships in a way it isn't normally revealed, because what is normally revealed is actually a decoy . . . all those words about love, etc. All that is always just a cover for hatred nourished by the fear of death: woman, for man, is death. This is actually the castration complex at its most effective: giving is really dicing with death.

Giving: there you have a basic problem, which is that masculinity is always associated – in the unconscious, which is after all what makes the whole economy function – with debt. Freud, in deciphering the latent antagonisms between parents and children, shows very well the extent to which the family is founded, as far as the little boy is concerned, on a fearful debt. The child *owes* his parents his life and his problem is exactly to *repay* them: nothing is more dangerous than obligation. Obligation is submission to the enormous weight of the other's generosity, is being threatened by a blessing . . . and a blessing is always an evil when it comes from someone else. For the moment you receive something you are effectively 'open' to the other, and if you are a man you have only one wish, and that is hastily to return the gift, to break the circuit of an exchange that could have no end . . . to be nobody's child, to owe no one a thing.

And so debt, what is always expressed in religions by laws like 'a tooth for a tooth', 'a gift for a gift', 'an eye for an eye', is a system of absolute equivalence . . . of no inequality, for inequality is always interpreted by the masculine as a difference of strength, and thus as a threat. This economy is ruled by price: there's a price to pay, life is dear, the price of life has to be paid. And here lies a difficulty in connection with love, in that, at coming, love starts escaping the system of equivalence in all sorts of ways. It's very hard to give back something you can't pin down. What's so frightening in relations between male and female at the moment of coming (*au niveau de la jouissance*) is the possibility that there might be more on one side than on the other and the Symbolic finds it really tough to know who wins and who loses, who gives more in a relationship of this sort. The memory of debt and the fear of having to recognize one's debt rise up straight-away. But the refusal to know is nonetheless ambivalent in its implications, for not knowing is threatening while at the same time (and this is where the castra-tion complex comes in) it reinforces the desire to know. So in the end woman, in man's desire, stands in the place of not knowing, the place of mystery. In this sense she is no good, but at the same time she is good because it's this mystery that leads man to keep overcoming, dominating, subduing, putting his manhood to the test, against the mystery he has to keep forcing back.

And so they want to keep woman in the place of mystery, consign her to mystery, as they say 'keep her in her place', keep her at a distance: she's always not quite there . . . but no one knows exactly where she is. She is kept in place in a quite characteristic way – coming back to Oedipus, the place of one who is too often forgotten,[3] the place of the sphinx . . . she's kept in the place of what we might call the 'watch-bitch' (*chienne chanteuse*). That is to say, she is outside the city, at the edge of the city – the city is man, ruled by masculine law – and there she is. In what way is she there? She is there not recognizing: the sphinx doesn't recognize herself, she it is who poses questions, just as it's man who holds the answer and furthermore, as you know, his answer is completely worthy of him: 'Man', simple answer . . . but it says everything. 'Watch-bitch', the sphinx was called: she's an animal and she sings out. She sings out because women do . . . they do utter a little, but they don't speak. Always keep in mind the distinction between speaking and talking. It is said, in philosophical texts, that women's weapon is the word, because they talk, talk endlessly, chatter, overflow, with sound, mouth-sound: but they don't actually *speak*, they have nothing to say. They always inhabit the place of silence, or at most make it echo with their singing. And neither is to their benefit, for they remain outside knowledge.

Silence: silence is the mark of hysteria. The great hysterics have lost speech, they are aphonic, and at times have lost more than speech: they are pushed to the point of choking, nothing gets through. They are decapitated, their tongues are cut off and what talks isn't heard because it's the body that talks, and man doesn't hear the body. In the end, the woman pushed to hysteria is the woman who disturbs and is nothing but disturbance. The master dotes on disturbance right from the moment he can subdue it and call it up at his command. Conversely the hysteric is the woman who cannot not ask the master what he wants her to want: she wants nothing, truly she wants nothing. She wants . . . she wants to want. But what is it she wants to want? So she goes to school: she asks the master: 'What should I want?' and 'What do you want me to want, so that I might want it?' Which is what happens in analysis.

Let's imagine that all this functioned otherwise, that it could function other-wise. We'd first have to imagine resistance to masculine desire conducted by woman as hysteric, as distracted. We'd first have to imagine her ceasing to support with her body what I call the realm of the proper. The realm of the proper in the sense of the general cultural heterosocial establishment in which man's reign is held to be proper: proper may be the opposite of improper, and also of unfitting, just as black and white are opposites. Etymologically, the 'proper' is 'property', that which is not separable from me. Property is proximity, nearness: we must love our neighbors, those close to us, as ourselves: we must draw close to the other so that we may love him/her, because we love ourselves most of all. The realm of the proper, culture, functions by the appropriation articulated, set into play, by man's classic fear of seeing himself expropriated, seeing himself deprived . . . by his refusal to be deprived, in a state of separation, by his fear of losing the prerogative, fear whose response is all of History. Everything must return to the masculine. 'Return': the economy is founded on a system of returns. If a man spends and is spent, it's on condition that his power returns. If a man should go out, if he should go out to the other, it's always done according to the Hegelian model, the model of the master-slave dialectic.

Woman would then have to start by resisting the movement of reappropriation that rules the whole economy, by being party no longer to the masculine return, but by proposing instead a desire no longer caught up in the death struggle, no longer implicated in the reservation and reckoning of the masculine economy, but breaking with the reckoning that 'I never lose anything except to win a bit more' . . . so as to put aside all negativeness and bring out a positiveness which might be called the living other, the rescued other, the other unthreatened by destruction. Women have it in them to organize this regeneration, this vitalization of the other, of otherness in its entirety. They have it in them to affirm the difference, *their* difference, such that nothing can destroy that difference, rather that it might be affirmed, affirmed to the point of strangeness. So much so that when sexual difference, when the preservation or dissolution of sexual difference, is touched on, the whole problem of destroying the strange, destroying all the forms of racism, all the exclusions, all those instances of outlaw and genocide that recur through History, is also touched on. If women were to set themselves to transform History, it can safely be said that every aspect of History would be completely altered. Instead of being made by man, History's task would be to make woman, to produce her. And it's at this point that work by women themselves on women might be brought into play, which would benefit not only women but all humanity.

But first she would have to *speak,* start speaking, stop saying that she has nothing to say! Stop learning in school that women are created to listen, to believe, to make no discoveries. Dare to speak her piece about giving, the possibility of a giving that doesn't take away, but *gives.* Speak of her pleasure and, God knows, she has something to say about that, so that she gets to unblock a sexuality that's just as much feminine as masculine, 'de-phallocentralize' the body, relieve man of his phallus, return him to an erogenous field and a libido that isn't stupidly organized round that monument, but appears shifting, diffused, taking on all the others of oneself. Very difficult: first we have to get rid of the systems of censorship that bear down on every attempt to speak in the feminine. We have to get rid of and also explain what all knowledge brings with it as its burden of power: to show in what ways, culturally, knowledge is the accomplice of power: that whoever stands in the place of knowledge is always getting a dividend of power: show that all thinking until now has been ruled by this dividend, this surplus value of power that comes back to him who knows. Take the philosophers, take their position of mastery, and you'll see that there is not a soul who dares to make an advance in thought, into the as-yet-unthought, without shuddering at the idea that he is under the surveillance of the ancestors, the grandfathers, the tyrants of the concept, without thinking that there behind your back is always the famous Name-of-the-Father, who knows whether or not you're writing whatever it is you have to write without any spelling mistakes.

Now, I think that what women will have to do and what they will do, right from the moment they venture to speak what they have to say, will of necessity bring about a shift in metalanguage. And I think we're completely crushed, especially in places like universities, by the highly repressive operations of metalanguage, the operations, that is, of the commentary on the commentary, the code, the operation that sees to it that the moment women open their mouths – women more often than men – they are immediately asked in whose name and from what theoretical standpoint they are speaking, who is their master and where they are coming from: they have, in short, to salute . . . and show their identity papers. There's work to be done against *class*, against categorization, against classification – classes. 'Doing classes' in France means doing military service. There's work to be done against military service, against all schools, against the pervasive masculine urge to judge, diagnose, digest, name . . . not so much in the sense of the loving precision of poetic naming as in that of the repressive censorship of philosophical nomination/conceptualization.

Women who write have for the most part until now considered themselves to be writing not as women but as writers. Such women may declare that sexual difference means nothing, that there's no attributable difference between masculine and feminine writing . . . What does it mean to 'take no position'? When someone says 'I'm not political' we all know what that means! It's just another way of saying: 'My politics are someone else's!' And it's exactly the case with writing! Most women are like this: they do someone else's – man's – writing, and in their innocence sustain it and give it voice, and end up producing writing that's in effect masculine. Great care must be taken in working on feminine writing not to get trapped by names: to be signed with a woman's name doesn't necessarily make a piece of writing feminine. It could quite well be masculine writing, and conversely, the fact that a piece of writing is signed with a man's name does not in itself exclude femininity. It's rare, but you can sometimes find femininity in writings signed by men: it does happen.

Which texts appear to be women-texts and are recognized as such today, what can this mean, how might they be read?[4] In my opinion, the writing being done now that I see emerging around me won't only be of the kinds that exist in print today, though they will always be with us, but will be something else as well. In particular we ought to be prepared for what I call the 'affirmation of the difference', not a kind of wake about the corpse of the mummified woman, nor a fantasy of woman's decapitation, but something different: a step forward, an adventure, an exploration of woman's powers: of her power, her potency, her ever-dreaded strength, of the regions of femininity. Things are starting to be written, things that will constitute a feminine Imaginary, the site, that is, of identifications of an ego no longer given over to an image defined by the masculine ('like the woman I love, I mean a dead woman'), but rather inventing forms of women on the march, or as I prefer to fantasize, 'in flight', so that instead of lying down, women will go forward by leaps in search of themselves.

There is work to be done on female sexual pleasure and on the production of an unconscious that would no longer be the classic unconscious. The unconscious is always cultural and when it talks it tells you the old stories, it tells you the old stories you've heard before because it consists of the repressed of culture. But it's also always shaped by the forceful return of a libido that doesn't give up that easily, and also by what is strange, what is outside culture, by a language which is a savage tongue that can make itself understood quite well. This is why, I think, *political* and not just literary work is started as soon as writing gets done by women that goes beyond the bounds of censorship, reading, the gaze, the masculine command, in that cheeky risk taking women can get into when they set out into the unknown to look for themselves.

This is how I would define a feminine textual body: as a *female libidinal economy*, a regime, energies, a system of spending not necessarily carved out by culture. A feminine textual body is recognized by the fact that it is always endless, without ending: there's no closure, it doesn't stop, and it's this that very often makes the feminine text difficult to read. For we've learned to read books that basically pose the word 'end'. But this one doesn't finish, a feminine text goes on and on and at a certain moment the volume comes to an end but the writing continues and for the reader this means being thrust into the void. These are texts that work on the beginning but not on the origin. The origin is a masculine myth: I always want to know where I come from. The question 'Where do children come from?' is basically a masculine, much more than a feminine, question. The quest for origins, illustrated by Oedipus, doesn't haunt a feminine unconscious. Rather it's the beginning, or beginnings, the manner of beginning, not promptly with the phallus in order to close with the phallus, but starting on all sides at once, that makes a feminine writing. A feminine text starts on all sides at once, starts twenty times, thirty times, over.

The question a woman's text asks is the question of giving – 'What does this writing give?' 'How does it give?' And talking about nonorigin and beginnings, you might say it 'gives a send-off' (*donne le départ*). Let's take the expression 'giving a send-off' in a metaphorical sense: giving a send-off is generally giving the *signal* to depart. I think it's more than giving the departure signal, it's really giving, making a *gift* of, departure, allowing departure, allowing breaks, 'parts', partings, separations . . . from this we break with the return-to-self, with the spec-ular relations ruling the coherence, the identification, of the individual. When a woman writes in nonrepression she passes on her others, her abundance of none-ego/s in a way that destroys the form of the family structure, so that it is defa-milialized, can no longer be thought of in terms of the attribution of roles within a social cell: what takes place is an endless circulation of desire from one body to another, above and across sexual difference, outside those relations of power and regeneration constituted by the family. I believe regeneration leaps, age leaps, time leaps . . . A woman-text gets across a detachment, a kind of disengagement, not the detachment that is immediately taken back, but a real capacity to lose hold and let go. This takes the metaphorical form of wandering, excess, risk of the unreckonable: no reckoning, a feminine text can't be predicted, isn't predictable, isn't knowable and is therefore very disturbing. It can't be anticipated, and I believe femininity is written outside anticipation: it really is the text of the unfore-seeable.

Let's look not at syntax but at fantasy, at the unconscious: all the feminine texts I've read are very close to the voice, very close to the flesh of language, much more so than masculine texts . . . perhaps because there's something in them that's freely given, perhaps because they don't rush into meaning, but are straightway at the threshold of feeling. There's *tactility* in the feminine text, there's touch, and this touch passes through the ear. Writing in the feminine is passing on what is cut out by the Symbolic, the voice of the mother, passing on what is most archaic. The most archaic force that touches a body is one that enters by the ear and reaches the most intimate point. This innermost touch always echoes in a woman-text. So the movement, the movement of the text, doesn't trace a straight line. I see it as an outpouring . . . which can appear in primitive or elementary texts as a fantasy of blood, of menstrual flow, etc., but which I prefer to see as vomiting, as 'throwing up', 'disgorging'. And I'd link this with a basic structure of property relations defined by mourning.

Man cannot live without resigning himself to loss. He has to mourn. It's his way of withstanding castration. He goes through castration, that is, and by subli-mation incorporates the lost object. Mourning, resigning oneself to loss, means not losing. When you've lost something and the loss is a dangerous one, you refuse to admit that something of your self might be lost in the lost object. So you 'mourn', you make haste to recover the investment made in the lost object. But I believe women *do not mourn*, and this is where their pain lies! When you've mourned, it's all over after a year, there's no more suffering. Woman, though, does not mourn, does not resign herself to loss. She basically *takes up the chal-lenge of loss* in order to go on living: she lives it, gives it life, is capable of unspar-ing loss. She does not hold onto loss, she loses without holding onto loss. This makes her writing a body that overflows, disgorges, vomiting as opposed to masculine incorporation . . . She loses, and doubtless it would be to the death were it not for the intervention of those basic movements of a feminine unconscious (this is how I would define *feminine sublimation*) which provide the capacity of passing above it all by means of a form of oblivion which is not the oblivion of burial or interment but the oblivion of *acceptance*. This is taking loss, seizing it, living it. Leaping. This goes with not withholding: she does not withhold. She does not withhold, hence the impression of constant return evoked by this lack of withholding. It's like a kind of open memory that ceaselessly makes way. And in the end, she will write this not-withholding, this not-writing: she writes of not-writing, not-happening . . . She crosses limits: she is neither outside nor in, whereas the masculine would try to 'bring the outside in, if possible'.[5]

And finally this open and bewildering prospect goes hand in hand with a certain kind of laughter. Culturally speaking, women have wept a great deal, but once the tears are shed, there will be endless laughter instead. Laughter that breaks out, overflows, a humour no one would expect to find in women – which is nonetheless surely their greatest strength because it's a humor that sees man much further away than he has ever been seen. Laughter that shakes the last chapter of my text *LA*,[6] 'she who laughs last'. And her first laugh is at herself.

Translated by Annette Kuhn

NOTES

This article first appeared as 'Le Sexe ou la tête?' in *Les Cahiers du GRIF*, no. 13 (1976), pp. 5–15. The text was transcribed from a conversation between Hélène Cixous and the editors of *Les Cahiers du GRIF* which took place in Brussels during 1975. The present translation follows the published transcript with two exceptions (signalled in nn. 4 and 5) and is published with the permission of Hélène Cixous. The approach and arguments are developed in Cixous's more recent work. See, e.g., *Vivre l'orange* (Paris: Editions des femmes, 1979), written in French and English, and *Illa* (Paris: Editions des femmes, 1980). Thanks are due to Elaine Marks for suggesting this translation of the title, to Keith Cohen for advice on specific points of translation, and to Chris Holmlund for bibliographical assistance.

1. Hélène Cixous and Catherine Clément, *La Jeune Née* (Paris: 10/18, 1975) [Translator's note].
2. Marguerite Duras, *Le Ravissement de Lol V. Stein* (Paris: Gallimard, 1964). There are two English translations of this work: *The Ravishing of Lol V. Stein*, trans. Richard Seaver (New York: Grove Press, 1966), and *The Rapture of Lol V. Stein*, trans. Eileen Ellenbogen (London: Hamish Hamilton, 1967) [Translator's note].
3. 'La place de celle qu'on oublie en français trop souvent parce qu'on dit "sphinx" au lieu de "sphinge" ': That is, the French form of the word would suggest that the sphinx is male, whereas the sphinx of the oedipal myth is in fact female [Translator's note].
4. There follows in the original a passage in which several categories of women's writing existing at the time (1975) are listed and discussed. These include: ' "the little girl's

story", where the little girl is getting even for a bad childhood,' 'texts of a return to a woman's own body', and texts which were a critical success, 'ones about madwomen, deranged, sick women'. The passage is omitted here, at the author's request, on the grounds that such a categorization is outdated, and that the situation with regard to women's writing is very much different now than it was five or six years ago [Translator's note].

5. The following passage, deleted from the main body of the text, is regarded by the author as expressing a position tangential to the central interest of her work, which has to do with homosexuality: 'And it's this being "neither out nor in", being "beyond the outside/inside opposition" that permits the play of "bisexuality". Female sexuality is always at some point bisexual. Bisexual doesn't mean, as many people think, that she can make love with both a man and a woman, it doesn't mean she has two partners, even if it can at times mean this. Bisexuality on an unconscious level is the possibility of extending into the other, of being in such a relation with the other that *I* move into the other without destroying the other: that I will look for the other where s/he is without trying to bring everything back to myself' [Translator's note].

6. Hélène Cixous, *LA* (Paris: Gallimard, 1976) [Translator's note].

17

About Chinese Women

Julia Kristeva

PART I: ON THIS SIDE
[. . .]

2 The War Between the Sexes

Yahweh Elohim created the world and concluded alliances by *dividing* (*karath*) light from darkness, the waters of the heavens from the waters of the earth, the earth from the seas, the creatures of the water from the creatures of the air, the animals each according to their kind and man (in His own image) from himself. It's also by division that He places them opposite each other: man and woman. Not without hesitation, though, for it is said at first that 'male and female created He them'. But this first version is quickly corrected by the story of Adam's rib. Later, the first female creature, due to the hesitation wherein man and woman are not all that separate, makes an ephemeral appearance in the form of the diabolical Lilith, an emanation of Sodom and Gomorrah (Isaiah xxxiv, 14), who crops up in several more or less heterodox exegeses, but not in the Bible itself.

Divided from man, made of that very thing which is lacking in him, the biblical woman will be wife, daughter or sister, or all of them at once, but she will rarely have a name. Her function is to assure procreation – the propagation of the race. But she has no direct relation with the law of the community and its political and religious unity: God generally speaks only to men. Which is not to say that woman doesn't know more about Him; indeed, she is the one who knows the material conditions, as it were, of the body, sex and procreation, which permit the existence of the community, its permanence and thus man's very dialogue with his God. Besides, is the entire community not the *bride* of God? But women's knowledge is corporal, aspiring to pleasure rather than tribal unity (the forbidden fruit seduces Eve's senses of *sight* and *taste*). It is an informulable knowledge, an ironic common sense (Sarah, pregnant at 90, laughs at this divine news); or else; when it serves social necessity, it's often in a roundabout way, after having violated the most ancient of taboos, that of incest (Sarah declared the sister of Abraham; Lot's daughters sleeping with their father).

Long before the establishment of the people of Israel, the Northern Semites worshipped maternal divinities. Even while such worship continued, though, these farmers and shepherds had already begun to isolate the principle of a male, paternal divinity and a pantheon in the image of the family (father–mother–son). But Judaism was founded through and beyond this tradition, when, around 2000 BC, Egyptian refugees, nomads, brigands and insurgent peasants banded together, it seems, without any coherent ethnic origin, without land or State, seeking at first merely to survive as a wandering community. Jewish monotheism is undoubtedly rooted in this will to create a community in the face of all the unfavourable concrete circumstances: an abstract, nominal, symbolic community beyond individuals and their beliefs, but beyond their political organization as well. In fact, the Kingdom of David survived only a short while after its foundation in 1000 BC, preceded by wars, and followed by discord, before becoming the vassal, and eventually the victim, of Babylonia. Devised to create a community, monotheism does not, however, accommodate itself to the political community that is the State; initially it doesn't even help it. Monotheism does survive the State, however, and determine the direction the latter will take, even much later, through Christianity up to the various forms of modern technocracies, both religious and secular. But this is not the problem that concerns us here. Let us note that by establishing itself as the principle of a symbolic, paternal community in the grip of the superego, beyond all ethnic considerations, beliefs or social loyalties, monotheism represses, along with paganism, the greater part of agrarian civilizations and their ideologies, women and mothers. The Syrian goddess who was worshipped up until the beginning of the Christian era in the Armenian city of Hieropolis-Menbidj, or the numerous sacrifices to Ishtar, survive the biblical expurgation only in the shape of Deborah, the inspired warrior who accompanied the soldiers and celebrated their deeds, or else in the mouths of prophets who deplore idolatry, such as Jeremiah, the last of the pre-exile prophets, who denounced the cult of the 'Queen of the Heavens'.

Consequently, no other civilization seems to have made the principle of sexual difference so crystal clear: between the two sexes a cleavage or abyss opens up. This gap is marked by their different relationship to the law (both religious and political), a difference which is in turn the very condition of their alliance. Monotheistic unity is sustained by a radical separation of the sexes: indeed, it is this very separation which is its prerequiste. For without this gap between the sexes, without this localization of the polymorphic, orgasmic body, desiring and laughing, in the *other* sex, it would have been impossible, in the *symbolic realm*, to isolate the principle of One Law – the One, Sublimating, Transcendent Guarantor of the ideal interests of the community. In the sphere of *reproductive relations*, at that time inseparably linked to relations of production, it would have been impossible to ensure the propagation of the species simply by turning it into the highest premium of pleasure.

There is one unity: an increasingly purified community discipline, that is isolated as a transcendent principle and which thereby ensures the survival of the group. This *unity* which is represented by the God of monotheism is sustained by a *desire* that pervades the community, a desire which is at once stirring and threatening. Remove this threatening desire, the dangerous support of cohesion, from man; place it beside him and create a supplement for what is lacking in this man who speaks to his God; and you have woman, who has no access to the word, but who appears as the pure desire to seize it, or as that which ensures the permanence of the divine paternal function for all humans: that is, the desire to continue the species.

This people of shepherds and nomads settled only temporarily to found their community by means of the only durable bond in the steppes and the desert: the word. The shepherd (Abel, for example) will therefore be sacrificed so that a lowly farmer can initiate the narrative of tribal wanderings. Invasions and exiles ensue: a sixth century BC of exodus, and a fifth century of temporary return to the land, with the invaders displaying a relative degree of tolerance. The word of the community will consequently oscillate between prophecy and legislation, but it will always be a word that aims to gather together this society which history is bent on dispersing. We must not employ some vulgar form of sociology in order to attribute to climatic or socio-historic conditions the privilege granted to the word and the monotheistic transcendence that represents its agency in the southern Mediterranean basin. But the discovery, by one of the peoples of this region, of the specific form of religiosity known as monotheism (which had failed in Egypt after the attempts of Amen-Hotep IV) on the one hand corresponds to the function of human symbolism, which is to provide an agency of communication and cohesion despite the fact that it works through interdiction and division (thing/word, body/speech, pleasure/law, incest/procreation . . .); while on the other hand it simultaneously represents the paternal function: patrilinear descent with transmission of the name of the father centralizes eroticism, giving it the single goal of procreation. It is thus caught in the grip of an abstract symbolic authority which refuses to recognize the growth of the child in the mother's body, something a matrilinear system of descent kept alive in the minds by leaving open certain possibilities of polymorphism, if *not* incest. If, with these two keys, one can consolidate a social group and make it resistant to any test of internal or external dissolution, one begins to understand that the monotheistic community acquires a vitality that allows it not only to survive geographic or historical threats, but to ensure an otherwise impossible development of productive forces by an infinite perfecting of goods and of means of production. This control ensures a productivist teleology: even if the threats of the prophets disturb this teleology and keep it from degenerating into profiteering and the enjoyment of wealth, this does not in any way preclude the advantage that the property-owning classes derive from it for the perfecting of their economic and political power.

The economy of this system requires that women be excluded from the single true and legislating principle, namely the Word, as well as from the (always paternal) element that gives procreation a social value: they are excluded from knowledge and power. The myth of the relationship between Eve and the serpent is the best summary of this exclusion. The serpent stands for the opposite of God, since he tempts Eve to transgress His prohibition. But he is also Adam's repressed desire to transgress, that which he dares not carry out, and which is his shame. The sexual symbolism helps us understand that the serpent is that which, in God or Adam, remains beyond or outside the sublimation of the Word. Eve has no relationship other than with that, and even then because she is its very opposite, the 'other race'.

When Yahweh says to the serpent, 'I will put enmity between thee and woman, and between thy seed (*zera*) and her seed (*zera*): it shall bruise thy head, and thou shalt bruise (*teshufenu*) its heel (*akev*)', He established the divergence – of race or 'seed' – between God and man on the one hand and woman on the other. Furthermore, in the second part of the sentence, woman disappears completely into seed: generation. But, even more essentially, Yahweh formulates the code of eroticism between the two seeds as though it were a code of war. An endless war, where *he* will lose his head (or his gland?), and *she* her trace, her limit, her succession (the threat, perhaps, to deprive her of descendants, if she takes herself to be all-powerful, and phallic?). It is a strange goal at all events, to follow on the heels of women, and one to be borne in mind when one is confronted with the bound feet of Chinese women, crushed in a way that is infinitely less decisive, but more painful and much more certain.

St Augustine returns to this function of the serpent and offers a definition when he points out that it represents the 'sense of the body' but 'belongs to the reason of science' and 'is dependent on cognition'; and when he thinks (must we believe that this is a consequence of the double nature of the 'sense of the body'?) that sexual difference, far from being a question of distinguishing between two individuals, 'can be discerned in a single human being':

> For this reason I have thought that the sense of the body should not be taken for the woman, since we see that it is common to us and beasts, and have preferred to take something which the beasts do not have, and have believed that it is more appropriate for the serpent to be understood as the sense of the body . . . for these are the senses of the rational nature and pertain to the intelligence, but that five-fold sense of the body by which the corporeal species and movement are perceived, not only by us but also by the beasts . . . Whenever that carnal or animal sense, therefore, introduces into this purpose of the mind, which uses the living force of reason in temporal and corporeal things for the purpose of carrying out its functions some inducement to *enjoy itself*, that is, to enjoy itself as a kind of *private* and *personal* good and not as a *public* and *common* good which is an *unchangeable good*, then the serpent, as it were, addresses the woman. But to consent to this inducement is to eat of the forbidden tree.[1]

If what woman desires is the very opposite of the sublimating Word and paternal legislation, she neither *has* nor *is* that opposite. All that remains for her is to pit herself constantly against that opposite in the very movement by which she desires it, to kill it repeatedly and then suffer endlessly: a radiant perspective on masochism, a masochism that is the price she must pay in order to be Queen. In a symbolic economy of production and reproduction centred on the paternal Word (the phallus, if you like), one can make a woman believe that she *is* (the phallus) even if she doesn't have it (the serpent, the penis): doesn't she have the child? In this way, social harmony is preserved: the structure functions, produces and reproduces. Without it, the very foundation of this society is endangered.

We must stress this last point, for its importance is overlooked. At best one is guilty of naïvety if one considers our modern societies as simply patrilinear, or class-structured, or capitalist-monopolist, and omits the fact that they are at the same time (and never one without the other) governed by a monotheism whose essence is best expressed in the Bible: the 'paternal Word' sustained by a fight to the death between the two races (men/women). In this naïvety, one forgets that whatever attacks this radical location of sexual difference, while still remaining *within the framework of our patrilinear, class-structured, capitalist societies*, is above all also attacking a fundamental discovery of Judaism that lies in the separation of the sexes and in their incompatibility: in castration, if you like – the support of monotheism and the source of its eroticism. To wish to deny this separation and yet remain within the framework of patrilinear capitalist society and its monotheistic ideology (even when disguised as humanism) necessarily plunges one back into the petty perversion of fetishism. And we know the role that the pervert, with his invincible belief in the maternal phallus and his obstinate refusal to recognize the existence of the other sex, has been able to play in anti-Semitism and the totalitarian movements that embrace it. Let us recall the fascist or social-fascist homosexual community (and all homosexual communities for whom there is no 'other race'), and the fact that it is inevitably flanked by a community of viragos who have forgotten the war of the sexes and identify with the paternal Word or its serpent. The feminist movements are equally capable of a similar perverse denial of biblical teaching. We must recognize this and be on our guard.

On the other hand, there are analysts who do recognize this and, faithful to Freudian pessimism, accept the abyss between the two races; yet they go on to preach the impossibility of communication between the two, the 'lack of relation'. Here it is no longer a question of the war between the sexes: doesn't every psychiatrist have as a companion a 'dead woman', an aphasic mother, an inaudible haven of procreation, that ensures and reassures the 'analytic word'?

The solution? To go on waging the war between the two races without respite, without a perverse denial of the abyss that marks sexual difference or a disillusioned mortification of the division. In the meantime, some other economy of the sexes installs itself, but not before it has transformed our entire logic of production (class) and reproduction (family). China will just be one more horizon, which we will be able to read once this transformation is complete. Before it has happened, however, that country is susceptible of functioning as just another perversion, another mortification (for example: the blindness of the left-winger who believes in Chinese chastity – the final discovery of a happiness that can be opposed to 'bourgeois morality').

3 The Virgin of the Word

Universalist as it is, Christianity does associate women with the symbolic community, but only provided they keep their *virginity*. Failing that, they can atone for their carnal *jouissance* with their martyrdom. Between these two extremes, the mother participates in the community of the Christian Word not by giving birth to her children, but merely by preparing them for baptism.

St Augustine once again offers a fairly cynical explanation for the basically economic reasons for this association of women with the Christian Word, which is secured at the price of the virginity represented by Mary and imitated by the female monastic orders. Quite simply, by the time of Augustine, the survival of the European community no longer depended on the accelerated propagation of the species, but rather on the participation by all men and women in the symbolic efforts (technical as well as ideological) to perfect the means and relations of production:

> But it would be very foolish, for the sake of enjoying marriage even at the present time, when the coming of Christ is not served through carnal genera- tion by the very begetting of children, to take upon oneself the burden of this tribulation of the flesh which the Apostle predicts for those who marry – unless those who cannot remain continent feared that under the temptation of Satan they would fall into sins leading to damnation.[2]

Between this historical constraint and the myth of the Virgin impregnated by the Word there is still a certain distance, which will be bridged by two psychoan- alytical processes, one relating to the role of the mother, the other to the workings of language.

The first consists in ceasing to repress the fact that the mother is *other*, has no penis, but experiences *jouissance* and bears children. But this is acknowledged only at the pre-conscious level: just enough to imagine that she bears children, while censuring the fact that she has experienced *jouissance* in an act of coitus, that there was a 'primal scene'. Once more, the vagina and the *jouissance* of the mother are disregarded, and immediately replaced by that which puts the mother on the side of the socio-symbolic community: childbearing and procreation in the name of the father. This operation of false recognition – mis-recognition – of maternal *jouissance* is accomplished by a process whose origins Ernest Jones was the first to understand. Too hastily categorized simply as the biographer of Freud, Jones in fact deserves credit not only for having proposed one of the most inter- esting concepts of female sexuality, but for having been the first to attempt an analysis of the sexual economy of the great Christian myths. So, in the Word and Breath celebrated by many religions of which Christianity is the chief, the psychoanalyst sees an emanation not of the glottal but of the anal sphincter. This sacrilegious theory, confirmed by the fantasies of analysands, tends to prove that impregnation by the fart (hiding behind its sublimation into Word) corresponds to the fantasy of anal pregnancy, of penetration or auto-penetration by an anal penis, and, in any case, of a confusion of anus and vagina: in short, to a denial of sexual difference. Such a scenario is probably more frequent among male subjects, and represents the way in which the small boy usurps the role of the mother, by denying his difference in order to submit himself in her place and as a woman to the father. In this homosexual economy, we can see that what Christianity recognizes in a woman, what it demands of her in order to include her within its symbolic order, is that by living or thinking of herself as a virgin impregnated by the Word, she should live and think of herself as a male homosexual. If, on the other hand, this identification with the homosexual does not succeed, if a woman is not a virgin, a nun, and chaste, but has orgasms and gives birth, her only means of gaining access to the symbolic paternal order is by engaging in an endless struggle between the orgasmic maternal body and the symbolic prohibition – a struggle that will take the form of guilt and mortification, and culminate in masochistic *jouissance*. For a woman who has not easily repressed her relationship with her mother, participation in the symbolic paternal order as Christianity defines it can only be masochistic. As St Augustine again so marvellously puts it: 'No-one, however, to my way of thinking, would ever prefer virginity to martyrdom' ('Holy Virginity', XLVII, 47). The *ecstatic* and the *melancholic*, two great female archetypes of Christianity, exemplify two ways in which a woman may participate in this symbolic Christian order.

In the first discourse, the maternal traits are attributed to the symbolic father, the mother is denied by this displacement of her attributes and the woman then submits herself to a sexually undifferentiated androygnous being:

> But when this most wealthy Spouse desires to enrich and comfort the Bride still more, He draws her so closely to Him that she is like one who swoons from excess of pleasure and joy and seems to be suspended in those Divine arms and drawn near to that sacred side and to those Divine breasts. Sustained by that Divine milk with which her Spouse continually nourishes her and growing in grace so that she may be enabled to receive His comforts, she can do nothing but rejoice. Awakening from that sleep and heavenly inebriation, she is like one amazed and stupefied; well, I think, may her sacred folly wring these words from her: 'Thy breasts are better than wine'.[3]

At the same time, in the second discourse, submission to the father is experienced as punishment, pain and suffering inflicted upon the heterogeneous body. Such a confrontation provokes a melancholic *jouissance* whose most emotive eulogy is perhaps to be found in Catherine of Siena's treatise on the sensuality of tears.

What is there in the psycho-sexual development of a little girl in monotheistic capitalist society that prepares her for this economy of which the *ecstatic* and the *melancholic* represent the two extremes of the attempt to gain access to the social order (to symbolism, power, knowledge)?

There is increasing insistence on the importance of pre-Oedipal phases, oral and anal, in the subsequent development of both boy and girl. The child is bound to the mother's body without the latter being, as yet, a 'separate object'. Instead, the mother's body acts with the child's as a sort of socio-natural continuum. This period is dominated by the oral and anal drives of incorporation and aggressive rejection: hence the pleasure is auto-erotic as well as inseparable from the mother's body. Through language, the Oedipal phase introduces the symbolic agency, the prohibition of auto-eroticism and the recognition of the paternal function. As Jones once again points out, the boy as well as the girl must renounce his or her own pleasure in order to find an object of the opposite sex, or renounce his or her own sex in order to find a homogeneous pleasure that has no *other* as its object. But if such is the rule, it is realized differently in boys and in girls. When the boy does not identify with his mother to submit like a woman to his father, he becomes his father's rival for the mother's love, and the castration he experiences is rather a fear of 'aphanisis': fear of not being able to satisfy both *her* and *himself.* The girl also finds herself faced with a choice: either she identifies with the mother, or she raises herself to the symbolic stature of the father. In the first case, the pre-Oedipal stages (oral and anal eroticism) are intensified. By giving herself a male object (a substitute for the father), she desires and appropriates him for herself through that which her mother has bequeathed her during the 'female' pre-Oedipal phase – i.e., through the oral-sadistic veil that accompanies the virginal *jouissance* of heterosexual woman. If we perceive a sort of fundamental female 'homosexuality' in this identification with the pre-Oedipal mother, we perceive at the same time that this has nothing whatever to do with male homosexuality, and is not superseded by the 'female heterosexual'. In the second case, identification with the father, the girl represses the oral-sadistic stage, and at the same time represses the vagina and the possibility of finding someone else as her partner. (This situation can come about, for instance, by refusing the male partner, by feminizing the male partner or by assuming either a male or a female role in a relationship with a female partner.) The sadistic component of such an economy is so violent as to obliterate the vagina. In her imagination, the girl obtains a real or imaginary penis for herself; the imaginary acquisition of the male organ seems here to be less important than the access she gains to the symbolic mastery which is necessary to censor the pre-Oedipal stage and wipe out all trace of dependence on the mother's body. Obliteration of the pre-Oedipal stage, identification with the father, and then: 'I'm looking, as a man would, for a woman'; or else, 'I submit myself, as if I were a man who thought he was a woman, to a woman who thinks she is a man.' Such are the double or triple twists of what is commonly called female homosexuality, or lesbianism. The oral-sadistic dependence on the mother has been so strong that it now represents not simply a veil over the vagina, but a veritable blockade. Thus the lesbian never discovers the vagina, but creates from this restitution of pre-Oedipal drives (oral/anal, absorption/rejection) a powerful mechanism of symbolization. Intellectual or artist, she wages a vigilant war against her pre-Oedipal dependence on her mother, which keeps her from discovering her own body as other, different, possessing a vagina. Melancholy – fear of aphanisis – punctuated by sudden bursts of energy marks the loss of the maternal body, this immediate investment of sadism in the symbolic.

It is interesting to note that, on the level of speech, the pre-Oedipal stage corresponds to an intense echolalia, first in rhythm and then in intonation, before a phonologico-syntactic structure is imposed on the sentence. This latter is only totally achieved at the end of the Oedipal phase. It is obvious, then, that a reactivation of the pre-Oedipal phase in a man (by homosexuality or imaginary incest) creates in his pre-sentence speech an explosion of rhythm, intonation and nonsense: nonsense invades sense, and creates laughter. When he flees the symbolic paternal order (through fear of castration, Freud would say, through fear of aphanisis, Jones would say), man can laugh. But the daughter, on the other hand, is rewarded by the symbolic order when she identifies with the father: only here is she recognized not as herself but in opposition to her rival, the mother with a vagina who experiences *jouissance.* Thus, at the price of censuring herself as a woman, she will be able to triumph in her henceforth sublimated sadistic attacks on the mother whom she has repressed and with whom she will always fight, either (as a heterosexual) by identifying with her, or (as a homosexual) by pursuing her erotically. Therefore the invasion of her speech by these unphrased, nonsensical, maternal rhythms, far from soothing her, or making her laugh, destroys her symbolic armour and makes her ecstatic, nostalgic or mad. Nietzsche would not have known how to be a woman. A woman has nothing to laugh about when the symbolic order collapses. She can take pleasure in it if, by identifying with the mother, the vaginal body, she imagines she is the sublime, repressed forces which return through the fissures of the order. But she can just as easily die from this upheaval, as a victim or a militant, if she has been deprived of a successful maternal identification and has found in the symbolic paternal order her one superficial, belated and easily severed link with life.

Faithful to a certain biblical tradition, Freud saw the fear of castration as the essential moment in the formation of any psyche, male or female. Closer to Christianity, but also to the post-Romantic psychology which defines all characters according to the amorous relations, Jones proposed to find the determining element in psychic structure in aphanisis (the fear of losing the possibility of *jouissance*), rather than in castration. Perhaps it would not merely be a resurgence of Greek or logico-phenomenological thought to suggest locating this fundamental event neither in castration nor in aphanisis (both of which would be only its fantasmic derivatives), but rather in *the process of learning the symbolic function* to which the human animal is subjected from the pre-Oedipal phase onward. By symbolic function we mean a system of signs (first, rhythmic and intonational difference, then signifier/signified) which are organized into logico-syntactic structures whose aim is to accredit social communication as exchange purified of pleasure. From the beginning, then, we are dealing with a training process, an inhibition, which already begins with the first echolalias, but fully asserts itself with language-learning. If the pre-Oedipal phase of this inhibition is still full of pleasure and not yet detached from the mother/child continuum, it already entails certain prohibitions: notably the training of the glottal and anal sphincters. And it is on the foundation of these prohibitions that the superego will be built.

The symbolic order functions in our monotheistic West by means of a *system of kinship* that involves transmission of the name of the father and a rigorous prohibition of incest, and a *system of speech* that involves an increasingly logical, simple, positive and 'scientific' form of communication, that is stripped of all stylistic, rhythmic and 'poetic' ambiguities. Such an order brings this *inhibition constitutive of the speaking animal* to a height never before attained, one logically assumed by the role of the father. The role of the 'mother' (the repressed element) includes not only the drives (of which the most basic is that of aggressive rejection) but also, through the education of the sphincters, the first training of these drives in the oral/anal phase, marked by rhythms, intonations and gestures which as yet have no significance.

Daughter of the father? Or daughter of the mother?

As the Sophoclean chorus says, 'Never was a daughter more her father's daughter' than Electra. Not only does she incite vengeance; she is also the principal agent in the murder of her mother, more so than Orestes himself, for in the murder scene, is it not the voices of the daughter and the mother we hear while the son remains silent? It is a delusion to think that Orestes, an anti-Oedipus, has killed his mother to wrest himself thus from the family and move into a new community that is supra-familial and political: the *city* whose cult was already becoming an economic and political necessity in Greece. Faced with this murder, thought-out and spoken by Electra, of which Orestes is only the agent, one wonders if anti-Oedipal man is not a fiction, or, at all events, if he is not always appended to the *jouissance* of a wife-sister. There would be no unavenged dead father – no Resurrection of the Father – if that father did not have a (virgin) daughter. A daughter does not put up with the murder of a father. That the father is made a symbolic power – that is, that he is dead, and thus elevated to the rank of a Name – is what gives meaning to her life, which will henceforth be an eternal vendetta. Not that this fixation does not drive her mad: in vain Electra says that 'only a madman could forget a father killed so heartlessly'; in vain does she accuse poor Chrysothemis, 'her mother's daughter', of being demented, of forgetting her father; she cannot stop herself from being driven mad by her own activity. But her own madness, contrary to Chrysothemis's passive clinging to her mother, is what the leader of the chorus will call, at the end, an 'effort that crowns history', for without it, there would be no 'freedom', and no 'history' for the city from which, as woman, she is none the less alienated. For, in fact, this pursuit of the father's cause has a darker side to it: hatred of the mother, or more precisely, hatred of her *jouissance*. Electra wants Clytemnestra dead, not because she is a mother who kills the father, but because she is a mistress (of Aegisthus). Let *jouissance* be forbidden to the mother: this is the demand of the father's daughter, fascinated by the mother's *jouissance*. And one can imagine how the city will depend on these fathers' daughters (given that a man can fulfil the office of daughter) in order to cover up the fact that the mother's *jouissance* is nourished by the war of the sexes and ends in the murder of the father. The Electras – 'deprived forever of their hymens' – militants in the cause of the father, frigid with exaltation – are they then dramatic figures emerging at the point where the social consensus corners any woman who wants to escape her condition: nuns, 'revolutionaries', even 'feminists'?

It takes a Mozart to make a comedy out of this fidelity of the daughter to the father. The dead father is retained in the guise of the Commander. Orestes is cut out and replaced with poor Ottavio. Aegisthus and Clytemnestra have no reason to exist: power and *jouissance*, following one upon the other in a radiant musical infinity, will be represented by Don Giovanni. So the heroic Electra becomes the pitiful, unhappy Donna Anna: the ill-treated hysteric, passionately in love with the death of her father, commemorating his murder – but without hope of revenge – in a hallucinatory monologue of bitterness and jubilation. Since history repeats itself only as farce, Donna Anna is a comic Electra: still a slave to her father, but to a father whose political and moral law are crumbling enough, by the eighteenth century, to allow Mozart not to treat it as tragedy.

4 Without Time

The symbolic order – the order of verbal communication, the paternal order of genealogy – is a temporal order. For the speaking animal, it is the clock of objective time: it provides the reference point, and, consequently, all possibilities of measurement, by distinguishing between a before, a now and an after. If *I* don't exist except in the speech I address to another, *I* am only *present* in the moment of that communication. In relation to this present of my being, there is that which precedes and that which follows. My family lineage will also be placed in this before and after: the number of ancestors and future generations. Within these coordinates I shall project myself: a journey on the axis centred by the moment of my speech, exemplified by its most intimate phenomenon, my own family tree. This projection will not be a mere displacement of my present on to the future or on to someone else: it may also overthrow the well-oiled order of communication (and thus of society) or of descent (and thus of the family), if I project not the moment of my fixed, governed word, ruled by a series of inhibitions and prohibitions (ranging from rules to sexual taboos and economic, political and ideological constraints), but rather the underlying causality that shapes it, which I repress in order that I may enter the socio-symbolic order, and which is capable of blowing up the whole construct.

'Underlying causality' – a figure of speech that alludes to the social contradictions that a given society can provisionally subdue in order to constitute itself as such. But a figure of speech that is also used to designate that 'other scene': the unconscious, drive-related and transverbal scene whose eruptions determine not only my speech or my interpersonal relationships, but even the complex relations of production and reproduction which we so frequently see only as dependent on, rather than shaping, the economy.

No reference point in the unconscious; I still don't speak there. No now, no before, no after. No true or false either. It [*ça*] displaces, condenses, distributes. It retains everything repressed by the word: by sign, by sense, by communication, by the symbolic order, in whatever is legislating, paternal and restrictive.

There is no time without speech. Therefore, there is no time without the father. That, incidentally, is what the Father is: sign and time. It is understandable, then, that what the father doesn't say about the unconscious, what sign and time repress in the drives, appears as their *truth* (if there is no 'absolute', what is truth, if not the unspoken of the spoken?) and that this truth can be imagined only as a *woman*.

A curious truth: outside time, with neither a before nor an after, neither true nor false; subterranean, it neither judges nor postulates, but refuses, displaces and breaks the symbolic order before it can re-establish itself.

If a woman cannot be part of the temporal symbolic order except by identifying with the father, it is clear that as soon as she shows any sign of that which, in herself, escapes such identification and acts differently, resembling the dream or the maternal body, she evolves into this 'truth' in question. It is thus that female specificity defines itself in patrilinear society: woman is a specialist in the unconscious, a witch, a baccanalian, taking her *jouissance* in an anti-Apollonian, Dionysian orgy.

A *jouissance* which breaks the symbolic chain, the taboo, the mastery. A *marginal discourse*, with regard to the science, religion and philosophy of the *polis* (witch, child, underdeveloped, not even a poet, at best his accomplice). A *pregnancy*: an escape from the temporality of day-to-day social obligations, an interruption of the regular monthly cycles, where the surfaces – skin, sight – are abandoned in favour of a descent into the depths of the body, where one hears, tastes and smells the infinitesimal life of the cells. Perhaps the notion that the period of gestation approaches *another temporality*, more cosmic and 'objective' than human and 'subjective', is just another myth designed to restore time (even if different) at the very moment when time breaks up, before its product (the child) emerges. The child: sole evidence, for the symbolic order, of *jouissance* and pregnancy, thanks to whom the woman will be coded in the chain of production and thus perceived as a temporalized parent. *Jouissance*, pregnancy, marginal discourse: this is the way in which this 'truth', hidden and cloaked [*dérobent et enrobent*] by the truth of the symbolic order and its time, functions through women.

The artist (that imaginary committer of incest) suspects that it is from the mother's side that the unverifiable atemporal 'truth' of the symbolic order and its time springs out and explodes. The Western artist (that fetishist), then, raises this 'truth' to the skies by finding its symbol in the female body. Let us not even speak about the endless 'Madonnas with Child'. Let us take something less evangelical: Tiepolo's *Time Disrobing Truth* (Museum of Fine Arts at Boston, Massachusetts) for example. A scene of abduction, or of coitus? The enigma is emphasized by the anomaly of the design. Truth has a right leg where her left should be, and this leg is thrust forward, between herself and the genitals of Time. But his pain and her air of majesty do not deceive: their gaze is caught by two others who do not speak: the infant and the parrot. The arrows (of love?) and a mask are there to indicate the borrowed and indirect means by which 'truth', so armed, can not only trample the globe underfoot, but steal Time's scythe [*faux*] and transform the latter into a fallen master, an angry servant. But in this fantasy, where a woman, intended to represent Truth, takes the place of the phallus (notably in Tiepolo's painting), she ceases to act as an atemporal, unconscious force, splitting, defying and breaking the symbolic and temporal order, and instead substitutes herself for it as solar mistress, a priestess of the absolute. Once it is disrobed in order to be presented in itself, 'truth' is lost 'in itself'; for in fact it has no self, it emerges only in the gaps of an identity. Once it is represented, even by the form of a woman, the 'truth' of the unconscious passes into the symbolic order, and even overshadows it, as fundamental fetish, phallus-substitute, support for all transcendental divinity. A crude but enormously effective trap for 'feminism': to acknowledge us, to turn us into the Truth of the temporal order, so as to keep us from functioning as its unconscious 'truth', an unrepresentable form beyond true and false, and beyond present-past-future.

Until now this trap has always worked in the West. It seems to me, however, that far from being simply the affair of 'others' stubbornly refusing the specificity of women, the dilemma arises from a very profound structural mechanism concerning the casting of sexual difference and even of discourse in the West. A woman finds herself caught here, and can't do much about it. But a few concrete results of this implacable structure can be noted.

We cannot gain access to the temporal scene, that is, to the political and historical affairs of our society, except by identifying with the values considered to be masculine (mastery, superego, the sanctioning communicative word that institutes stable social exchange). From Louise Michel to Alexandra Kollontai, to cite only two fairly recent examples – not to speak of the suffragettes or their contemporary Anglo-Saxon sisters, some of whom are more threatening than the father of the primitive horde – we have been able to serve or overthrow the socio-historic order by playing at being supermen. A few enjoy it: the most active, the most effective, the 'homosexual' women (whether they know it or not). Others, more bound to the mother, and more tuned into their unconscious drives, refuse this role and sullenly hold back, neither speaking nor writing, in a permanent state of expectation, occasionally punctuated by some kind of outburst: a cry, a refusal, 'hysterical symptoms'. These two extremes condemn us either to being the most passionate servants of the temporal order and its apparatus of consolidation (the new wave: women ministers), or of subversion (the other new wave, always a little behind the first: the promotion of women in left-wing parties). Or else we will forever remain in a sulk in the face of history, politics and social affairs: symptoms of their failure, but symptoms destined for marginality or for a new mysticism.

Let us refuse both these extremes. Let us know that an ostensibly masculine, paternal identification, because it supports symbol and time, is necessary in order to have a voice in the chapter of politics and history. Let us achieve this identification in order to escape a smug polymorphism where it is so easy and comfortable for a woman to remain; and let us in this way gain entry to social practice. Let us right away be wary of the premium on narcissism that such an integration can carry; let us reject the development of a 'homologous' woman, who is finally capable and virile; and let us rather act on the socio-politico-historical stage as her negative: that is, act first with all those who refuse and 'swim against the tide' – all who rebel against the existing relations of production and reproduction. But let us not take the role of Revolutionary either, whether male or female: let us on the contrary refuse all roles to summon this 'truth' situated outside time, a truth that is neither true nor false, that cannot be fitted in to the order of speech and social symbolism, that is an echo of our *jouissance*, of our mad words, of our pregnancies. But how can we do this? By listening; by recognizing the unspoken in all discourse, however Revolutionary, by emphasizing at each point whatever remains unsatisfied, repressed, new, eccentric, incomprehensible, that which disturbs the mutual understanding of the established powers.

A constant alternation between time and its 'truth', identity and its loss, history and that which produces it: that which remains extraphenomenal, outside the sign, beyond time. An impossible dialectic of two terms, a permanent alternation: never the one without the other. It is not certain that anyone here and now is capable of this. An analyst conscious of history and politics? A politician tuned into the unconscious? Or, perhaps, a woman . . .

5 I Who Want Not To Be

For a woman, the call of the mother is not only a call from beyond time, or beyond the socio-political battle. With family and history at an impasse, this call troubles the word: it generates hallucinations, voices, 'madness'. After the superego, the ego founders and sinks. It is a fragile envelope, incapable of staving off the irruption of this conflict, of this love which had bound the little girl to her mother, and which then, like black lava, had lain in wait for her all along the path of her desperate attempts to identify with the symbolic paternal order. Once the moorings of the word, the ego, the superego, begin to slip, life itself can't hang on: death quietly moves in. Suicide without a cause, or sacrifice without fuss for an apparent cause which, in our age, is usually political: a woman can carry off such things without tragedy, even without drama, without the feeling that she is fleeing a well-fortified front, but rather as though it were simply a matter of making an inevitable, irresistible and self-evident transition.

I think of Virginia Woolf, who sank wordlessly into the river, her pockets weighed down with stones. Haunted by voices, waves, lights, in love with colours – blue, green – and seized by a strange gaiety that would bring on the fits of strangled, screeching laughter recalled by Miss Brown. Or I think of the dark corner of the deserted farmhouse in the Russian countryside where, a few months later in that same year of 1914, Maria Tsvetaeva, fleeing the war, hanged herself: the most rhythmic of Russian poets, whose drumbeats went further back in the memory of the Russian language than those of Mayakovsky, and who wrote: 'My problem (in writing verse, and my reader's problem in understanding it) consists in the impossibility of my task: for example, to express the sigh a-a- with words (that is, meaning). With words/meanings to say the sound. Such that all that remains in the ear is a-a-a.'

Or Sylvia Plath, another of those women disillusioned with meanings and words, who took refuge in lights, rhythms and sounds: a refuge that already announces, for those who know how to read her, her silent departure from life:

> Axes
> After whose stroke the wood rings
> And the echoes!
> Echoes travelling
> Off from the centre like horses.
> Words dry and riderless,
> the indefatigable hoof-taps.
> While
> From the bottom of the pool fixed stars
> Govern a life.[4]

When Dostoevsky's Kirilov commits suicide, it's to prove that his will is stronger than God's. By proving thus that the human ego possesses supreme power, he believes he is emancipating Man by putting him in the place of God. ('If I kill myself I become God' – 'God is necessary and therefore He must exist'.)

Something entirely different is at stake in Tsvetaeva's suicide: not *to be*, that is, in the final instance, *to be God*; but to dissolve being itself, to free it of the word, of the self, of God. 'I don't want to die. I want not to be', she writes in her notes.

In an analogous situation a man can imagine an all-powerful, though always insignificant, mother in order to 'legitimize' himself: to make himself known, to lean on her and be guided by her through the social labyrinth, though not without his own occasional ironic commentary. Méry-Laurent for Mallarmé, Madame Straus for 'little Marcel', Miss Weaver for Joyce, the series of fiancées taken and rejected by Kafka . . . For a woman, as soon as the father is not calling the tune and language is being torn apart by rhythm, no mother can serve as an axis for the sacred or for farce. If she tries to provide it herself, the result is so-called female homosexuality, identification with virility, or a tight rein on the least pre-Oedipal pleasure. And if no paternal legitimation comes along to dam up the inexhaustible non-symbolized drive, she collapses into psychosis or suicide.

The triumph of narcissism? But that would be the most primal form of narcissism: the most archaic death-drive, that which precedes and therefore surpasses any identity, sign, order or belief. As a motive for revolutionary action, this drive, if it is strangled in the throat of history, can destroy the body itself. For Tsvetaeva, the failure of the Revolution, Soviet bureaucracy and the war are all features to be considered. But without faith – without testament.

When, striving for access to the word and to time, she identifies with the father, she becomes a support for transcendence. But when she is inspired by that which the symbolic order represses, isn't a woman also the most radical atheist, the most committed anarchist? In the eyes of this society, such a posture casts her as a victim. But elsewhere?

Translated by Seán Hand

NOTES

1. St Augustine, *The Trinity*, tr. S. McKenna (Washington, DC: The Catholic University of America Press, 1963), p. 362 and pp. 359–60. My [Kristeva's] emphasis.
2. St Augustine, 'Holy Virginity', in *Treatises on Marriage and Other Subjects*, tr. J. McQuade (New York: Fathers of the Church, 1955), p. 159.
3. St Teresa of Jesus, 'Conceptions of the love of God', in *The Complete Works*, tr. and ed. E. Allison Peers (London: Sheed & Ward, 1946), vol. II, p. 384.
4. S. Plath, *Ariel* (London: Faber, 1968), p. 86.

18

This Sex Which Is Not One[1]

Luce Irigaray

Female sexuality has always been conceptualized on the basis of masculine parameters. Thus the opposition between 'masculine' clitoral activity and 'feminine'
vaginal passivity, an opposition which Freud – and many others – saw as stages,
or alternatives, in the development of a sexually 'normal' woman, seems rather
too clearly required by the practice of male sexuality. For the clitoris is conceived
as a little penis pleasant to masturbate so long as castration anxiety does not exist
(for the boy child), and the vagina is valued for the 'lodging' it offers the male
organ when the forbidden hand has to find a replacement for pleasure-giving.

In these terms, woman's erogenous zones never amount to anything but a
clitoris-sex that is not comparable to the noble phallic organ, or a hole-envelope
that serves to sheathe and massage the penis in intercourse: a non-sex, or a
masculine organ turned back upon itself, self-embracing.

About woman and her pleasure, this view of the sexual relation has nothing to
say. Her lot is that of 'lack', 'atrophy' (of the sexual organ), and 'penis envy', the
penis being the only sexual organ of recognized value. Thus she attempts by every
means available to appropriate that organ for herself: through her somewhat
servile love of the father-husband capable of giving her one, through her desire
for a child-penis, preferably a boy, through access to the cultural values still
reserved by right to males alone and therefore always masculine, and so on.
Woman lives her own desire only as the expectation that she may at last come to
possess an equivalent of the male organ.

Yet all this appears quite foreign to her own pleasure, unless it remains within
the dominant phallic economy. Thus, for example, woman's autoeroticism is very
different from man's. In order to touch himself, man needs an instrument: his
hand, a woman's body, language . . . And this self-caressing requires at least a
minimum of activity. As for woman, she touches herself in and of herself without
any need for mediation, and before there is any way to distinguish activity from
passivity. Woman 'touches herself' all the time, and moreover no one can forbid
her to do so, for her genitals are formed of two lips in continuous contact. Thus,
within herself, she is already two – but not divisible into one(s) – that caress each
other.

This autoeroticism is disrupted by a violent break-in: the brutal separation of the two lips by a violating penis, an intrusion that distracts and deflects the woman from this 'self-caressing' she needs if she is not to incur the disappearance of her own pleasure in sexual relations. If the vagina is to serve *also*, but *not only*, to take over for the little boy's hand in order to assure an articulation between autoeroticism and heteroeroticism in intercourse (the encounter with the totally other always signifying death), how, in the classic representation of sexuality, can the perpetuation of autoeroticism for woman be managed? Will woman not be left with the impossible alternative between a defensive virginity, fiercely turned in upon itself, and a body open to penetration that no longer knows, in this 'hole' that constitutes its sex, the pleasure of its own touch? The more or less exclusive – and highly anxious – attention paid to erection in Western sexuality proves to what extent the imaginary that governs it is foreign to the feminine. For the most part, this sexuality offers nothing but imperatives dictated by male rivalry: the 'strongest' being the one who has the best 'hard-on', the longest, the biggest, the stiffest penis, or even the one who 'pees the farthest' (as in little boys' contests). Or else one finds imperatives dictated by the enactment of sadomasochistic fantasies, these in turn governed by man's relation to his mother: the desire to force entry, to penetrate, to appropriate for himself the mystery of this womb where he has been conceived, the secret of his begetting, of his 'origin'. Desire/need, also to make blood flow again in order to revive a very old relationship – intrauterine, to be sure, but also prehistoric – to the maternal.

Woman, in this sexual imaginary, is only a more or less obliging prop for the enactment of man's fantasies. That she may find pleasure there in that role, by proxy, is possible, even certain. But such pleasure is above all a masochistic prostitution of her body to a desire that is not her own, and it leaves her in a familiar state of dependency upon man. Not knowing what she wants, ready for anything, even asking for more, so long as he will 'take' her as his 'object' when he seeks his own pleasure. Thus she will not say what she herself wants; moreover, she does not know, or no longer knows, what she wants. As Freud admits, the beginnings of the sexual life of a girl child are so 'obscure', so 'faded with time', that one would have to dig down very deep indeed to discover beneath the traces of this civilization, of this history, the vestiges of a more archaic civilization that might give some clue to woman's sexuality. That extremely ancient civilization would undoubtedly have a different alphabet, a different language . . . Woman's desire would not be expected to speak the same language as man's; woman's desire has doubtless been submerged by the logic that has dominated the West since the time of the Greeks.

Within this logic, the predominance of the visual, and of the discrimination and individualization of form, is particularly foreign to female eroticism. Woman takes pleasure more from touching than from looking, and her entry into a dominant scopic economy signifies, again, her consignment to passivity: she is to be the beautiful object of contemplation. While her body finds itself thus eroticized, and called to a double movement of exhibition and of chaste retreat in order to stimulate the drives of the 'subject', her sexual organ represents *the horror of nothing to see*. A defect in this systematics of representation and desire. A 'hole' in its scoptophilic lens. It is already evident in Greek statuary that this nothing-to-see has to be excluded, rejected, from such a scene of representation. Woman's genitals are simply absent, masked, sewn back up inside their 'crack'.

This organ which has nothing to show for itself also lacks a form of its own. And if woman takes pleasure precisely from this incompleteness of form which allows her organ to touch itself over and over again, indefinitely, by itself, that pleasure is denied by a civilization that privileges phallomorphism. The value granted to the only definable form excludes the one that is in play in female auto-eroticism. The *one* of form, of the individual, of the (male) sexual organ, of the proper name, of the proper meaning . . . supplants, while separating and dividing, that contact of *at least two* (lips) which keeps woman in touch with herself, but without any possibility of distinguishing what is touching from what is touched.

Whence the mystery that woman represents in a culture claiming to count everything, to number everything by units, to inventory everything as individualities. *She is neither one nor two*. Rigorously speaking, she cannot be identified either as one person, or as two. She resists all adequate definition. Further, she has no 'proper' name. And her sexual organ, which is not *one* organ, is counted as *none*. The negative, the underside, the reverse of the only visible and morphologically designatable organ (even if the passage from erection to detumescence does pose some problems): the penis.

But the 'thickness' of that 'form', the layering of its volume, its expansions and contractions and even the spacing of the moments in which it produces itself as form – all this the feminine keeps secret. Without knowing it. And if woman is asked to sustain, to revive, man's desire, the request neglects to spell out what it implies as to the value of her own desire. A desire of which she is not aware, moreover, at least not explicitly. But one whose force and continuity are capable of nurturing repeatedly and at length all the masquerades of 'feminity' that are expected of her.

It is true that she still has the child, in relation to whom her appetite for touch, for contact, has free rein, unless it is already lost, alienated by the taboo against touching of a highly obsessive civilization. Otherwise her pleasure will find, in the child, compensations for and diversions from the frustrations that she too often encounters in sexual relations *per se*. Thus maternity fills the gaps in a repressed female sexuality. Perhaps man and woman no longer caress each other except through that mediation between them that the child – preferably a boy – represents? Man, identified with his son, rediscovers the pleasure of maternal fondling; woman touches herself again by caressing that part of her body: her baby-penis-clitoris.

What this entails for the amorous trio is well known. But the Oedipal inter-diction seems to be a somewhat categorical and factitious law – although it does provide the means for perpetuating the authoritarian discourse of fathers – when it is promulgated in a culture in which sexual relations are impracticable because man's desire and woman's are strangers to each other. And in which the two desires have to try to meet through indirect means, whether the archaic one of a sense-relation to the mother's body, or the present one of active or passive exten-sion of the law of the father. These are regressive emotional behaviors, exchanges of words too detached from the sexual arena not to constitute an exile with respect to it: 'mother' and 'father' dominate the interactions of the couple, but as social roles. The division of labor prevents them from making love. They produce or reproduce. Without quite knowing how to use their leisure. Such little as they have, such little indeed as they wish to have. For what are they to do with leisure? What substitute for amorous resource are they to invent? Still . . .

Perhaps it is time to return to that repressed entity, the female imaginary. So woman does not have a sex organ? She has at least two of them, but they are not identifiable as ones. Indeed, she has many more. Her sexuality, always at least double, goes even further: it is *plural*. Is this the way culture is seeking to char-acterize itself now? Is this the way texts write themselves/are written now? Without quite knowing what censorship they are evading? Indeed, woman's plea-sure does not have to choose between clitoral activity and vaginal passivity, for example. The pleasure of the vaginal caress does not have to be substituted for that of the clitoral caress. They each contribute, irreplaceably, to woman's plea-sure. Among other caresses . . . Fondling the breasts, touching the vulva, spread-ing the lips, stroking the posterior wall of the vagina, brushing against the mouth of the uterus, and so on. To evoke only a few of the most specifically female plea-sures. Pleasures which are somewhat misunderstood in sexual difference as it is imagined – or not imagined, the other sex being only the indispensable comple-ment to the only sex.

But *woman has sex organs more or less everywhere*. She finds pleasure almost anywhere. Even if we refrain from invoking the hystericization of her entire body, the geography of her pleasure is far more diversified, more multiple in its differ-ences, more complex, more subtle, than is commonly imagined – in an imaginary rather too narrowly focused on sameness.

'She' is indefinitely other in herself. This is doubtless why she is said to be whimsical, incomprehensible, agitated, capricious . . . not to mention her language, in which 'she' sets off in all directions leaving 'him' unable to discern the coherence of any meaning. Hers are contradictory words, somewhat mad from the standpoint of reason, inaudible for whoever listens to them with ready-made grids, with a fully elaborated code in hand. For in what she says, too, at least when she dares, woman is constantly touching herself. She steps ever so slightly aside from herself with a murmur, an exclamation, a whisper, a sentence left unfinished . . . When she returns, it is to set off again from elsewhere. From another point of pleasure, or of pain. One would have to listen with another ear, as if hearing *an 'other meaning' always in the process of weaving itself, of embracing itself with words, but also of getting rid of words in order not to become fixed, congealed in them.* For if 'she' says something, it is not, it is already no longer, identical with what she means. What she says is never identical with anything, moreover; rather, it is contiguous. *It touches (upon).* And when it strays too far from that proximity, she breaks off and starts over at 'zero': her body-sex.

It is useless, then, to trap women in the exact definition of what they mean, to make them repeat (themselves) so that it will be clear; they are already elsewhere in that discursive machinery where you expected to surprise them. They have returned within themselves. Which must not be understood in the same way as within yourself. They do not have the interiority that you have, the one you perhaps suppose they have. Within themselves means *within the intimacy of that silent, multiple, diffuse touch.* And if you ask them insistently what they are thinking about, they can only reply: Nothing. Everything.

Thus what they desire is precisely nothing, and at the same time everything. Always something more and something else besides that *one* – sexual organ, for example – that you give them, attribute to them. Their desire is often interpreted, and feared, as a sort of insatiable hunger, a voracity that will swallow you whole. Whereas it really involves a different economy more than anything else, one that upsets the linearity of a project, undermines the goal-object of a desire, diffuses the polarization toward a single pleasure, disconcerts fidelity to a single discourse . . .

Must this multiplicity of female desire and female language be understood as shards, scattered remnants of a violated sexuality? A sexuality denied? The question has no simple answer. The rejection, the exclusion of a female imaginary certainly puts woman in the position of experiencing herself only fragmentarily, in the little-structured margins of a dominant ideology, as waste, or excess, what is left of a mirror invested by the (masculine) 'subject' to reflect himself, to copy himself. Moreover, the role of 'femininity' is prescribed by this masculine specula(riza)tion and corresponds scarcely at all to woman's desire, which may be recovered only in secret, in hiding, with anxiety and guilt.

But if the female imaginary were to deploy itself, if it could bring itself into play otherwise than as scraps, uncollected debris, would it represent itself, even so, in the form of *one* universe? Would it even be volume instead of surface? No. Not unless it were understood, yet again, as a privileging of the maternal over the feminine. Of a phallic maternal, at that. Closed in upon the jealous possession of its valued product. Rivalling man in his esteem for productive excess. In such a race for power, woman loses the uniqueness of her pleasure. By closing herself off as volume, she renounces the pleasure that she gets from the *non-suture of her lips*: she is undoubtedly a mother, but a virgin mother; the role was assigned to her by mythologies long ago. Granting her a certain social power to the extent that she is reduced, with her own complicity, to sexual impotence.

(Re-)discovering herself, for a woman, thus could only signify the possibility of sacrificing no one of her pleasures to another, of identifying herself with none of them in particular, *of never being simply one*. A sort of expanding universe to which no limits could be fixed and which would not be incoherence nonetheless – nor that polymorphous perversion of the child in which the erogenous zones would lie waiting to be regrouped under the primacy of the phallus.

Woman always remains several, but she is kept from dispersion because the other is already within her and is autoerotically familiar to her. Which is not to say that she appropriates the other for herself, that she reduces it to her own property. Ownership and property are doubtless quite foreign to the feminine. At least sexually. But not *nearness*. Nearness so pronounced that it makes all discrimination of identity, and thus all forms of property, impossible. Woman derives pleasure from what is *so near that she cannot have it, nor have herself*. She herself enters into a ceaseless exchange of herself with the other without any possibility of identifying either. This puts into question all prevailing economies: their calculations are irremediably stymied by woman's pleasure, as it increases indefinitely from its passage in and through the other.

However, in order for woman to reach the place where she takes pleasure as woman, a long detour by way of the analysis of the various systems of oppression brought to bear upon her is assuredly necessary. And claiming to fall back on the single solution of pleasure risks making her miss the process of going back through a social practice that *her* enjoyment requires.

For woman is traditionally a use-value for man, an exchange value among men; in other words, a commodity. As such, she remains the guardian of material substance, whose price will be established, in terms of the standard of their work and of their need/desire, by 'subjects': workers, merchants, consumers. Women are marked phallically by their fathers, husbands, procurers. And this branding determines their value in sexual commerce. Woman is never anything but the locus of a more or less competitive exchange between two men, including the competition for the possession of mother earth.

How can this object of transaction claim a right to pleasure without removing her/itself from established commerce? With respect to other merchandise in the marketplace, how could this commodity maintain a relationship other than one of aggressive jealousy? How could material substance enjoy her/itself without provoking the consumer's anxiety over the disappearance of his nurturing ground? How could that exchange – which can in no way be defined in terms 'proper' to woman's desire – appear as anything but a pure mirage, mere foolishness, all too readily obscured by a more sensible discourse and by a system of apparently more tangible values?

A woman's development, however radical it may seek to be, would thus not suffice to liberate woman's desire. And to date no political theory or political practice has resolved, or sufficiently taken into consideration, this historical problem, even though Marxism has proclaimed its importance. But women do not constitute, strictly speaking, a class, and their dispersion among several classes makes their political struggle complex, their demands sometimes contradictory.

There remains, however, the condition of underdevelopment arising from women's submission by and to a culture that oppresses them, uses them, makes of them a medium of exchange, with very little profit to them. Except in the quasi monopolies of masochistic pleasure, the domestic labor force, and reproduction. The powers of slaves? Which are not negligible powers, moreover. For where pleasure is concerned, the master is not necessarily well served. Thus to reverse the relation, especially in the economy of sexuality, does not seem a desirable objective.

But if women are to preserve and expand their autoeroticism, their homo-sexuality, might not the renunciation of heterosexual pleasure correspond once again to that disconnection from power that is traditionally theirs? Would it not involve a new prison, a new cloister, built of their own accord? For women to undertake tactical strikes, to keep themselves apart from men long enough to learn to defend their desire, especially through speech, to discover the love of other women while sheltered from men's imperious choices that put them in the position of rival commodities, to forge for themselves a social status that compels recognition, to earn their living in order to escape from the condition of prostitute . . . these are certainly indispensable stages in the escape from their proletarization on the exchange market. But if their aim were simply to reverse the order of things, even supposing this to be possible, history would repeat itself in the long run, would revert to sameness: to phallocratism. It would leave room neither for women's sexuality, nor for women's imaginary, nor for women's language to take (their) place.

NOTE

1. This text was originally published as 'Ce sexe qui n'en est pas un', in *Cahiers du Grif*, no. 5. English translation: 'This Sex Which Is Not One', trans. Claudia Reeder, in *New French Feminisms*, ed. Elaine Marks and Isabelle de Courtivron (New York, 1981), pp. 99–106.

Suggested Further Reading

As already noted, Lacan's own work can be difficult and opaque; a persevering reader who resists intimidation may also grow to find it exciting and nuanced. Juliet Mitchell and Jacqueline Rose's *Feminine Sexuality* (1985) provides a selection of Lacan's writing and seminars (by Lacan and those of his School) as well as illuminating introductions from each of these editors.

Malcolm Bowie's chapter on Lacan in John Sturrock's *Structuralism and Since* (1979) is a succinct and accessible introduction to his work. Jane Gallop's *Reading Lacan* (1985) or Elizabeth Grosz's *Jacques Lacan: A Feminist Introduction* (1990) provide a more sustained critical commentary.

The work of 'new French feminists', here namely Julia Kristeva, Hélène Cixous and Luce Irigaray, is now widely available in translation. The Bibliography at the end of the book cites a relevant selection of primary sources. *New French Feminisms: An Anthology* edited by Elaine Marks and Isabelle de Courtivron (1981) presents representative, albeit brief, extracts from these three theorists and others. Anthologies on specific theorists include:

    T. Moi, (ed.), *The Kristeva Reader* (1986);
    H. Cixous, and C. Clément, *The Newly Born Woman* (1986);
    M. Whitford, (ed.), *The Irigaray Reader* (1991).

'The Laugh of the Medusa' (1976) by Hélène Cixous provides an interesting companion piece to her 'Castration and Decapitation' (1981) collected here.

Again, an indispensable resource for readers of Freud and Lacan is J. Laplanche and J. B. Pontalis, *The Language of Psychoanalysis* (1988).

PART 5:
POSTMODERNISMS/
POSTFEMINISMS

The essays and extracts brought together in this final section of the anthology cannot be collected under any single 'ism', nor do they pay tribute to any one particular fore*father*,[1] unlike earlier sections in this collection. This discontinuity in itself may be read as an encouraging and hard-won accomplishment. The terms 'postmodernism' and 'postfeminism' will be used loosely here – themselves being subject to much conceptual debate; and none of the essays which follow are specifically polemical about, or explicitly aligned with, either of these terms. In an earlier part (not included here) of the chapter from *Gender Trouble*, Judith Butler, for example, only goes so far as to make a provisional claim:

> Perhaps there is an opportunity at this juncture of cultural politics, a period that some would call 'postfeminist', to reflect from within a feminist perspective on the injunction to construct a subject of feminism.[2]

Jane Flax makes a similar point in the essay which follows, situating psychoanalysis and its presumed subject in the context of a postmodern world which refutes such presumptions.

What the pieces in this section typically have in common is the eclecticism of their influences so that poststructuralism and object relations, de Beauvoir and Lacan, Masters and Johnson, and Madonna are to be found here, variously and without 'discipline' or discrimination (the popular is as valid as the scientific), in overlapping and contesting ways. Lacan is a most obvious and consistent influence (even when Camille Paglia names him only to denounce him) – and so too, of course, is Freud. The longevity and persistence of Freud's influence, in its various guises and emphases, is revealed here. Another common feature of these otherwise seemingly disparate texts is the attention they pay to issues of representation, and particularly of visual representation. In an era undoubtedly dominated by visual media and media theory, the ubiquitous construction of the (male) gaze[3] builds on Freud's own work on scopophilia (looking as 'fetishistic or voyeuristic mechanisms to circumvent' the threat of castration).[4] The cultural predominance of visual semiotics and the 'knowingness' of media-imaging – wittingly psychoanalytic or unwitting but imitative, such is pervasiveness of the idiom – in the construction and reconstruction of desiring subjects are fore-grounded issues particularly with regard to sighting the site (or vice versa) of womanhood.

While all the essays in the section have been written in the last third of the twentieth century, not all the arguments are novel: many will be familiar to, or resonant for, the reader who has explored earlier chapters of this book. For instance, a persistent debate focuses on the problems of discerning and interpret-ing the 'natural' and the 'artificial'. Thus we have here, on the one hand, Monique Wittig arguing for a 'practical' deconstruction of those categories of sex perceived and named as 'natural': 'there [is] no natural group "women"'; but then, on the other, Camille Paglia warning that 'there is a limit to what she [woman] can alter in herself and in man's relation to her . . . nature's burden falls more heavily on one sex . . . nature's cycles are woman's cycles'. Paglia insists that she is not simply a biological determinist, persistently asserting, as on the first page of *Sexual Personae,* that sexuality is 'the intricate intersection of nature and culture'. She claims, however, that it has been a recent fallacy that one could think about sex and gender without considering nature. While sexuality is prob-lematized by Paglia, she is categorical, in the extract collected here, about sex and bodies and hormones:

> Woman's body is a sea acted upon by the month's lunar wave-motion. Sluggish and dormant, her fatty tissues are gorged with water, then suddenly cleansed at hormonal high tide . . . . Every month for women is a new defeat of the will . . . Man is sexually compartmentalized. Genitally, he is condemned to a perpetual pattern of linearity, focus, aim, directedness. He must learn to aim. Without aim, urination and ejaculation end in infantile soiling . . .

Thus Paglia contends with persistent dualisms including female/male, nature/culture, earth-cult/sky-cult and Dionysian/Apollonian. In other respects she is much more 'deconstructive', resistant to categorization and an advocate of various 'personae', enactments which negotiate and contest what they cannot ignore: nature. As Paglia explains in the essay 'No Law in the Arena: A Pagan Theory of Sexuality' she is also committed to :

> . . . not only the right but the obligation to defy nature's tyranny. The highest human identity consists precisely in such assertions of freedom against mate-rial limitation . . . A pagan design for living would be a sexual mosaic . . . I encourage bisexual experimentation, and I want a world in which people, throughout their lives, freely cross the gender lines in love.[5]

An obligatory reference point in the long-standing feminist debate about sex/gender and nature/culture, and about the being and role of 'woman', is Sherry Ortner's 1972 essay, 'Is Female to Male as Nature is to Culture?'[6] (not included here because, being anthropological in its focus, it makes virtually no reference to psychoanalysis, apart from citing some of Nancy Chodorow's work on the psycho-sociological implications of familial structures). The essay lends credence to Paglia's claim that, while there has been a good deal of talk about culture, gender and symbolization, sex has too often been ignored.[7] Mary Jane Sherfey's essay (which is included here), on the other hand, is precisely about sex, and about woman's 'natural' and unrivalled orgasmic capacity, which is repressed and rendered 'unnatural' in order to preserve and maintain the western nuclear and biological family. Judith Butler, however, recuperates the category of sex – only to question it out of its 'natural' existence:

> . . . what is 'sex' anyway? Is it natural, anatomical, chromosomal, or hormonal, and how is a feminist critic to assess the scientific discourses which purport to establish such 'facts' . . . does sex have a history?

She provides a response (with an intertextual gesture to Sherry Ortner's essay mentioned above) by challenging the originary and determinant power of 'sex':

> . . . gender is not to culture as sex is to nature; gender is also the discursive/cultural means by which 'sexed nature' or 'a natural sex' is produced and established as 'prediscursive', prior to culture, a politically neutral surface *on which* culture acts. This [is the] construction of 'sex' as the radically unconstructed . . . .[8]

In her later text on 'the subject', *Bodies that Matter* (1993), Butler tries further to clarify her claim that, while there are undeniably material bodies, there is no natural, definitive, pre-discursive sex prior to gender-construction:

> Thus, the question is . . . through what regulatory norms is sex itself material-ized? And how is it that treating the materiality of sex as a given presupposes and consolidates the normative conditions of its own emergence? . . . As a sedimented effect of a reiterative or ritual practice, sex acquires its naturalized effect . . . . To claim that discourse is formative is not to claim that it origi-nates, causes, or exhaustively composes that which it concedes; rather, it is to claim that there is no reference to a pure body which is not at the same time a further formation of that body.[9]

In an earlier engagement with 'sex', 'Sexuality in the Field of Vision' (1986), Jacqueline Rose discusses the 'imperfect construction' of sexual difference (and Freud's own theorizing of precisely that):

... Freud's writing shows that sexual difference is indeed such a hesitant and imperfect construction. Men and women take up positions of symbolic and polarized opposition against the grain of a multifarious and bisexual disposition . . . The lines of that division are fragile in exact proportion to the rigid insistence with which our culture lays them down; they constantly converge and threaten to coalesce.

While Rose's essay anticipates or prefigures Butler's in a number of respects, it is perhaps her attention to visual perception which is closest in its implications. If material bodies are sexed immediately they are perceived, then perception itself must be problematized. Might it be that we find what we are predisposed to look for and name? Is the 'fact' of perception as discursively constructed as the sex it perceives and then constructs: 'visual space as more than the domain of simple recognition'?

In the last essay in the section, 'Final Analysis: Can Psychoanalysis Survive in the Postmodern West?', Jane Flax addresses the status of psychoanalysis by *analysing* its own discursive formations. Psychoanalysis, rather than continuing to try to validate itself as an exact science, must take some of its own, often repressed, polymorphous medicine ('obsession with this topic repeats rather than interprets Freud's own fixation on Enlightenment thinking'). The 'deconstructive' theories to which psychoanalysis has given rise must, argues Flax in a passage prior to the piece presented here, be reflexively applied:

It must become more conscious of and self-reflective about the politics of its theories, clinical practices, and its relations to other forms of power and knowledge. *Within its own disciplinary practices it will have to find new ways to develop and highlight the qualities psychoanalysts recommend to their patients* [my emphasis]. These include a tolerance for ambiguity, ambivalence, and difference and the ability to flourish within an increasingly multiple and contradictory external world.[10]

Flax posits a somewhat monolithic notion of 'feminism' (as we have seen, there are more feminisms than one and recent theorists as diverse as Butler and Paglia are keen to indict some of its 'phallacious' premises and projects). She also argues that psychoanalysis, despite its own legitimating anxieties, has always been 'deconstructive', and hence – before the event – postmodern. Again, her notion of the postmodern may also appear rather too unitary and consensual, but it challenges any clinical practice which persists in talking of 'cure'. Notions of cure, like the categories of sexual difference, have a history. 'Cure', like 'sex', like 'woman', is a complex imposition (and imposture) which demands acquiescence and regulates allegiance to a normative milieu; 'being cured' may be a masquerade, too. A sceptical assessment of the notion of cure, combined with a compassionate sense of disease and abjection, may stimulate instead, a political attention to the difference between 'healing' and 'curing'.[11] A subject *may* be healed in any context, in any body, and the assessment of the healing may be largely subjective and necessarily always 'in process'. Of course, and as I myself learnt – sometimes painfully and by witnessing others' pain – from teaching a course on psychoanalytic theory, the issues addressed by psychoanalysis and by clinical practice are *not* merely theoretical abstractions: indeed, it is obnoxious to deny or belie the lived experience of abjection, despair, abuse and injury. Clinical practice will have to continue to change; the power-relations of the analyst and analysand, as with other power relations, must be seen to be provisional and contingent. Sonu Shamdasani, one of the editors of a recent collection of essays, *Speculations after Freud: Psychoanalysis, philosophy and culture*, acknowledges the problems attendant on such disruptions:

> The first step that these [essays] require would be to risk a momentary suspension of the verities of contemporary practice. For some, it is this move, perceived as cavalierly overriding the exigencies of the suffering and the demand for its alleviation that are daily brought to the therapeutic situation, that provokes censure. If clinicians turn to theory as the safeguard amidst the turmoil and the strain of the clinical encounter, serious tampering with this frame is assumed to threaten the survival of both participants. From another angle, it is precisely because so much potentially rides upon the stakes of this encounter that rigorous questioning is necessitated: such questioning would then be seen not as an avoidance of the call of suffering, but as an attempt to allow it the time of another hearing. A recognition of the necessity of something like psychoanalysis, whilst at the same time recognizing the impoverishment of its means.[12]

'Psychoanalysis', continues Shamdasani, 'is not One, cannot be owned, or adequately appropriated.'[13] Certainly, the essays collected in the present *Reader*, and not merely in this final section, attest to this.

NOTES

1. Male theorists are dominant in 'postmodernism' – Jean-François Lyotard, Frederic Jameson and Jean Baudrillard, for example – but the essays presented here are more concerned with theorizing the *effects* of post-modernity on psychoanalysis.
2. Judith Butler, *Gender Trouble: Feminism and the Subversion of Identity* (NY and London: Routledge, 1990), p. 5.
3. Laura Mulvey, *Visual and Other Pleasures* (London: Macmillan, 1989), pp. 25–6. Laura Mulvey's work, especially 'Visual Pleasure and Narrative Cinema', first published in *Screen* in 1975, has also been particularly significant in this context. John Berger, too, in *Ways of Seeing* (London and Harmondsworth: BBC and Penguin, 1972), p. 47, made the point that, because of the domination of a gaze that is 'male', woman *look* that way – in both senses of the word: '. . . men *act* and women *appear*.

Men look at women. Women watch themselves being looked at . . . . The surveyor of woman in herself is male: the surveyed female. Thus she turns herself into an object of vision; a sight.'

4. See, for example, S. Freud, 'Three Essays on the Theory of Sexuality' (1905), PFL 7, pp. 69–70.

5. Camille Paglia, 'No Law in the Arena: A Pagan Theory of Sexuality', *Vamps and Tramps*, (Harmondsworth: Penguin, 1995), pp. 71–82.

6. Sherry B. Ortner, 'Is Female to Male as Nature is to Culture?', *Feminist Studies,* Vol. 1, no. 2, Fall, 1972, and collected in Mary Evans (ed.), *The Woman Question: Readings on the Subordination of Women,* (Oxford: Fontana, 1982).

7. Cf., for example, C. Paglia, op. cit., p. 258.

8. Judith Butler, *Gender Trouble*, op. cit., pp. 6–7.

9. Judith Butler, *Bodies that Matter: On the Discursive Limits of 'Sex'* (London and New York: Routledge, 1993), p. 10.

10. Jane Flax, 'Final Analysis: Can Psychoanalysis survive in the Postmodern West?', *disputed subjects: essays on psychoanalysis, politics and philosophy* (London and New York: Routledge, 1993), p. 38.

11. I have taken this distinction from Dr Christiane Northrup, who outlines the difference in medical terms; see C. Northrup, *Women's Bodies, Women's Wisdom* (London: Piatkus, 1995), p. 39. Some of what she says is obviously germane to a psychoanalytic project, although her claims are holistic and humanistic ('healing is a natural process'), and therefore might well be called into question by the arguments outlined in the present collection.

12. Sonu Shamdasani, 'Introduction: the censure of the speculative', S. Shamdasani and M. Munchow, (eds), *Speculations After Freud: Psychoanalysis, Philosophy and Culture,* (London and New York: Routledge, 1994), p. xiv.

13. Ibid., p. xv.

19

A Theory on Female Sexuality

Mary Jane Sherfey

No doubt the most far-reaching hypothesis extrapolated from biological data is the existence of the universal and physically normal condition of women's inability ever to reach complete sexual satiation in the presence of the most intense, repetitive orgasmic experiences, no matter how produced. Theoretically, a woman could go on having orgasms indefinitely if physical exhaustion did not intervene.

It is to be understood that repetitive orgasms leading to the satiation-in-satiation state will be most apt to occur in parous and experienced women during the luteal phase of the menstrual cycle. It is one of the most important ways in which the sexuality of the primate and human female differs from the primate and human male at the physical level; and this difference exists only because of the female's capacity to produce the fulminating pelvic congestion and edema. This capacity is mediated by specific hormonal combinations with high fluid-imbibing action which are found only in certain primates and, probably, a very few other mammalian species.

I must stress that this condition does not mean a woman is always consciously unsatisfied. There is a great difference between satisfaction and satiation. A woman may be emotionally satisfied to the full in the absence of *any* orgasmic expression (although such a state would rarely persist through years of frequent arousal and coitus without some kind of physical or emotional reaction formation). Satiation-in-insatiation is well illustrated by Masters' statement, 'A woman *will usually* be satisfied with three to five orgasms . . .' I believe it would rarely be said, 'A man will usually be satisfied with three to five ejaculations.' The man *is* satisfied. The woman *usually wills* herself to be satisfied because she is simply unaware of the extent of her orgasmic capacity. However, I predict that this hypothesis will come as no great shock to many women who consciously realize, or intuitively sense, their lack of satiation . . .

It seems that the vast majority of cases of coital frigidity are due simply to the absence of frequent, prolonged coitus. This statement is supported by unpublished data which Masters and Johnson are now accumulating. Following this logical conclusion of their previous research, they began treating a series of couples with severe, chronic frigidity or impotence. All had received prior medical and, often, psychiatric treatment to no avail. For the women, none of

whom had ever experienced orgasms after five or more years of marriage, treatment consisted of careful training of the husband to use the proper technique
essential to all women and the specific ones required by his wife. In many cases
this in itself was sufficient. In the others, daily sessions were instigated of marital coitus followed by prolonged use of the artificial phallus (three to four hours
or more). Thus far, with about fifty women treated, every woman but one
responded within three weeks at most and usually within a few days. They began
at once to experience intense, multiple orgasms; and once this capacity was
achieved after the exposure to daily prolonged coitus, they were able to respond
with increasing ease and rapidity so that the protracted stimulation was no longer
necessary. It is too early for thorough follow-ups, but initial impressions are most
favourable.

Should these preliminary findings hold, an almost total biological aetiology of
coital frigidity will be proved. The inordinate sexual, orgasmic capacity of the
human female will fall in line with that of the other higher primates – and the
magnitude of the psychological and social problems facing modern mankind is
difficult to contemplate.

HISTORICAL PERSPECTIVE AND CULTURAL DILEMMA

The nature of female sexuality as here presented makes it clear that, just as the
vagina did not evolve for the delivery of big-headed babies, so women's inordinate
orgasmic capacity did not evolve for monogamous, sedentary cultures. It is unreasonable to expect that this inordinate sexual capacity could be, even in part, given
expression within the confines of our culture; and it is particularly unreasonable to
expect the delayed blooming of the sexuality of many women after the age of thirty
or so to find adequate avenues of satisfaction. Less than one hundred years ago, and
in many places today, women regularly had their third or fourth child by the time
they were eighteen or nineteen, and the life span was no more than thirty-five to
forty years. It could well be that the natural synchronization of the peak periods for
sexual expression in men and women has been destroyed only in recent years.

These findings give ample proof of the conclusion that neither men nor
women, but especially not women, are biologically built for the single-spouse,
monogamous marital structure or for the prolonged adolescence which our society can now bestow upon both of them. Generally, men have never accepted strict
monogamy except in principle. Women have been forced to accept it; but not, I
submit, for the reasons usually given.

The human mating system, with its permanent family and kinship ties, was
absolutely essential to man's becoming – and remaining – man. In every culture
studied, the crucial transition from the nomadic. hunting, and food-gathering
economy to a settled, agricultural existence was the beginning of family life,
modern civilization, and civilized man. In the pre-agricultural societies, life was

precarious, population growth slow, and infanticide often essential to group survival. With the domestication of animals and the agriculture revolution, for the first time in all time, the survival of a species lay in the extended family with its private property, kinship lineages, inheritance laws, social ordinances, and, most significantly, many surviving children. Only in that carefully delineated and rigidly maintained large-family complex could the individual find sufficient security to allow his uniquely human potentialities to be developed through the long years of increasingly helpless childhood – and could populations explode into the first little villages and towns.

Many factors have been advanced to explain the rise of the patriarchal, usually polygamous, system and its concomitant ruthless subjugation of female sexuality (which necessarily subjugated her entire emotional and intellectual life). However, if the conclusions reached here are true, it is conceivable that the *forceful* suppression of women's inordinate sexual demands was a prerequisite to the dawn of every modern civilization and almost every living culture. Primitive woman's sexual drive was too strong, too susceptible to the fluctuating extremes of an impelling, aggressive eroticism to withstand the disciplined requirements of a settled family life – where many living children were necessary to a family's well-being and where paternity had become as important as maternity in maintaining family and property cohesion. For about half the time, women's erotic needs would be insatiably pursued; paternity could never be certain; and with lactation erotism, constant infant care would be out of the question.

There are many indications from the prehistory studies in the Near East that it took perhaps five thousand years or longer for the subjugation of women to take place. All relevant data from the 12,000 to 8,000 BC period indicate that pre-civilized woman enjoyed full sexual freedom and was often totally incapable of controlling her sexual drive.[1] Therefore, I propose that one of the reasons for the long delay between the earliest development of agriculture (*c.* 12,000 BC) and the rise of urban life and the beginning of recorded knowledge (*c.* 8,000–5,000 BC) was the ungovernable cyclic sexual drive of women. Not until these drives were gradually brought under control by rigidly enforced social codes could family life become the stabilizing and and creative crucible from which modern civilized man could emerge.

Although then (and now) couched in superstitious, religious and rationalized terms, behind the subjugation of women's sexuality lay the inexorable economics of cultural evolution which finally forced men to impose it and women to endure it. If that suppression has been, at times, unduly oppressive or cruel, I suggest the reason has been neither man's sadistic, selfish infliction of servitude upon helpless women nor women's weakness or inborn masochism. The strength of the drive determines the force required to suppress it.

The hypothesis that women possess a *biologically determined*, inordinately high, cyclic sexual drive is too significant to be accepted without confirmation from every field of science touching the subject. Assuming this analysis of the nature of women's sexuality is valid, we must ask ourselves if the basic intensity of women's sexual drive has abated appreciably as the result of the past seven thousand years of suppression (which has been, of course, only partial suppression for most of that time). Just within the very recent past, a decided lifting of the ancient social injunctions against the free expression of female sexuality has occurred. This unprecedented development is born of the scientific revolution, the product of both efficient contraceptives, and the new social equality and emotional honesty sweeping across the world (an equality and honesty which owe more to the genius of Sigmund Freud than to any other single individual). It is hard to predict what will happen should this trend continue – except one thing is certain: if women's sexual drive has not abated, and they prove incapable of controlling it, thereby jeopardizing family life and child care, a return to the rigid, enforced suppression will be inevitable and mandatory. Otherwise the biological family will disappear and what other patterns of infant care and adult relationships could adequately substitute cannot now be imagined.

Should the hypothesis be true that one of the requisite cornerstones upon which all modern civilizations were founded was *coercive* suppression of women's inordinate sexuality, one looks back over the long history of women and their relationships to men, children, and society since the Neolithic revolution with a deeper, almost awesome, sense of the ironic tragedy in the triumph of the human condition.

SUMMARY

Recent embryological research has demonstrated conclusively that the concept of the initial anatomical bisexuality or equipotentiality of the embryo is erroneous. All mammalian embryos, male and female, are anatomically female during the early stages of fetal life. In humans, the differentiation of the male from the female form by the action of fetal androgen begins about the sixth week of embryonic life and is completed by the end of the third month. Female structures develop autonomously without the necessity of hormonal differentiation. If the fetal gonads are removed from a genetic female before the first six weeks, she will develop into a normal female, even undergoing normal pubertal changes if, in the absence of ovaries, exogenous hormones are supplied. If the fetal gonads are similarly removed from a genetic male, he will develop into a female, also undergoing normal female pubertal changes if exogenous hormones are supplied. The probable relationship of the autonomous female anatomy to the evolution of viviparity is described.

From this surprising discovery of modern embryology and other biological data, the hypothesis is suggested that the female's relative lack of differentiating hormones during embryonic life renders her more sensitive to hormonal conditioning in later life, especially to androgens, since some embryonic and strong maternal estrogenic activity is present during embryonic life. This ready androgen responsivity provides the physiological means whereby androgen-sensitive structures could evolve to enhance the female's sexual capacity. In the primates, the marked development of the clitoral system, certain secondary sexual characteristics including skin erotism, and the extreme degree of perineal sexual edema (achieved in part by progesterone with its strong androgenic properties) are combined in various species to produce an intense aggressive sexual drive and an inordinate, insatiable capacity for copulations during estrus. The breeding advantage would thus go to the females with the most insatiable sexual capacity. The infrahuman female's insatiable sexual capacity could evolve only if it did not interfere with maternal care. Maternal care is insured by the existence of the extreme sexual drive only during estrus and its absence during the prolonged postpartum anestrus of these animals.

The validity of these considerations and their relevance to the human female are strongly supported by the demonstration of comparable sexual physiology and behaviour in women. This has been accomplished by the research of Masters and Johnson, and a summary of their findings of the actual nature of the sexual response cycle in women is presented. Their most important observations are:

A. There is no such thing as a vaginal orgasm distinct from a clitoral orgasm. The nature of the orgasm is the same regardless of the erotogenic zone stimulated to produce it. The orgasm consists of the rhythmic contractions of the extravaginal musculature against the greatly distended circumvaginal venous plexi and vestibular bulbs surrounding the lower third of the vagina.

B. The nature of the labial-preputial-glandar mechanism which maintains continuous stimulation of the retracted clitoris during intravaginal coition has been described. By this action, clitoris, labia minora, and lower third of the vagina function as a single, smoothly integrated unit when traction is placed on the labia by the male organ during coitus. Stimulation of the clitoris is achieved by the rhythmical pulling on the edematous prepuce. Similar activation of the clitoris is achieved by preputial friction during direct clitoral area stimulation.

C. With full sexual arousal, women are normally capable of many orgasms. As many as six or more can be achieved with intravaginal coition. During clitoral area stimulation, when a woman can control her sexual tension and maintain prolonged stimulation, she may attain up to fifty or more orgasms in an hour's time.

From these observations and other biological data, especially from primatology, I have advanced four hypotheses:

1. The erotogenic potential of the clitoral glans is probably greater than that of the lower third of the vagina . . . The evolution of primate sexuality has occurred primarily through selective adaptations of the perineal edema and the clitoral complex, not the vagina.

2. Under optimal arousal conditions, women's orgasmic potential may be similar to that of the primates described. In both, orgasms are best achieved only with the high degree of pelvic vasocongestion and edema associated with estrus in the primates and the luteal phase of the menstrual cycle in women or with prolonged, effective stimulation. Under these conditions, each orgasm tends to increase pelvic vasocongestion; thus the more orgasms achieved, the more can be achieved. Orgasmic experiences may continue until physical exhaustion intervenes.

3. In these primates and in women, an inordinate cyclic sexual capacity has thus evolved leading to the paradoxical state of sexual insatiation in the presence of the utmost sexual satiation. The value of this state for evolution is clear: with the breeding premium going to the primate females with the greatest pelvic edema, the most effective clitoral erotism, and the most aggressive sexual behavior, the satiation-in-insatiation state may have been an important factor in the adaptive radiation of the primates leading to man – and a major barrier to the evolution of modern man.

4. The rise of modern civilization, while resulting from many causes, was contingent on the suppression of the inordinate cyclic sexual drive of women because (*a*) the hyperhormonalization of the early human females associated with the hypersexual drive and the prolonged pregnancies was an important force in the escape from the strict estrus sexuality and the much more important escape from lactation asexuality. Women's uncurtailed continuous hypersexuality would drastically interfere with maternal responsibilities; and (*b*) with the rise of the settled agriculture economies, man's territorialism became expressed in property rights and kinship laws. Large families of known parentage were mandatory and could not evolve until the inordinate sexual demands of women were curbed.

Finally, the data on the embryonic female primacy and the Masters and Johnson research on the sexual cycle in women will require amendations of psychoanalytic theory. These will be less than one might think at first sight. Other than concepts based on innate bisexuality, the rigid dichotomy between masculine and feminine sexual behaviour, and derivative concepts of the clitoral-vaginal transfer theory, psychoanalytic theory will remain. Much of the theory concerning the 'masculine' components of female sexuality will also remain but will be based on a different biological conception. Certainly, much of present and past sexual symbolism will take on richer meanings.

It is my strong conviction that these fundamental biological findings will, in fact, strengthen psychoanalytic theory and practice in the area of female sexuality. Without the erroneous biological premises, the basic sexual constitution and its many manifestations will be seen as highly moldable by hormonal influences, which in turn are so very susceptible to all those uniquely human emotional, intellectual, imaginative, and cultural forces upon which psychoanalysis has cast so much light. The power of the psychic processes will stand the stronger. Therefore it may be safely predicted that these new biological findings will not 'blow away'

Freud's 'artificial structure of hypotheses' but will transpose it to a less artificial and more effective level.

In any event, and regardless of the validity of my own conclusions, it is my hope that this presentation of recent major contributions from biology and gynecology bearing on female sexual differentiation and adult functioning will aid in the integration of psychological and biological knowledge and will provide a firm biological foundation upon which all future theories of female psychosexuality must rest.

NOTES

[This note has been renumbered for the present volume.]

1. 'Today it is unfashionable to talk about former more matriarchal orders of society. Nevertheless, there is evidence from many parts of the world that the role of women has weakened since earlier times in several sections of social structure.' The evidence given here lends further support to this statement by J. Hawkes and L. Woolley. See *History of Mankind, Vol. I: Prehistory and the Beginning of Civilization* (New York: Harper & Row, 1963). However, I must make it clear that the biological data presented support only the thesis on the intense, insatiable erotism in women. Such erotism could be contained within one or possibly several types of social structures which would have prevailed through most of the Pleistocene period.

   I am indebted to Prof. Joseph Mazzeo of Columbia University for calling my attention to the fact that the first study on the existence of a pre-Neolithic matriarchal society was published in 1861: Bachofen's *Das Mutterrecht* (Basel: B. Schwabe, 1897). Indeed, Bachofen's work remains an unsurpassed, scholarly analysis of the mythologies of the Near East, hypothesizing both a matriarchal society and the inordinate erotism of women. His entire thesis was summarily rejected by twentieth-century anthropologists for lack of objective evidence (and cultural bias). On several scores, the ancient myths have proved more accurate than the modern scientists' theories. I suspect this will be another instance in which the myths prove faithful reflections of former days.

20

One Is Not Born a Woman

Monique Wittig

A materialist feminist[1] approach to women's oppression destroys the idea that women are a 'natural group': 'a racial group of a special kind, a group perceived *as natural*, a group of men considered as materially specific in their bodies'.[2] What the analysis accomplishes on the level of ideas, practice makes actual at the level of facts: by its very existence, lesbian society destroys the artificial (social) fact constituting women as a 'natural group'. A lesbian society[3] pragmatically reveals that the division from men of which women have been the object is a political one and shows that we have been ideologically rebuilt into a 'natural group'. In the case of women, ideology goes far since our bodies as well as our minds are the product of this manipulation. We have been compelled in our bodies and in our minds to correspond, feature by feature, with the *idea* of nature that has been established for us. Distorted to such an extent that our deformed body is what they call 'natural', what is supposed to exist as such before oppression. Distorted to such an extent that in the end oppression seems to be a consequence of this 'nature' within ourselves (a nature which is only an *idea*). What a materialist analysis does by reasoning, a lesbian society accomplishes practically: not only is there no natural group 'women' (we lesbians are living proof of it), but as individuals as well we question 'woman', which for us, as for Simone de Beauvoir, is only a myth. She said: 'One is not born, but becomes a woman. No biological, psychological, or economic fate determines the figure that the human female presents in society: it is civilization as a whole that produces this creature, intermediate between male and eunuch, which is described as feminine.'[4]

However, most of the feminists and lesbian-feminists in America and elsewhere still believe that the basis of women's oppression *is biological as well as historical*. Some of them even claim to find their sources in Simone de Beauvoir.[5] The belief in mother right and in a 'prehistory' when women created civilization (because of a biological predisposition) while the coarse and brutal men hunted (because of a biological predisposition) is symmetrical with the biologizing interpretation of history produced up to now by the class of men. It is still the same method of finding in women and men a biological explanation of their division, outside of social facts. For me this could never constitute a lesbian approach to women's oppression, since it assumes that the basis of society or the beginning of society lies in heterosexuality. Matriarchy is no less heterosexual than patriarchy: it is only the sex of the oppressor that changes. Furthermore, not only is this conception still imprisoned in the categories of sex (woman and man), but it holds onto the idea that the capacity to give birth (biology) is what defines a woman. Although practical facts and ways of living contradict this theory in lesbian society, there are lesbians who affirm that 'women and men are different species or races (the words are used interchangeably): men are biologically inferior to women; male violence is a biological inevitability . . .'[6] By doing this, by admitting that there is a 'natural' division between women and men, we naturalize history, we assume that 'men' and 'women' have always existed and will always exist. Not only do we naturalize history, but also consequently we naturalize the social phenomena which express our oppression, making change impossible. For example, instead of seeing giving birth as a forced production, we see it as a 'natural', 'biological' process, forgetting that in our societies births are planned (demography), forgetting that we ourselves are programmed to produce children, while this is the only social activity 'short of war'[7] that presents such a great danger of death. Thus, as long as we will be 'unable to abandon by will or impulse a lifelong and centuries-old commitment to childbearing as *the* female creative act',[8] gaining control of the production of children will mean much more than the mere control of the material means of this production: women will have to abstract themselves from the definition 'woman' which is imposed upon them.

A materialist feminist approach shows that what we take for the cause or origin of oppression is in fact only the *mark*[9] imposed by the oppressor: the 'myth of woman',[10] plus its material effects and manifestations in the appropriated consciousness and bodies of women. Thus, this mark does not predate oppression: Colette Guillaumin has shown that before the socioeconomic reality of black slavery, the concept of race did not exist, at least not in its modern meaning, since it was applied to the lineage of families. However, now, race, exactly like sex, is taken as an 'immediate given', a 'sensible given', 'physical features', belonging to a natural order. But what we believe to be a physical and direct perception is only a sophisticated and mythic construction, an 'imaginary formation',[11] which reinterprets physical features (in themselves as neutral as any others but marked by the social system) through the network of relationships in which they are perceived. (They are seen as *black*, therefore they *are* black; they are seen as *women*, therefore, they *are* women. But before being *seen* that way, they first had to be *made* that way.) Lesbians should always remember and acknowledge how 'unnatural', compelling, totally oppressive, and destructive being 'woman' was for us in the old days before the women's liberation movement. It was a political constraint, and those who resisted it were accused of not being 'real' women. But then we were proud of it, since in the accusation there was already something like a shadow of victory: the avowal by the oppressor that 'woman' is not something that goes without saying, since to be one, one has to be a 'real' one. We were at the same time accused of wanting to be men. Today this double accusation has been taken up again with enthusiasm in the context of the women's liberation movement by some feminists and also, alas, by some lesbians whose political goal seems somehow to be becoming more and more 'feminine'. To refuse to be a woman, however, does not mean that one has to become a man. Besides, if we take as an example the perfect 'butch', the classic example which provokes the most horror, whom Proust would have called a woman/man, how is her alienation different from that of someone who wants to become a woman? Tweedledum and Tweedledee. At least for a woman, wanting to become a man proves that she has escaped her initial programming. But even if she would like to, with all her strength, she cannot become a man. For becoming a man would demand from a woman not only a man's external appearance but his consciousness as well, that is, the consciousness of one who disposes by right of at least two 'natural' slaves during his life span. This is impossible, and one feature of lesbian oppression consists precisely of making women out of reach for us, since women belong to men. Thus a lesbian *has* to be something else, a not-woman, a not-man, a product of society, not a product of nature, for there is no nature in society.

The refusal to become (or to remain) heterosexual always meant to refuse to become a man or a woman, consciously or not. For a lesbian this goes further than the refusal of the *role* 'woman'. It is the refusal of the economic, ideological and political power of a man. This, we lesbians, and non-lesbians as well, knew before the beginning of the lesbian and feminist movement. However, as Andrea Dworkin emphasizes, many lesbians recently 'have increasingly tried to transform the very ideology that has enslaved us into a dynamic, religious, psychologically compelling celebration of female biological potential'.[12] Thus, some avenues of the feminist and lesbian movement lead us back to the myth of woman which was created by men especially for us, and with it we sink back into a natural group. Having stood up to fight for a sexless society,[13] we now find ourselves entrapped in the familiar deadlock of 'woman is wonderful'. Simone de Beauvoir underlined particularly the false consciousness which consists of selecting among the features of the myth (that women are different from men) those which look good and using them as a definition for women. What the concept 'woman is wonderful' accomplishes is that it retains for defining women the best features (best according to whom?) which oppression has granted us, and it does not radically question the categories 'man' and 'woman', which are political categories and not natural givens. It puts us in a position of fighting within the class 'women' not as the other classes do, for the disappearance of our class, but for the defense of 'woman' and its reinforcement. It leads us to develop with complacency 'new' theories about our specificity: thus, we call our passivity 'non-violence', when the main and emergent point for us is to fight our passivity (our fear, rather, a justified one). The ambiguity of the term 'feminist' sums up the whole situation. What does 'feminist' mean? Feminist is formed with the word 'femme', 'woman', and means: someone who fights for women. For many of us it means someone who fights for women as a class and for the disappearance of this class. For many others it means someone who fights for woman and her defense – for the myth, then, and its reinforcement. But why was the word 'feminist' chosen if it retains the least ambiguity? We chose to call ourselves 'feminists' ten years ago, not in order to support or reinforce the myth of woman, nor to identify ourselves with the oppressor's definition of us, but rather to affirm that our movement had a history and to emphasize the political link with the old feminist movement.

It is, then, this movement that we can put in question for the meaning that it gave to feminism. It so happens that feminism in the last century could never resolve its contradictions on the subject of nature/culture, woman/society. Women started to fight for themselves as a group and rightly considered that they shared common features as a result of oppression. But for them these features were natural and biological rather than social. They went so far as to adopt the Darwinist theory of evolution. They did not believe like Darwin, however, 'that women were less evolved than men, but they did believe that male and female natures had diverged in the course of evolutionary development and that society at large reflected this polarization'.[14] 'The failure of early feminism was that it only attacked the Darwinist charge of female inferiority, while accepting the foundations of this charge – namely, the view of woman as "unique".'[15] And finally it was women scholars – and not feminists – who scientifically destroyed this theory. But the early feminists had failed to regard history as a dynamic process which develops from conflicts of interests. Furthermore, they still believed as men do that the cause (origin) of their oppression lay within themselves. And therefore after some astonishing victories the feminists of this first front found themselves at an impasse out of a lack of reasons to fight. They upheld the illogical principle of 'equality in difference', an idea now being born again. They fell back into the trap which threatens us once again: the myth of woman.

Thus it is our historical task, and only ours, to define what we call oppression in materialist terms, to make it evident that women are a class, which is to say that the category 'woman' as well as the category 'man' are political and economic categories not eternal ones. Our fight aims to suppress men as a class, not through a genocidal, but a political struggle. Once the class 'men' disappears, 'women' as a class disappear as well, for there are no slaves without masters. Our first task, it seems, is to always thoroughly dissociate 'women' (the class within which we fight) and 'woman', the myth. For 'woman' does not exist for us: it is only an imaginary formation, while 'women' is the product of a social relationship. We felt this strongly when everywhere we refused to be called a '*woman's* liberation movement'. Furthermore, we have to destroy the myth inside and outside ourselves. 'Woman' is not each one of us, but the political and ideological formation which negates 'women' (the product of a relation of exploitation). 'Woman' is there to confuse us, to hide the reality 'women'. In order to be aware of being a class and to become a class we first have to kill the myth of 'woman' including its most seductive aspects (I think about Virginia Woolf when she said the first task of a woman writer is to kill 'the angel in the house'). But to become a class we do not have to suppress our individual selves, and since no individual can be reduced to her/his oppression we are also confronted with the historical necessity of constituting ourselves as the individual subjects of our history as well. I believe this is the reason why all these attempts at 'new' definitions of woman are blossoming now. What is at stake (and of course not only for women) is an individual definition as well as a class definition. For once one has acknowledged oppression, one needs to know and experience the fact that one can constitute oneself as a subject (as opposed to an object of oppression), that one can become *someone* in spite of oppression, that one has one's own identity. There is no possible fight for someone deprived of an identity, no internal motivation for fighting, since, although I can fight only with others, first I fight for myself.

The question of the individual subject is historically a difficult one for everybody. Marxism, the last avatar of materialism, the science which has politically formed us, does not want to hear anything about a 'subject'. Marxism has rejected the transcendental subject, the subject as constitutive of knowledge, the 'pure' consciousness. All that thinks per se, before all experience, has ended up in the garbage can of history, because it claimed to exist outside matter, prior to matter, and needed God, spirit, or soul to exist in such a way. This is what is called 'idealism'. As for individuals, they are only the product of social relations, therefore their consciousness can only be 'alienated'. (Marx, in *The German Ideology*, says precisely that individuals of the dominating class are also alienated, although they are the direct producers of the ideas that alienate the classes oppressed by them. But since they draw visible advantages from their own alienation they can bear it without too much suffering.) There exists such a thing as class consciousness, but a consciousness which does not refer to a particular subject, except as participating in general conditions of exploitation at the same time as the other subjects of their class, all sharing the same consciousness. As for the practical class problems – outside of the class problems as traditionally defined – that one could encounter (for example, sexual problems), they were considered 'bourgeois' problems that would disappear with the final victory of the class struggle. 'Individualistic', 'subjectivist', 'petit bourgeois', these were the labels given to any person who had shown problems which could not be reduced to the 'class struggle' itself.

Thus Marxism has denied the members of oppressed classes the attribute of being a subject. In doing this, Marxism, because of the ideological and political power this 'revolutionary science' immediately exercised upon the workers' movement and all other political groups, has prevented all categories of oppressed peoples from constituting themselves historically as subjects (subjects of their struggle, for example). This means that the 'masses' did not fight for themselves but for *the* party or its organizations. And when an economic trans- formation took place (end of private property, constitution of the socialist state), no revolutionary change took place within the new society, because the people themselves did not change.

For women, Marxism had two results. It prevented them from being aware that they are a class and therefore from constituting themselves as a class for a very long time, by leaving the relation 'women/men' outside of the social order, by turning it into a natural relation, doubtless for Marxists the only one, along with the relation of mothers to children, to be seen this way, and by hiding the class conflict between men and women behind a natural division of labor (*The German Ideology*). This concerns the theoretical (ideological) level. On the practical level, Lenin, *the* party, all the communist parties up to now, including all the most radical political groups, have always reacted to any attempt on the part of women to reflect and form groups based on their own class problem with an accusation of divisiveness. By uniting, we women are dividing the strength of the people. This means that for the Marxists women *belong* either to the bourgeois class or to the proletariat class, in other words, to the men of these classes. In addition, Marxist theory does not allow women any more than other classes of oppressed people to constitute themselves as historical subjects, because Marxism does not take into account the fact that a class also consists of individuals one by one. Class consciousness is not enough. We must try to understand philosophically (politically) these concepts of 'subject' and 'class consciousness' and how they work in relation to our history. When we discover that women are the objects of oppression and appropriation, at the very moment that we become able to perceive this, we become subjects in the sense of cognitive subjects, through an operation of abstraction. Consciousness of oppression is not only a reaction to (fight against) oppression. It is also the whole conceptual re-evaluation of the social world, its whole reorganization with new concepts, from the point of view of oppression. It is what I would call the science of oppression created by the oppressed. This operation of understanding reality has to be undertaken by every one of us: call it a subjective, cognitive practice. The movement back and forth between the levels of reality (the conceptual reality and the material reality of oppression, which are both social realities) is accomplished through language.

It is we who historically must undertake the task of defining the individual subject in materialist terms. This certainly seems to be an impossibility since materialism and subjectivity have always been mutually exclusive. Nevertheless, and rather than despairing of ever understanding, we must recognize the *need* to reach subjectivity in the abandonment by many of us to the myth 'woman' (the myth of woman being only a snare that holds us up). This real necessity for everyone to exist as an individual, as well as a member of a class, is perhaps the first condition for the accomplishment of a revolution, without which there can be no real fight or transformation. But the opposite is also true; without class and class consciousness there are no real subjects, only alienated individuals. For women to answer the question of the individual subject in materialist terms is first to show, as the lesbians and feminists did, that supposedly 'subjective', 'individual', 'private' problems are in fact social problems, class problems; that sexuality is not for women an individual and subjective expression, but a social institution of violence. But once we have shown that all so-called personal problems are in fact class problems, we will still be left with the question of the subject of each singular woman – not the myth, but each one of us. At this point, let us say that a new personal and subjective definition for all humankind can only be found beyond the categories of sex (woman and man) and that the advent of individual subjects demands first destroying the categories of sex, ending the use of them, and rejecting all sciences which still use these categories as their fundamentals (practically all social sciences).

To destroy 'woman' does not mean that we aim, short of physical destruction, to destroy lesbianism simultaneously with the categories of sex, because lesbianism provides for the moment the only social form in which we can live freely. Lesbian is the only concept I know of which is beyond the categories of sex (woman and man), because the designated subject (lesbian) is *not* a woman, either economically, or politically, or ideologically. For what makes a woman is a specific social relation to man, a relation that we have previously called servitude,[16] a relation which implies personal and physical obligation as well as economic obligation ('forced residence',[17] domestic corvée, conjugal duties, unlimited production of children, etc.), a relation which lesbians escape by refusing to become or to stay heterosexual. We are escapees from our class in the same way as the American runaway slaves were when escaping slavery and becoming free. For us this is an absolute necessity; our survival demands that we contribute all our strength to the destruction of the class of women within which men appropriate women. This can be accomplished only by the destruction of heterosexuality as a social system which is based on the oppression of women by men and which produces the doctrine of the difference between the sexes to justify this oppression.

NOTES

1. Christine Delphy, 'Pour un féminisme matérialiste', *L'Arc* 61 (1975). Translated as 'For a Materialist Feminism', *Feminist Issues* 1, no. 2 (Winter 1981).
2. Colette Guillaumin, 'Race et Nature: Système des marques, idée de groupe naturel et

rapports sociaux', *Pluriel* no. 11 (1977). Translated as 'Race and Nature: The System of Marks, the Idea of a Natural Group and Social Relationships,' *Feminist Issues* 8, no. 2 (Fall 1988).

3. I use the word society with an extended anthropological meaning; strictly speaking, it does not refer to societies, in that lesbian societies do not exist completely autonomously from heterosexual social systems.
4. Simone de Beauvoir, *The Second Sex* (New York: Bantam, 1952), p. 249.
5. Redstockings, *Feminist Revolution* (New York: Random House, 1978), p. 18.
6. Andrea Dworkin, 'Biological Superiority: The World's Most Dangerous and Deadly Idea', *Heresies* 6:46.
7. Ti-Grace Atkinson, *Amazon Odyssey* (New York: Links Books, 1974), p. 15.
8. Dworkin, op. cit.
9. Guillaumin, op. cit.
10. de Beauvoir, op. cit.
11. Guillaumin, op. cit.
12. Dworkin, op.cit.
13. Atkinson, p. 6: 'If feminism has any logic at all, it must be working for a sexless society.'
14. Rosalind Rosenberg, 'In Search of Woman's Nature', *Feminist Studies* 3, no. 1/2 (1975): 144.
15. Ibid., p. 146.
16. In an article published in *L'Idiot International* (mai 1970), whose original title was 'Pour un mouvement de libération des femmes' ('For a Women's Liberation Movement').
17. Christiane Rochefort, *Les stances à Sophie* (Paris: Grasset, 1963).

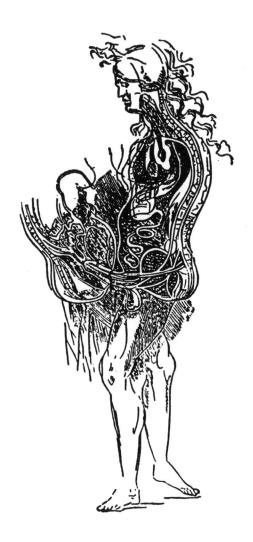

Drawing attributed to Leonardo da Vinci and discussed by Freud in *Leonardo da Vinci, A Memory of His Childhood* (1910).

21

Sexuality in the Field of Vision

Jacqueline Rose

In an untypical moment Freud accuses Leonardo of being unable to draw.[1] A drawing done in anatomical section of the sexual act is inaccurate. What is more it is lacking in pleasure: the man's expression is one of disgust, the position is uncomfortable, the woman's breast is unbeautiful (she does not have a head). The depiction is inaccurate, uncomfortable, undesirable and without desire. It is also inverted: the man's head looks like that of a woman, and the feet are the wrong way around according to the plane of the picture – the man's foot pointing outwards where the woman's foot should be, and her foot in his place. In fact, most of Freud's monograph on Leonardo is addressed to the artist's *failure*, that is, to the restrictions and limitations which Leonardo himself apparently experienced in relation to his potential achievement. Freud takes failure very seriously, even when it refers to someone who, to the gaze of the outside world, represents the supreme form of artistic success. But in this footnote on the sexual drawing, Freud goes beyond the brief of the largely psychobiographical forms of interpretation that he brings to Leonardo's case. He relates – quite explicitly – a failure to depict the sexual act to bisexuality and to a problem of representational space. The uncertain sexual identity muddles the plane of the image so that the spectator does not know where she or he stands in relationship to the picture. A confusion at the level of sexuality brings with it a disturbance of the visual field.

An artistic practice which sets itself the dual task of disrupting visual form and questioning the sexual certainties and stereotypes of our culture can fairly return to this historical moment (historical analytically as well as artistically, since the reference to Leonardo is now overlaid with the reference to the beginnings of psychoanalysis itself). Not for authority (authority is one of the things being questioned here), but for its suggestiveness in pointing up a possible relation between sexuality and the image. We know that Freud's writing runs parallel to the emergence of 'modern' art; he himself used such art as a comparison for the blurred fields of the unconscious psychic processes which were the object of his analytic work.[2] But in this footnote on Leonardo's failure in the visual act, we can already see traced out a specific movement or logic: that there can be no work on the image, no challenge to its powers of illusion and address, which does not simultaneously challenge the fact of sexual difference, whose self-evidence Leonardo's drawing had momentarily allowed to crumble.[3]

The rest of Freud's writing shows that sexual difference is indeed such a hesitant and imperfect construction. Men and women take up positions of symbolic and polarized opposition against the grain of a multifarious and bisexual disposition, which Freud first identified in the symptom (and genius . . .) before recognizing its continuing and barely concealed presence across the range of normal adult sexual life. The lines of that division are fragile in exact proportion to the rigid insistence with which our culture lays them down; they constantly converge and threaten to coalesce. Psychoanalysis itself can therefore explain the absence of that clear and accomplished form of sexuality that Freud himself had unsuccessfully searched for in the picture.

Freud often related the question of sexuality to that of visual representation. Describing the child's difficult journey into adult sexual life, he would take as his model little scenarios, or the staging of events, which demonstrated the complexity of an essentially visual space, moments in which perception *founders* (the boy child refuses to believe the anatomical difference that he sees)[4] or in which pleasure in looking tips over into the register of *excess* (witness to a sexual act in which he reads his own destiny, the child tries to interrupt by calling attention to his presence).[5] Each time the stress falls on a problem of seeing. The sexuality lies less in the content of what is seen than in the subjectivity of the viewer, in the relationship between what is looked at and the developing sexual knowledge of the child. The relationship between viewer and scene is always one of fracture, partial identification, pleasure and distrust. As if Freud found the aptest analogy for the problem of our identity as human subjects in failures of vision or in the violence which can be done to an image as it offers itself to view. For Freud, with an emphasis that has been picked up and placed at the centre of the work of Jacques Lacan, our sexual identities as male or female, our confidence in language as true or false, and our security in the image we judge as perfect or flawed, are fantasies.[6] And these archaic moments of disturbed visual representation, these troubled scenes, which expressed and unsettled our groping knowledge in the past, can now be used as theoretical prototypes to unsettle our certainties once again. Hence one of the chief drives of an art which today addresses the presence of the sexual in representation – to expose the fixed nature of sexual identity as a fantasy and, in the same gesture, to trouble, break up, or rupture the visual field before our eyes.

The encounter between psychoanalysis and artistic practice is therefore *staged*, but only in so far as that staging has *already taken place*. It is an encounter which draws its strength from that repetition, working like a memory trace of something we have been through before. It gives back to repetition its proper meaning and status: not lack of originality or something merely derived (the commonest reproach to the work of art), nor the more recent practice of appropriating artistic and photographic images in order to undermine their previous status; but repetition as insistence, that is, as the constant pressure of something hidden but not forgotten – something that can only come into focus now by blurring the field of representation where our normal forms of self-recognition take place.

The affinity between representation and sexuality is not confined to the visual image. In fact, in relation to other areas of theoretical analysis and activity, recognition of this affinity in the domain of the artistic image could be said to manifest something of a lag.[7] In one of his most important self-criticisms,[8] Barthes underlined the importance of psychoanalysis in pushing his earlier exposé of ideological meanings into a critique of the possibility of meaning itself. In his case studies Freud had increasingly demonstrated that the history of the patient did not consist of some truth to be deciphered behind the chain of associations which emerged in the analytic setting; it resided within that chain and in the process of emergence which the analysis brought into effect. Lacan immediately read in this the chain of language which slides from unit to unit, producing meaning out of the relationship between terms; its truth belongs to that movement and not to some prior reference existing outside its domain. The divisions of language are in themselves arbitrary and shifting: language rests on a continuum which gets locked into discrete units of which sexual difference is only the most strongly marked. The fixing of language and the fixing of sexual identity go hand in hand; they rely on each other and share the same forms of instability and risk. Lacan read Freud through language, but he also brought out, by implication, the sexuality at work in all practices of the sign. Modernist literary writing could certainly demonstrate, alongside the syntactic and narrative shifts for which it is best known, oscillations in the domain of sexuality, a type of murking of the sexual proprieties on which the politer world of nineteenth-century realist fiction had been based. Although the opposition between the two forms of writing has often been overstated, it is no coincidence that, in order to illustrate this tension between 'readerly' and 'writerly' fiction, Barthes chose a story in which the narrative enigma turns on a castrato (Balzac's *Sarrasine*).[9] The indecipherable sexuality of the character makes for the trouble and the joy of the text.

It is worth pausing over the implications of this for a modernist and postmodernist artistic practice which is increasingly understood in terms of a problematic of reading and a theory of the sign. Again, the historical links are important. Freud takes modern painting as the image of the unconscious. But the modernist suspension of the referent, with its stress on the purity of the visual signifier, belongs equally with Saussure who, at the same time, was criticizing the conception of language as reference and underlining the arbitrary nature of the sign (primacy to the signifier instead of language as a nomenclature of the world). Lacan's move then simply completes the circuit by linking Saussure back to Freud. The unconscious reveals that the normal divisions of language and sexuality obey the dictates of an arbitrary law undermining the very possibility of reference for the subject since the 'I' can no longer be seen to correspond to some pre-given and permanent identity of psycho-sexual life. The problem of psychic identity is therefore immanent to the problem of the sign.

The same link (of language and the unconscious) can be made to that transition to postmodernism which has been read as a return of the referent, but the referent as a problem, not as a given.[10] Piles of cultural artefacts bring back something we recognize but in a form which refuses any logic of the same. The objects before the spectator's eyes cannot be ordered: in their disjunctive relation, they produce an acuter problem of vision than the one which had resulted when reference was simply dropped from the frame. Above all – to return to the analogy with the analytic scene – these images require a reading which neither coheres them into a unity, nor struggles to get behind them into a realm of truth. The only possible reading is one which repeats their fragmentation of a cultural world they both echo and refuse.

At each point of these transitions – artistic and theoretical – something is called into question at the most fundamental level of the way we recognize and respond to our own subjectivity and to a world with which we are assumed to be familiar, a world we both do and do not know. Yet in each of these instances, it is precisely the psychoanalytic concepts of the unconscious and sexuality, specifically in their relationship to language, which seem to be lost.

Thus the modernist stress on the purity of the visual signifier easily dissolves into an almost mystic contemplation. Language can be used to rupture the smoothness of the visual image but it is language as pure mark uninformed by the psychoanalytic apprehension of the sign. Cultural artefacts are presented as images within images to rob them of the values they seem naturally to embody, but the fundamental sexual polarity of that culture is not called into account. Finally, meaning is seen to reside in these images as supplement, allegory or fragment, but with no sexual residue or trace – the concept of textuality is lifted out of psychoanalytic and literary theory but without the sexual definition that was its chief impetus and support.

Across a range of instances, language, sexuality and the unconscious *in their mutual relation* appear as a present-absence which all these moments seem to brush against, or elicit, before falling away. The elisions can be summarized schematically:

– purity of the visual signifier and the unconscious as mystique (no language);

– language as rupture of the iconicity of the visual sign (no unconscious);

– cultural artefacts as indictment of the stereotype (no sexual difference);

– reading as supplement, process or fragment (no sexual determinacy of the signifier or of visual space).

Artists engaged in sexual representation (representation *as* sexual) come in at precisely this point, calling up the sexual component of the image, drawing out an emphasis that exists *in potentia* in the various instances they inherit and of which they form a part.[11] Their move is not therefore one of (moral) corrective. They draw on the tendencies they also seek to displace, and clearly belong, for example, within the context of that postmodernism which demands that reference, in its problematized form, re-enter the frame. But the emphasis on sexuality produces specific effects. First, it adds to the concept of cultural artefact or stereotype the political imperative of feminism which holds the image accountable for the reproduction of norms. Secondly, to this feminist demand for scrutiny of the image, it adds the idea of a sexuality which goes beyond the issue of content to take in the parameters of visual form (not just what we see but how we see – visual space as more than the domain of simple recognition). The image therefore submits to the sexual reference, but only in so far as reference itself is questioned by the work of the image. And the aesthetics of pure form are implicated in the less pure pleasures of looking, but these in turn are part of an aesthetically extraneous political space. The arena is simultaneously that of aesthetics and sexuality, and art and sexual politics. The link between sexuality and the image produces a particular dialogue which cannot be covered adequately by the familiar opposition between the formal operations of the image and a politics exerted from outside.

The engagement with the image therefore belongs to a political intention. It is an intention which has also inflected the psychoanalytic and literary theories on which such artists draw. The model is not one of applying psychoanalysis to the work of art (what application could there finally be which does not reduce one field to the other or inhibit by interpretation the potential meaning of both?). Psychoanalysis offers a specific account of sexual difference but its value (and also its difficulty) for feminism, lies in the place assigned to the woman in that differentiation. In his essay on Leonardo, Freud himself says that once the boy child sees what it is to be a woman, he will 'tremble for his masculinity' henceforth.[12] If meaning oscillates when a castrato comes onto the scene, our sense must be that it is in the normal image of the man that our certainties are invested and, by implication, in that of the woman that they constantly threaten collapse.

A feminism concerned with the question of looking can therefore turn this theory around and stress the particular and limiting opposition of male and female which any image seen to be flawless is serving to hold in place. More simply, we know that women are meant to *look* perfect, presenting a seamless image to the world so that the man, in that confrontation with difference, can avoid any apprehension of lack. The position of woman as fantasy therefore depends on a particular economy of vision (the importance of 'images of women' might take on its fullest meaning from this).[13] Perhaps this is also why only a project which comes via feminism can demand so unequivocally of the image that it renounce all pretensions to a narcissistic perfection of form.

At the extreme edge of this investigation, we might argue that the fantasy of absolute sexual difference, in its present guise, could be upheld only from the point when painting restricted the human body to the eye.[14] That would be to give the history of the image in Western culture a particularly heavy weight to bear. For, even if the visual image has indeed been one of the chief vehicles through which such a restriction has been enforced, it could only operate like a law which always produces the terms of its own violation. It is often forgotten that psycho-analysis describes the psychic law to which we are subject, but only in terms of its *failing*. This is important for a feminist (or any radical) practice which has often felt it necessary to claim for itself a wholly other psychic and representa-tional domain. Therefore, if the visual image in its aesthetically acclaimed form serves to maintain a particular and oppressive mode of sexual recognition, it does so only partially and at a cost. Our previous history is not the petrified block of a singular visual space since, looked at obliquely, it can always be seen to contain its moments of unease.[15] We can surely relinquish the monolithic view of that history, if doing so allows us a form of resistance which can be articulated *on this side of* (rather than beyond) the world against which it protests.

Among Leonardo's early sketches, Freud discovers the heads of laughing women, images of exuberance which then fall out of the great canon of his art. Like Leonardo's picture of the sexual act, these images appear to unsettle Freud as if their pleasure somehow correlated with the discomfort of the sexual drawing (the sexual drawing through its failure, the heads of laughing women for their excess). These images, not well known in Leonardo's canon, now have the status of fragments, but they indicate a truth about the tradition which excludes them, revealing the presence of something strangely insistent to which these artists return. '*Teste di femmine, che ridono*'[16] – laughter is not the emphasis here, but the urgent engagement with the question of sexuality persists now, as it did then. It can no more be seen as the beginning, than it should be the end, of the matter.

NOTES

1. Sigmund Freud, 'Leonardo da Vinci and a Memory of his Childhood', [SE XI] p. 70n; [PFL 14] p. 159n. This essay was written for the catalogue of the exhibition *Difference: On Representation and Sexuality*, held at the New Museum of Contemporary Art, New York, December–February 1984–5 and at the Institute of Contemporary Arts, London, September–October 1985, pp. 31–3. The exhibition, curated by Kate Linker, included works by Ray Barrie, Victor Burgin, Hans Haacke, Mary Kelly, Silvia Kolbowski, Barbara Kruger, Sherry Levine, Yve Lomax, Jeff Wall and Marie Yates. There was also a film and video exhibition in conjunction with the art exhibition in New York, curated by Jane Weinstock. Only part of the drawing discussed here is now attributed to Leonardo, see 'Leonardo da Vinci', [PFL 14], p. 161n.
2. Freud, 'The Dissection of the Psychical Personality' [SE XXII] p. 79;]PFL 2] p. 112 (passage retranslated by Samuel Weber in *The Legend of Freud*, p. 1).
3. Peter Wollen makes a similar point on the relationship between perceptual and sexual contradiction in Manet's Olympia in 'Manet – Modernism and Avant-Garde', *Screen* 21: 2, Summer 1980, p. 21.
4. Freud, 'Some Physical Consequences of the Anatomical Distinction between the Sexes;, [SE XIX] p. 252, [PFL] pp. 335–6.

5. Freud, *From the History of an Infantile Neurosis*, [SE XVII] pp. 29–47; [PFL 9] pp. 80–1.

6. On the centrality of the visual image in Lacan's topography of psychic life, and on enunciation and the lying subject, see 'The Imaginary' and 'Dora – Fragment of an Analysis', note 24 in this collection [*Sexuality in the Field of Vision*].

7. For discussion of these issues in relation to film, see Laura Mulvey's crucial article, 'Visual Pleasure and Narrative Cinema', and also Jane Weinstock's article in *Difference: On Representation and Sexuality*.

8. Roland Barthes, 'Change the Object Itself'.

9. Barthes, *S/Z*.

10. Leo Steinberg defined postmodernism as the transition from nature to culture; this is reinterpreted by Craig Owens, 'The Allegorical Impulse – Towards a Theory of Postmodernism', *October* 12–13, Spring and Summer 1980, esp. pp. 79–80, and also Douglas Crimp, 'On the Museum's Ruins', *October* 13, Summer 1980. Craig Owens has recently used Freud's account of the creative impulse in a critical appraisal of the Expressionist revival, 'Honor, Power and the Love of Women', *Art and Artists*, January 1983.

11. For a discussion of some of these issues in relation to feminist art, see Mary Kelly, 'Re-viewing Modernist Criticism', *Screen* 22: 3, Autumn 1981.

12. 'Leonardo da Vinci and a Memory of his Childhood', op. cit., p. 95; pp. 186–7.

13. The status of the woman as fantasy in relation to the desire of the man was a central concern of Lacan's later writing; see *Encore*, especially 'God and the Jouissance of Woman' and 'A Love Letter' in *Feminine Sexuality*, and the commentary, 'Feminine Sexuality – Jacques Lacan and the *école freudienne*', in *Sexuality in the Field of Vision* (London and New York: Verso, 1986).

14. Norman Bryson describes post-Albertian perspective in terms of such a restriction in *Vision and Painting: The Logic of the Gaze* (London 1983).

15. See Lacan on death in Holbein's 'The Ambassadors', *The Four Fundamental Concepts*, pp. 85–90.

16. 'Leonardo da Vinci and a Memory of his Childhood', [SE XI] p. 111; [PFL 14] p. 203. An exhibition entitled *The Revolutionary Power of Women's Laughter*, including works by Barbara Kruger and Mary Kelly, was held at Protetch McNeil, New York, January 1983.

22

Sex and Violence, or Nature and Art

Camille Paglia

In the beginning was nature. The background from which and against which our ideas of God were formed, nature remains the supreme moral problem. We cannot hope to understand sex and gender until we clarify our attitude toward nature. Sex is a subset to nature. Sex is the natural in man.

Society is an artificial construction, a defense against nature's power. Without society, we would be storm-tossed on the barbarous sea that is nature. Society is a system of inherited forms reducing our humiliating passivity to nature. We may alter these forms, slowly or suddenly, but no change in society will change nature. Human beings are not nature's favorites. We are merely one of a multitude of species upon which nature indiscriminately exerts its force. Nature has a master agenda we can only dimly know.

Human life began in flight and fear. Religion rose from rituals of propitiation, spells to lull the punishing elements. To this day, communities are few in regions scorched by heat or shackled by ice. Civilized man conceals from himself the extent of his subordination to nature. The grandeur of culture, the consolation of religion absorb his attention and win his faith. But let nature shrug, and all is in ruin. Fire, flood, lightning, tornado, hurricane, volcano, earthquake – anywhere at any time. Disaster falls upon the good and bad. Civilized life requires a state of illusion. The idea of the ultimate benevolence of nature and God is the most potent of man's survival mechanisms. Without it, culture would revert to fear and despair.

Sexuality and eroticism are the intricate intersection of nature and culture. Feminists grossly oversimplify the problem of sex when they reduce it to a matter of social convention: readjust society, eliminate sexual inequality, purify sex roles, and happiness and harmony will reign. Here feminism, like all liberal movements of the past two hundred years, is heir to Rousseau. *The Social Contract* (1762) begins: 'Man is born free, and everywhere he is in chains.' Pitting benign Romantic nature against corrupt society, Rousseau produced the progressivist strain in nineteenth-century culture, for which social reform was the means to achieve paradise on earth. The bubble of these hopes was burst by the catastrophes of two world wars. But Rousseauism was reborn in the postwar generation of the sixties, from which contemporary feminism developed.

Rousseau rejects original sin, Christianity's pessimistic view of man born unclean, with a propensity for evil. Rousseau's idea, derived from Locke, of man's innate goodness led to social environmentalism, now the dominant ethic of American human services, penal codes, and behaviorist therapies. It assumes that aggression, violence, and crime come from social deprivation – a poor neighborhood, a bad home. Thus feminism blames rape on pornography and, by a smug circularity of reasoning, interprets outbreaks of sadism as a backlash to itself. But rape and sadism have been evident throughout history and, at some moment, in all cultures.

This book takes the point of view of Sade, the most unread major writer in western literature. Sade's work is a comprehensive satiric critique of Rousseau, written in the decade after the first failed Rousseauist experiment, the French Revolution, which ended not in political paradise but in the hell of the Reign of Terror. Sade follows Hobbes rather than Locke. Aggression comes from nature; it is what Nietzsche is to call the will-to-power. For Sade, getting back to nature (the Romantic imperative that still permeates our culture from sex counseling to cereal commercials) would be to give free rein to violence and lust. I agree. Society is not the criminal but the force which keeps crime in check. When social controls weaken, man's innate cruelty bursts forth. The rapist is created not by bad social influences but by a failure of social conditioning. Feminists, seeking to drive power relations out of sex, have set themselves against nature. Sex *is* power. Identity is power. In western culture, there are no non-exploitative relationships. Everyone has killed in order to live. Nature's universal law of creation from destruction operates in mind as in matter. As Freud, Nietzsche's heir, asserts, identity is conflict. Each generation drives its plow over the bones of the dead.

Modern liberalism suffers unresolved contradictions. It exalts individualism and freedom and, on its radical wing, condemns social orders as oppressive. On the other hand, it expects government to provide materially for all, a feat manageable only by an expansion of authority and a swollen bureaucracy. In other words, liberalism defines government as tyrant father but demands it behave as nurturant mother. Feminism has inherited these contradictions. It sees every hierarchy as repressive, a social fiction; every negative about woman is a male lie designed to keep her in her place. Feminism has exceeded its proper mission of seeking political equality for women and has ended by rejecting contingency, that is, human limitation by nature or fate.

Sexual freedom, sexual liberation. A modern delusion. We are hierarchical animals. Sweep one hierarchy away, and another will take its place, perhaps less palatable than the first. There are hierarchies in nature and alternate hierarchies in society. In nature, brute force is the law, a survival of the fittest. In society, there are protections for the weak. Society is our frail barrier against nature. When the prestige of state and religion is low, men are free, but they find freedom intolerable and seek new ways to enslave themselves, through drugs or depression. My theory is that whenever sexual freedom is sought or achieved, sadomasochism will not be far behind. Romanticism always turns into decadence. Nature is a hard taskmaster. It is the hammer and the anvil, crushing individuality. Perfect freedom would be to die by earth, air, water, and fire.

Sex is a far darker power than feminism has admitted. Behaviorist sex therapies believe guiltless, no-fault sex is possible. But sex has always been girt round with taboo, irrespective of culture. Sex is the point of contact between man and nature, where morality and good intentions fall to primitive urges. I called it an intersection. This intersection is the uncanny crossroads of Hecate, where all things return in the night. Eroticism is a realm stalked by ghosts. It is the place beyond the pale, both cursed and enchanted.

This book shows how much in culture goes against our best wishes. Integration of man's body and mind is a profound problem that is not about to be solved by recreational sex or an expansion of women's civil rights. Incarnation, the limitation of mind by matter, is an outrage to imagination. Equally outrageous is gender, which we have not chosen but which nature has imposed upon us. Our physicality is torment, our body the tree of nature on which Blake sees us crucified.

Sex is daemonic. This term, current in Romantic studies of the past twenty-five years, derives from the Greek *daimon*, meaning a spirit of lower divinity than the Olympian gods (hence my pronunciation 'daimonic'). The outcast Oedipus becomes a daemon at Colonus. The word came to mean a man's guardian shadow. Christianity turned the daemonic into the demonic. The Greek daemons were not evil – or rather they were both good and evil, like nature itself, in which they dwelled. Freud's unconscious is a daemonic realm. In the day we are social creatures, but at night we descend to the dream world where nature reigns, where there is no law but sex, cruelty, and metamorphosis. Day itself is invaded by daemonic night. Moment by moment, night flickers in the imagination, in eroticism, subverting our strivings for virtue and order, giving an uncanny aura to objects and persons, revealed to us through the eyes of the artist.

The ghost-ridden character of sex is implicit in Freud's brilliant theory of 'family romance'. We each have an incestuous constellation of sexual personae that we carry from childhood to the grave and that determines whom and how we love or hate. Every encounter with friend or foe, every clash with or submission to authority bears the perverse traces of family romance. Love is a crowded theater, for as Harold Bloom remarks, 'We can never embrace (sexually or otherwise) a single person, but embrace the whole of her or his family romance.'[1] We still know next to nothing of the mystery of cathexis, the investment of libido in certain people or things. The element of free will in sex and emotion is slight. As poets know, falling in love is irrational.

Like art, sex is fraught with symbols. Family romance means that adult sex is always representation, ritualistic acting out of vanished realities. A perfectly humane eroticism may be impossible. Somewhere in every family romance is hostility and aggression, the homicidal wishes of the unconscious. Children are monsters of unbridled egotism and will, for they spring directly from nature, hostile intimations of immorality. We carry that daemonic will within us forever. Most people conceal it with acquired ethical precepts and meet it only in their dreams, which they hastily forget upon waking. The will-to-power is innate, but the sexual scripts of family romance are learned. Human beings are the only creatures in whom consciousness is so entangled with animal instinct. In western culture, there can never be a purely physical or anxiety-free sexual encounter. Every attraction, every pattern of touch, every orgasm is shaped by psychic shadows.

The search for freedom through sex is doomed to failure. In sex, compulsion and ancient Necessity rule. The sexual personae of family romance are obliterated by the tidal force of regression, the backwards movement toward primeval dissolution, which Ferenczi identifies with ocean. An orgasm is a domination, a surrender, or a breaking through. Nature is no respecter of human identity. This is why so many men turn away or flee after sex, for they have sensed the annihilation of the daemonic. Western love is a displacement of cosmic realities. It is a defense mechanism rationalizing forces ungoverned and ungovernable. Like early religion, it is a device enabling us to control our primal fear.

Sex cannot be understood because nature cannot be understood. Science is a method of logical analysis of nature's operations. It has lessened human anxiety about the cosmos by demonstrating the materiality of nature's forces, and their frequent predictability. But science is always playing catch-up ball. Nature breaks its own rules whenever it wants. Science cannot avert a single thunderbolt. Western science is a product of the Apollonian mind; its hope is that by naming and classification, by the cold light of intellect, archaic night can be pushed back and defeated.

Name and person are part of the west's quest for form. The west insists on the discrete identity of objects. To name is to know; to know is to control. I will demonstrate that the west's greatness arises from this delusional certitude. Far Eastern culture has never striven against nature in this way. Compliance, not confrontation is its rule. Buddhist meditation seeks the unity and harmony of reality. Twentieth-century physics, going full circle back to Heracleitus, postulates that all matter is in motion. In other words, there is no thing, only energy. But this perception has not been imaginatively absorbed, for it cancels the west's intellectual and moral assumptions.

The westerner knows by seeing. Perceptual relations are at the heart of our culture, and they have produced our titanic contributions to art. Walking in nature, we see, identify, name, *recognize*. This recognition is our apotropaion, that is, our warding off of fear. Recognition is ritual cognition, a repetition-compulsion. We say that nature is beautiful. But this aesthetic judgment, which not all peoples have shared, is another defense formation, woefully inadequate for encompassing nature's totality. What is pretty in nature is confined to the thin skin of the globe upon which we huddle. Scratch that skin, and nature's daemonic ugliness will erupt.

Our focus on the pretty is an Apollonian strategy. The leaves and flowers, the birds, the hills are a patchwork pattern by which we map the known. What the west represses in its view of nature is the chthonian, which means 'of the earth' – but earth's bowels, not its surface. Jane Harrison uses the term for pre-Olympian Greek religion, and I adopt it as a substitute for Dionysian, which has become contaminated with vulgar pleasantries. The Dionysian is no picnic. It is the chthonian realities which Apollo evades, the blind grinding of subterranean force, the long slow suck, the murk and ooze. It is the dehumanizing brutality of biology and geology, the Darwinian waste and bloodshed, the squalor and rot we must block from consciousness to retain our Apollonian integrity as persons. Western science and aesthetics are attempts to revise this horror into imaginatively palatable form.

The daemonism of chthonian nature is the west's dirty secret. Modern humanists made the 'tragic sense of life' the touchstone of mature understanding. They defined man's mortality and the transience of time as literature's supreme subjects. In this I again see evasion and even sentimentality. The tragic sense of life is a partial response to experience. It is a reflex of the west's resistance to and misapprehension of nature, compounded by the errors of liberalism, which in its Romantic nature-philosophy has followed the Rousseauist Wordsworth rather than the daemonic Coleridge.

Tragedy is the most western literary genre. It did not appear in Japan until the late nineteenth century. The western will, setting itself up against nature, dramatized its own inevitable fall as a human universal, which it is not. An irony of literary history is the birth of tragedy in the cult of Dionysus. The protagonist's destruction recalls the slaughter of animals and, even earlier, of real human beings in archaic ritual. It is no accident that tragedy as we know it dates from the Apollonian fifth century of Athens' greatness, whose cardinal work is Aeschylus' *Oresteia*, a celebration of the defeat of chthonian power. Drama, a Dionysian mode, turned against Dionysus in making the passage from ritual to mimesis, that is, from action to representation. Aristotle's 'pity and fear' is a broken promise, a plea for vision without horror.

Few Greek tragedies fully conform to the humanist commentary on them. Their barbaric residue will not come unglued. Even in the fifth century, as we shall see, a satiric response to Apollonianized theater came in Euripides' decadent plays. Problems in accurate assessment of Greek tragedy include not only the loss of three-quarters of the original body of work but the lack of survival of any complete satyr-play. This was the finale to the classic trilogy, an obscene comic burlesque. In Greek tragedy, comedy always had the last word. Modern criticism has projected a Victorian and, I feel, Protestant high seriousness upon pagan culture that still blankets teaching of the humanities. Paradoxically, assent to savage chthonian realities leads not to gloom but to humor. Hence Sade's strange laughter, his wit amid the most fantastic cruelties. For life is not a tragedy but a comedy. Comedy is born of the clash between Apollo and Dionysus. Nature is always pulling the rug out from under our pompous ideals.

Female tragic protagonists are rare. Tragedy is a male paradigm of rise and fall, a graph in which dramatic and sexual climax are in shadowy analogy. Climax is another western invention. Traditional eastern stories are picaresque, horizontal chains of incident. There is little suspense or sense of an ending. The sharp vertical peaking of western narrative, as later of orchestral music, is exemplified by Sophocles' *Oedipus Rex*, whose moment of maximum intensity Aristotle calls *peripeteia*, reversal. Western dramatic climax was produced by the agon of male will. Through action to identity. Action is the route of the escape from nature, but all action circles back to origins, the womb-tomb of nature, Oedipus, trying to escape his mother, runs straight into her arms. Western narrative is a mystery story, a process of detection. But since what is detected is unbearable, every revelation leads to another repression.

The major women of tragedy – Euripides' Medea and Phaedra, Shakespeare's Cleopatra and Lady Macbeth, Racine's Phèdre – skew the genre by their disruptive relation to male action. Tragic woman is less moral than man. Her will-to-will power is naked. Her actions are under a chthonian cloud. They are a conduit of the irrational, opening the genre to intrusions of the barbaric force that drama shut out at its birth. Tragedy is a western vehicle for testing and purification of the male will. The difficulty in grafting female protagonists onto it is a result not of male prejudice but of instinctive sexual strategics. Woman introduces untransformed cruelty into tragedy because she is the problem that the genre is trying to correct.

Tragedy plays a male game, a game it invented to snatch victory from the jaws of defeat. It is not flawed choice, flawed action, or even death itself which is the ultimate human dilemma. The gravest challenge to our hopes and dreams is the messy biological business-as-usual that is going on within us and without us at every hour of every day. Consciousness is a pitiful hostage of its flesh-envelope, whose surges, circuits, and secret murmurings it cannot stay or speed. This is the chthonian drama that has no climax but only an endless round, cycle upon cycle. Microcosm mirrors macrocosm. Free will is stillborn in the red cells of our body, for there is no free will in nature. Our choices come to us pre-packaged and special delivery, molded by hands not our own.

Tragedy's inhospitality to woman springs from nature's inhospitality to man. The identification of woman with nature was universal in prehistory. In hunting or agrarian societies dependent upon nature, femaleness was honored as an immanent principle of fertility. As culture progressed, crafts and commerce supplied a concentration of resources freeing men from the caprices of weather or the handicap of geography. With nature at one remove, femaleness receded in importance.

Buddhist cultures retained the ancient meanings of femaleness long after the west renounced them. Male and female, the Chinese yang and yin, are balanced and interpenetrating powers in man and nature, to which society is subordinate. This code of passive acceptance has its roots in India, a land of sudden extremes where a monsoon can wipe out 50,000 people overnight. The femaleness of fertility religions is always double-edged. The Indian nature-goddess Kali is creator *and* destroyer, granting boons with one set of arms while cutting throats with the other. She is the lady ringed with skulls. The moral ambivalence of the great mother goddesses has been conveniently forgotten by those American feminists who have resurrected them. We cannot grasp nature's bare blade without shedding our own blood.

Western culture from the start has swerved from femaleness. The last major western society to worship female powers was Minoan Crete. And significantly, that fell and did not rise again. The immediate cause of its collapse – quake, plague, or invasion – is beside the point. The lesson is that cultic femaleness is no guarantee of cultural strength or viability. What did survive, what did vanquish circumstance and stamp its mind-set on Europe was Mycenaean warrior culture, descending to us through Homer. The male will-to-power: Mycenaeans from the south and Dorians from the north would fuse to form Apollonian Athens, from which came the Greco-Roman line of western history.

Both the Apollonian and Judeo-Christian traditions are transcendental. That is, they seek to surmount or transcend nature. Despite Greek culture's contrary Dionysian element, which I will discuss, high classicism was an Apollonian achievement. Judaism, Christianity's parent sect, is the most powerful of protests against nature. The Old Testament asserts that a father god made nature and that differentiation into objects and gender was after the fact of his maleness. Judeo-Christianity, like Greek worship of the Olympian gods, is a sky-cult. It is an advanced stage in the history of religion, which everywhere began as earth-cult, veneration of fruitful nature.

The evolution from earth-cult to sky-cult shifts woman into the nether realm. Her mysterious procreative powers and the resemblance of her rounded breasts, belly and hips to earth's contours put her at the center of early symbolism. She was the model for the Great Mother figures who crowded the birth of religion worldwide. But the mother cults did not mean social freedom for women. On the contrary, as I will show in a discussion of Hollywood in the sequel to this book, cult-objects are prisoners of their own symbolic inflation. Every totem lives in taboo.

Woman was an idol of belly-magic. She seemed to swell and give birth by her own law. From the beginning of time, woman has seemed an uncanny being. Man honored but feared her. She was the black maw that had spat him forth and would devour him anew. Men, bonding together, invented culture as a defense against female nature. Sky-cult was the most sophisticated step in this process, for its switch of the creative locus from earth to sky is a shift from belly-magic to head-magic. And from this defensive head-magic has come the spectacular glory of male civilization, which has lifted woman with it. The very language and logic modern woman uses to assail patriarchal culture were the invention of men.

Hence the sexes are caught in a comedy of historical indebtedness. Man, repelled by his debt to a physical mother, created an alternate reality, a heterocosm to give him the illusion of freedom. Woman, at first content to accept man's protections but now inflamed with desire for her own illusory freedom, invades man's systems and suppresses her indebtedness to him as she steals them. By head-magic she will deny there ever was a problem of sex and nature. She has inherited the anxiety of influence.

The identification of woman with nature is the most troubled and troubling term in this historical argument. Was it ever true? Can it still be true? Most feminist readers will disagree, but I think this identification not myth but reality. All the genres of philosophy, science, high art, athletics, and politics were invented by men. But by the Promethean law of conflict and capture, woman has a right to seize what she will and to vie with man on his own terms. Yet there is a limit to what she can alter in herself and in man's relation to her. Every human being must wrestle with nature. But nature's burden falls more heavily on one sex. With luck, this will not limit woman's achievement, that is, her action in male-created social space. But it must limit eroticism, that is, our imaginative lives in sexual space, which may overlap social space but is not identical with it.

Nature's cycles are woman's cycles. Biologic femaleness is a sequence of circular returns, beginning and ending at the same point. Woman's centrality gives her a stability of identity. She does not have to become but only to be. Her centrality is a great obstacle to man, whose quest for identity she blocks. He must transform himself into an independent being, that is, a being free of her. If he does not, he will simply fall back into her. Reunion with the mother is a siren call haunting our imagination. Once there was bliss, and now there is struggle. Dim memories of life before the traumatic separation of birth may be the source of Arcadian fantasies of a lost golden age. The western idea of history as a propulsive movement into the future, a progressive or Providential design climaxing in the revelation of a Second Coming, is a male formulation. No woman, I submit, could have coined such an idea, since it is a strategy of evasion of woman's own cyclic nature, in which man dreads being caught. Evolutionary or apocalyptic history is a male wish list with a happy ending, a phallic peak.

Woman does not dream of transcendental or historical escape from natural cycle, since she *is* that cycle. Her sexual maturity means marriage to the moon, waxing and waning in lunar phases. Moon, month, menses: same word, same world. The ancients knew that woman is bound to nature's calendar, an appointment she cannot refuse. The Greek pattern of free will to hubris to tragedy is a male drama, since woman has never been deluded (until recently) by the mirage of free will. She knows there is no free will, since she is not free. She has no choice but acceptance. Whether she desires motherhood or not, nature yokes her into the brute inflexible rhythm of procreative law. Menstrual cycle is an alarming clock that cannot be stopped until nature wills it.

Woman's reproductive apparatus is vastly more complicated than man's, and still ill-understood. All kinds of things can go wrong or cause distress in going right. Western woman is in an agonistic relation to her own body: for her, biologic normalcy is suffering, and health an illness. Dysmenorrhea, it is argued, is a disease of civilization, since women in tribal cultures have few menstrual complaints. But in tribal life, woman has an extended or collective identity; tribal religion honors nature and subordinates itself to it. It is precisely in advanced western society, which attempts to improve or surpass nature and which holds up individualism and self-realization as a model, that the stark facts of woman's condition emerge with painful clarity. The more woman aims for personal identity and autonomy, the more she develops her imagination, the fiercer will be her struggle with nature – that is, with the intractable physical laws of her own body. And the more nature will punish her: do not dare to be free! for your body does not belong to you.

The female body is a chthonian machine, indifferent to the spirit who inhabits it. Organically, it has one mission, pregnancy, which we may spend a lifetime staving off. Nature cares only for species, never individuals: the humiliating dimensions of this biologic fact are most directly experienced by women, who probably have a greater realism and wisdom than men because of it. Woman's body is a sea acted upon by the month's lunar wave-motion. Sluggish and dormant, her fatty tissues are gorged with water, then suddenly cleansed at hormonal high tide. Edema is our mammalian relapse into the vegetable. Pregnancy demonstrates the deterministic character of woman's sexuality. Every pregnant woman has body and self taken over by a chthonian force beyond her control. In the welcome pregnancy, this is a happy sacrifice. But in the unwanted one, initiated by rape or misadventure, it is a horror. Such unfortunate women look directly into nature's heart of darkness. For a fetus is a benign tumor, a vampire who steals in order to live. The so-called miracle of birth is nature getting her own way.

Every month for women is a new defeat of the will. Menstruation was once called 'the curse', a reference to the expulsion from the Garden, when woman was condemned to labor pains because of Eve's sin. Most early cultures hemmed in menstruating women by ritual taboos. Orthodox Jewish women still purify themselves from menstrual and uncleanness in the *mikveh*, a ritual bath. Women have borne the symbolic burden of man's imperfections, his grounding in nature. Menstrual blood is the stain, the birthmark of original sin, the filth that transcendental religion must wash from man. Is this identification merely phobic, merely misogynistic? Or is it possible there *is* something uncanny about menstrual blood, justifying its attachment to taboo? I will argue that it is not menstrual blood per se which disturbs the imagination – unstaunchable as that red flood may be – but rather the albumen in the blood, the uterine shreds, placental jellyfish of the female sea. This is the chthonian matrix from which we rose. We have an evolutionary revulsion from slime, our site of biologic origins. Every month, it is woman's fate to face the abyss of time and being, the abyss which is herself.

The Bible has come under fire for making woman the fall guy in man's cosmic drama. But in casting a male conspirator, the serpent, as God's enemy, Genesis hedges and does not take its misogyny far enough. The Bible defensively swerves from God's true opponent, chthonian nature. The serpent is not outside Eve but in her. She is the garden *and* the serpent. Anthony Storr says of witches, 'At a very primitive level, all mothers are phallic.'[2] The Devil is a woman. Modern emancipation movements, discarding stereotypes impeding woman's social advance, refuse to acknowledge procreation's daemonism. Nature is serpentine, a bed of tangled vines, creepers and crawlers, probing dumb fingers of fetid organic life which Wordsworth taught us to call pretty. Biologists speak of man's reptilian brain, the oldest part of our upper nervous system, killer survivor of the archaic era. I contend that the premenstrual woman incited to snappishness or rage is hearing signals from the reptilian brain. In her, man's latent perversity is manifest. All hell breaks loose, the hell of chthonian nature that modern humanism denies and represses. In every premenstrual woman struggling to govern her temper, sky-cult wars again with earth-cult.

Mythology's identification of woman with nature is correct. The male contribution to procreation is momentary and transient. Conception is a pinpoint of time, another of our phallic peaks of action, from which the male slides back uselessly. The pregnant woman is daemonically, devilishly complete. As an ontological entity, she needs nothing and no one. I shall maintain that the pregnant woman, brooding for nine months upon her own creation, is the pattern of all solipsism, that the historical attribution of narcissism to women is another true myth. Male bonding and patriarchy were the recourse to which man was forced by his terrible sense of woman's power, her imperviousness, her archetypal confederacy with chthonian nature. Woman's body is a labyrinth in which man is lost. It is a walled garden, the medieval *hortus conclusus*, in which nature works its daemonic sorcery. Woman is the primeval fabricator, the real First Mover. She turns a gob of refuse into a spreading web of sentient being, floating on the snaky umbilical by which she leashes every man.

Feminism has been simplistic in arguing that female archetypes were politically motivated falsehoods by men. The historical repugnance to woman has a rational basis: disgust is reason's proper response to the grossness of procreative nature. Reason and logic are the anxiety-inspired domain of Apollo, premiere god of sky-cult. The Apollonian is harsh and phobic, coldly cutting itself off from nature by its superhuman purity. I shall argue that western personality and western achievement are, for better or worse, largely Apollonian. Appollo's great opponent Dionysus is ruler of the chthonian whose law is procreative femaleness.

As we shall see, the Dionysian is liquid nature, a miasmic swamp whose proto-
type is the still pond of the womb.

[. . .]

NOTES

1. Harold Bloom, *The Anxiety of Influence: A Theory of Poetry* (New York, 1973), p. 94.
2. Anthony Storr, *Sexual Deviation* (Harmondsworth, Middx, 1964) p. 63.

23

Subjects of Sex/Gender/Desire

Judith Butler

[. . .]

THEORIZING THE BINARY, THE UNITARY, AND BEYOND
[. . .]

Feminist critique ought to explore the totalizing claims of a masculinist signifying economy, but also remain self-critical with respect to the totalizing gestures of feminism. The effort to identify the enemy as singular in form is a reverse-discourse that uncritically mimics the strategy of the oppressor instead of offering a different set of terms. That the tactic can operate in feminist and anti-feminist contexts alike suggests that the colonizing gesture is not primarily or irreducibly masculinist. It can operate to effect other relations of racial, class and heterosexist subordination, to name but a few. And clearly, listing the varieties of oppression, as I began to do, assumes their discrete, sequential coexistence along a horizontal axis that does not describe their convergences within the social field. A vertical model is similarly insufficient; oppressions cannot be summarily ranked, causally related, distributed among places of 'originality' and 'derivativeness'.[1] Indeed, the field of power structured in part by the imperializing gesture of dialectical appropriation exceeds and encompasses the axis of sexual difference, offering a mapping of intersecting differentials which cannot be summarily hierarchized either within the terms of phallogocentrism or any other candidate for the position of 'primary condition of oppression'. Rather than an exclusive tactic of masculinist signifying economies, dialectical appropriation and suppression of the Other is one tactic among many, deployed centrally but not exclusively in the service of expanding and rationalizing the masculinist domain.

The contemporary feminist debates over essentialism raise the question of the universality of female identity and masculinist oppression in other ways. Universalistic claims are based on a common or shared epistemological standpoint, understood as the articulated consciousness or shared structures of oppression or in the ostensibly transcultural structures of femininity, sexuality, and/or *écriture feminine*. The opening discussion in this chapter argued that this globalizing gesture has spawned a number of criticisms from women who claim that the category of 'woman' is normative and exclusionary and is invoked with the unmarked dimensions of class and racial privilege intact. In other words, the insistence upon the coherence and unity of the category of women has effectively refused the multiplicity of cultural, social, and political intersections in which the concrete array of 'women' are constructed.

Some efforts have been made to formulate coalitional politics which do not assume in advance what the content of 'women' will be. They propose instead a set of dialogic encounters by which variously positioned women articulate separate identities within the framework of an emergent coalition. Clearly, the value of coalitional politics is not to be underestimated, but the very form of coalition, of an emerging and unpredictable assemblage of positions, cannot be figured in advance. Despite the clearly democratizing impulse that motivates coalition building, the coalitional theorist can inadvertently reinsert herself as sovereign of the process by trying to assert an ideal form for coalitional structures *in advance*, one that will effectively guarantee unity as the outcome. Related efforts to determine what is and is not the true shape of a dialogue, what constitutes a subject-position, and, most importantly, when 'unity' has been reached, can impede the self-shaping and self-limiting dynamics and coalition.

The insistence in advance on coalitional 'unity' as a goal assumes that solidarity, whatever its price, is a prerequisite for political action. But what sort of politics demands that kind of advance purchase on unity? Perhaps a coalition needs to acknowledge its contradictions and take action with those contradictions intact. Perhaps also part of what dialogic understanding entails is the acceptance of divergence, breakage, splinter, and fragmentation as part of the often tortuous process of democratization. The very notion of 'dialogue' is culturally specific and historically bound, and while one speaker may feel secure that a conversation is happening, another may be sure it is not. The power relations that condition and limit dialogic possibilities need first to be interrogated. Otherwise, the model of dialogue risks relapsing into a liberal model that assumes that speaking agents occupy equal positions of power and speak with the same presuppositions about what constitutes 'agreement' and 'unity' and, indeed, that those are the goals to be sought. It would be wrong to assume in advance that there is a category of 'women' that simply needs to be filled in with various components of race, class, age, ethnicity, and sexuality in order to become complete. The assumptions of its essential incompleteness permits that category to serve as a permanently available site of contested meanings. The definitional incompleteness of the category might then serve as a normative ideal relieved of coercive force.

Is 'unity' necessary for effective political action? Is the premature insistence on the goal of unity precisely the cause of an ever more bitter fragmentation among the ranks? Certain forms of acknowledged fragmentation might faciliate coalitional action precisely because the 'unity' of the category of women is neither presupposed nor desired. Does 'unity' set up an exclusionary norm of solidarity at the level of identity that rules out the possibility of a set of actions which disrupt the very borders of identity concepts, or which seek to accomplish precisely that disruption as an explicit political aim? Without the presupposition or goal of 'unity', which is, in either case, always instituted at a conceptual level, provisional unities might emerge in the context of concrete actions that have purposes other than that articulation of identity. Without the compulsory expectation that feminist actions must be instituted from some stable, unified, and agreed upon identity, those actions might well get a quicker start and seem more congenial to a number of 'women' for whom the meaning of the category is permanently moot.

This anti-foundationalist approach to coalitional politics assumes neither that 'identity' is a premise nor that the shape or meaning of a coalitional assemblage can be known prior to its achievement. Because the articulation of an identity within available cultural terms instates a definition that forecloses in advance the emergence of new identity concepts in and through politically engaged actions, the foundationalist tactic cannot take the transformation or expansion of existing identity concepts as a normative goal. Moreover, when agreed-upon identities or agreed-upon dialogic structures, through which already established identities are communicated, no longer constitute the theme or subject of politics, then identities can come into being and dissolve depending on the concrete practices that constitute them. Certain political practices institute identities on a contingent basis in order to accomplish whatever aims are in view. Coalitional politics requires neither an expanded category of 'women' nor an internally multiplicitous self that offers its complexity at once.

Gender is a complexity whose totality is permanently deferred, never fully what it is at any given juncture in time. An open coalition, then, will affirm identities that are alternately instituted and relinquished according to the purposes at hand; it will be an open assemblage that permits of multiple convergences and divergences without obedience to a normative telos of definitional closure.

IDENTITY, SEX, AND THE METAPHYSICS OF SUBSTANCE

What can be meant by 'identity', then, and what grounds the presumption that identities are self-identical, persisting through time as the same, unified and internally coherent? More importantly, how do these assumptions inform the discourses on 'gender identity'? It would be wrong to think that the discussion of 'identity' ought to proceed prior to a discussion of gender identity for the simple reason that 'persons' only become intelligible through becoming gendered in conformity with recognizable standards of gender intelligibility. Sociological discussions have conventionally sought to understand the notion of the person in terms of an agency that claims ontological priority to the various roles and functions through which it assumes social visibility and meaning. Within philosophical discourse itself, the notion of 'the person' has received analytic elaboration on the assumption that whatever social context the person is 'in' remains somehow externally related to the definitional structure of personhood, be that consciousness, the capacity for language, or moral deliberation. Although that literature is not examined here, one premise of such inquiries is the focus of critical exploration and inversion. Whereas the question of what constitutes 'personal identity' within philosophical accounts almost always centers on the question of what internal feature of the person establishes the continuity or self-identity of the person through time, the question here will be: To what extent do *regulatory practices* of gender formation and division constitute identity, the internal coherence of the subject, indeed, the self-identical status of the person? To what extent is 'identity' a normative ideal rather than a descriptive feature of experience? And how do the regulatory practices that govern gender also govern culturally intelligible notions of identity? In other words, the 'coherence' and 'continuity' of 'the person' are not logical or analytic features of personhood, but, rather, socially instituted and maintained norms of intelligibility. Inasmuch as 'identity' is assured through the stabilizing concepts of sex, gender, and sexuality, the very notion of 'the person' is called into question by the cultural emergence of those 'incoherent' or 'discontinuous' gendered beings who appear to be persons but who fail to conform to the gendered norms of cultural intelligibility by which persons are defined.

'Intelligible' genders are those which in some sense institute and maintain relations of coherence and continuity among sex, gender, sexual practice, and desire. In other words, the spectres of discontinuity and incoherence, themselves thinkable only in relation to existing norms of continuity and coherence, are constantly prohibited and produced by the very laws that seek to establish causal or expressive lines of connection among biological sex, culturally constituted genders, and the 'expression' or 'effect' of both in the manifestation of sexual desire through sexual practice.

The notion that there might be a 'truth' of sex, as Foucault ironically terms it, is produced precisely through the regulatory practices that generate coherent identities through the matrix of coherent gender norms. The heterosexualization of desire requires and institutes the production of discrete and asymmetrical oppositions between 'feminine' and 'masculine', where these are understood as expressive attributes of 'male' and 'female'. The cultural matrix through which gender identity has become intelligible requires that certain kinds of 'identities' cannot 'exist' – that is, those in which gender does not follow from sex and those in which the practices of desire do not 'follow' from either sex or gender. 'Follow' in this context is a political relation of entailment instituted by the cultural laws that establish and regulate the shape and meaning of sexuality. Indeed, precisely because certain kinds of 'gender identities' fail to conform to those norms of cultural intelligibility, they appear only as developmental failures or logical impossibilities from within that domain. Their persistence and proliferation, however, provide critical opportunities to expose the limits and regulatory aims of that domain of intelligibility and, hence, to open up within the very terms of that matrix of intelligibility rival and subversive matrices of gender disorder.

Before such disordering practices are considered, however, it seems crucial to understand the 'matrix of intelligibility'. Is it singular? Of what is it composed? What is the peculiar alliance presumed to exist between a system of compulsory heterosexuality and the discursive categories that establish the identity concepts of sex? If 'identity' is an *effect* of discursive practices, to what extent is gender identity, construed as a relationship among sex, gender, sexual practice, and desire, the effect of a regulatory practice that can be identified as compulsory heterosexuality? Would that explanation return us to yet another totalizing frame in which compulsory heterosexuality merely takes the place of phallogocentrism as the monolithic cause of gender oppression?

Within the spectrum of French feminist and poststructuralist theory, very different regimes of power are understood to produce the identity concepts of sex. Consider the divergence between those positions, such as Irigaray's, that claim there is only one sex, the masculine, that elaborates itself in and through the production of the 'Other', and those positions, Foucault's, for instance, that assume that the category of sex, whether masculine or feminine, is a production of a diffuse regulatory economy of sexuality. Consider also Wittig's argument that the category of sex is, under the conditions of compulsory heterosexuality, always feminine (the masculine remaining unmarked and, hence, synonomous with the 'universal'). Wittig concurs, however paradoxically, with Foucault in claiming that the category of sex would itself disappear and, indeed, *dissipate* through the disruption and displacement of heterosexual hegemony.

The various explanatory models offered here suggest the very different ways in which the category of sex is understood depending on how the field of power is articulated. Is it possible to maintain the complexity of these fields of power and think through their productive capacities together? On the one hand, Irigaray's theory of sexual difference suggests that women can never be understood on the model of a 'subject' within the conventional representational systems of Western culture precisely because they constitute the fetish of representation and, hence, the unrepresentable as such. Women can never 'be', according to this ontology of substances, precisely because they are the relation of difference, the excluded, by which that domain marks itself off. Women are also a 'difference' that cannot be understood as the simple negation or 'Other' of the always-already-masculine subject. As discussed earlier, they are neither the subject nor its Other, but a difference from the economy of binary opposition, itself a ruse for a monologic elaboration of the masculine.

Central to each of these views, however, is the notion that sex appears within hegemonic language as a *substance*, as, metaphysically speaking, a self-identical being. This appearance is achieved through a performative twist of language and/or discourse that conceals the fact that 'being' a sex or a gender is fundamentally impossible. For Irigaray, grammar can never be a true index of gender relations precisely because it supports the substantial model of gender as a binary relation between two positive and representable terms.[2] In Irigaray's view, the substantive grammar of gender, which assumes men and women as well as their attributes of masculine and feminine, is an example of a binary that effectively masks the univocal and hegemonic discourse of the masculine, phallogocentrism, silencing the feminine as a site of subversive multiplicity. For Foucault, the substantive grammar of sex imposes an artificial binary relation between the sexes, as well as an artificial internal coherence within each term of that binary. The binary regulation of sexuality suppresses the subversive multiplicity of a sexuality that disrupts heterosexual, reproductive, and medicojuridical hegemonies.

For Wittig, the binary restriction on sex serves the reproductive aims of a system of compulsory heterosexuality; occasionally, she claims that the overthrow of compulsory heterosexuality will inaugurate a true humanism of 'the person' freed from the shackles of sex. In other contexts, she suggests that the profusion and diffusion of a nonphallocentric erotic economy will dispel the illusions of sex, gender, and identity. At yet other textual moments it seems that 'the lesbian' emerges as a third gender that promises to transcend the binary restriction on sex imposed by the system of compulsory heterosexuality. In her defense of the 'cognitive subject', Wittig appears to have no metaphysical quarrel with hegemonic modes of signification or representation; indeed, the subject, with its attribute of self-determination, appears to be the rehabilitation of the agent of existential choice under the name of the lesbian: 'the advent of individual subjects demands first destroying the categories of sex . . . the lesbian is the only concept I know of which is beyond the categories of sex.'[3] She does not criticize 'the subject' as invariably masculine according to the rules of an inevitably patriarchal Symbolic, but proposes in its place the equivalent of a lesbian subject as language-user.[4]

The identification of women with 'sex', for Beauvoir as for Wittig, is a conflation of the category of women with the ostensibly sexualized features of their bodies and hence, a refusal to grant freedom and autonomy to women as it is purportedly enjoyed by men. Thus, the destruction of the category of sex would be the destruction of an *attribute*, sex, that has, through a misogynist gesture of synecdoche, come to take the place of the person, the self-determining *cogito*. In other words, only men are 'persons', and there is no gender but the feminine:

> Gender is the linguistic index of the political opposition between the sexes. Gender is used here in the singular because indeed there are not two genders. There is only one: the feminine, the 'masculine' not being a gender. For the masculine is not the masculine, but the general.[5]

Hence, Wittig calls for the destruction of 'sex' so that women can assume the status of a universal subject. On the way toward that destruction, 'women' must assume both a particular and a universal point of view.[6] As a subject who can realize concrete universality through freedom, Wittig's lesbian confirms rather than contests the normative promise of humanist ideals premised on the metaphysics of substance. In this respect, Wittig is distinguished from Irigaray, not only in terms of the now familiar oppositions between essentialism and materialism,[7] but in terms of the adherence to a metaphysics of substance that confirms the normative model of humanism as the framework for feminism. Where it seems that Wittig has subscribed to a radical project of lesbian emancipation and enforced a distinction between 'lesbian' and 'woman', she does this through the defense of the pregendered 'person', characterized as freedom. This move not only confirms the presocial status of human freedom, but subscribes to that metaphysics of substance that is responsible for the production and naturalization of the category of sex itself.

The metaphysics of substance is a phrase that is associated with Nietzsche within the contemporary criticism of philosophical discourse. In a commentary on Nietzsche, Michel Haar argues that a number of philosophical ontologies have been trapped within certain illusions of 'Being' and 'Substance' that are fostered by the belief that the grammatical formulation of subject and predicate reflects the prior ontological reality of substance and attribute. These constructs, argues Haar, constitute the artificial philosophical means by which simplicity, order, and identity are effectively instituted. In no sense, however, do they reveal or represent some true order of things. For our purposes, this Nietzschean criticism becomes instructive when it is applied to the psychological categories that govern much popular and theoretical thinking about gender identity. According to Haar, the critique of the metaphysics of substance implies a critique of the very notion of the psychological person as a substantive thing:

> The destruction of logic by means of its genealogy brings with it as well the ruin of the psychological categories founded upon this logic. All psychological categories (the ego, the individual, the person) derive from the illusion of substantial identity. But this illusion goes back basically to a superstition that deceives not only common sense but also philosophers – namely, the belief in language and, more precisely, in the truth of grammatical categories. It was grammar (the structure of subject and predicate) that inspired Descartes' certainty that 'I' is the subject of 'think', whereas it is rather the thoughts that come to 'me': at bottom, faith in grammar simply conveys the will to be the 'cause' of one's thoughts. The subject, the self, the individual, are just so many false concepts, since they transform into substances fictitious unities having at the start only a linguistic reality.[8]

Wittig provides an alternative critique by showing that persons cannot be signified within language without the mark of gender. She provides a political analysis of the grammar of gender in French. According to Wittig, gender not only designates persons, 'qualifies' them, as it were, but constitutes a conceptual episteme by which binary gender is universalized. Although French gives gender to all sorts of nouns other than persons, Wittig argues that her analysis has consequences for English as well. At the outset of 'The Mark of Gender' (1984), she writes:

> The mark of gender, according to grammarians, concerns substantives. They talk about it in terms of function. If they question its meaning, they may joke about it, calling gender a 'fictive sex'. . . . as far as the categories of the person are concerned, both [English and French] are bearers of gender to the same extent. Both indeed give way to a primitive ontological concept that enforces in language a division of beings into sexes. . . . As an ontological concept that deals with the nature of Being, along with a whole nebula of other primitive concepts belonging to the same line of thought, gender seems to belong primarily to philosophy.[9]

For gender to 'belong to philosophy' is, for Wittig, to belong to 'that body of self-evident concepts without which philosophers believe they cannot develop a line of reasoning and which for them go without saying, for they exist prior to any thought, any social order, in nature'.[10] Wittig's view is corroborated by that popular discourse on gender identity that uncritically employs the inflectional attribution of 'being' to genders and to 'sexualities'. The unproblematic claim to 'be' a woman and 'be' heterosexual would be symptomatic of that metaphysics of gender substances. In the case of both 'men' and 'women', this claim tends to subordinate the notion of gender under that of identity and to lead to the conclusion that a person *is* a gender and *is* one in virtue of his or her sex, psychic sense of self, and various expressions of that psychic self, the most salient being that of sexual desire. In such a prefeminist context, gender, naively (rather than critically) confused with sex, serves as a unifying principle of the embodied self and maintains that unity over and against an 'opposite sex' whose structure is presumed to maintain a parallel but oppositional internal coherence among sex, gender, and desire. The articulation 'I feel like a woman' by a female or 'I feel like a man' by a male presupposes that in neither case is the claim meaninglessly redundant. Although it might appear unproblematic *to be* a given anatomy (although we shall later consider the way in which that project is also fraught with difficulty), the experience of a gendered psychic disposition or cultural identity is considered an achievement. Thus, 'I feel like a woman' is true to the extent that Aretha Franklin's invocation of the defining Other is assumed: 'You make me feel like a natural woman'.[11] This achievement requires a differentiation from the opposite gender. Hence, one is one's gender to the extent that one is not the other gender, a formulation that presupposes and enforces the restriction of gender within that binary pair.

Gender can denote a *unity* of experience, of sex, gender, and desire, only when sex can be understood in some sense to necessitate gender – where gender is a psychic and/or cultural designation of the self – and desire – where desire is heterosexual and therefore differentiates itself through an oppositional relation to that other gender it desires. The internal coherence or unity of either gender, man or woman, thereby requires both a stable and oppositional heterosexuality. That institutional heterosexuality both requires and produces the univocity of each of the gendered terms that constitute the limit of gendered possibilities within an oppositional, binary gender system. This conception of gender presupposes not only a causal relation among sex, gender, and desire, but suggests as well that desire reflects or expresses gender and that gender reflects or expresses desire. The metaphysical unity of the three is assumed to be truly known and expressed in a differentiating desire for an oppositional gender – that is, in a form of oppositional heterosexuality. Whether as a naturalistic paradigm which establishes a causal continuity among sex, gender, and desire, or as an authentic-expressive paradigm in which some true self is said to be revealed simultaneously or successively in sex, gender, and desire, here 'the old dream of symmetry', as Irigaray has called it, is presupposed, reified, and rationalized.

This rough sketch of gender gives us a clue to understanding the political reasons for the substantializing view of gender. The institution of a compulsory and naturalized heterosexuality requires and regulates gender as a binary relation in which the masculine term is differentiated from a feminine term, and this differentiation is accomplished through the practices of heterosexual desire. The act of differentiating the two oppositional moments of the binary results in a consolidation of each term, the respective internal coherence of sex, gender, and desire.

The strategic displacement of that binary relation and the metaphysics of substance on which it relies presuppose that the categories of female and male, woman and man, are similarly produced within the binary frame. Foucault implicitly subscribes to such an explanation. In the closing chapter of the first volume of *The History of Sexuality* and in his brief but significant introduction to *Herculine Barbin, Being the Recently Discovered Journals of a Nineteenth-Century Hermaphrodite*,[12] Foucault suggests that the category of sex, prior to any categorization of sexual difference, is itself constructed through a historically specific mode of *sexuality*. The tactical production of the discrete and binary categorization of sex conceals the strategic aims of that very apparatus of production by postulating 'sex' as 'a cause' of sexual experience, behavior, and desire. Foucault's genealogical inquiry exposes this ostensible 'cause' as 'an effect', the production of a given regime of sexuality that seeks to regulate sexual experience by instating the discrete categories of sex as foundational and causal functions within any discursive account of sexuality.

Foucault's introduction to the journals of the hermaphrodite, Herculine Barbin, suggests that the genealogical critique of these reified categories of sex is the inadvertent consequence of sexual practices that cannot be accounted for within the medicolegal discourse of a naturalized heterosexuality. Herculine is not an 'identity', but the sexual impossibility of an identity. Although male and female anatomical elements are jointly distributed in and on this body, that is not the true source of scandal. The linguistic conventions that produce intelligible gendered selves find their limit in Herculine precisely because she/he occasions a convergence and disorganization of the rules that govern sex/gender/desire. Herculine deploys and redistributes the terms of a binary system, but that very redistribution disrupts and proliferates those terms outside the binary itself. According to Foucault, Herculine is not categorizable within the gender binary as it stands; the disconcerting convergence of heterosexuality and homosexuality in her/his person are only occasioned, but never caused, by his/her anatomical discontinuity. Foucault's appropriation of Herculine is suspect,[13] but his analysis implies the interesting belief that sexual heterogeneity (paradoxically foreclosed by a naturalized 'hetero'-sexuality) implies a critique of the metaphysics of substance as it informs the identitarian categories of sex. Foucault imagines Herculine's experience as 'a world of pleasures in which grins hang about without the cat'.[14] Smiles, happinesses, pleasures, and desires are figured here as qualities without an abiding substance to which they are said to adhere. As free-floating attributes, they suggest the possibility of a gendered experience that cannot be grasped through the substantializing and hierarchizing grammar of nouns (*res extensa*) and adjectives (attributes, essential and accidental). Through his cursory reading of Herculine, Foucault proposes an ontology of accidental attributes that exposes the postulation of identity as a culturally restricted principle of order and hierarchy, a regulatory fiction.

If it is possible to speak of a 'man' with a masculine attribute and to understand that attribute as a happy but accidental feature of that man, then it is also possible to speak of a 'man' with a feminine attribute, whatever that is, but still to maintain the integrity of the gender. But once we dispense with the priority of 'man' and 'woman' as abiding substances, then it is no longer possible to subordinate dissonant gendered features as so many secondary and accidental characteristics of a gender ontology that is fundamentally intact. If the notion of an abiding substance is a fictive construction produced through the compulsory ordering of attributes into coherent gender sequences, then it seems that gender as substance, the viability of *man* and *woman* as nouns, is called into question by the dissonant play of attributes that fail to conform to sequential or causal models of intelligibility.

The appearance of an abiding substance or gendered self, what the psychiatrist Robert Stoller refers to as a 'gender core',[15] is thus produced by the regulation of attributes along culturally established lines of coherence. As a result, the exposure of this fictive production is conditioned by the deregulated play of attributes that resist assimilation into the ready made framework of primary nouns and subordinate adjectives. It is of course always possible to argue that dissonant adjectives work retroactively to redefine the substantive identities they are said to modify and, hence, to expand the substantive categories of gender to include possibilities that they previously excluded. But if these substances are nothing other than the coherences contingently created through the regulation of attributes, it would seem that the ontology of substances itself is not only an artificial effect, but essentially superfluous.

In this sense, *gender* is not a noun, but neither is it a set of free-floating attributes, for we have seen that the substantive effect of gender is performatively produced and compelled by the regulatory practices of gender coherence. Hence, within the inherited discourse of the metaphysics of substance, gender proves to be performative – that is, constituting the identity it is purported to be. In this sense, gender is always a doing, though not a doing by a subject who might be said to preexist the deed. The challenge for rethinking gender categories outside of the metaphysics of substance will have to consider the relevance of Nietzsche's claim in *On the Genealogy of Morals* that 'there is no "being" behind doing, effecting, becoming "the doer" is merely a fiction added to the deed – the deed is everything'.[16] In an application that Nietzsche himself would not have anticipated or condoned, we might state as a corollary: There is no gender identity behind the expressions of gender; that identity is performatively constituted by the very 'expressions' that are said to be its results.

LANGUAGE, POWER, AND THE STRATEGIES OF DISPLACEMENT

[. . .]

Within the terms of feminist sexual theory, it is clear that the presence of power dynamics within sexuality is in no sense the same as the simple consolidation or augmentation of a heterosexist or phallogocentric power regime. The 'presence' of so-called heterosexual conventions within homosexual contexts as well as the proliferation of specifically gay discourses of sexual difference, as in the case of 'butch' and 'femme' as historical identities of sexual style, cannot be explained as chimerical representations of originally heterosexual identities. And neither can they be understood as the pernicious insistence of heterosexist constructs within gay sexuality and identity. The repetition of heterosexual constructs within sexual cultures both gay and straight may well be the inevitable site of the denaturalization and mobilization of gender categories. The replication of heterosexual constructs in non-heterosexual frames brings into relief the utterly constructed status of the so-called heterosexual original. Thus, gay is to straight *not* as copy is to original, but, rather, as copy is to copy. The parodic repetition of 'the original' [. . .] reveals the original to be nothing other than a parody of the *idea* of the natural and the original.[17] Even if heterosexist constructs circulate as the available sites of power/discourse from which to do gender at all, the question remains: What possibilities of recirculation exist? Which possibilities of doing gender repeat and displace through hyperbole, dissonance, internal confusion, and proliferation the very constructs by which they are mobilized?

Consider not only that the ambiguities and incoherences within and among heterosexual, homosexual, and bisexual practices are suppressed and redescribed within the reified framework of the disjunctive and asymmetrical binary of masculine/feminine, but that these cultural configurations of gender confusion operate as sites for intervention, exposure, and displacement of these reifications. In other words, the 'unity' of gender is the effect of a regulatory practice that seeks to render gender identity uniform through a compulsory heterosexuality. The force of this practice is, through an exclusionary apparatus of production, to restrict the relative meanings of 'heterosexuality,' 'homosexuality', and 'bisexuality' as well as the subversive sites of their convergence and resignification. That the power regimes of heterosexism and phallogocentrism seek to augment themselves through a constant repetition of their logic, their metaphysic, and their naturalized ontologies does not imply that repetition itself ought to be stopped – as if it could be. If repetition is bound to persist as the mechanism of the cultural reproduction of identities, then the crucial question emerges: What kind of subversive repetition might call into question the regulatory practice of identity itself?

If there is no recourse to a 'person', a 'sex', or a 'sexuality' that escapes the matrix of power and discursive relations that effectively produce and regulate the intelligibility of those concepts for us, what constitutes the possibility of effective inversion, subversion, or displacement within the terms of a constructed identity? What possibilities exist *by virtue of* the constructed character of sex and gender? Whereas Foucault is ambiguous about the precise character of the 'regulatory practices' that produce the category of sex, and Wittig appears to invest the full responsibility of the construction to sexual reproduction and its instrument, compulsory hetrosexuality, yet other discourses converge to produce this categorial fiction for reasons not always clear or consistent with one another. The power relations that infuse the biological sciences are not easily reduced, and the medicolegal alliance emerging in nineteenth-century Europe has spawned categorial fictions that could not be anticipated in advance. The very complexity of the discursive map that constructs gender appears to hold out the promise of an inadvertent and generative convergence of these discursive and regulatory structures. If the regulatory fictions of sex and gender are themselves multiply contested sites of meaning, then the very multiplicity of their construction holds out the possibility of a disruption of their univocal posturing.

Clearly this project does not propose to lay out within traditional philosophical terms an *ontology* of gender whereby the meaning of *being* a woman or a man is elucidated within the terms of phenomenology. The presumption here is that the 'being' of gender is *an effect*, an object of a genealogical investigation that maps out the political parameters of its construction in the mode of ontology. To claim that gender is constructed is not to assert its illusoriness or artificiality, where those terms are understood to reside within a binary that counterposes the 'real' and the 'authentic' as oppositional. As a genealogy of gender ontology, this inquiry seeks to understand the discursive production of the plausibility of that binary relation and to suggest that certain cultural configurations of gender take the place of 'the real' and consolidate and augment their hegemony through that felicitious self-naturalization.

If there is something right in Beauvoir's claim that one is not born, but rather *becomes* a woman, it follows that *woman* itself is a term in process, a becoming, a constructing that cannot rightfully be said to originate or to end. As an ongoing discursive practice, it is open to intervention and resignification. Even when gender seems to congeal into the most reified forms, the 'congealing' is itself an insistent and insidious practice, sustained and regulated by various social means. It is, for Beauvoir, never possible finally to become a woman, as if there were a *telos* that governs the process of acculturation and construction. Gender is the repeated stylization of the body, a set of repeated acts within a highly rigid regulatory frame that congeal over time to produce the appearance of substance, of a natural sort of being. A political genealogy of gender ontologies, if it is successful, will deconstruct the substantive appearance of gender into its constitutive acts and locate and account for those acts within the compulsory frames set by the various forces that police the social appearance of gender. To expose the contingent acts that create the appearance of a naturalistic necessity, a move which has been a part of cultural critique at least since Marx, is a task that now takes on the added burden of showing how the very notion of the subject, intelligible only through its appearance as gendered, admits of possibilities that have been forcibly foreclosed by the various reifications of gender that have constituted its contingent ontologies. . . .

NOTES

[The notes have been renumbered for this volume.]

1. See the argument against 'ranking oppressions' in Cherríe Moraga, 'La Güera', in *his Bridge Called My Back: Writings of Radical Women of Color*, eds Gloria Anzaldua and Cherríe Moraga (New York: Kitchen Table, Women of Color Press, 1982).

2. For a fuller elaboration of the unrepresentability of women in phallogocentric discourse, see Luce Irigaray, 'Any Theory of the "Subject" Has Always Been Appropriated by the Masculine', in *Speculum of the Other Woman*, trans. Gillian C. Gill (Ithaca: Cornell University Press, 1985). Irigaray appears to revise this argument in her discussion of 'the feminine gender' in *Sexes et parentés*.

3. Monique Wittig, 'One is Not Born a Woman', *Feminist Issues*, Vol. 1, No. 2, Winter 1981, p. 53.

4. The notion of the 'Symbolic' is discussed at some length in Section Two of this text. It is to be understood as an ideal and universal set of cultural laws that govern kinship and signification and, within the terms of psychoanalytic structuralism, govern the production of sexual difference. Based on the notion of an idealized 'paternal law', the Symbolic is reformulated by Irigaray as a dominant and hegemonic discourse of phallogocentrism. Some French feminists propose an alternative language to one governed by the Phallus or the paternal law, and so wage a critique against the Symbolic. Kristeva proposes the 'semiotic' as a specifically maternal dimension of language, and both Irigaray and Hélène Cixous have been

associated with *écriture feminine*. Wittig, however, has always resisted that movement, claiming that language in its structure is neither misogynist nor feminist, but an *instrument* to be deployed for developed political purposes. Clearly her belief in a 'cognitive subject' that exists prior to language facilitates her understanding of language as an instrument, rather than as a field of significations that preexist and structure subject-formation itself.

5. Monique Wittig, 'The Point of View: Universal or Particular?' *Feminist Issues*, Vol. 3, No. 2, Fall 1983, p. 64.

6. 'One must assume both a particular *and* a universal point of view, at least to be part of literature', Monique Wittig, 'The Trojan Horse', *Feminist Issues*, Vol. 4, No. 2, Fall 1984, p. 68.

7. The journal, *Questions Feministes*, available in English translation as *Feminist Issues*, generally defended a 'materialist' point of view which took practices, institution, and the constructed status of language to be the 'material grounds' of the oppression of women. Wittig was part of the original editorial staff. Along with Monique Plaza, Wittig argued that sexual difference was essentialist in that it derived the meaning of women's social function from their biological facticity, but also because it subscribed to the primary signification of women's bodies as maternal and, hence, gave ideological strength to the hegemony of reproductive sexuality.

8. Michel Haar, 'Nietzsche and Metaphysical Language', *The New Nietzsche: Contemporary Styles of Interpretation*, ed. David Allison (New York: Delta, 1977), pp. 17–18.

9. Monique Wittig, 'The Mark of Gender', *Feminist Issues*, Vol. 5, No. 2, Fall 1985, p. 4.

10. Ibid., p. 3.

11. Aretha's song, originally written by Carole King, also contests the naturalization of gender. 'Like a natural woman' is a phrase that suggests that 'naturalness' is only accomplished through analogy or metaphor. In other words, 'You make me feel like a metaphor of the natural', and without 'you', some denaturalized ground would be revealed. For a further discussion of Aretha's claim in light of Simone de Beauvoir's contention that 'one is not born, but rather becomes a woman', see my 'Beauvoir's Philosophical Contribution', in (eds) Ann Garry and Marjorie Pearsall, *Women, Knowledge, and Reality* (Rowman and Allenheld, forthcoming).

12. Michel Foucault, ed., *Herculine Barbin, Being the Recently Discovered Memoirs of a Nineteenth-Century Hermaphrodite*, trans. Richard McDougall (New York: Colophon, 1980), originally published as *Herculine Barbin, dite Alexina B. presenté par Michel Foucault* (Paris: Gallimard, 1978). The French version lacks the introduction supplied by Foucault with the English translation.

13. See chapter 2, section ii.

14. Foucault, ed., *Herculine Barbin*, p. x.

15. Robert Stoller, *Presentations of Gender*, (New Haven: Yale University Press, 1985), pp. 11–14.

16. Friedrich Nietzsche, *On the Genealogy of Morals*, trans. Walter Kaufmann (New York: Vintage, 1969), p. 45.

17. If we were to apply Fredric Jameson's distinction between parody and pastiche, gay identities would be better understood as pastiche. Whereas parody, Jameson argues, sustains some sympathy with the original of which it is a copy, pastiche disputes the possibility of an 'original' or, in the case of gender, reveals the 'original' as a failed effort to 'copy' a phantasmatic ideal that cannot be copied without failure. See Fredric Jameson, 'Postmodernism and Consumer Society', in *The Anti-Aesthetic: Essays on Postmodern Culture*, ed. Hal Foster (Port Townsend, WA: Bay Press, 1983).

24

Final Analysis: Can Psychoanalysis Survive in the Postmodern West?

Jane Flax

[. . .]

PSYCHOANALYSIS AND WESTERN LEGITIMATION CRISES

Psychoanalytic discourse has attained considerable success in normalizing its domain. However, challenges to its legitimacy are strengthening. Lacan's questioning of the authority of the analyst, the training and legitimation procedures within psychoanalysis, and the status of its knowledge is no longer unusual. Psychoanalytic theory, clinical treatment, and disciplinary practices all face strong intra- and extra-discursive challenges. The social-political context of psychoanalysis compounds its difficulties. Profound crises of cultural identity, subjectivity, meaning, authority, and status pervade the postmodern world. Contemporary political and intellectual developments are especially disruptive to the white, relatively rich Westerner's sense of identity and confidence. These persons have been the primary subjects/objects of psychoanalytic discourse.

Until recently, the United States was the dominant location of psychoanalysis. White, well-off Americans, the primary practitioners and clientele of psychoanalysis, are facing a particular sort of disillusionment. The fantasy that our social history is exempt from the disorder and tragedy experienced by others is disintegrating. The long string of events beginning with the assassinations of (among others) President Kennedy, Robert F. Kennedy, Martin Luther King, and Malcom X, urban uprisings, the war in Vietnam, Watergate, and the resignation of President Nixon continue to affect us. The accelerating decay of civility and urban life also disrupts this fantasized sense of immunity and intensifies our sense of inefficacy. The United States no longer appears as the 'land of promise' free from the suffering and mistakes of other cultures.

These disruptions occur within the context of global ones. The Holocaust, contests for power within the West and between it and Japan, the collapse of the Soviet system, anti-colonialist revolts, and challenges to racism and male-dominance continue to undermine expectations of order, continuity, and stability. These political shifts alter the circulation of knowledge and power in many ways. The meanings – or even existence – of Enlightenment ideas (reason, history, science, progress, power, gender, and the inherent superiority of Western culture), including those upon which psychoanalysis depends, are subject to increasingly corrosive attacks.

Internal dissent has further disrupted the epistemological security of Western thinkers. Postmodernists and feminists undermine the foundations of Western thought. They expose the essential contestability of its constituting notions. This exposure creates a legitimation crisis, since these notions then appear as mere humanly created artifacts for whose effects and consequences we alone are responsible. If knowledge is an effect of discrete, historical human action, it can no longer underwrite or guarantee neutrality. Its relation to any larger truth or transcendental Reality appears at best highly contingent, contestable, and underdetermined. The circuits of power and their relations with the production of truth are more evident.

As we will see, these philosophic and political developments pose profound challenges to some of the most cherished and legitimating psychoanalytic ideas. Two foundational notions now appear particularly problematic. One notion is the belief that psychoanalysis is an empirical science because it can rely on clinical 'data' to validate theory. The other is that analytic treatment (or its legitimating theories) can be politically neutral.

1. Postmodernism and the Powers of Knowledge

Postmodernists challenge Enlightenment ideas about truth, knowledge, power, history, self, and language still predominant in the West.[1] The power of reason to apprehend the truth is a central theme in Enlightenment stories about knowledge. One of the most important and definitive abilities of reason is its intrinsic capacity to recognize truth. Truth emerges out of a properly conducted relation between subject and object. Any rational subject apprehending or operating properly on the same object would arrive at the identical truth about it. The philosophy of knowledge can identify the optimum methods and rules for conducting this relation. It can provide accounts of how truth is generated and general standards by which truth claims can be more effectively produced and evaluated.[2]

Postmodernists' stories about truth do not focus on reason, method, and the relationships between subject and object. They treat truth as an effect of multiple and various discursive practices, including the circulation of power. They also question the ideas of mind, language, and the Real that underlie and ground any transcendental, empirical or foundational claims.[3] Intrinsic to either transcendental or empirical epistemologies is the belief that the mind can register data or ideas accurately. Our theoretical assumptions, methods, and mental processes need not in principle obscure the mind's reception of information about reality.

For example, an empiricist analyst would claim that in listening to the patient's free associations, she or he is directly observing bits of the patient's unconscious processes. Unless countertransference intervenes, reliable information accumulates over time. The analyst can increase the sum of our accurate knowledge about the unconscious by reporting data gleaned from the analytic situation. Particular tenets of psychoanalytic theory can be tested against this data. Our theories can then be brought into line with the data, thereby increasing their accuracy and truth content.

A postmodernist would claim that the empiricist's view rests on fundamentally mistaken ideas. Postmodernists stress the dependence of thought on language and the epistemological consequences of this reliance. Language, a primary medium of psychoanalysis, cannot be a transparent, passive, or neutral instrument. Language is not a simple matter of putting the appropriate labels on objects. Each of us is born into an ongoing set of language games. We must learn these games to be understood by and to understand others. In acquiring linguistic skills we take on a way of life and enter into specific circuits of power. This emphasis on power distinguishes postmodernists from hermeneutic thinkers. The hermeneutic approach does not locate linguistic practices within discrete discursive formations in which knowledge and power are interdependent. Hermeneutic philosophers also believe that a text has a deep meaning (or meanings) against which particular interpretations can be evaluated. Postmodernists reject this idea and claim the *meanings* of a text are multiple and indeterminant.[4]

Language partially constructs our personhood including the structure, categories, and content of thought. The dependence of thought on language means that it and the mind itself are partially socially and historically (pre-)constituted. Language necessarily affects the *meanings* of our experiences and understandings of them, including interpretations of clinical data and analyses of it. To speak of experience near knowledge is mistaken, since without language we can neither conceptualize an event as experience nor communicate it to another. The linguistic constitution of experience is simultaneously a social and theoretical organization of it. Experience cannot speak for itself or directly to us. Language speaks us as much as we speak it. Its effects are often hidden and inaccessible to us.

Postmodernists also deny the possibility that an ahistorical or transcendental standpoint could exist. How could we acquire and maintain universal, transcendental, or *a priori* mental categories or ideas? The human mind is not homogeneous, unitary, lawful, or internally consistent in or over time. Attaining a transcendental standpoint would require cleansing the mind of all its social and linguistic determinants and acquiring a 'god's-eye' view. What mental agency could carry out such a cleansing? All the sense data, ideas, intentions, or perceptions we have are already constituted. They only occur in and reflect linguistically and socially determined practices.

Lacking such a standpoint, even if the Real existed, we could never immediately apprehend or directly report it. Even if we could attain a god's eye view, what use would it be in making sense of our messy, contingent lives? Rather than mourn the inaccessibility of the Real, postmodernists investigate the sources of desire for it. They regard wishes for order or an eternal, homogeneous real with suspicion. Unity is an effect of domination, repression, and the temporary success of particular rhetorical strategies. They hope to open up possibilities and create spaces in which multiple differences can flourish.

However, it would be incorrect to assume that postmodernism is a form of relativism. Relativism has meaning only as the partner of its binary opposite – universalism. The relativist assumes the lack of an absolute standard is significant. If there is no one thing against which to measure all claims, then 'everything is relative'. If the hankering for a universal standard disappears, 'relativism' would lose its meaning. We could turn our attention to the limits and possibilities of local productions of truth. The god's-eye view will be displaced by admittedly partial and fragmentary multiples of one.[5]

2. Feminism and the Instabilities of Gender

Feminists define gender as a changeable set of social relations that pervade many aspects of human experience from the constitution of the 'inner self' and family life to the 'public worlds' of the state, the economy, and knowledge production. Gender is not a consequence or effect of 'natural sexual differences'. It cannot be explained by reference to anatomical or biological attributes, although the relations of gender to embodiment are an interesting and controversial question. Gender is an indispensable category in the analysis of current Western cultures.[6]

Definitions of gender in feminist accounts often differ from psychoanalytic ones. Feminists stress the role of relations of domination in the production and maintenance of gender. They analyse gender as complex, historically contingent and determinative relations in and through which both masculinity and femininity are constituted. Gender is not the same as the 'woman problem'. It cannot be understood nor its problems addressed solely by studying the psychology of women. This approach does not relieve women of their positions as deviant others. Incorporation of more material about women into existing discourses is insufficient and may be counterproductive. Such incorporation allows the operation of gendered claims within existing discourses to remain undisturbed.

Feminists claim that neither men nor women within contemporary Western cultures exist outside gender systems. One of their effects is the constitution of masculinity/femininity as exclusionary and unequal opposites. Power and domination partially constitute and maintain these relations. In relations of domination, no subject can simply or voluntarily switch sides. We receive certain privileges or suffer certain injuries depending on our structural positions, no matter what our subjective intent or purposes may be. Men can no more easily resign from masculinity and its effects than I can from being a white woman.

Gender and race relations mark both men and women, although in different and unequal ways.

By situating men as well as women within gender relations, we remove their purity/privilege. The social production of reason and knowledge production becomes more evident. Rather than insisting that women's reason can be as 'pure' as men's, it is more productive to question the purity of reason itself and the claim that no valuable or truthful knowledge can arise from the activities traditionally associated with women or the passions.

We can also investigate the motives for insisting on such splits and this hierarchical ordering of human qualities. The insights derived from feminist object relations psychoanalysis are especially helpful in this investigation.[7] Children develop in and through the contexts of relations with others. Given the current sexual division of labor, the subjectivities of both men and women initially evolve partially through interactions with a woman – a mother and/or other female relations. The predominant role women must assume in our early caretaking and in our fantasies generates problems for both genders. To some extent, male identity emerges out of oppositional moves.[8] Men must become not-female as they acquire masculinity. In a culture where gender is an asymmetric binary relation, men must guard against the return of the repressed – their identification with mother and those 'female' qualities within them. This provides a powerful unconscious incentive for identifying with and overvaluing the abstract and the impersonal. It is a strong motive for reinforcing gender segregation, including within intellectual work, to ensure that women will never again have power over men.

IMPLICATIONS FOR PSYCHOANALYSIS

1. Theory

Psychoanalysis' relation to recent intellectual and political developments in the postmodern West is profoundly ambivalent. Freud and some contemporary analysts remain powerfully attracted to Enlightenment notions of knowledge. They share its belief in the emancipatory potential of science and rational thought. Nonetheless, Freud and subsequent analysts such as Winnicott and Klein contribute to the undermining of confidence in the integrity and powers of reason. Freud's post-1920s writings on the structure of the mind as intrinsically conflicted and simultaneously psychic and somatic are especially important. Winnicott's notions of the psyche-soma and the transitional space as the locus of culture suggest many alternatives to rationalism. Klein's positing of an epistemophiliac instinct also hints at directions worth pursuing.[9]

Within psychoanalytic accounts, psychic structures and processes appear increasingly fragmented, multidetermined, fluid, and subject to complex and often unconscious alterations. Unlike many philosophers, analysts such as Freud,

Klein, and Winnicott conceptualize the mind as fully embodied,[10] inherently conflict ridden, dynamic, heterogeneous, and constituted in and through processes that are intrinsically discordant. These processes cannot be synthesized or organized into a permanent, hierarchical organization of functions or control. The equation of mind and conscious thought or reason or the psychical and consciousness becomes untenable.

Their ideas subvert the dualisms such as mind/body, subject/object, thought/passion, and rational/irrational that pervade some forms of modern philosophy and science and impede the success of their own projects. Psychoanalysts also challenge Enlightenment ontological premises by positing various forms of desire (for objects, drive satisfaction, mirroring, or the Other) rather than reason as the definitive and motivating core of our being.

Psychoanalytic theories of mind also contradict and challenge many contemporary epistemologies. Both the rationalist's faith in the powers of reason and the empiricist's belief in the reliability of sense perception and observation are grounded in and depend upon assumptions about the mind. It must have the capacity to be at least partially undetermined by the effects of the body, passions, and social authority or convention. However, psychoanalysis throws into doubt all epistemologies that rely on the possibility of accurate self-observation and direct, reliable access to and control over the mind and its activities.

Psychoanalysis identifies forces whose effects and boundaries can never be transparent to us. These forces, which include bodily experience, libidinal wishes, authority relations, and cultural conventions perpetually affect thought. Insight into the mind's operations will remain incomplete and provisional, because even aspects of the observing ego are repressed.

We cannot not 'control for' bias if its source is in the dynamically unconscious repressed material to which the conscious mind lacks direct access. The agency of our knowing is contaminated by the influence of these unconscious forces, including desire and authority. Being able to give reasons for one's choice of action or definition of self-interest is not straightforward evidence of rationality or freedom from the unconscious. A 'rational reconstruction' of the reasons for a choice or belief may be an elaborate rationalization of or reparation for an irrational wish or fear.

This complicated view also challenges those who portray mental life as the epiphenomena of a relatively simple series of electrochemical processes and networks. The subjective meanings of, say, delusions will never be captured within the discourse of neural firing. However, the rich content of such phenomena is clearly important in understanding the intricacies of subjectivity.

While psychoanalysts have much to contribute to conversations about subjectivity, they are vulnerable to challenges to the validity of their truth claims. Analysts cannot solve this dilemma by claiming that psychoanalysis is or could (given certain specified conditions) be a science. In my view, this approach is profoundly erroneous for several reasons. It undermines the confidence of others, including philosophers and practitioners of the natural sciences, in psychoanalysis. Such claims merely generate endless and unproductive debates about the scientific status of psychoanalysis. Instead, we should question the beliefs behind the assumption that this is a crucial matter. What could this status mean, and what would it add to the content or usefulness of psychoanalytic theory?

Obsession with this topic repeats rather than interprets Freud's own fixation on Enlightenment thinking. 'Real' knowledge and science are still equated. Such arguments arise out of outmoded and inaccurate views of what science is and how it produces its own truth claims. Most importantly, it obscures, avoids, and retards addressing a problem faced by all discursive formations – how to generate discourse-specific means and tests for the production of knowledge. For psychoanalysis, this project will require better accounts of the knowledge that clinical experience generates and of the qualities of clinical relations and treatment. Psychoanalysts could contribute much more to epistemology, philosophies of mind, and to stories of human development, subjectivity, and the importance of human relations within them if they could provide better accounts of psychoanalytic processes.

2. Clinical Treatment

Psychoanalytic thinkers such as Freud and Lacan also undermine the Enlightenment belief in the intrinsic or necessary relationships between reason, self-determination, and freedom or emancipation. Contrary to the great hope of Enlightenment, use of one's own reason will not necessarily make us free. If the conscious/rational self is 'not even master in its own house, but must content itself with scanty information of what is going on unconsciously in its mind',[11] the possibilities for autonomous action are quite constrained. The ego does not necessarily express or ensure the possibility of an autonomous or rational will. Analysis may increase one's capacity for self-reflection. Decrease of the powers of rationalization and the influences of unconscious deference to authority will not necessarily follow. In its relations with the id, the ego 'too often yields to the temptation to become sycophantic, opportunist and lying, like a politician who sees the truth but wants to keep his place in popular favor'.[12]

Analysts may track the complicity between ego and superego forces, including political authority. However, they are often more reluctant to explore the impact of such influences on their own theories and practices. One of the important lessons of both postmodernism and feminism for psychoanalysis is that clinical treatment cannot be politically or socially neutral. The knowledge that informs psychoanalytic practices, like all knowledge, contains traces of the relations of power that circulate through it.

Psychoanalysis has played an important part in generating categories of identity and standards of normalcy and health, especially for practices of sexuality, child rearing, and gender. The normalizing veils of scientific language and claims to the objective discovery of 'natural' forces, identities, or drives disguise the operation of these standards. More critical examination reveals the congruence of these identities and standards, especially those of femininity/masculinity, good/bad mother, healthy/deviant, and homosexuality/heterosexuality, with the practices and commitments of other dominant power/knowledge configurations.

In its normalizing and regulatory aspects, psychoanalysis is empowered by and contributes to a modern form of power, 'biopower'. Biopower signals and reflects shifts in the constitution of modern Western states and their legitimating discourses. The legitimacy of these states now rests and depends upon the politics of life rather than those of death.[13] Older forms of the state exercised juridical power. In these states, the ultimate and definitive expression of state power was its right to kill those who transgressed its law. While these aspects of power have not disappeared, a new one has gradually become pivotal – the power of life, or biopower. The legitimacy of the state is now grounded in and depends upon its ability to maintain and improve the health and welfare of its citizens. Thus it is not surprising that issues such as health care or the treatment of AIDS often dominate contemporary political discourses.

The concrete and precise character of the modern state's knowledge of and interest in human bodies is unusual. The humanistic rubric of the state's interest in and obligation to the creation and protection of the 'well-being' of its inhabitants justifies increasingly pervasive surveillance of them. Biopower is based in and effects a 'real and effective "incorporation"' of power. It circulates through and roots itself in the concrete lives of individuals and populations through multiple and variegated means.[14] The production of new sorts of truth and particular disciplinary and confessional practices generate and constitute biopower. These practices are supported and exercised both by the state and by newly elaborated discursive formations, especially medicine and the human sciences. The state needs experts to amass the knowledge it requires and to execute the policies said to effect and maximize this well-being and protection. Instances of such knowledge and associated practices include medicine, education, public health, prisons, and schools.

One purpose of biopower is to ensure a more tractable public body. The heterogeneous elements of a population can be made less dissonant through practices of 'normalization'. Concepts of deviancy, illness, maladjustment, and so forth are products of the same discourses that create the normal. These concepts also name the dangers the normal must be protected against. They justify the need for new and better knowledge to control the problems and for the exercise of power. This knowledge is simultaneously individual and global. It entails the study of specific 'traits' possessed by individuals that cause their deviations and the search for methods that can be applied to all such individuals to effect the desired disciplinary results in the populations as a whole. 'Prevention' of disease or crime requires the at least potential extension of these knowledges and practices to everyone.

The state's interest is in ensuring regularity of behavior, not only in punishing crimes after the fact. The more peaceful (e.g., controlled) the population, the more the state's power is legitimated and ensured. As the state becomes more powerful, it can dispense disciplinary legitimacy. It supports, regulates, and enforces the monopoly of certain professions over specific domains and practices. Failure of disciplinary practices becomes the basis for 'experts' to ask for more resources and power to pursue and exercise their knowledge for the public good.

Along with the processes of normalization and discipline, the individual subject is created through confessional practices. The primary exemplars of these practices are psychoanalysis and psychiatry. Psychoanalysts and others believe in the existence of a particular form of being, the 'individual'. They teach us we have an individual 'self' about which knowledge is possible. This individual has certain 'natural', or 'true' traits. These discourses create the idea that there is something 'deep inside' us, something hidden but at least partially knowable by consciousness, a source of both pleasure and danger. We experience this self as true and foundational.

However, the constitution of this individual and our belief in its existence is an effect of biopower. Such experience is not 'true' in some ontological or essentialist sense. It is an effect of a subjectivity constituted in and through certain discourses, including psychoanalysis. In other discourses such notions and experiences might not exist.

The discourses of biopower produce dangerous forces within us such as sexuality, controllable only by the person exercising surveillance upon her- or himself. The surveillance is said to lead to 'self-knowledge' and freedom from the effect of these forces. However, to attain such self-knowledge and self-control, the individual must consult an expert whose knowledge provides privileged access to this dangerous aspect of the person's 'self'. By transforming pleasure into 'sexuality', these confessional discourse/practices generate further practices/knowledge of self-control and self-knowledge. Simultaneously they ensure their own replication and an expansion of their domain.

While psychoanalysis contributes to and benefits from biopower, it also subverts it. The norms it posits and the categories it produces are notoriously ambiguous.[15] Unlike many other discourses, excess and excluded material are readily accessible and available to disrupt conversation or move it in a different direction. This is a strength of psychoanalytic discourse. Analysts should exploit this ambiguity rather than trying to standardize the meanings of its concepts and occlude their productive instability. Psychoanalysts claim tolerance of ambiguity as a sign of psychological well-being. It should become a norm for the health of psychoanalytic discourse as well.

Clinical practice subverts biopower in other ways. It can offer relationships that escape such modern binary oppositions as subject/object, work/play, instrumental/affective, child/adult, inner/outer, and public /private. Analysis is a form of relational work. It is an open-ended and mutually constituted field of activity in which multiple aspects of activity and experience come into play. Language, visual images, dreams, passion, reason, bodily experience, childlike wishes, and adult responsibility are all components of analytic discourse. Analytic time is not linear. Analysis is not oriented to material production, nor is it governed by a precise definition of output. Cost/benefit analysis cannot capture the utility or qualities of its activities or effects. This complexity is one of the strengths of analysis. Analysts err and even risk destroying analysis when they try to exercise order or control by marking one aspect as the true, foundational, or curative one.

The multiplicity of analysis and its emphasis on relationships help to account for the devaluation, identity crises, and current social dislocations of psychoanalysis. Its relational qualities place it within the female side of gendered circuits of identity and power. The confounding of binary oppositions disrupts its potential place within discursive formations, for example, some empirical sciences, whose knowledge and practices produce and depend upon their existence and stability.

3. Disciplinary Training and Practices

If psychoanalysts try to cling to the medical model and to establish analysis as clinical science, psychoanalysis will not survive in the postmodern West. The knowledge-producing practices of psychoanalysis cannot meet the regulatory standards of other discourses, such as medicine or biochemistry, nor should they. Without discourse-specific standards, questions such as who should be authorized to practise analysis cannot be resolved. Satisfactory answers will require more discursive consensus about which knowledge legitimates analytic practices.

If psychoanalysis is to survive in the postmodern world, it must broaden the topics considered legitimate within its discursive conversations. It should increase the number and kinds of partners with whom it converses and explore the implications of their knowledge for analysis. Analysts can have productive conversations among themselves and with others concerning the discourse-specific qualities of their own knowledge and practices and the implications of these for other discursive formations. Such conversations should address the politics of psychoanalytic knowledge and practices and the complex networks of discipline, confession, and resistance within which psychoanalysis circulates. These networks are components of both the internal practices of psychoanalysis and its relations with other discourses.

The paradoxical existence of increasing fragmentation and concentration of disciplinary practices and powers pervades the postmodern world. Psychoanalysis cannot be immune from the consequences all citizens of such a world must face. We find ourselves sometimes in an inadvertent but unavoidable complicity with powers whose ethical and political practices are ambiguous at best. Simultaneously we experience both vulnerabilities and responsibilities to other discursive communities whose practices are (if we are lucky) only partially compatible with ours. Perhaps more than ever, psychoanalysts need to establish new colleges of psychoanalysis. In itself this will not be sufficient for psychoanalysis to survive, much less to flourish. However, intolerance of difference, disorder, and complexity or a wistful political innocence will doom the discourse of psychoanalysis to increasing marginality and obscurity in the postmodern world.

NOTES

[The notes have been renumbered for this volume.]

1. The term *postmodernist* is controversial and ill-defined. I have discussed it extensively in my *Thinking Fragments* (Berkeley: University of California Press, 1990). My account here includes a probably misleading condensation of some of the ideas of Michel Foucault, Jacques Derrida, Jean-Francois Lyotard and Richard Rorty.

2. When philosophers such as Adolf Grunbaum evaluate the epistemological liabilities or scientific status of psychoanalysis without paying attention to or giving a justification of the warrant for their own practices, they operate within this discourse.

3. On this point, see Jacques Derrida, 'Violence and Metaphysics', in his *Writing and Difference* (Chicago: University of Chicago Press, 1978); and Richard Rorty, *Philosophy and the Mirror of Nature* (Princeton: Princeton University Press, 1979).

4. Spence and Schafer are among the most important advocates of hermeneutic approaches in psychoanalysis. For an example from philosophy see Hans-Georg Gadamer, *Truth and Method* (New York: Crossroad Publishing, 1984).

5. On what a postmodernist philosopher might do, see the essays in *The Institution of Philosophy*, edited by Avner Cohen and Marcelo Dascal (La Salle, Ill: Open Court, 1989); *After Philosophy: End or Transformation*, edited by Kenneth Baynes, James Bohman, and Thomas McCarthy (Cambridge: MIT Press, 1987); Rorty, ch. 8; Richard Rorty, *Consequences of Pragmatism* (Minneapolis: University of Minnesota Press, 1982); Jacques Derrida, *Positions* (Chicago: University of Chicago Press, 1981); Michel Foucault, *Politics, Philosophy, Culture* (New York: Routledge, 1988); and Nancy Fraser, *Unruly Practices: Power, Discourse and Gender in Contemporary Social Theory* (Minneapolis: University of Minnesota Press, 1989).

6. See the essays in *Gender/Body/Knowledge*, edited by Alison M. Jaggar and Susan R. Bordo (New Brunswick: Rutgers University Press, 1989); *Feminist Challenges: Social and Political Theory*, edited by Carole Pateman and Elizabeth Gross (Boston: Northeastern Press, 1986); *Third World Women and the Politics of Feminism*, edited by Chandra Talpade Mohanty, Ann Russo, and Lourdes Torres (Bloomington: Indiana University Press, 1991); and *Feminists Theorize the Political*, edited by Judith Butler and Joan Scott (New York: Routledge, 1992).

7. Especially the work of Nancy Chodorow, *The Reproduction of Mothering* (Berkeley: University of California Press, 1978); Dorothy Dinnerstein, *The Mermaid and the Minotaur* (New York: Harper and Row, 1976); and Irene Fast, *Gender Identity: A Differentiation Model* (Hillsdale: Analytic Press, 1984). Many psychoanalysts continue to ignore this work, or it is marginalized as having relevance solely to an understanding of the psychology of women. For example, despite the title of his recent book, Stephen A. Mitchell, *Relational Concepts of Psychoanalysis* (Cambridge: Harvard University Press, 1988) mentions none of these authors. He (as is common

with many analysts) does not discuss gender as a crucial social relation in the constitution of modern subjectivity. Object relations theory has many other gender biases.

8. I discuss some of the difficulties in mother–daughter relations and their consequences for women's subjectivities in 'The Conflict between Nurturance and Autonomy', *Feminist Studies* 4, 2 (June 1978): 171–189; and 'Mothers and Daughters Revisited', in this volume [*disputed subjects*, 1993].

9. Sigmund Freud, *The Ego and the Id* (New York: W. W. Norton, 1960) [SE XIX; PFL II]; Melanie Klein, 'Early Stages of the Oedipus Conflict', in *Love, Guilt and Reparation*; D. W. Winnicott, *Playing and Reality* (New York: Basic Books, 1971); and D. W. Winicott, 'Mind and its Relation to Psyche-Soma', in his *Through Paediatrics to Psycho-Analysis* (New York: Basic Books, 1975).

10. Cf. the discussion of the bodily ego in Sigmund Freud, 'The Unconscious', in *Collected Papers*, v. 4, edited by James Strachey (New York: Basic Books, 1959). [SEXIV; PFL 11]

11. Sigmund Freud, 'Analysis Terminable and Interminable', *Collected Papers*, v. 5 (New York: Basic Books, 1959), 353. [SE XXIII]

12. Freud, *The Ego and the Id*, p. 46.

13. Michel Foucault, *The History of Sexuality, Volume I, An Introduction* (New York: Vintage, 1980), especially part 5.

14. Michel Foucault, 'Truth and Power', in his *Power/Knowledge*; and Michel Foucault, *History of Sexuality*.

15. For example, Sigmund Freud, *Three Essays on the Theory of Sexuality* (New York: Basic Books, 1975) [SE VII; PFL 7] is an exemplar of ambiguity. It would be quite revealing to track the eruptions of tension and multiple definitions of crucial terms throughout this text.

Suggested Further Reading

The following texts have been chosen as indicative further reading on these complex and diffuse subjects:

Diana Fuss, *Essentially Speaking: Feminism, Nature and Difference* (1989);
Linda J. Nicholson, ed., *Feminism/Postmodernism* (1990);
Jane Flax, *Thinking Fragments: Psychoanalysis, Feminism, and Postmodernism in the Contemporary West* (1990);
Judith Butler, *Gender Trouble: Feminism and the Subversion of Identity* (1990);
Camille Paglia, *Sex, Art and American Culture* (1993);
Thomas Domenici and Ronnie C. Lesser (eds) *Disorienting Sexuality: Psychoanalytic Reappraisals of Sexual Identities* (1995).

Bibliography

Abraham, K., 'Manifestations of the Female Castration Complex', *International Journal of Psycho-Analysis*, III, 1922.

Abraham, N. and Torok, M., *The Shell and the Kernel*. Volume One (trans. and ed.), Nicholas T. Rand (Chicago and London: University of Chicago Press, 1994).

——, *The Wolf Man's Magic Word: A Cryptonomy*, trans. and ed., Nicholas T. Rand (Minneapolis: University of Minnesota Press, 1986).

Adams, P. and Cowie, E. (eds), *The Woman in Question* (London and New York: Verso, 1990).

Andermatt Coneley, V., *Hélène Cixous: Writing the Feminine* (Lincoln: University of Nebraska Press, 1984).

——, *Hélène Cixous* (London: Harvester Wheatsheaf, 1992).

Appignanesi, L. and Forrester, J., *Freud's Women* (London: Virago, 1993).

Armstrong, I. and Carr, H. (eds), *Positioning Klein*, special edition of *Women: A Cultural Review*, Vol. 1, 2, Summer 1990.

Balint, A., 'Love for the Mother and Mother Love', *International Journal of Psycho-Analysis*, XXX, 1949 and collected in M. Balint (ed.), *Primary Love and Psycho-Analytic Technique* (New York: Liveright Publishing, 1965).

Balint, M., 'Critical Notes on the Theory of the Pregenital Organizations of the Libido' (1935) in M. Balint (ed.), *Primary Love and Psycho-Analytic Technique* (New York: Liveright Publishing, 1965).

——, 'Perversions and Genitality' in M. Balint (ed.), *Primary Love and Psycho-Analytic Technique* (New York: Liveright Publishing, 1965).

Balmary, M., *Psychoanalysing Psychoanalysis: Freud and the Hidden Fault of the Father* (Baltimore: Johns Hopkins University Press, 1982).

Baruch, E., *Women Analyse Women* (New York: New York University Press, 1991).

Benjamin, J., *The Bonds of Love: Psychoanalysis, feminism and the problem of domination* (London: Virago, 1990).

Berger, J., *Ways of Seeing* (London: British Broadcasting Corporation and Penguin Books, 1972).

Bernard, J., *The Future of Marriage* (New York: Bantam, 1972).

——, *The Future of Motherhood* (New York: Penguin, 1974).

Bernheimer, C. and Kahane, C., *In Dora's Case: Freud, Hysteria, Feminism* (London: Virago, 1985).

Bettelheim, B., *Symbolic Wounds: Puberty Rites and the Envious Male* (London: Thames and Hudson, 1955).

Bion, W. R., *Second Thoughts: Selected Papers on Psycho-Analysis* (London: Karnac, 1961).

Boothby, R., *Death and Desire: Psychoanalytic Theory in Lacan's Return to Freud* (London: Routledge, 1991).

Bowie, M., *Lacan* (London: Fontana, 1991).

——, *Psychoanalysis and the Future of Theory* (Oxford: Blackwell, 1993).

Brennan, T. (ed.), *Between Feminism and Psychoanalysis* (London and New York: Routledge, 1989).

—— , *The Interpretation of the Flesh: Freud and Femininity* (London: Routledge, 1992).

Bronfen, E., *Over Her Dead Body: Death, femininity and the aesthetic* (Manchester: Manchester University Press, 1992).

Brooks, P., *Body Work: Objects of Desire in Modern Narrative* (Cambridge, Mass. & London: Harvard University Press, 1993).

Brunswick, R. M., 'The Pre-Oedipal Phase of Libido Development' (1940) in *The Psycho-Analytic Reader* (ed.) Robert Fleiss (London: Hogarth, 1950).

Burgin, V., Donald, J. and Kaplan, C. (eds), *Formations of Fantasy* (London and New York: Methuen, 1986).

Butler, J., *Bodies that Matter: On the Discursive Limits of 'Sex'* (London and New York: Routledge, 1993).

—— , *Gender Trouble: Feminism and the Subversion of Identity* (London and New York: Routledge, 1990).

—— , 'Gender as Performance: An Interview with Judith Butler', with Peter Osborne and Lynne Segal, *Radical Philosophy*, 67, Summer, 1994.

—— , 'Gender Trouble, Feminist Theory, and Psychoanalytic Discourse' in *Feminism/Postmodernism*, (ed.) Linda J. Nicholson (London and New York: Routledge, 1990).

—— , 'The Lesbian Phallus and the Morphological Imaginary', *differences: a Journal of Feminist Cultural Studies*, 4, 1, 1992.

—— , *The Psychic Life of Power: Theories in Subjection* (Stanford: Stanford University Press, 1997).

Carotenuto, A., *A Secret Symmetry: Sabina Spielrein Between Freud and Jung* (New York: Pantheon, 1982).

Chasseguet-Smirgel, J., 'Feminine Guilt and the Oedipus Complex' (1964), in *Female Sexuality* (ed.) J. Chasseguet-Smirgel (Ann Arbor: University of Michigan Press, 1970).

Chodorow, N., *Femininities, Masculinities, Sexualities* (London: Free Association Books, 1994).

—— , *Feminism and Psychoanalysis* (Cambridge: Polity, 1989).

—— , *The Reproduction of Mothering: Psychoanalysis and the Sociology of Gender* (Berkeley, Los Angeles, London: University of California Press, 1978).

Cixous, H., 'The Laugh of the Medusa', *Signs*, Summer, 1976.

—— , 'Castration and Decapitation', *Signs*, Autumn, 1981.

Cixous, H. and Clément, C., *The Newly Born Woman*, (trans.) Betsy Wing (Manchester: Manchester University Press, 1986).

Clément, C., *The Weary Sons of Freud* (London: Verso, 1987).

Copjec, J., 'The Sartorial Superego', *October*, 50, 1989.

Coward, R., *Our Treacherous Hearts* (London: Faber & Faber, 1992).

Derrida, J., 'Semiology and Grammatology: Interview with Julia Kristeva', Positions (trans. and ed.) Alan Bass (London: Athlone Press, 1981).

Deutsch, H., *Confrontations with Myself* (New York: Norton, 1973).

—— , 'On Female Homosexuality', *International Journal of Psycho-Analysis*, XIII, 1932.

—— , *Psychology of Women*, Vols 1 & 2 (New York: Grune and Stratton, 1944 and 1945).

—— , The Psychology of Women in Relation to the Functions of Reproduction', *International Journal of Psycho-Analysis*, VI, 1925.

—— , 'The Significance of Masochism in the Mental Life of Women', *International Journal of Psycho-Analysis*, XI, 1930.

—— , *The Therapeutic Process, The Self and Female Psychology: Collected Psychoanalytic Papers*, (ed.) Paul Roazen (New Brunswick and London: Transaction, 1992).

Dinnerstein, D., *The Mermaid and the Minotaur: Sexual Arrangements and Human Malaise* (New York: Harper and Row, 1976).

—— , *The Rocking of the Cradle and the Ruling of the World* (London: Souvenir Press, 1978).

Doane, J. and Hodges, D., *From Klein to Kristeva: Psychoanalytic Feminism and the Search for the 'Good Enough' Mother* (Ann Arbor: University of Michigan, 1992).

Domenici, T. and Lesser, R. C., (eds), *Disorienting Sexuality: Psychoanalytic Reappraisals of Sexual Identities* (London and New York: Routledge, 1995).

Elliott, A., *Psychoanalytic Theory* (Oxford: Blackwell, 1994).

Ellmann, M. (ed.), *Psychoanalytic Literary Criticism* (London: Longman, 1994).

Erikson, E. H., 'Womanhood and Inner Space' (1968) in *Women and Analysis*, (ed.) J. Strouse (New York: Grossman, 1974).

—— , 'Once More the Inner Space: Letter to a Former Student' (1974) in *Women and Analysis* (ed.) J. Strouse (New York: Grossman, 1974).

Evans, M. (ed.), *The Woman Question: Readings on the Subordination of Women* (Oxford: Fontana, 1982).

Feldstein, R. and Roof, J. (eds), *Feminism and Psychoanalysis* (Ithaca: Cornell University Press, 1989).

Felman, S., *What does a Woman Want?* (Baltimore: Johns Hopkins University Press, 1993).

Felman, S. (ed.), *Literature and Psychoanalysis – The Question of Reading: Otherwise* (Baltimore and London: Johns Hopkins University Press, [1977] 1982).

Ferenczi, S., *Thalassa: A Theory of Genitality* (1924) (New York: Norton, 1968).

Flax, J., *disputed subjects: essays on psychoanalysis, politics and philosophy* (New York and London: Routledge, 1993).

—— , *Thinking Fragments: Psychoanalysis, Feminism, and Postmodernism in the Contemporary West* (Berkeley: University of California Press, 1990).

Fletcher, J. and Benjamin, A. (eds), *Abjection, Melancholia and Love: the Work of Julia Kristeva* (London and New York: Routledge, 1990).

Fliess, R. (ed.), *The Psycho-Analytic Reader* (London: Hogarth, 1950).

Forrester, J., *The Seductions of Psychoanalysis: Freud, Lacan and Derrida* (Cambridge: CUP, 1990).

von Franz, M., *The Feminine in Fairy Tales* (1972) (Boston: Shambhala, 1993).

—— , *The Golden Ass of Apuleius: the Liberation of the Feminine in Man* (Boston: Shambhala, 1992).

Fraser, N. and Bartky, S. L. (eds), *Revaluing French Feminism: Critical Essays on Difference, Agency and Culture* (Bloomington: Indiana University Press, 1992).

Freud, S., Standard Edition (SE) (London: Hogarth Press and The Institute of Psycho-Analysis, 24 volumes; 1953–74).

—— , Pelican Freud Library (PFL) [subsequently Penguin Freud Library] (Harmondsworth: Penguin, 15 volumes; from 1973).

Fuss, D., *Essentially Speaking: Feminism, Nature and Difference* (New York and London: Routledge, 1989).

Gallop, J., *Feminism and Psychoanalysis: The Daughter's Seduction* (London: Macmillan, 1982).

—— , *Reading Lacan* (Ithaca: Cornell University Press, 1985).

—— , 'Reading the Mother Tongue: Psychoanalytic Feminist Criticism' in *The Trial(s) of Psychoanalysis* (ed.) Françoise Metzer (Chicago and London: Chicago University Press, 1988).

—— , *Thinking Through the Body* (London: Routledge, 1990).

Garber, M., *Vested Interests: Cross-Dressing and Cultural Anxiety* (Harmondsworth: Penguin, 1992).

Gardiner, M. (ed.), *The Wolf-Man and Sigmund Freud* (Harmondsworth: Penguin, 1973).

Garner, S. N., Kahane, C. and Sprengnether, M., (eds), *The (M)Other Tongue: Essays in Feminist Psychoanalytic Interpretation* (Ithaca: Cornell University Press, 1985).

Gilligan, C., *In a Different Voice: Psychological Theory and Women's Development* (Cambridge, Mass., and London: Harvard University Press, 1982).

Goldenberg, N. R., *Resurrecting the Body: Feminism, Religion and Psychoanalysis* (New York: Crossroad, 1990).

Grosz, E., *Jacques Lacan: A Feminist Introduction* (London: Routledge, 1990).

—— , *Sexual Subversions: Three French Feminists* (Sydney: Allen & Unwin, 1989).

Grunberger, B., 'Outline for a Study of Narcissism in Female Sexuality' in J. Chasseguet-Smirgel (ed.), *Female Sexuality* (Ann Arbor: University of Michigan Press, 1970).

Haraway, D., 'A Manifesto for Cyborgs: Science, Technology, and Socialist Feminism in the 1980s' in Nicholson, L. J. (ed.), *Feminism/Postmodernism* (New York and London: Routledge, 1990).

Harding, E. M., *The Way of All Women* [1933] (London: Rider, 1983).

—— , *Women's Mysteries, Ancient and Modern* (New York: Rider, 1955).

Heath, S., 'Joan Riviere and the Masquerade' in V. Burgin, J. Donald and C. Kaplan (eds), *Formations of Fantasy* (London and New York: Methuen, 1986).

—— , *The Sexual Fix* (London: Macmillan, 1982).

Heiman, P., Isaacs, S., Klein, M. and Riviere, J. (eds), *Developments in Psycho-Analysis* (London: Hogarth, 1952).

Hinshelwood, R. D., *A Dictionary of Kleinian Thought* (London: Free Association Books, 1989).

Hirsch, M., *The Mother/Daughter Plot: Narrative, Psychoanalysis, Feminism* (Bloomington: Indiana University Press, 1989).

Horney, K., 'The Flight from Womanhood', *International Journal of Psycho-Analysis*, VII, 1926.

—— , *Feminine Psychology* (New York: Norton, 1967).

Irigaray, L., *Elemental Passions*, trans. J. Collie and J. Still (London: Athlone Press, 1992).

—— , *An Ethics of Sexual Difference*, trans. C. Burke and G. Gill (London: Athlone Press, 1993).

—— , *Speculum of the Other Woman*, trans. G. Gill (Ithaca, New York: Cornell University Press, 1985).

—— , *This Sex Which is not One* (1977), trans. C. Porter and C. Burke (Ithaca, New York: Cornell University Press, 1985).

—— , *Sexes and Genealogies*, trans. G. Gill (New York: Columbia University Press, 1993).

Jardine, A., *Gynesis: Configurations of Women and Modernity* (Ithaca, New York: Cornell University Press, 1985).

Jones, E., 'Notes on Dr Abraham's Article on the Female Castration Complex'. *International Journal of Psycho-Analysis*, III, 1922.

—— , 'The Early Development of Female Sexuality', *International Journal of Psycho-Analysis*, VIII, 1927.

—— , 'Early Female Sexuality', *International Journal of Psycho-Analysis*, XVI, 1935.

—— , *Collected Papers on Psychoanalysis* (London: Ballière, Tindall & Cox, 1948).

Jung, C. G., *Aspects of the Feminine*, trans. R. F. C. Hull (London: Ark (Routledge), 1982).

—— , *Memories, Dreams and Reflections* (ed.) A. Jaffé; trans. R. and C. Winston (New York: Vintage Books, 1961).

—— , *Collected Works: 20 volumes*, trans. R. F. C. Hull (except Volume 2) (London: Routledge and Kegan Paul, 1957 ff.).

Jung, C. G. (ed.), *Man and His Symbols* (1964) (London: Picador, 1978).

Keiser, S., 'Discussion of Sherfey's Paper on Female Sexuality', *Journal of the American Psychoanalytic Association*, 16, 1968.

Kernberg, O., *Borderline Conditions and Pathological Narcissism* (New York: Jason Aronson, 1975).

Kerr, J., *A Most Dangerous Method: The Story of Jung, Freud, & Sabina Spielrein* (London: Sinclair-Stevenson, 1994).

King, P. and Steiner, R. (eds), *The Freud-Klein Controversies, 1941–45* (London and New York: Tavistock/Routledge, 1990).

Klein, M., Envy and Gratitude and other works (London: Virago, 1989).

—— , *Love, Guilt and Reparation and other works 1921–1945* (London: Virago, 1989).

—— , *The Psycho-Analysis of Children* (London: Virago, 1989).

—— , *Narrative of a Child Analysis* (London: Virago, 1989).

—— , 'Early Stages of the Oedipus Complex', *International Journal of Psycho-Analysis*, XII, 1928.

Kofman, S., *The Enigma of Woman: Woman in Freud's Writings* (Ithaca, New York: Cornell University Press, 1985).

Kristeva, J., *Black Sun: Depression and Melancholia* (trans.) Léon S. Roudiez (New Columbia University Press, 1989).

—— , *In the Beginning Was Love: Psychoanalysis and Faith* (New York: Columbia University Press, 1989).

—— , *Powers of Horror: An Essay on Abjection* (trans.) Léon S. Roudiez (New York: Columbia University Press, 1982).

—— , *Revolution in Poetic Language* (1974) (New York: Columbia University Press, 1984).

—— , *Strangers to Ourselves*, trans. Léon S. Roudiez (New York: Columbia University Press, 1991).

—— , *Tales of Love* (New York: Columbia University Press, 1987).

Lacan, J., *Écrits: A Selection* (London: Tavistock, 1974).

—— , *The Four Fundamental Concepts of Psychoanalysis* (ed.) J. Alain-Miller (trans.) A. Sheridan (London: Hogarth and the Institute of Psychoanalysis, 1977).

Lampl de Groot, J., 'The Evolution of the Oedipus Complex in Women', *International Journal of Psycho-Analysis*, IX, 1928.

Laplanche, J. and Pontalis, J. B., *The Language of Psychoanalysis* (London: Karnac, 1988).

Lechte, J., *Julia Kristeva* (London: Routledge, 1990).

Lodge, D. (ed.), *Modern Criticism and Theory: A Reader* (London and New York: Longman, 1988).

McClellan, J., 'The extensions of woman', 'Life', *Observer*, 17 April 1994.

Marks, E. and de Courtivron, I. (eds), *New French Feminisms: An Anthology* (Brighton: Harvester, 1981).

Masson, J. M., *The Assault on Truth: Freud's Suppression of the Seduction Theory* (Harmondsworth: Penguin, 1985).

Metz, C., *The Imaginary Signifier* (Bloomington: Indiana University Press, 1981).

Miller, A., *The Drama of Being A Child and the Search for the True Self* (London: Virago, 1987).

Miller, J. B. (ed.), *Psychoanalysis and Women* (New York: Penguin, 1973).

Minsky, R. (ed.), *Psychoanalysis and Gender: An Introductory Reader* (London and New York: Routledge, 1996).

Mitchell, J., *Psychoanalysis and Feminism: A Radical Reassessment of Freudian Psychoanalysis* (Harmondsworth: Penguin [1975], 1986).

Mitchell, J., *Women: The Longest Revolution* (London: Virago, 1984).

Mitchell, J. (ed.), *The Selected Melanie Klein* (Harmondsworth: Penguin, 1986).

Mitchell, J. and Rose, J. (eds), *Feminine Sexuality: Jacques Lacan & The École Freudienne* (London: Macmillan, 1985).

Moi, T., *Sexual/Textual Politics* (London: Methuen, 1985).

Moi, T. (ed.), *The Kristeva Reader* (Oxford: Blackwell, 1986).

Morgan, R., *Sisterhood is Powerful: An Anthology of Writings from the Women's Liberation Movement* (New York: Vintage, 1970).

Mulvey, L., *Visual and Other Pleasures* (London: Macmillan, 1989).

Nicholson, L. J. (ed.), *Feminism/Postmodernism* (New York and London: Routledge, 1990).

Northrup, C., *Women's Bodies, Women's Wisdom* (London: Piatkus, 1995).

Nye, R. A. (ed.), *Sexuality* (Oxford: Oxford University Press, 1999).

O'Connor, N. and Ryan, J., *Wild Desires and Mistaken Identities: Lesbianism and Psychoanalysis* (London: Virago, 1993).

Ortner, S. B., 'Is Female to Male as Nature is to Culture?', *Feminist Studies*, vol. 1, no. 2, Fall, 1972 and collected in Mary Evans, (ed.), *The Woman Question: Readings on the Subordination of Women*, (Oxford: Fontana, 1982).

Pacteau, F., 'The Impossible Referent: representations of the androgyne' in V. Burgin, J. Donald and C. Kaplan (eds), *Formations of Fantasy* (London and New York: Methuen, 1994).

Paglia, C., *Sex, Art and American Culture* (Harmondsworth: Penguin, 1993).

—— *Sexual Personae: Art and Decadence from Nefertiti to Emily Dickinson* (Harmondsworth: Penguin, 1991).

——, *Vamps and Tramps* (Harmondsworth: Penguin, 1995).

Phillips, J. and Stonebridge, L. (eds), *Reading Melanie Klein* (London and New York: Routledge, 1998).

Raphael-Leff, J. and Perelberg, R. J. (eds), *Female Experience: Three Generations of British Women Psychoanalysts on Work with Women* (London and New York: Routledge, 1997).

Rich, A., *Blood, Bread and Poetry* (London: Virago, 1987).

——, *Of Woman Born: Motherhood as Experience and Institution* (London: Virago, 1976).

Riviere, J., *The Inner World and Joan Riviere: Collected Papers* (ed.) Athol Hughes, (London and New York, Karnac, 1991).

——, 'Womanliness as a Masquerade', *International Journal of Psycho-Analysis*, X, 1929 and collected in V. Burgin, T. Donald and C. Kaplan (eds), *Formations of Fantasy*, (London and New York: Methuen, 1986).

Roazen, P. (ed.), *The Therapeutic Process, The Self and Female Psychology: Collected Psychoanalytic Papers* (New Brunswick and London: Transaction, 1992).

Rosaldo, M. Z. and Lamphere, L. (eds), *Woman, Culture and Society* (Stanford: Stanford University Press, 1974).

Rose, J., *Sexuality in the Field of Vision* (London and New York: Verso, 1986).

——, *Why War? – Psychoanalysis, Politics, and the Return to Melanie Klein* (Oxford: Blackwell, 1993).

Ruitenbeek, H. M. (ed.), *Psychoanalysis and Female Sexuality* (New Haven: College and University Press Services, 1966).

Rustin, M., *The Good Society and the Inner World* (London: Verso, 1991).

Rycroft, C., *Psychoanalysis and Beyond* (London: Chatto & Windus, 1985).

——, *A Critical Dictionary of Psychoanalysis* (Harmondsworth: Penguin, 1995).

Samuels, A. (ed.), *Psychopathology: Contemporary Jungian Perspectives* (London: Karnac, 1989).

Samuels, A., Shorter, B. and Plaut, F. (eds), *A Critical Dictionary of Jungian Analysis* (London and New York: Routledge and Kegan Paul, 1986).

de Saussure, F., *Course in General Linguistics* (Glasgow: Fontana/Collins, [1915] 1974).

Sayers, J., *Mothering Psychoanalysis: Helene Deutsch, Karen Horney, Anna Freud and Melanie Klein* (London: Hamish Hamilton, 1991).

—— , *Sexual Contradictions: Psychology, Psychoanalysis, and Feminism* (London: Tavistock, 1987).

Schwartz, A. E., *Sexual Subjects: Lesbians, Gender and Psychoanalysis* (London and New York: Routledge, 1998).

Segal, H., *Introduction to the Work of Melanie Klein* (London: Hogarth, 1964).

—— , *The Work of Hannah Segal: A Kleinian Approach to Clinical Practice* (New York and London: Jason Aronson, 1981).

Segal, J., *Melanie Klein* (London: Sage, 1993).

Segal, L., *Is the Future Female?* (London: Virago, 1992).

—— , *Sex Exposed* (London: Virago, 1992).

—— , *Slow Motion: Changing Masculinities, Changing Men* (London: Virago, 1990).

—— , *Straight Sex* (London: Virago, 1992).

Sellers, S., *Writing Differences: Reading from the Seminar of Hélène Cixous* (Milton Keynes: Open University Press, 1988).

Sexton, A., *The Complete Poems* (Boston: Houghton Miffin, 1982).

Shamdasani, S., 'Jung, gifted and blackened', *Times Higher Education Supplement,* 6 March 1998.

—— , *Cult Fictions: C. G. Jung and the Founding of Analytical Psychology* (London and New York: Routledge, 1998).

Shamdasani, S. and Münchow, M. (eds), *Speculations After Freud: psychoanalysis, philosophy and culture* (New York and London: Routledge, 1994).

Sherfey, M. J., 'The Evolution and Nature of Female Sexuality in Relation to Psychoanalytic Theory', *Journal of the American Psychoanalytic Association,* 14, 1966 and collected in R. Morgan, *Sisterhood is Powerful: An Anthology of Writings from the Women's Liberation Movement* (New York: Vintage, 1970).

Shiach, M., *Hélène Cixous: A Politics of Writing* (London: Routledge, 1991).

Singer, J., *Androgyny* (London: Routledge & Kegan Paul, 1976).

Souter, T., 'The Third Sex', *Independent on Sunday,* 9 October 1994.

Spivak, G. C., 'French Feminism in an International Frame', *Yale French Studies,* 62, 1981.

—— , *In Other Worlds* (New York and London: Routledge, 1987).

Stanton, D. C., 'Difference on Trial: A Critique of Maternal Metaphor in Cixous, Irigaray, and Kristeva' in Nancy K. Miller (ed.), *The Poetics of Gender* (New York: Columbia University Press, 1986).

Strouse, J., *Women and Analysis: Dialogues on Psychoanalytic Views of Femininity* (New York: Grossman, 1974).

Sturrock, J. (ed.), *Structuralism and Since: From Lévi Strauss to Derrida* (New York and Oxford: Oxford University Press, 1979).

Sulieman, S. R., *The Female Body in Western Culture: Contemporary Perspectives* (Cambridge, Mass. and London: Harvard University Press, 1986).

Torok, M., 'The Meaning of Penis Envy in Women' (1963), *differences: A Journal of Feminist Cultural Studies,* 4, 1992 and in Abraham, N. and Torok, M., *The Shell and the Kernel.*

Vice, S. (ed.), *Psychoanalytic Criticism: A Reader* (Cambridge: Polity, 1996).

Wheelright, J., 'I'm just a sweet transgenderist', *Independent,* 27 March 1995.

Wehr, D. S., *Jung and Feminism: Liberating Archetypes* (London: Routledge and Kegan Paul, 1988).

Whitford, M., *Luce Irigaray: Philosophy in the Feminine* (London: Routledge, 1991).

—— , *Knowing the Difference* (London: Routledge, 1994).

Whitford, M. (ed.), *The Irigaray Reader* (Oxford: Blackwell, 1991).

Wittig, M., *The Straight Mind and Other Essays* (Hemel Hempstead: Harvester Wheatsheaf, 1992).

Wolff, C., *Love Between Women* (New York: Harper & Row, 1971).

Wollstonecraft, M., *Vindication of Rights of Woman* (1792), (ed.) M. B. Kramnick (Harmondsworth: Penguin, 1983).

Woodman, M., *The Pregnant Virgin: A Process of Psychological Transformation* (Toronto: Inner City Books, 1985).

—— , *The Ravaged Bridegroom: Masculinity in Women* (Toronto: Inner City Books, 1990).

—— , *Leaving My Father's House: A journey to conscious femininity* (London: Rider, 1993).

Woodman, M. and Dickson, E., *Dancing in the Flames: The Dark Goddess in the Transformation of Consciousness* (Dublin: Gill & Macmillan, 1996).

Wright, E., *Psychoanalytic Criticism: Theory In Practice* (London and New York: Methuen, 1984).

Wright, E., (ed.), *Feminism and Psychoanalysis: A Critical Dictionary* (Oxford: Blackwell, 1992).

Young-Bruel, E., *Anna Freud* (London: Macmillan, 1988).

—— , *Freud on Women* (London: Hogarth, 1990).

Zilboorg, G., 'Masculine and Feminine: Some Biological and Cultural Aspects' (1944) in J. B. Miller (ed.), *Psychoanalysis and Women*.

Notes on Contributors

Judith Butler is the Maxine Elliot Professor of Rhetoric and Comparative Literature at the University of California, Berkeley. She is well known as a theorist on gender, sexuality, identity politics and queer theory.

Nancy Chodorow is Professor of Sociology at the University of California, Berkeley. She has a background in social anthropology and is also a practising psychoanalyst.

Hélène Cixous is a novelist, dramatist, essayist and founding theorist of contemporary French feminism. She is the Head of the Centre d'Etudes Féminines and Professor of English Literature at the Université de Paris VIII – Vincennes.

Helene Deutsch (1884–1982) was born Helene Rosenbach in Polish-speaking Galicia on the Ukrainian border of the Austro-Hungarian Empire. Her Jewish liberal father, to whom she was extremely devoted, was a prominent lawyer and a representative at the Federal Court in Vienna. Helene's relationship with her restrictive mother was, on the other hand, very problematic – as outlined in Deutsch's autobiography, *Confrontations with Myself* (1973), written when she was in her late eighties. She began studying medicine at the University of Vienna, completing her degree in Munich. Here she married Felix Deutsch who was later to become Freud's doctor. Helene began her analysis with Freud in 1918, having become an elected member of the Psycho-Analytical Society in the same year. When her analysis was terminated by Freud she continued with Karl Abraham. In 1934 she left Vienna to live and continue her career in Boston, Massachusetts, and ultimately, to settle in America.

Jane Flax is Professor of Political Science at Howard University, specializing in political theory. She is also a psychotherapist in private practice.

Sigmund Freud (1856–1939) was born in Moravia but spent most of his life – until a year before his death – in Vienna. He began his career and medical training with work on anatomy and on the nervous system. He had a period of study with Charcot at the Salpêtriere in Paris after which his interests began to turn, slowly (his clinical work continued for years) but thoroughly, to psychology. His work on hysteria, conducted with a colleague, Joseph Breuer, gives evidence of this progression. In 1896, Freud introduced the term and began to adumbrate a new method: 'psychoanalysis'. His consideration of infant sexuality, the interpretation of dreams and the strategies human subjects unconsciously develop in order to negotiate trauma and repressions has made a striking and pervasive impact on twentieth-century thinking and being – and this, more persistently *outside* the discourses of medicine and psychology. In 1938, driven by Hitler's invasion of Austria and suffering from cancer, he moved to London where he died the following year.

Esther Harding (1888–1971) was born in England and studied medicine at the London School of Medicine for Women. She gained her degree from the University of London and in 1922 went to Zurich to work with Jung. She moved to New York in 1923 where she started her own practice and where she was to be a founding member of the Analytical Psychology Club of New York, the medical Society of Analytical Psychology of America, and the C. G. Jung Foundation of New York. She was also a Patron of the C. G. Jung Institute.

Karen Horney (1885–1952) was born in Hamburg, Germany. She studied at the University of Berlin and in 1913 received her medical degree. From 1914–18 she continued her studies in psychiatry and from 1918–32 taught at the Berlin Psychoanalytic Institute. She went to the United States in 1932 and was an Associate Director of the Psychoanalytic Institute in Chicago for two years. Moving to New York in 1934, she taught at the New York Psychoanalytic Institute until 1941. She was a founder of the Association for the Advancement of Psychoanalysis and the American Institute for Psychoanalysis.

Luce Irigaray is a French feminist philosopher, writer and practising psychoanalyst with doctorates in both linguistics and philosophy. She is Director of Research at the Centre National de Recherche Scientifique, Paris.

Carl Gustav Jung (1875–1961) was born in Switzerland, the son of a country parson. He attended boarding school in Basel and showed a particular facility in languages. Despite an early interest in archaeology he studied medicine at the University of Basel. He chose to study psychiatry after a period studying with Krafft-Ebing, the renowned neurologist, and became a lecturer in psychiatry at the University of Zurich. He is known as the founder of Analytical Psychology, developed after a short period of collaboration with Sigmund Freud. He became increasingly devoted to his private practice and his own research which reflected his interests in myth, alchemical studies, comparative religions and in religious experience, including synchronicity and the paranormal. He was a prolific writer and committed traveller. His autobiography, *Memories, Dreams and Reflections* was published in the year of his death, 1961.

Melanie Klein (1882–1960) was born in Vienna. Rather than pursuing the university training and medical career she at times considered, she married at twenty-one and had three children. Klein's own mother was severely dominating and it was upon her mother's death that she first sought analysis. Living in Budapest at the time, she began a training analysis with one of Freud's colleagues Sándor Ferenczi. She left Budapest for Berlin in 1921 and continued her analysis with Karl Abraham. She was a pioneer in the analysis of children and the interpretation of their play. Her difference of emphasis, particularly in relation to a much earlier instigation of the Oedipus complex and thus its affects, led to some factionalism and dispute in psychoanalytic circles. In 1925 she gave a course of lectures in London as a guest of the British Psycho-Analytical Society. Shortly thereafter, in 1926, she moved to London, where she remained until her death. A distinctive Kleinian School is now well-established.

Julia Kristeva was one of the founding figures of 'New French Feminism' in the 1960s and 70s. She continues to write on a broad range of topics including semiotics, political philosophy, abjection and clinical depression. She is a Professor at the Université de Paris VII and is a practising psychoanalyst.

Born in Paris, **Jacques Lacan** (1901–81) spent most of his life and his career in the same city. He studied medicine and psychiatry and in 1934 joined the Paris Psychoanalytic Society. He had an involvement, too, in the early 1930s, in the French Surrealist movement. He continued his practice as an analyst in Paris until 1952. In the 1950s he began to steer his psychoanalytic work in the direction of linguistics and structuralism and then, post-structuralism. His career as an analyst became increasingly controversial but his theoretical work and in particular his seminars, had enthusiastic and multi-disciplinary support. He left the Paris Psychoanalytic Society in 1953 and founded the French Society of Psychoanalysis. After his expulsion in 1961 from the International Psychoanalytic Association he reformed his own society as the L'École Freudienne de Paris. In 1980, he suddenly and unilaterally dissolved L'École Freudienne and formed another society, excluding many of his former colleagues: La cause Freudienne.

The daughter of a wealthy Dutch family, **Jeanne Lampl de Groot** (1895–1987) studied medicine. In 1922, as a young doctor, she began a training analysis with Sigmund Freud, becoming a long-term friend of both Freud and his daughter Anna. She was a co-founder of the Psychoanalytic Institute training programme in the Netherlands and wrote particularly on female sexuality and on the effects of Oedipal development on women. She is known for her continued loyalty to Freud and many of his premises and rather less known for the now acknowledged influence of her ideas on his.

Juliet Mitchell was a lecturer in English literature from 1962 to 1970. She has been a freelance writer and lecturer in Britain and abroad and is now a trained psychoanalyst practising in London. She is a full member of the British Psychoanalytic Society. She is also Lecturer in Gender and Society at the University of Cambridge and has recently been appointed Fellow of Jesus College at Cambridge.

Noreen O'Connor undertook her training at the Philadelphia Psychoanalytic Psychotherapy Association in London and is now on the Training Committee of the Association. She has been a psychotherapist in the public sector and presently works in full-time private practice. Her PhD, from Cork University, was in contemporary European philosophy and she has published widely on topics both philosophical and psychoanalytical.

Camille Paglia gained a doctorate in English in 1974 from Yale University under the tutelage of Harold Bloom. She has taught at Bennington College and at Wesleyan and Yale universities. She is presently Professor of Humanities at the University of the Arts in Philadelphia. She is known for her controversial writing, both academic and general, and for her various television appearances where she displays her own interests in media, sexual politics and cultural artefacts/institutions.

Born in Brighton, Sussex, **Joan Riviere** (1883–1962) (née Verrall) came from a family well connected in literary and intellectual spheres. Her uncle was the Cambridge classicist, A. W. Verrall and as a young woman she participated in her uncle's social gatherings and meetings. As part of her schooling Joan was sent to Germany to learn its language – something which was to prove invaluable to her work as a translator of Freud and of Melanie Klein, in particular. After her father's death, her physical and mental suffering brought her to analysis with the British Freudian psychoanalyst, Ernest Jones, in 1916. By 1918 she had begun to practise as a lay analyst herself, was a member of the newly formed British Psycho-Analytical Society and a translator into English of Freud's *Introductory Lectures*.

She had a year of analysis with Freud in 1922. In 1924 she became friends with Melanie Klein and continued as her advocate, colleague and translator. Riviere's own papers were much influenced by Klein although she also always remained an admirer of Freud. As a lecturer, teacher and writer she was a leading member of British psychoanalysis.

Jacqueline Rose is Professor of English at Queen Mary and Westfield College, University of London, specializing in feminism and psychoanalysis and modern literature.

Joanna Ryan studied for a PhD in psychology at the University of Cambridge and trained at the Philadelphia Psychoanalytic Psychotherapy Association, London. She has worked as a psychoanalytic psychotherapist both in community health organizations and in private practice. She writes and publishes on psychoanalysis and lesbian issues.

Mary Jane Sherfey was a resident psychiatrist at the Payne Whitney Clinic, New York City Hospital in the 1950s and 1960s, the period when she was developing her views on female sexuality in relation to psychoanalytic theory.

Maria Torok practised clinical psychoanalysis from 1956 after completing her training as an analyst. She gained membership, with her colleague and co-author Nicolas Abraham (1919–75), of the Paris Psychoanalytic Society and continues to work as an analyst in Paris.

Marie-Louise von Franz (1915–98) was born in Munich, Germany, into a family in which her father was a baron and an Austrian colonel. She gained a PhD in classical languages from the University of Zurich, Switzerland, in 1940 but she had begun to train and to work closely with C. G. Jung in 1934. From 1948 she was a Jungian analyst and a teacher at the C. G. Jung Institute in Zurich. She lectured throughout the world and published widely. She had worked with Jung on his investigations into alchemy and archetype and this she extended into her own work on myths, fairy-tales and folk-tales.

Monique Wittig was involved in the Mouvement de Liberation Féminine and in theorizing radical separatist lesbianism in Paris in the 1960s and 70s. She now prefers to live and work in the United States. She teaches at the University of Tucson, Arizona.

Marion Woodman is a Jungian analyst practising in Toronto, Ontario, Canada. She trained at the C. G. Jung Institute in Zurich and has taught and written extensively on Jungian analysis and feminine consciousness.

Index